# The Problems of a Political Animal

# The Problems of a Political Animal

*Community, Justice, and Conflict in Aristotelian Political Thought*

Bernard Yack

UNIVERSITY OF CALIFORNIA PRESS
*Berkeley · Los Angeles · London*

This book is a print-on-demand volume. It is manufactured using toner in place of ink. Type and images may be less sharp than the same material seen in traditionally printed University of California Press editions.

University of California Press
Berkeley and Los Angeles, California

University of California Press, Ltd.
London, England

© 1993 by
The Regents of the University of California

Library of Congress Cataloging-in-Publication Data

Yack, Bernard, 1952–
   The problems of a political animal : community, justice, and conflict in Aristotelian political thought / Bernard Yack.
      p.   cm.
   Includes bibliographical references and index.
   ISBN 0-520-08166-8 (alk. paper). — ISBN 0-520-08167-6 (pbk. : alk. paper)
   1. Aristotle—Contributions in political science.   2. Community.   3. Justice.
4. Social conflict.   I. Title.
JC71.A7Y34   1993
320′.01′1—dc20                                                                  92-23296
                                                                                      CIP

Printed in the United States of America

The paper used in this publication meets the minimum requirements of American National Standard for Information Sciences—Permanence of Paper for Printed Library Materials, ANSI Z39.48-1984. ∞

*In memory of Judith Nisse Shklar (1929–1992)*

# Contents

| | |
|---|---|
| Acknowledgments | ix |
| Introduction | 1 |
|    *Political Community as a Term of Distinction* | 5 |
|    *Distorted Images of Aristotelian Politics* | 10 |
|    *Interpretive Approaches* | 18 |
| 1. Community | 25 |
|    *The Communal Animal* | 27 |
|    *The Forms of Friendship and Justice* | 33 |
|    *Aristotelian Community and Modern Social Theory* | 43 |
| 2. Political Community | 51 |
|    *The Defining Characteristics of Political Community* | 53 |
|    *The Political Animal* | 62 |
|    *The Ancient Polis and Modern Political Communities* | 71 |
|    *Appendix. Monarchy and Political Community* | 85 |
| 3. Political Teleology | 88 |
|    *The Naturalness of the Polis* | 90 |
|    *Politics and the Good Life* | 96 |
|    *An Anthropocentric Universe?* | 100 |
|    *The Good Life in Imperfect Political Communities* | 102 |
| 4. Political Friendship | 109 |
|    *Neither Brothers nor Comrades* | 110 |
|    *The Dangers of Political Intimacy* | 118 |
|    *Political Friendship and the Inconveniences of Political Life* | 122 |

5. Political Justice     128
   *Political Justice and Reciprocity*     133
   *Natural and Conventional Right*     140
   *The Subject of Justice*     149
   *General and Distributive Justice*     157
   *A Political Conception of the Common Good*     166

6. The Rule of Law     175
   *What Is Law?*     178
   *Adjudication*     184
   *A Political Conception of the Rule of Law*     194

7. Class Conflict and the Mixed Regime     209
   *Class Conflict in Ancient Greece*     210
   *A Political Understanding of Class Conflict*     215
   *Perceived Injustice and Class Interests*     218
   *Political Friends, Class Enemies*     224
   *The Mixed Regime and Political Justice*     231
   *Appendix. "Political Revolution": A Missing Aristotelian Category*     239

8. The Good Life in Political Context     242
   *Moral Character in Political Context*     243
   *Misfortune and the Asymmetry Between Praise and Blame*     251
   *Moral Conflict in Political Context*     259

9. The Good Life in Extrapolitical Context     268
   *How Good Is the Aristotelian Good Life?*     269
   *The Tensions Within a Good Human Life*     277

Conclusion     281

Bibliography     285

Index of Citations from Aristotle's Works     301

General Index     305

# Acknowledgments

Earlier versions of arguments presented in chapters 2, 3, 5, 8, and 9 have appeared in articles published in *The Review of Politics* 47, no. 1 (Jan. 1985): 92–112; *History of Political Thought* 12 (1991): 15–34; *Political Theory* 18 (May 1990): 16–37; and *Soundings* 72, no. 4 (Winter 1989): 607–29. I'd like to thank these journals for allowing me to alter and reprint portions of these articles.

I owe a great debt to all those friends and colleagues who read parts of this book as it developed over the years and who shared their insights with me. I'd especially like to thank Peter Euben, William Galston, Harvey Goldman, Jack Gunnell, Don Herzog, Stephen Holmes, Bernard Manin, Harvey C. Mansfield, Jr., Martha Nussbaum, Stephen Salkever, Arlene Saxonhouse, Lauren Schulz, Gary Shiffman, Judith Shklar, and Jeffrey Stout.

It has been my great good fortune in life to be able to share my ideas with Marion Smiley. In good times and bad, her extraordinary intelligence and intellectual honesty have been my constant inspiration.

# Introduction

The shared sentiments and commitments that constitute a community are often the source of its deepest conflicts. Anyone who has lived in a family rather than merely longed for a home knows that all too well. Strangers may cheat you, but only brothers or sisters, comrades or colleagues can betray you. In the end, intense and ugly forms of distrust and conflict are part of the price we pay for the pleasures of communal life.

Aristotle, unlike many of his contemporary followers, is deeply aware of the special conflicts associated with human communities. The intensity of our conflicts, he notes, increases with the closeness of our relationships. Anger is something that individuals "express more strongly against their companions, when they think they have been treated unjustly.... Hence the sayings 'Cruel are the wars of brothers' and 'Those who love extravagantly will hate extravagantly as well.' ... And it is reasonable," Aristotle concludes, "that this should happen. For, in addition to the injury, they also consider themselves robbed of this [companionship]" (*Politics* [hereafter *Pol.*] 1328a10).[1]

Critics of modern liberal democracies often invoke Aristotle's understanding of political community when they complain that our political

---

1. See Aristotle, *Rhetoric* 1379b2 and *Nicomachean Ethics* 1160a3, for similar remarks. Like Georg Simmel, Aristotle is familiar with "the wholly disproportionate violence to which normally well-controlled people can be moved within their relations to those closest to them"; G. Simmel, *Conflict*, 43–44.

1

life is nothing but "civil war carried on by other means," "a war of all against all . . . we make for ourselves, not out of whole cloth but out of an intentional distortion of our social natures."[2] But for Aristotle political community signifies a conflict-ridden reality rather than a vision of lost or future harmony. It is the scene of political conflict rather than its remedy. All the cruel, mindless, and selfish actions that we, sadly, associate with ordinary political life are included prominently among "the political things" (*ta politika*) that Aristotle sets out to study; he does not restrict his study to just the occasional moments of warmth and heroism. Just as there are peaks of virtue and cooperation that can be found only among citizens, so there are forms of distrust, conflict, and competition that only citizens experience. Accordingly, an Aristotelian account of politics must explain the problems of political life as well as its proudest achievements. And it must, as I try to show, use the bonds created by political community to help explain these problems rather than treat them as a consequence of the absence or weakening of communal bonds themselves. In other words, Aristotle insists on what we might call a communitarian account of political conflict and competition.

The very idea of a communitarian account of political conflict and competition may seem strange or paradoxical, given the general association of the term *communitarian* with aspirations toward social harmony and integration. Most contemporary communitarians see political community as a remedy for political conflict rather than one of its sources. But if, as communitarians insist, our shared practices and sentiments largely constitute our identity and character, then it seems sensible to look, as I suggest Aristotle does, to the way in which we share things in order to help explain our continuing social and political conflicts.

Aristotle also insists that a proper understanding of the achievements and opportunities made possible by political community must take due note of the imperfect and conflict-ridden conditions in which those achievements arise. He argues that although the political community comes into being for the sake of survival and comfort, its highest and final purpose is to enable us to lead the good life of rational and virtuous behavior. In particular, the political community provides us with the laws that help us acquire the virtues and the shared practices that

---

2. A. MacIntyre, *After Virtue*, 263; B. Barber, *Strong Democracy*, 75.

allow us to exercise and perfect them. Without it the Aristotelian good life is impossible.

Nevertheless, the political communities that enable us to lead the good life are the same imperfect and conflict-ridden communities described above. No actual political community has ever approached the requirements of the ideal regime outlined in book 7 of the *Politics*.[3] Aristotle cannot even cite an example of one that meets the less exacting standards of the correct (*orthos*)—or unqualifiedly just—regimes laid down in book 3. Hence, if we insist, as some do, that "without the ideal city, there will be no good men,"[4] then we must conclude that there have never have been and most likely never will be any virtuous individuals in this world. That cannot, of course, be Aristotle's conclusion.[5] But it is an unavoidable conclusion unless we can identify, as I try to do in this book, the ways in which ordinary, imperfect political communities can enable us to lead a good life.[6]

Unlike the majority of modern moral philosophers, Aristotle has a profound sense of the social and political constraints that condition ethical behavior. The Aristotelian good life is built on highly contingent and fragile foundations.[7] Unfavorable conditions can keep us from ever achieving it; unforeseen and uncontrollable circumstances can steal part or all of it away from us.

Such is the world in which the Aristotelian good life develops, a world in which nature gives us the tools—reasoning, speech, and the political community—with which to build the good life but, at the same time, erects innumerable and often overwhelming obstacles to realizing it. The problems and the opportunities of ordinary political life are thus inseparable for Aristotle. We need to understand political community in order to explain political conflict, and we need to understand political conflicts in order to identify and explain the nature of the good life as actually led.

---

3. On the utopian character of Aristotle's best regime, see C. Rowe, "Aims and Method," 69; R. Bodéüs, "Law and the Regime," 237–38.

4. T. Irwin, *Aristotle's First Principles*, 410.

5. If Aristotle did not believe that relatively virtuous individuals could emerge from the imperfect regimes of the ordinary political world, then he would have no audience for his lectures on ethics, for he insists that the only proper audience for such lectures consists of individuals who are already disposed by their upbringing to the virtuous life; *Nicomachean Ethics* 1095b4.

6. See below, esp. chapters 2 and 3.

7. Martha Nussbaum reconstructs this aspect of Aristotle's philosophical vision with wonderful clarity and insight in *The Fragility of Goodness*.

Unfortunately, the modern division of politics and ethics into separate disciplines makes it difficult to recognize this Aristotelian approach to the study of political conflict and human flourishing. Moral philosophers devote the bulk of their attention to the analysis and evaluation of concepts, leaving the study of social structures and contingencies to social and political theorists. They usually take note of the social contexts of ethical actions only when they talk of applying their conclusions to specific situations, as in the field of "applied ethics." As a result, they tend, unlike Aristotle, to see social structures and contingencies as factors that constrain the application of ethical concepts rather than as partly constitutive of these concepts. Even when contemporary commentators insist on the unity of Aristotelian ethical and political philosophy, they usually subordinate politics to ethics and underestimate the extent to which political contingencies constrain ethical choices and development.[8]

In this study I attempt to reconstruct Aristotle's understanding of the characteristic mixture of problems and opportunities created by life in ordinary political communities. I explore Aristotle's account of life in imperfect and conflict-ridden political communities—the only kind of political life that human beings have ever known. I try to show that we can gain new and interesting insights into the structure, constraints, and possibilities of ordinary political life by viewing them, as Aristotle does, as a mixture of inconveniences and opportunities that follow from our political nature.

My aim is to identify and explore the most interesting of these insights rather than offer a comprehensive commentary on or sustained defense of Aristotle's political philosophy. In the first part of the book (chapters 1–4) I consider a number of basic concepts in Aristotelian political philosophy: community, political community, political teleology, and political friendship. I try to show that these concepts are geared to explaining the nature of everyday political life rather than, as most

---

8. A particularly striking example of this subordination of Aristotelian politics to ethics appears in Terence Irwin's recent book, *Aristotle's First Principles*. Despite his own arguments against separating the two fields—part of a brilliant effort to unify the whole range of Aristotle's philosophical concerns—Irwin minimizes the political constraints on the achievement of the good life. "The Aristotelian virtues," he suggests, "rationally pursue the common good, and, in moderately favourable conditions, secure it"; *Aristotle's First Principles*, 447. Because he also insists that "without the ideal city there will be no good men" (ibid., 409), it seems that "moderately favourable conditions" include the highly improbable and never experienced conditions of Aristotle's best regime. Despite his insistence on the unity of politics and ethics, the political constraints on the development of the Aristotelian good life almost completely disappear in Irwin's account.

commentators assume, the moral achievements of Aristotle's best regime. Viewed in this way, Aristotelian concepts such as community and political friendship suggest some new and interesting ideas about the nature of social cooperation and conflict, ideas that are far more relevant to contemporary social life than Aristotelian political thought has been generally thought to be.

In the second part of the book (chapters 5–7) I discuss the key concepts that Aristotle uses to evaluate everyday political life: justice, the rule of law, and the mixed regime. I offer reinterpretations of each of these Aristotelian concepts that emphasizes the political problems that they are designed to explain and challenge. (In the case of the mixed regime examined in chapter 7, my reinterpretation requires an extended discussion of Aristotle's understanding of class conflict, the problem that the mixed regime is designed to address.) The key to these reinterpretations is my emphasis on the way in which the shared expectations of members of political communities shape and constrain concepts, such as justice and the rule of law, that are most often treated as having independent moral foundations. Much of my effort in these chapters is devoted to reasserting the political context in which Aristotle presents these concepts, a context that most interpreters ignore in order to integrate Aristotelian ideas into contemporary debates about justice and law.

Finally, in the third part of the book I discuss the constraints that our political nature puts on the achievement and enjoyment of the Aristotelian good life. In chapter 8 I explore the moral conflicts that arise for creatures that depend, as we do according to Aristotle, on our political communities for the moral training that makes the good life possible. In chapter 9 I discuss the limitations that Aristotle sees in a life that depends on the fragile and unreliable foundation of human politics.

I repeat that my aim is to identify and explore the most interesting of Aristotle's insights rather than offer a general commentary on his political work. I deal with specific concepts or problems concerning which Aristotle has some insight worth exploring, rather than with specific sections of his works. To highlight these insights, I devote considerable space in each chapter to showing how they can help us recognize limitations in the most influential approaches to a variety of issues in moral and political philosophy. Thus, although I hope that my efforts will alter the general image of Aristotle's political thought, I offer a series of explorations of related issues rather than a comprehensive reinterpretation of his political philosophy.

## POLITICAL COMMUNITY AS A TERM OF DISTINCTION

Scholars have paid relatively little attention to the elements of Aristotelian political philosophy reconstructed in this study. The widespread association of Aristotle's conception of community with contemporary longings for communal integration and harmony has led most contemporary commentators to minimize the significance of conflict and competition in his political philosophy.[9] Even Alisdair MacIntyre, one of Aristotle's most enthusiastic contemporary partisans, chides Aristotle for ignoring "the centrality of opposition and conflict in human life."[10] Despite the fact that Aristotle devotes the core of the *Politics*, books 3–6, to an extended analysis of political conflict and competition, most contemporary scholars would probably agree with MacIntyre.

This widespread misimpression grows out of, among other things, a relatively narrow and superficial understanding of Aristotle's claim about the naturalness of the political community. In the textbook accounts, this claim makes Aristotle a defender of the naturalness of cooperation among human beings and an opponent of those, like Hobbes, who insist that natural impulses drive human beings into conflict with each other.[11] Because Aristotle's claim about the naturalness of political community contrasts so much more sharply with widespread modern opinions than does anything he has to say about political conflict, his understanding of the nature—indeed, the naturalness—of political conflict is often ignored by modern scholars.

Aristotle does, of course, insist that human beings are by nature political animals. In doing so, he asserts that the way the Greeks live, engaged in the new and peculiar kind of activity we call politics, develops naturally out of human needs and inclinations and, more significantly, represents the only way in which human beings can fully develop their highest natural capacities. But this assertion has an important implication that, in spite of all the commentary and controversy it has inspired, has escaped most of Aristotle's commentators:[12] nature seems to have chosen a most imperfect and inconvenient way for human beings to develop and perfect their characteristic capacities. For *no* actual po-

---

9. Michael Stocker's *Plural and Conflicting Values* and Martha Nussbaum's *The Fragility of Goodness* provide valuable exceptions to the general underestimation of Aristotle's interest in moral and political conflict.

10. A. MacIntyre, *After Virtue*, 153.

11. For a typical comparison along these lines, see R. Dahl, *Modern Political Analysis*, 18.

12. A recent exception is S. Salkever, *Finding the Mean*, 19.

litical community is well-ordered according to Aristotle; consequently, "human affairs [*pragmatōn*] most often work out badly" (*Pol.* 1260b35, *Rhetoric* [hereafter *Rhet.*] 1389b16). All actual political regimes fall short of unqualified justice, and Aristotle's recommendations for improvement would still leave them short of the mark. Even Sparta, one of the only regimes in which Aristotle can find something to praise, pursues virtue for the sake of a dangerous and incorrect end: military power (*Pol.* 1271b1, 1333b–34b). One of the few actual regimes that Aristotle praises thus treats the virtues as if they exist for the sake of success at war, a view that he does not hesitate to condemn as "absolutely murderous" (*Nicomachean Ethics* [hereafter *NE*] 1177b10).

Aristotle concludes that "living together and sharing any human concern is always difficult" (*Pol.* 1263a15), and he recognizes that this difficulty increases in proportion to the extent and importance of what we share. In the political community human beings share something of the greatest importance: the endeavor to make possible the good life in which human beings most fully develop and perfect their natural capacities. Living together in political communities is thus especially difficult. If we need the political community to develop and perfect our nature, then nature has thrust us into a most problematic and precarious position. We are not, of course, the only social species. But we are, it seems, the only social species that depends for its development on a form of community so internally unstable and unreliable.

The concept of political community thus provides the key to Aristotle's understanding of ordinary political life. It is the first concept that Aristotle examines in the *Politics*, and it helps him define and explain all of the social phenomena he examines there. A political community is, according to Aristotle, a self-sufficient group of free and relatively equal individuals who have the opportunity to engage in regular and public discussion about which laws and policies should direct their activities and who take turns, according to regular and recognized rules, in ruling and being ruled.[13] Politics, as Aristotle understands it, concerns only the actions and interactions of members of such communities. Few nations and societies have participated in it, since the great majority of societies have been ruled by monarchs, emperors, dictators, and priests.

Aristotle would probably agree with Moses Finley's description of

---

13. I defend and explore this definition of political community in the second section of chapter 2.

politics as practiced by ancient Greeks as one of "the rarer of human activities."[14] Since the demise of the Greek polis, political activity, as Aristotle understands it, has frequently disappeared, reappearing occasionally among medieval and Renaissance city-states and more extensively among the liberal democratic republics of the modern world. Political community has sometimes emerged suddenly, with great noise and fanfare, as in France in 1789 or in Eastern Europe two hundred years later. Just as frequently it has died a violent death. Aristotle's concept of political community, I argue, can help us understand the structure of shared dispositions and expectations that shapes communal life in all places where political community has emerged and survived.[15]

"The political things" (*ta politika*) represent for Aristotle, as for most Greeks, the things that are associated with the Greek polis. But the Greek polis represents only one instance of the concept of political community that Aristotle constructs. It is the only instance with which Aristotle is himself familiar; but merely because he abstracts from the polis certain characteristics of a political community, there is no reason to assume that no other forms of political community are possible. Indeed, I argue in the final section of chapter 2 that the majority of modern republican nation-states share these characteristics and thus would be described by Aristotle as political communities. Smallness of size and population, which is often assumed to be an essential characteristic of Aristotelian political community, is only an essential feature of the best political community, the one sketched in book 7 of the *Politics*.

Nevertheless, Aristotle's relatively exclusive definition of politics is far narrower than those definitions popular among most contemporary students of politics.[16] Most of these students agree that politics is a universal activity, an activity that has a prominent place in every age and every independent community. The major debate among them is about whether or not politics plays a part in the organization of every group and society within an independent community. Some follow Max Weber in associating politics primarily with the state and its monopoly

---

14. M. Finley, *Politics in the Ancient World*, 52–53. See also C. Meier, *The Greek Discovery of the Political*; M. Gagarin, *Early Greek Law*, 144–46.
15. I defend this controversial assertion in later sections of the book.
16. Aristotle's definition of politics, however, is not as restrictive within political communities as those contemporary definitions that focus on state authority. Though relatively few independent communities have experienced political activity, according to Aristotle, within those few communities politics permeates well beyond governmental institutions into the general fabric of life. He certainly exempts the family from politics, but that is only because, given his claims about the status of women and slaves, the family community is not a place where citizens interact with each other.

on the legitimate use of violent force. Others speak of the politics of nonstate organizations, from families and unions to corporations and football teams.[17] Neither group follows Aristotle in treating politics as a term of distinction among the ways in which authority is exercised in autonomous communities.

Among twentieth-century political theorists, especially among those who are dissatisfied with liberal political theory and practice, there has been some resistance to the extremely broad understanding of politics favored by contemporary political scientists. Some political theorists, sometimes relying on Aristotelian ideas, have offered even more exclusive definitions of politics and the public realm than Aristotle's. Most often these definitions reserve the term *political* for actions that in some way transcend the special selfish interests of individuals and groups. According to these definitions, it is a mistake to describe contemporary liberal democracies as political communities or to expect to find any genuine political activity within them.

Hannah Arendt developed the most famous and influential of these definitions in *The Human Condition*. She argues there that politics is an activity in which we seek to overcome the biological constraints that in other activities tie us to narrower family and economic interests. For Arendt the public realm is a common space in which we express our freedom from biological and economic necessity.[18] The prevalence of a pluralist form of politics in which different groups determine public policy by balancing their economic and personal interests represents, from this point of view, the elimination of true political activity from modern life. In recent years an increasing number of political theorists have invoked republican or "civic humanist" rhetoric to make similar claims about the ways in which individualism and interest group politics have destroyed the public realm. In these criticisms, the defining feature of true public activity is discussion of and devotion to a truly *common* good.[19]

The existence of this countercurrent has, as Hanna Pitkin notes, introduced two very different ways of talking about politics into contem-

---

17. See, for example, the articles collected in A. Leftwich, *What Is Politics?* and R. Dahl, *Modern Political Analysis*, 5–6.
18. H. Arendt, *The Human Condition*, 9–69.
19. For recent statements of "civic republican" ideals, see W. Sullivan, *Reconstructing Public Philosophy*; A. Oldfield, *Citizenship and Community*; R. Bellah et al., *Habits of the Heart*. The revival of civic republican theorizing was inspired, to a great extent, by the reconstruction of the venerable tradition of republican rhetoric by J. G. A. Pocock, *The Machiavellian Moment*, and the reinterpretation of the American Founders' rhetoric by Gordon Wood, *The Creation of the American Republic*.

porary scholarly discourse. In one, politics describes one ordinary empirical feature of every independent community, if not of every form of human association. In the other, politics describes a substantive moral standard of behavior, a standard that contemporary political behavior clearly fails to meet.[20]

Because the advocates of the more exclusive moral conception of politics often build their arguments on Aristotelian ideas, most contemporary readers associate Aristotle's relatively exclusive understanding of politics with theirs. One of my major goals in the following chapters is to dissolve that association. Aristotle has a much more exclusive definition of politics than most contemporary social scientists do. Politics, as he conceives of it, occurs only in a relatively small portion of human social groups. Nevertheless, Aristotelian political community is not an ideal that we approach the more we eliminate the influence of selfish individual interests. Self-serving actions, just as much as self-sacrificing actions, can express the shared expectations and identity introduced by this form of communal life.[21]

A reconstruction of Aristotle's account of ordinary political life can improve our understanding of politics in at least two ways. Negatively, it might help undermine the recurring temptation to dismiss the imperfect politics of everyday life in the name of romantic and moralistic images of political community. More positively, however, it might encourage us to take imperfect politics far more seriously than we may now be inclined to do. By showing how even the imperfect politics of actual political communities can make human flourishing possible, it encourages us to use our understanding of the problems of a political community to identify the real possibilities for a good human life.

## DISTORTED IMAGES OF ARISTOTELIAN POLITICS

Despite the considerable space that Aristotle devotes to the study of actual Greek politics, most scholars view him as too much the teleological moralist to be a trustworthy guide to the structure and conflicts of ordinary political life. As noted earlier, even a contemporary champion of Aristotelian ethics such as Alisdair MacIntyre complains that Aristotle has too elevated and harmonious an understanding of political

---

20. H. Pitkin, *Wittgenstein and Justice*, 208–9. See also B. Fay, *Social Theory and Political Practice*, 54–55, where this understanding of politics, endorsed by a number of modern theorists, including Arendt, is described as the "Aristotelian vision of politics"; C. Meier, *The Greek Discovery of the Political*, 7.

21. These are controversial claims that run counter to a large body of commentary on Aristotle's work. I develop and defend them throughout the book.

life.²² Hence, before proceeding with my reconstruction of Aristotle's understanding of the problems of ordinary political life, I need to identify and challenge the various sources of this widely shared image of Aristotelian political philosophy.

Many contemporary scholars believe that it was Hannah Arendt's great achievement "to recover and restore the ancient conception of the public realm."²³ Her views have, accordingly, played a very large role in shaping contemporary images of ancient politics, images that often reflect her overly heroic view of both Aristotelian political theory and ancient Greek political practice.

Although Arendt does not eliminate conflict from her account of political life, political conflict, as she understands it, takes place on a very elevated plain where men and women break free of concerns about biological and economic necessity in order to compete for eternal fame. The Greeks, she claims, recognized that debates about the distribution of goods are not, properly speaking, political subjects. In the modern world, in contrast, we have allowed these "social" concerns, with their degrading ties to natural necessities, to pollute the free air of public discourse. As a result, both politics and the public realm have virtually disappeared from the modern world.²⁴

> What all Greek philosophers, no matter how opposed to polis life, took for granted is that freedom is exclusively located in the political realm, that necessity is primarily a prepolitical phenomenon, characteristic of the private household organization.... The "good life," as Aristotle called the life of the citizen, was not merely better, more carefree or nobler than ordinary life, but of an altogether different quality. It was "good" to the extent that by having mastered the necessities of sheer life, by being freed from labour and work, and by overcoming the innate urge of all living creatures for their own survival, it was no longer bound to the biological life process.²⁵

In this passage Arendt attributes to Aristotle and the Greeks a dichotomy between politics, freedom, and humanity on the one hand and social needs, biological necessity, and nature on the other. This dichotomy has become so influential that descriptions of Aristotelian and ancient Greek politics as an effort to transcend nature and biological necessity have become commonplace among contemporary scholars.²⁶

22. A. MacIntyre, *After Virtue*, 153.
23. S. Dossa, *The Public Realm*, 139.
24. H. Arendt, *The Human Condition*, 23–65, 286–97.
25. Ibid., 29, 33.
26. For example, Stephen Holmes (*Benjamin Constant*, 58, 58n23) complains about "Aristotle's view of total citizenship as a glorious triumph of the best in man over a

Unfortunately, few dichotomies could be more foreign to the letter or spirit of Aristotelian philosophy. Aristotle does distinguish between the household (*oikos* or *oikia*) and the polis. But Arendt's parallel distinctions between humanity and nature and between the good life of politics and "the biological life-process" directly contradict Aristotle's understanding of nature and humanity. Aristotle clearly states in the opening book of the *Politics* that both our distinctiveness as human beings and our attachment to political life grow out of our biological nature. We are by nature political creatures because we are naturally inclined to live in communities and because our natural capacity for speech and argument lead us to form specifically *political* communities.[27] Although we need to assist nature to establish political communities and promote moral virtue, in doing so we work with our natural capacities rather than against them. A life in which we somehow succeeded in "overcoming the innate urge of all living for their own survival," a life in which we were "no longer bound to the biological life process," might be divine or beastly, according to Aristotle. But it would not be a human, let alone a political, life.

Arendt's dichotomies have a far greater affinity to post-Kantian German philosophy, from which they were drawn, than to Aristotelian political philosophy, let alone Greek political practice.[28] Ever since Kant drew his famous distinction between a phenomenal world of nature governed by necessary causal laws and a noumenal world of human reason governed by self-imposed moral laws, German philosophers have tended to see humanity as an achievement to be won against nature.

---

sniveling desire for mere life," but he cites Arendt, rather than Aristotle, as his reference. E. M. Wood (*Mind and Politics*, 174–75) also suggests, but more approvingly, that "for the Greeks the realm of politics was the realm of freedom, the truly human, in which man raised himself above the natural order." Wood, however, has come in her later study of Athenian democracy (*Peasant-Citizen and Slave*, 40–41) to recognize the "gross misapprehensions" of Arendt's account of Greek politics. She wonders "how different her [Arendt's] historical judgments might have been had she been forced to attribute the glories of ancient Athens . . . to the baleful influence of its 'banausic' citizens," that is, the poor citizens who continued to struggle with nature to satisfy biological necessities.

27. I develop this argument fully in the second section of chapter 2.

28. See S. Salkever, *Finding the Mean*, 173–74, for similar criticisms of Arendt's interpretation of Aristotle. On occasion, Arendt seems to misrepresent Aristotelian opinions deliberately, as when she quotes his discussion of "the possibility of immortalizing" as support for her claim that "the polis was for the Greeks . . . their guarantee against the futility of individual life, the space protected against this futility and reserved for the relative permanence, if not immortality, of mortals." She notes here, correctly, that this passage "occurs very properly in his [Aristotle's] political writings" (*The Human Condition*, 51). But she neglects to mention that it is part of a description of the contemplative life, a description that explicitly contrasts the "immortalizing" aims of contemplation with the all-too-mortal limitations of political life (*NE* 1177b31).

One problem they wrestle with again and again is how to realize our humanity and freedom in a world that seems to be dominated by nature and necessity.[29] Arendt's conception of politics represents another attempt to describe a way in which we can realize our humanity in a natural world that resists our efforts. Whatever its virtues, it has little to do with Aristotle's understanding of political life or with ancient Greek political life itself.

The central focus of political conflict in Aristotle's *Politics,* as in Athenian political life itself, is disagreement about the distribution of goods and power. Yet this is precisely the kind of activity that Arendt insists has no place in the public realm. As Pitkin has noted, Arendtian politics replaces debate about distributive justice with a kind of schoolboy competition about who has more contempt for degrading natural necessities.[30] Aristotelian politics, in contrast, never severs its roots in nature and natural necessity and the debates about distributive justice that those roots nourish. For Aristotle, our political virtues reflect our natural capacities and our political problems reflect our natural needs and limitations.

If Arendt's conception of politics is so foreign to Aristotle's conceptual vocabulary, what accounts for the widespread acceptance of her image of Aristotelian political philosophy? The main reason, I suggest, is that her claims are read within the context of an older and broader controversy about the nature of political community, a controversy that inclines modern scholars to exaggerate the nobility and harmony of Aristotelian politics. I am referring here to the debates that have grown up around communitarian critiques of liberal individualism.

When one reads the *Politics* with these debates in mind, Aristotle's statements about the priority of the political community to the individual seem the most striking and important. Hence, Aristotle's interpreters often identify his arguments with the numerous objections that political philosophers have raised against liberal individualism. Since these

---

29. I discuss the way in which Kant's freedom-nature dichotomy shapes a large part of radical German social criticism, from Schiller and the young Hegel through Marx and Nietzsche, in *The Longing for Total Revolution;* see esp. ch. 3, "The Social Discontent of the Kantian Left." Arendt's understanding of politics and the active life fits very well into the "left Kantian" tradition of social criticism I reconstruct there. Her version of the realization of humanity in the natural world, with its emphasis on the longing to immortalize oneself (*The Human Condition,* 50–51), takes its cue from Heidegger's understanding of the way in which human beings are distinguished from the rest of nature: their awareness of death and finitude, an awareness that leads Heidegger to describe human existence as "being-toward-death" (M. Heidegger, *Being and Time,* 279–311).
30. H. Pitkin, "Justice."

philosophers often make their complaints in the name of lost ancient political theories and practices, opponents and proponents of liberal individualism often identify Aristotle with these complaints. Eric Havelock, a defender of liberal individualism, goes so far in his identification of Aristotle's arguments with those of contemporary anti-individualists that he assumes that Aristotle must have been directing his arguments against a vigorous tradition of liberal individualism among the ancient Greeks. That tradition, Havelock suggests, disappeared from the written record due, in no small part, to Aristotle's efforts to conceal it.[31]

Rousseau was the first and certainly the most influential of the social critics to invoke ancient theory and practice against liberal individualism. Building on Montesquieu's reinterpretation of republican virtue, he constructed a vision of ancient citizenship and public education in which the political community's laws "denature man" by replacing the independence of the natural man with the human freedom and generalized social dependence of the citizen.[32] That vision continues to shape the way in which scholars understand ancient political theory and practice, even when they do not explicitly invoke Rousseau and the general will. Defenders of the civic republican tradition may trace the origins of that tradition back to Aristotle. But when they describe republican politics as "a collective enterprise in self-transformation,"[33] they are using a Rousseauian political vocabulary that is completely out of place in the Aristotelian understanding of politics.

Aristotle, unlike Rousseau, did not believe that human beings need the denaturing exercise in "self-transformation" that Rousseau and civic republicans celebrate. We certainly need law and moral education in order to live a fully human life, according to Aristotle. Without them we are unlikely to develop the virtues that are the foundation of a good

31. E. Havelock, *The Liberal Temper*, esp. 371. See the critiques of Havelock in L. Strauss, "The Liberalism"; S. Holmes, "Aristippus," 115n6.

32. J.-J. Rousseau, *Emile*, 39–40, and *On the Social Contract*, book 1, ch. 7. Anyone familiar with Rousseau's works will recognize that this vision of virtuous citizenship represents only one side of Rousseauian political thought, a side that is, depending on one's point of view, balanced or contradicted by the much more individualistic understanding of human freedom presented in works such as his *Discourse on the Origins of Inequality* and *Reveries of a Solitary Walker*.

33. W. Sullivan, *Reconstructing Public Philosophy*, 158. Contemporary defenders of the civic republican tradition rarely note how profoundly Rousseau altered traditional understandings of citizenship, civic virtue, and political community. As a result, they tend to write Rousseauian conceptions of republican politics back into ancient and Renaissance conceptions. See B. Yack, *The Longing for Total Revolution*, for a discussion of the ways in which Rousseau broke with and distorted earlier conceptions of republican politics and civic virtue (35–81) and for a discussion of Arendt's debt to this new Rousseauian conception of citizenship (70–72).

life (*NE* 1103a–b, 1179b–80a). But the training of the virtues is not for Aristotle a fight against nature, and certainly not a struggle to transform naturally self-regarding beings into other-regarding citizens. It is instead a process in which we draw out and build on human beings' natural capacities and natural impulses for communal living.[34]

As already noted, it is not surprising that Aristotle's political thought is often associated with modern critiques of liberal individualism, given his claims about the priority of the community to the individual as well as the extensive criticism that many liberal theorists direct at these claims. But this association misleads many scholars into exaggerating Aristotle's hostility to social conflict and social differentiation. Aristotle does not develop his conception of political community as an answer to the celebrations of social differentiation and competition found in the writings of modern liberal individualists. If anything, he writes to counter the extreme communitarianism of Plato's *Republic,* a book that, he complains, makes social unity the measure of political health (*Pol.* 1261–62).[35] Aristotle argues against Plato that the elimination of social heterogeneity threatens to eliminate political community itself; *community* signifies for Aristotle a combination of sharing and differentiation rather than social unity (*Pol.* 1261a14–1261b15).[36] Aristotle's conception of political community seeks to explain rather than eliminate social differentiation and the conflicts that arise therefrom. As long as we identify his communitarianism with contemporary assaults on individualism and social differentiation, we will seriously misunderstand his account of political life.

I am not, however, insisting on removing the layers of communitarian interpretation that have settled on Aristotelian ideas solely in the name of textual fidelity. After all, one may prefer creative distortions to more faithful readings of texts, especially when one challenges, as do so many contemporary readers, the very notion of more or less authentic interpretations. I attempt to dig beneath overly communitarian readings because I believe that what we find there can help us analyze and resolve conceptual and theoretical difficulties that are, in large part, a legacy of the polemics between individualists and their communitarian critics.

---

34. On Aristotelian moral education, see M. Burnyeat, "Aristotle on Learning"; C. Lord, *Education and Culture;* N. Sherman, *The Fabric of Character.*

35. As R. F. Stalley ("Aristotle's Critique of Plato's *Republic,*" 184–85) notes, Aristotle seems more concerned in his account of Plato's *Republic* to correct our understanding of community than to present a full assessment of Plato's arguments.

36. I elaborate on this argument in chapters 1 and 2 and in "Community and Conflict."

Aristotle built his understanding of ordinary political life on the soundest of communitarian premises: the social construction of individual identities and aspirations. But unlike contemporary communitarians, he had no need to enlist this premise in a polemical war against advocates of liberal individualism. As a result, his communitarian conception of politics has none of the exaggerated hopes for moral harmony and elevated behavior associated with contemporary communitarianism. If one is seeking to construct an adequate communitarian understanding of ordinary political life, or even if one is interested only in seeing what might be learned from such an understanding, then one could do no better than to start with Aristotle.

Another, more textually based reason for the general assumption that Aristotle downplays the significance of political conflict is a widespread misunderstanding of his understanding of political teleology. According to Aristotle's teleological understanding of nature, it is the completed and perfected form of a species that accurately displays its nature. If, as Aristotle asserts, the polis is natural, then, most commentators conclude, the true political community must be its best and most perfect form: the best regime described by Aristotle in books 7 and 8 of *Politics*. We must deny, according to this understanding of Aristotelian political teleology, that actual political regimes, all of which fall short of this standard, are properly described as political communities at all, since they fail to grow into their complete and natural form. Instead of teaching us about a genuine political community, they merely manifest, as it were, the diseases and defects that prevent most political communities from maturing into healthy and fully functioning members of their species. From this perspective, the problems of ordinary political life tell us no more about a truly human life than a severely retarded child and a rotten acorn tell us about the inherent capacities of human beings and oaks.

In the third chapter of this book I try to demonstrate that this widely shared view represents a misunderstanding of Aristotle's political teleology. The polis itself, I argue, does not have a nature, according to Aristotle, and thus does not have its own natural end as a completed and perfected form. The polis derives its naturalness, instead, from properties of human nature. The end of the polis is thus not to develop itself into a complete and perfected form but rather to contribute to the development and perfection of human beings into their complete and natural form. Aristotle makes this end clear with his repeated claim that the polis exists for the sake of the good life. Unlike natural species, the political community exists for the sake of something else, not for the sake of its own development. It measures up to its natural form as long as it makes the contribution to human development without which human beings cannot complete themselves. Showing that the imperfect and conflict-ridden regimes of ordinary political life can make this contribution—though not, of course, as well as the best regime could do—is one of the primary aims of this book.

There is also a widely held view, developed first by Werner Jaeger, that Aristotle's theory of the good life and his empirical approach to the study of actual political life represent inconsistent strands in his political philosophy, strands written at different periods of his philosophical development.[37] But this view rests less on any historical evidence of Aristotle's development than on the assumption that the two approaches are as inconsistent as Platonic idealism and modern scientific empiricism. The acceptance of this assumption has contributed greatly to the paucity of theoretically interesting commentary on Aristotle's political thought in this century. In the middle years of this century, most scholars were more concerned with identifying when and in what order Aristotle expressed his thoughts about politics than with what we might learn from them.[38] By ascribing the most unexpected combinations of ideas in his political works to different periods in his development, they stripped his texts of some of their most interesting insights and thought-provoking problems. My reinterpretation of Aristotle's political teleology should diminish the need for this theoretically uninteresting genetic approach by minimizing the appearance of inconsistency that originally inspired it.[39]

Finally, the tendency of most contemporary scholars to treat politics and ethics as separate disciplines also poses an obstacle to an appreciation of the relationship between Aristotle's theory of the good life and the imperfections of ordinary political life. With the notable exception of the final pages of the *Nicomachean Ethics,* Aristotle's so-called ethical writings contain few direct references to the conflicts and constraints of ordinary political life. If one treats these writings as the foundation of a separate science of ethics, then it is easy to get the impression that

37. W. Jaeger, *Aristotle,* 269–92.
38. For example, see the articles collected in P. Steinmetz, *Schriften zu den Politika.*
39. In recent years students of Aristotle's political thought have increasingly challenged Jaeger's genetic approach to interpreting Aristotle's political writings. See, for example, A. Kamp, *Die Politische Philosophie des Aristoteles,* 124; R. Bodéüs, *Le philosophe et la cité,* 12, 133; G. Huxley, "On Aristotle's Best State," 144–46; C. Johnson, *Aristotle's Theory of the State,* xvi, 20–21; C. Rowe, "Aims and Methods."

the imperfections and untidiness of ordinary political life have little to do with Aristotle's understanding of ethical action. This is especially true if, like most English-speaking scholars, one is far more interested in the ideas expressed in the ethical writings than in those found in the so-called political writings.[40]

But Aristotle, unlike the majority of his contemporary interpreters, never distinguishes a science of ethics from a science of politics, nor does he treat ethics and politics as subdivisions of a more comprehensive science.[41] He states plainly in the opening pages of the *Nicomachean Ethics* that he is about to begin "an investigation of political matters" and that the study of the virtues belongs to "politics," the science that teaches us how to attain and safeguard the good for an entire people (*NE* 1094a27–1094b12). The Aristotelian virtues develop within the structures created by political communities. Without those structures they would neither grow nor find the opportunity for expression. Interpreting these virtues without reference to Aristotle's understanding of the political structure within which they operate fundamentally alters their meaning. If the ethical virtues require political communities in order to develop and prosper, and if, as Aristotle clearly believes, almost all actual political communities are badly constituted, then the good life will depend to a certain extent on imperfect political regimes. The good life as actually lived and the imperfections of ordinary political life are thus tied tightly together.

## INTERPRETIVE APPROACHES

One of the most important reasons for engaging in careful analysis of texts from older and foreign cultures is to gain some critical distance on the predominant ideas and institutions of our own time. When we set out to challenge these ideas and institutions directly, we still must use the conceptual vocabulary that they have shaped. Older and foreign

---

40. The number of English books and articles on Aristotelian ethics is many times that of books and articles on his political philosophy. The great majority of the former make little or no reference to political problems (although with the recent growth of interest in Aristotle's political thought this situation is beginning to change). We do not find the same separation of ethical and political analysis among German scholars. See, for example, Joachim Ritter's articles on Aristotle in *Metaphysik und Politik*; G. Bien, *Die Grundlagen der Politische Philosophie bei Aristoteles*; M. Riedel, *Metaphysik und Metapolitik*; E. Schütrumpf, *Die Analyse der Polis*; A. Kamp, *Die Politische Philosophie des Aristoteles*.

41. See R. Bodéüs, *Le philosophe et la cité*, 55–91, for a comprehensive and persuasive defense of this claim. See also J. Burnet, *The Ethics of Aristotle*; S. Cashdollar, "Aristotle's Politics of Morals".

texts, in contrast, do not owe anything to that vocabulary. Looking at our ideas and institutions from the point of view embodied in them provides us with a unique opportunity to identify the questions and premises that limit our vocabulary and the range of alternatives we normally consider. From this perspective, seemingly irreconcilable disagreements among contemporary schools of thought often reveal themselves as family squabbles, and some of our unspoken assumptions begin to emerge into view. Paradoxically, one of the most effective ways of promoting new ideas about familiar subjects is to look at them from the perspective of older thinkers such as Aristotle. It is to gain this critical distance on some of our political ideas that I attempt my reconstruction of Aristotle's view of ordinary political life.

One major problem with this approach to reading texts is that it threatens to transform them into mere negative images of contemporary conceptions, a transformation that distorts their meaning as surely as if we viewed them as mirrors of contemporary conceptions. To a certain extent, the danger of this kind of distortion is unavoidable in interpretation. We need to refer to our own conceptions in order to make sense of what we read, even if only to provide the contrasts that make a text intelligible. Every attempt to recreate exactly the pattern of thought that guided an earlier author is bound to fail at some point since our experiences do not exactly match those of the author. Modern readers inevitably contrast Aristotle's political ideas with those of Machiavelli and Hobbes and all the other authors with whom they, unlike Aristotle, are familiar. Even if they make the most scrupulous efforts to avoid writing later ideas into their understanding of Aristotle's words, their interpretations will reflect contrasts that Aristotle himself did not consider.[42] That is one reason why "history knows no repetitions of the same."[43] Renaissances lead either to innovation or sterility.

Does that mean we are deluding ourselves when we believe that consideration of ancient texts can give us some critical distance on the ideas and vocabulary of our time? I think not. The critical distance I am speaking of does not require us to occupy some Archimedean point completely outside of our culture. We need our own conceptions to interpret the conceptions of others. They are, after all, our only access to foreign conceptions. But if we make an effort to move back and forth

---

42. See H.-G. Gadamer, *Truth and Method*, 482–85. In this passage Gadamer is challenging Leo Strauss's arguments about the need to interpret texts, especially classical Greek texts, as their authors understood them.
43. H. Blumenberg, *The Legitimacy of the Modern Age*, 596.

between the two sets of conceptions and, especially, to look at our own from the point of view of those to which we have gained access, then we can learn something about ourselves as well as others. To gain a critical distance on our own conceptions, we cannot rest satisfied with posing a series of questions to the older texts that we possess; we must also try to reconstruct the questions that their authors would ask about us and our questions. By trying to imagine how these authors would view the questions we initially pose to their texts, we may identify some of the unrecognized assumptions that shaped our initial attempt at understanding them. Such a dialogic approach to interpretation can expand our self-awareness without asserting the possibility of escaping our preconceptions in reading older and foreign texts. We may not be able to break Gadamer's famous "hermeneutic circle,"[44] but we can certainly expand its circumference. Engaging in dialogue with the authors of older and foreign texts is one way of broadening the range of questions and preconceptions that we can bring to the interpretation of any phenomenon.

This dialogic approach to interpretation guides my reconstruction of Aristotle's view of ordinary political life. It requires that I engage both in close and careful reading of Aristotelian texts and in attempts to imagine how Aristotle would respond to later intellectual approaches and political innovations. By engaging Aristotle in such a dialogue, I do run the risk of distorting Aristotle's ideas and thus losing the critical distance on our own conceptions that I originally sought. But, I would argue, by remaining self-conscious about the role that contemporary questions play in any interpretation of older texts, we can both minimize this risk and lengthen that critical distance.

One might argue that the best way of minimizing the risk of distorting older texts is not to refer to later ideas and events at all when interpreting them. But the disadvantage of this approach is that without serious reflection on how an author would respond to later ideas and events, it becomes much more difficult to identify and compensate for the preconceptions that we ourselves bring to the interpretation of older texts. No method of interpretation can completely secure an older text from anachronistic distortion. By helping us to identify our preconceptions, my more dialogic approach to interpretation provides an alternative method of dealing with the risks of anachronistic distortions.

Engaging Aristotle in this kind of dialogue clearly moves my inter-

---

44. H.-G. Gadamer, *Truth and Method*, 235–40, 258–67.

pretation beyond the relatively strict adherence to Aristotle's explicit arguments favored by most students of his works. Like the great majority of Aristotle's commentators, I do try to justify most of my interpretations by citing explicit statements from his texts, but I also present two other kinds of interpretive argument. On the one hand, I sometimes develop and defend new interpretations by juxtaposing Aristotelian passages that have not previously been brought together. On the other hand, I often construct arguments based on the implications of Aristotelian insights, even when Aristotle himself never explicitly endorses or discusses these implications.

I make use of both kinds of argument in the reconstruction of Aristotle's understanding of community with which my book begins. Aristotle devotes to community (*koinōnia*) nothing like the explicit and sustained attention that he gives to the concept of political community. Indeed, Aristotle's most important remarks about community are incidental to his discussion of friendship in book 8 of the *Nicomachean Ethics*. Nevertheless, when we reconsider his discussions of social and political phenomena such as justice and friendship in the light of these remarks, new and intriguing ideas about social and political interaction quickly suggest themselves. I try both to identify these ideas and explore their implications in my discussion of Aristotle's understanding of community, even though direct appeal to Aristotle's words cannot conclusively confirm that he would accept this understanding as his own. In the end, I am more concerned about the intrinsic value of this understanding of community than in proving *conclusively* that Aristotle advocates it.

This approach to interpretation is bound to be somewhat controversial, especially among students of Aristotle's works. Questions about interpretation provoke some of the most heated controversies among contemporary social and political theorists; indeed, answers to these questions are often far more controversial than the interpretations they support. Nevertheless, these controversies are often repetitive and unnecessary. We could avoid many of them if interpreters would make a greater effort to make clear to themselves and to their audiences the interests that guide their interpretations.

Like the majority of Aristotle's commentators, my reconstruction of his arguments will be based on close and careful analysis of the Aristotelian canon. It is only through careful analysis of Aristotle's words that we can use them to gain a critical distance on later ideas and events. Where I may differ from many contemporary commentators is in the interest that I bring to close reading of Aristotelian texts. My own interest in Aristotle's writings lies in the recovery and reconsideration of unfamiliar insights into the nature of ordinary political life. This interest often leads me to choose, when there is more than one plausible interpretation of an Aristotelian passage or argument, the most original and theoretically provocative interpretation. Scholars who aim at constructing as accurate as possible an account of what Aristotle intended to say or who seek insight into the political ideas and practices characteristic of fourth-century Athens might well make different choices and are welcome to them.

Every interpretation requires such choices. All interpreters have to limit the meaning of the texts that they consider. Even those who seek to render as exact as possible an account of an author's intended meaning do not canvass all the possible meanings of the text. That would be an impossible task, since it would require considering the text from the perspective of every conceivable interest that it could inspire. Instead, they usually construct a limited context within which to determine the author's intended meaning: for example, the common meaning of terms at a given period or within the covers of the given text.[45] In either case, interest in the reconstruction of the author's intended meaning leads them to make choices that exclude possible and plausible meanings. What distinguishes my approach from theirs is the theoretical interest that guides my choice of interpretations rather than a cavalier attitude toward Aristotle's intended meaning.

One might still object, however, that the somewhat speculative interpretive approach used in this book, while legitimate in itself, is less appropriate for an interpretation of Aristotelian texts than it is in many other cases. After all, Aristotle, unlike his more flamboyant teacher, has left us treatises rather than dialogues—we have only fragments of his dialogues—and treatises communicate ideas much more directly than dramatic dialogues do. As a result, most commentators seem to assume that interpretation of Aristotle's works requires much less imagination than interpretation of Plato's does. They sometimes proceed as if, unlike Plato, Aristotle attempted to make explicit everything he intended to say, so that his interpreters' primary task is to pull together and render consistent (or declare inconsistent) the Aristotelian passages relevant to the issue that they choose to consider. In any case, few contem-

---

45. On the construction of explanatory contexts in the interpretation of texts, see B. Yack, *The Longing for Total Revolution,* xiv-xvi.

porary studies of Aristotle contain anything like the imaginative discussions of textual interpretation that appear in most books on the Platonic dialogues.

I believe, however, that the sharp contrast between Platonic dialogues and Aristotelian treatises has led us to exaggerate the explicitness of Aristotle's arguments. After all, we exaggerate a little when we say that we possess Aristotelian treatises. Drafts of treatises, lectures, lecture notes prepared by Aristotle or taken down by his students, a combination of all or some of the above by later redactors—we cannot be sure what we have in Aristotle's extant works.[46] We can be sure, however, that the great extant Aristotelian works are not, in contrast to the Platonic dialogues, finished pieces of writing meant for publication. We do not know how Aristotle, had he polished and published his treatises, would have connected the often disconnected arguments within each text, let alone the related arguments in different texts. It is, however, safe to assume, at the very least, that he provided his students with explanations and illustrations of these arguments that we do not see in his extant works.

The form of Aristotle's writings thus encourages us to pursue questions and connections that he does not explicitly ask and make. When reading Plato's works, we need to use our imagination to identify the implicit ideas and arguments toward which the author seeks to guide us by his explicit portrayal of setting, character, and argument. When reading Aristotle, in contrast, we need to use our imagination to fill in gaps in his explicit but unfinished arguments. We have to ask, for example, how Aristotle's discussions of related phenomena fit together, even if Aristotle himself does not explicitly note any connection between these discussions, and why he starts his treatment of various topics where he does, even when he offers no explicit explanation of his starting points.

It is far wiser, in my opinion, to admit openly the need for imaginative reconstruction of Aristotle's arguments than to pretend that his texts provide final, explicit standards against which to measure his meanings. Even if we were solely interested in recapturing the intended meaning of Aristotle's words, we could not refrain from such reconstruction. Those of us who seek new theoretical insights from his works depend even more on imaginative reconstructions of his ideas.

---

46. See A.-H. Chroust, *Aristotle*. For a lively and informative account of the posthumous fate of Aristotle's manuscripts and library, see L. Canfora, *The Vanished Library*, 26–29, 51–58, 173–82.

CHAPTER ONE

# Community

Aristotle begins the *Politics* with the assertion that "every polis is some sort of community [*koinōnia*]" (*Pol.* 1252a1). In the pages that follow, he has a great deal to say about just what "sort of community" the polis is. He does not, however, devote much attention in the *Politics* to questions about what sort of thing a "community" is.

Because the majority of Aristotle's remarks about community appear in his discussion of friendship in the *Nicomachean Ethics*, rather than in the *Politics*, they receive little attention in most accounts of his political thought. These accounts generally begin, like the *Politics* itself, with a discussion of the nature of the polis. Curtis Johnson, for example, has recently suggested that the nature of the state (or, more specifically, the nature of the political regime [*politeia*]) is the "first-order question" of Aristotelian political philosophy, the question we must answer before we can address "second-order" questions about how to evaluate various forms of the state.[1] But because Aristotle describes the polis as a species of the genus *community*, we have good reason to give priority to questions about community over questions about the nature of the state,[2] unless it turns out that Aristotle has little of importance or interest to say about the concept.

1. C. Johnson, *Aristotle's Theory of the State*, xv–xviii, 16–20.
2. Whether or not we describe a question about the nature of community, instead of a question about the nature of the state, as the "first-order" question is another matter. As I note in the final section of the Introduction, the framing and order of questions inevitably reflect our interpretive interests in a particular subject.

In this chapter I try to show that Aristotle has an original and insightful understanding of the nature and sources of communal life in general, even if we have to reconstruct that understanding from distinct and unsystematic discussions.³ Moreover, my reconstruction of Aristotle's understanding of community provides the foundation for many of the reinterpretations of familiar Aristotelian concepts (political community, political friendship, justice, the rule of law, and the mixed regime) that I present in the following chapters. Many of Aristotle's most familiar arguments begin to take on an unfamiliar and theoretically provocative appearance when we look at them in the light of what he has to say about community.

Overly romantic and moralistic images of Aristotelian politics owe a great deal to lack of familiarity with Aristotle's own understanding of community. Because modern commentators pay little attention to Aristotle's scattered remarks about community, they usually fall back on more familiar current conceptions of community when discussing his moral and political arguments. But, as I argue in this chapter, Aristotle differs from most modern social theorists in that he treats community as a generic rather than a specific social category. He uses it to characterize *all* social groups rather than to characterize one especially close and highly integrated form of social life. When we replace the modern understandings of community that shape most interpretations of Aristotle's political thought with this Aristotelian conception, his account of politics loses much of its romantic and moralistic glow and some of his most interesting insights into everyday political life emerge more clearly.

Unfortunately, Aristotle's commentators rarely distinguish clearly enough between his concepts of community and political community to recognize, let alone elaborate on, his implicit approach to social theory.⁴ When modern scholars invoke Aristotle's words, as they frequently do, to support their arguments about the *social* nature of human beings, they usually refer to his description of human beings as *political* animals and simply ignore the Aristotelian distinction between community and political community emphasized in this chapter.⁵ But

3. See W. L. Newman, *The Politics of Aristotle* 1:41.
4. The most interesting treatment of Aristotle's understanding of community can be found in M. Finley, "Aristotle and Economic Analysis," 144.
5. Some of Aristotle's most perceptive readers do notice that Aristotle extends the natural sociality of human beings well beyond the boundaries of the political community. But even they have, for the most part, tried to account for the whole range of human sociality within his concept of political community. To do so, they provide elaborate

by conflating Aristotle's understanding of our communal and political nature, these commentators lose sight of his distinctive understanding of both. Aristotle's most interesting and original insights into social and political life appear only when we clearly distinguish between his concepts of community and political community.

Finally, in addition to its contribution to Aristotle's understanding of political life, the Aristotelian understanding of community offers a number of intriguing ideas about how best to construct a theory of social interaction. Because Aristotle devotes the bulk of his attention to political community, these insights into the nature of social life have, for the most part, gone unnoticed. But while Aristotle is primarily a political philosopher, he also offers us, at least implicitly, an interesting and original approach to social theory. Reflection on this approach to social theory can, I argue in the final section of this chapter, help us gain much-needed critical distance on a number of modern controversies about the nature and value of community.

## THE COMMUNAL ANIMAL

Aristotle uses *koinōnia* as a generic term for all social groups.[6] *Koinōniai* emerge out of almost every kind of social interaction. They can be as fleeting as a business deal or as enduring as religious customs, as small as a nuclear family or as large as a nation. Wherever individuals hold something in common (*koinon*), be it a household, a contract, a destination, or a political regime, they participate in a *koinōnia* (*NE* 1132b31–1133b, 1159b25–1160a).[7]

I translate *koinōnia* as "community," even though Aristotle often

---

glosses on Aristotle's description of the *zōon politikon* that suggest that "social animal" would be the best rendering of that expression. See, for example, W. Kullmann, "Die Politische Philosophie des Aristoteles," 71–72; P. Rybicki, *Aristote et la pensée sociale moderne*, 39; T. Aquinas, "On Princely Government," in Aquinas, *Selected Political Writings*, 2–3; T. Aquinas, "Commentary on the Nicomachean Ethics," in *Selected Political Writings*, 190–91. Rybicki's book provides the best and most extended attempt to develop an Aristotelian approach to social theory. Unfortunately, its insights are limited by its failure to go beyond the *Politics* to Aristotle's discussion of friendship and community in his ethical writings in order to work out this Aristotelian understanding of social theory.

6. As Niklas Luhmann notes, we could translate *koinōnia* as "social system" if that modern generic term did not connote a degree of abstraction wholly absent from Aristotelian social theory; N. Luhmann, *Soziologische Aufklärung*, 138.

7. The former passage cited here (*NE* 1132b31–33b) describes parties to ordinary exchanges of goods as members of a *koinōnia*. (See also *NE* 1164a1.) For an especially insightful commentary on this passage, see M. Finley, "Aristotle and Economic Analysis," 144–46. See also E. M. and N. Wood, *Class Ideology*, 227.

uses it—for example, in describing parties to an exchange of goods—when we would be much more comfortable with terms such as "partnership" or "association."[8] I do so, first of all, in order to preserve the etymological relation between *koinon* (common) and *koinōnia* (community), a relation that is central to Aristotle's understanding of community.[9] Second, although I believe that we should try to distance Aristotle's understanding of community from the images of personal warmth and intimacy that we associate with the word "community," other familiar connotations of the word are very much worth preserving. One of the most striking features of Aristotle's understanding of community is that he associates with *all* social groups many social phenomena, such as friendship ties, that we usually associate only with smaller and highly integrated communities. By preserving this association in our translation of *koinōnia*, we draw attention to the distinctiveness of Aristotle's understanding of human sociability.

Although he focuses most of his attention on the political community, Aristotle insists that the human being is a "communal animal" (*zoōn koinōnikon*) as well as a political animal (*Eudemian Ethics* [hereafter *EE*] 1242a25).[10] He notes that human beings are naturally disposed to share a wide variety of communal goods and activities, not just those associated with political community. "Men strive to live together even when they have no need of assistance from one another, though it is also the case that the common advantage brings them together" (*Pol.* 1278b19). Human beings, he suggests, generally shun a solitary existence and find pleasure in regular interaction with each other. Moreover, they are equipped with the reasoning ability to see the mutual advantage to be gained from participating in groups. As a result, they are naturally disposed to establish and maintain a wide range of communities.

Apparently, Aristotle deems the communal nature of human beings to be so self-evident that he sees no need to offer proof of its existence.[11]

---

8. Even Carnes Lord, who strives in his translation of the *Politics* for a literal rendition of Aristotle's words, finds it necessary to use more than one term for *koinōnia*. Lord translates *koinōnia* as "partnership" in the opening sentence of the *Politics* and shifts between "community" and "partnership" throughout; Aristotle, *Politics*, translated by C. Lord, 35.
9. As does R. Mulgan, *Aristotle's Political Theory*, 16. See also M. Finley, *The Ancient Economy*, 152.
10. See the insightful commentary on this passage by M. Defourny, *Études sur la Politique d'Aristote*, 385–89.
11. Unlike many modern social theorists, Aristotle was not spurred on by competing social and political theories that deny the naturalness of human sociability to provide such

In the opening pages of the *Politics* he simply assumes our communal nature and rushes on to demonstrate that nature makes us political animals as well. Nevertheless, Aristotle's assumptions about our communal nature have important implications for his account of political life, as becomes clear when we examine his discussion of community in other texts. Some social theorists argue that Aristotle's persistent focus on politics rules out the use of Aristotle's "generic concept *koinōnia* as the subject of social predication."[12] But if we are willing to use some imagination in exploring Aristotle's scattered remarks about *koinōnia*, then we should be able to distinguish it from his understanding of political community.

Four key features characterize *community* as Aristotle uses the term. (1) A community consists of individuals who differ from each other in some significant way (*Pol.* 1261a–b). (2) These individuals share something: some good, activity, feature of their identity, or any combination thereof (*Pol.* 1252a1; *NE* 1156a–57b). (3) They engage in some interaction related to what they share. (4) Perhaps most important, they are bound to each other, to a greater or lesser extent, by some sense of friendship (*philia*) and some sense of justice (*NE* 1159b27).[13]

The first of these features, the heterogeneity of community members, may seem like a commonplace, but it plays an important role in Aristotle's understanding of community. As he makes clear in his critique of Plato's *Republic,* this notion leads Aristotle to conceive of community in terms of the kinds of things that different individuals share rather than in terms of collective identities.[14] Aristotle ridicules Plato for treating collective identity as the measure of communal health. If we took Plato's standards seriously, he complains, we would have to conclude that the ideal community would be a single individual, since only then could we be sure that we have rid ourselves of the social tensions created by heterogeneity (*Pol.* 1261a). Once we recognize the absurdity of Plato's ideal of collective identity, we must, Aristotle argues, acknowledge that heterogeneity is a necessary element of community rather than

---

proof. He did, however, feel the challenge of theories that denied the naturalness of political community and responded with his famous argument about our political nature.

12. M. Riedel, "Gesellschaft, Gemeinschaft," 804; M. Riedel, *Metaphysik und Metapolitik,* 39; N Luhmann, "Moderne Systemtheorien," 7.

13. This sketch of Aristotle's conception of *koinōnia* combines features of similar sketches by Moses Finley and W. L. Newmann. See M. Finley, "Aristotle and Economic Analysis," 144; W. L. Newman, *The Politics of Aristotle* 1:41–42.

14. As R. F. Stalley points out ("Aristotle's Critique of Plato's *Republic*," 182–99, 184–85), Aristotle seems far more interested in exploring the nature of community in this passage than in presenting a careful analysis of Plato's arguments.

the obstacle to social harmony that community seeks to overcome. Men and women, farmers and shoemakers, sailors and passengers, aristocratic and peasant families—such are the members of Aristotelian communities. The creative—and sometimes destructive—tension that emerges from combinations of sharing and difference is one of the most important features of community, as Aristotle conceives of it. Eliminate differences in social identity in the name of easing this tension and you destroy community itself (*Pol.* 1261b5).[15]

Aristotle does, of course, insist on the priority of the political community, among other communities, to the individual (*Pol.* 1253a19). But in doing so, he is illustrating the necessary role that communities play in the full development of the natural capacities of human beings, not the subordination of individual to collective identities. Nowhere will you find in Aristotle's writings the lyric celebration of such subordination that Rousseau, among others, has taught us to associate with community. Nor will you find a discussion of Rousseau's favorite passion, love of country, in Aristotle's account of the passions in the *Rhetoric*. One can hardly imagine a Rousseauian—or any "civic republican"—account of rhetoric that omitted love of country from the list of popular passions![16] Yet Aristotle finds no place for it in the *Rhetoric*, despite the fact that the *Rhetoric* is devoted to identifying the ways in which orators exploit the passions in order to sway their audience in the courts or the assembly. He omits it, I suspect, because a passion for collective identity plays little role in his understanding of community.

Because Aristotle describes business and traveling groups, indeed, all instrumental associations based on shared interest, as communities (*NE* 1132b31, 1159b25), he clearly does not identify community with collective identity. Instead, he identifies it with the kind of sharing—whether of goods, such as property, pleasure, or virtue, or of activities, such as politics, profit making, or religious worship—that bring individuals together. Of course, shared identities may also bring individuals together, according to Aristotle. The members of families, poleis, and many other communities (even members of the human race as a whole [*NE* 1155a29])[17] often see in each other a certain reflection of themselves, a

---

15. On this point, see M. Nussbaum, "Shame, Separateness, and Political Unity," 395–435; A. Saxonhouse, "Family, Polity, and Unity"; M. Nichols, *Socrates and the Political Community,* 153–80.

16. I discuss how and why Rousseau imposed the idea of such a passion on the ancient political philosophers in *The Longing for Total Revolution,* 62–72.

17. The further one stretches a sense of shared identity, the weaker it is likely to be, as Aristotle makes clear in his critique of Plato's proposal to turn the city into one family

reflection that leads them to devote special attention to each other (*Pol* 1262b23). But unless we clearly distinguish this sharing of social identity from collective identity, we are bound to misunderstand Aristotle's account of communal life.

Shared identity refers to common elements in the way in which a group of individuals identify themselves. Collective identity, in contrast, refers to the association of one's own identity with a collective will or actor, such as Rousseau's general will. Although Aristotle has a great deal to say about the social identities people share and the common goods that are often associated with such sharing, he does not speak of communities as collective actors expressing a "general will."[18] It is always individual actors—for example, fathers, ship captains, oligarchs, demagogues, or tyrants—who speak in the name of Aristotelian communities. These individuals may seek to persuade us that the policies that they choose are for our own or the common good. They may possess the kind of power or superior knowledge that make such persuasion unnecessary. But their choices, even when their decisions genuinely promote the common good of a community, remain the choices of particular individuals, choices that we may or may not be disposed to accept. Sharing some identity—for example, membership in a family, tribe, or class—with these individuals may make us more likely to accept the choices they make. But it does not presume the existence of a collective identity and will, nor does Aristotle ever suggest that it does. "Who rules?" and "Which individuals and groups would rule best?" are the questions that Aristotle asks in his analysis of communities; he does not ask, "Who best represents the general will with which we would all identify if only we could abstract from particular interests?"

Aristotle never confuses the intense sense of belonging to a group, what Herman Schmalenbach calls "*bund*" (communion),[19] with community itself. As Schmalenbach points out, those who actually live in communities, as opposed to those who yearn for them, rarely have an intense awareness of collective identity. For them, community "is noth-

---

(*Pol.* 1262a). Thus the sense of friendship and community shared by the human race as a whole is bound to be very weak. Nevertheless, it is not negligible. In some circumstances it may inspire a very strong, if temporary, bond with other individuals.

18. The passage that comes closest to an account of collective identity is Aristotle's discussion, at the beginning of *Politics,* book 3, about whether a political community derives its identities from its form (its constitution or regime) or its matter (its individual citizens). However, this is in fact a discussion about how we identify communities, not how individuals identify themselves.

19. H. Schmalenbach, "Communion." See also A. Black, *State, Community, and Human Desires,* 50–51.

ing but a fact" of life, "an existential circumstance or is simply evident. Life in a family or on the farm makes no explicit claims for community."[20] There is little sense of collective identity among community members precisely because their individual identities are shaped by the communities in which they live. "In the fact that the unconscious is the basis of community, we can consciously apprehend the strongest differentiating quality from communion."[21]

Those who experience "communion," in contrast, consciously experience the loss of separate identity that often comes with an intense sense of belonging to a group. This experience can arise in many different kinds of groups and situations—for example, among soldiers sharing adversity in the trenches, among travelers on a ship who share the pleasures of a cruise, even among people who, like the characters in Thomas Mann's *Magic Mountain,* share nothing but their boredom.[22] But it tends to be a fragile and transitory experience, an experience that comes and goes unexpectedly. (As with a sense of spontaneity, if you seek it, you will probably never experience it.)[23] Communions arise out of the ordinary experiences of social interaction that shape individual character and identity. Given their relatively settled personal identities, "those who grow up in a community easily come to mistrust such communions," when, as is often the case, they are "proposed to a community by someone who is not part of the community."[24]

The failure to distinguish clearly between community and communion (or collective identity) helps explain the romanticization of community life that appears in the works of so many modern social and political theorists since Rousseau, a romanticization that these theorists often read into Aristotle's works as well. Those who participate in communion lose their sense of distinction from one another and are, if only for a brief time, disposed toward high levels of mutual trust and relatively rare forms of cooperation. Those who participate in community,

---

20. H. Schmalenbach, "Communion," 78.
21. Ibid.
22. One of Schmalenbach's major points is that communion is just as likely to arise out of the voluntary and instrumental associations that Tönnies and other social theorists characterize as "societies" as from the more closely knit and constitutive social groups that they describe as "communities."
23. A. Black, *State, Community, and Human Desires,* 50–51.
24. H. Schmalenbach, "Communion," 91. To confirm Schmalenbach's point, imagine the suspicion that Rousseau would inspire were he living in a peasant village or in ancient Sparta. Many of the modern intellectuals, like Rousseau, who yearn for community would probably undermine it where it already exists, since it is an identity-dissolving communion, rather than community, that they really seek.

in contrast, do not lose this sense of distinction from one another, even if they share important elements of their identities.

As a result, community does not necessarily provide us with the source of increased trust and cooperation that we find in communion. The members of a traditional peasant village may share a relatively familiar and stable sense of who and what they are. But this sharing, as Oscar Lewis has noted, hardly eliminates "distrust, suspicion, envy, violence, reserve, and withdrawal" in "small peasant societies"; it merely channels social conflicts in directions that are relatively unfamiliar to participants in more diffuse, urban cultures.[25] Few conflicts are more intense than those between brothers over an inheritance or between peasant neighbors over a piece of land. But as Schmalenbach points out, such conflicts take place within the community that brothers and peasants share. Despite their conflicts, "neighbors and brothers remain neighbors and brothers. Neighborliness and brotherhood also persist [among them] psychically.... Those who oppose one another are not merely enemies. There is probably no better example anywhere to demonstrate how minor a role feelings play as a basis of community."[26]

Once we distinguish community from communion and collective identity, it becomes clear that for Aristotle community is a structural feature of everyday social interactions rather than an ideal of solidarity and harmonious living. Sentiments of love, sympathy, and solidarity will often develop in Aristotelian communities. But they will grow out of the same sources as much of the conflict and competition in communal life: the sharing of goods, activities, and identities by different kinds of individuals.

## THE FORMS OF FRIENDSHIP AND JUSTICE

Perhaps the most striking feature of Aristotle's understanding of community is his claim that some form of both friendship and justice binds the members of every kind of community.

> In every community there is thought to be some form of justice, and friendship too; at least men address as friends their fellow-voyagers and fellow-soldiers, and so too those sharing with them in any other kind of community.

25. O. Lewis, "The Folk-Urban Ideal Types," 498. Lewis goes on to suggest that "in some villages peasants can live out their lives without any deep knowledge or understanding of the people whom they 'know' in face-to-face relationships. By contrast, in modern Western cities, there may be more give and take about one's private, intimate life at a single 'sophisticated' cocktail party than would occur in years in a peasant village."
26. H. Schmalenbach, "Communion," 82.

> And the extent of their community is the extent of their friendship, as it is the extent to which justice exists between them.
>
> (*NE* 1159b27–31)

Because *community* is Aristotle's generic term for *all* social groups, it follows from this claim that participants in every kind of social group, even in the relatively fleeting and impersonal communities formed by exchangers and travelers, develop some form of both friendship and justice. Clearly, this sort of claim cuts right across the modern dichotomies—such as the distinctions between community and society or between altruism and self-interest—that often shape our social imagination. Contrary to the way in which we ordinarily describe social relations, Aristotle can speak of social phenomena such as the form of friendship that develops among those who exchange goods or the form of justice that develops among family members. We will seriously misunderstand his account of social and political life unless we make an effort to counter our reliance on these familiar dichotomies.

By *friendship* Aristotle means a disposition to give individuals what is good for them. "We may describe friendly feeling [*to philein*] toward anyone as wishing for him what you believe to be good things, not for your own sake but for his, and being inclined, as far as you can, to bring these things about" (*Rhet.* 1380b36). In every form of friendship "one wishes what is good for the friend," whether that good is profit, pleasure, or virtue. "For friendship asks us to do what we can, not what is due" (*EE* 1244a21; *NE* 1163b15).

Justice, in contrast, asks us to give precisely "what is due" to others (*NE* 1163b15). If friendship asks us to do all that we *can* to help another, justice asks us to do all that some standard of merit *obliges* us to do. For Aristotle, a sense of mutual concern among individuals is thus the mark of friendship, a sense of mutual obligation the mark of justice. Friendship maintains community by disposing individuals to seek each other's good in some way and to expect solicitude from each other. Justice brings individuals together by disposing them to hold each other accountable to standards of mutual obligation.

Friendship and justice inspire the emotional bonds that maintain Aristotelian communities. The pursuit of pleasure and advantage naturally leads individuals to associate with each other, according to Aristotle. But pleasure and advantage are not sufficient motivations to maintain the communities established in this way. They offer little incentive to maintain communal actions and goals when alternative, conflicting sources of pleasure and advantage appear, as they inevitably do. Aristotle would probably agree with Jon Elster that a combination of rational pursuit of individual self-interest and emotional attachment to social norms provides "the cement of society."[27] But he would note, in addition, that we would better understand the bewildering variety of social norms that emerges among any collection of human beings if we focused more of our attention on the different forms of friendship and justice promoted by different kinds of sharing.[28]

Clearly, Aristotle uses the Greek word *philia*—which I have been translating as "friendship"—to describe a much broader range of relationships than we are accustomed to using the word "friendship" to describe. Aristotle's concept of friendship possesses a sociological breadth that is quite foreign to both our theoretical and everyday vocabulary.[29] Indeed, Aristotle seems to use *philia* as a generic term for all expressions of human sympathy and mutual concern.

To a certain extent, Aristotle's concept of friendship reflects ordinary Greek usage, in which *philia* refers to a very broad range of personal relationships, not just to those based on personal intimacy between non-kin.[30] It is therefore tempting to translate *philia* by some term other

27. J. Elster, *The Cement of Society*, 15, 97.
28. Aristotle's discussion of friendship and justice bears some similarity to a number of later theories about the social passions that temper the individual's pursuit of pleasure and self-interest. Adam Smith, for example, speaks of "beneficence and justice" as the two dispositions that maintain society. He too distinguishes the obligations that we are disposed to impose on other individuals from the friendly but unenforceable concern for others that we also come to expect from them; A. Smith, *The Theory of Moral Sentiments*, 155–60. Similarly, Amartya Sen speaks of "sympathy" and "commitment" as the two social passions that maintain our communities by restricting self-interest; A. Sen, "Rational Fools." 31. What distinguishes Aristotle's account of friendship and justice from theirs is his claim that some sense of *both* friendship and justice, however limited in depth and breadth, develops in *every* social group, from families and religious societies to cities and business partnerships.
29. Modern sociological studies of friendship generally focus on a far narrower range of relationships—voluntary relationships expressing personal intimacy of some sort—than Aristotle considers. They usually explore the social influences on the way in which individuals form such relationships. For an overview, see, for example, G. Allen, *A Sociology of Friendship and Kinship*; G. Allen, *Friendship*; G. Suttles, "Friendship as a Social Institution." For a very insightful account of the social context shaping friendship ideals in different historical periods, see A. Silver, "Friendship and Trust." In "Friendships and Friendly Relations" Suzanne Kurth notes that we have "friendly relations" with a much larger and broader range of individuals than those with whom we have the intimate and noninstrumental ties that we ordinarily associate with friendship. Kurth's concept of "friendly relations" comes closer to Aristotle's understanding of the majority of nonintimate friendships, though it remains considerably more selective. Contemporary studies of patron-client relations cover some of the sociological ground covered by Aristotle's account of instrumental friendship. I discuss some of these studies when I turn to Aristotle's understanding of class conflict in chapter 7.
30. On problems in translating *philia* and *philos*, see D. Whitehead, *The Demes of Attica*, 231–32. W. R. Connor, *The New Politicians*, 30–31. For the Greek understanding of friendship in general, see J. C. Fraisse, *Philia*.

than "friendship" when Aristotle applies it to nonintimate relationships such as those between buyers and sellers of goods.[31] But it would be unfortunate if we gave in to this temptation, for we would then lose Aristotle's clear sense that all expressions of mutual concern, from those expressed by contractors to those expressed by kin and by intimate friends, have something important in common.

Aristotle does not merely follow Greek usage when he applies the concept of *philia* to such a broad range of relationships. He also provides the basis for an explanation of our social interactions that might justify that usage. Aristotle's discussion of friendship and community suggests that the emotional attachments formed by intimate friends, family members, travelers, and exchangers of goods are all properly described by one term, *philia*, because they all flow from a similar source: the disposition of human beings to develop a sense of concern for the good of individuals with whom they share goods, identities, and activities. The wide range in depth, breadth, and intensity of these attachments reflects the wide range of goods, identities, and activities that human beings share. Accordingly, Aristotle classifies forms of friendship with reference to the ends shared by individuals: pleasure, advantage, and virtuous activity (*NE* 1156a–57b).

Aristotle's concept of friendship thus reflects a fundamental premise of his approach to social theory, as well as common Greek usage. Friendship is for Aristotle a "state of soul"—that is, a settled disposition or character trait rather than a passion like love (*NE* 1157b28)[32]— that develops wherever individuals share ends and actions. "The proverb 'What friends have is common property' expresses the truth," Aristotle notes. "For friendship depends on community" and "the extent of their community is the extent of their friendship" (*NE* 1159b30–32). Sharing ends and actions disposes individuals to express a sense of selective concern for each other, a sense of concern that varies in its

---

31. I suspect that the only reason commentators have not offered such alternative translations of *philia* is that they devote most of their attention to Aristotle's best form of friendship—the friendship between virtuous individuals—the form of Aristotelian friendship that most closely conforms to modern notions of friendship. For exceptions, see J. Cooper, "Aristotle on the Forms of Friendship"; J. Cooper, "Aristotle on Friendship"; K. D. Alpern, "Aristotle on the Friendships of Utility and Pleasure"; R. Paine, "Anthropological Approaches to Friendship." Contemporary philosophical study of friendship— an increasingly popular topic—also tends to focus on the moral value of such intimate relationships. See, for example, L. Bluhm, *Friendship, Altruism, and Morality*; A. W. Price, *Love and Friendship*.

32. In this respect, friendship resembles virtue for Aristotle, which helps explain why he discusses it, following his discussion of the virtues, in his ethical writings.

degree of depth and intensity in proportion to the kinds of ends and actions they share. One reason we maintain our communities is because we are, in ways and to an extent that varies in different communities naturally disposed to aid those with whom we share ends, activities and identities.

That this kind of mutual concern develops in the more tightly knit communities, such as families and other intimate associations, seems undeniable. But do we have any evidence to confirm the plausibility of Aristotle's claim that we will find something like this sense of mutual concern even in more impersonal and transitory social groups? I think that we have. Consider, to begin with, a relatively easy case: our behavior when traveling with strangers. We are usually far more inclined to put ourselves out to help someone with whom we are sharing a plane or bus ride than we are willing to do after we have reached our destination. When we share a journey, the sense of being "all in the same boat"—the sense that we are all unavoidably stuck, whatever our differences, with the difficulties and inconveniences created by our shared means of transport—disposes us to make much more of an effort than we ordinarily make to help strangers.

Moving to the more difficult case of contractual and exchange relations, it is not as implausible as it might at first seem to assert that participants in exchanges and other economic dealings develop a limited sense of mutual concern. Exchangers, unlike thieves, engage in activities that they see as mutually advantageous—though, they hope, as more advantageous to themselves than to the other parties. Consequently, they tend to associate their own gain with the—preferably smaller—gains achieved by their partners. Exchangers hardly seek to maximize the good of their exchange partners, and self-interest, of course, often colors individuals' perceptions of what is good for others. But their participation in what they see as mutually advantageous activity may dispose them, however weakly, to prefer the well-being of their exchange partners as long as it does not directly harm their own interests. Even the relatively impersonal exchange of goods over the supermarket counter could dispose us to this kind of mutual concern. To the extent that we think of ourselves as acting to promote each other's advantage in such exchanges, we come to be more disposed, however minimally and momentarily, to help each other in ways we would not be disposed to do were we not exchanging with each other.[33]

---

33. Exchange friendship would probably not develop where there is no social interaction between individuals, as, say, in an electronic transfer of stocks or funds generated

Exchange relations manifest, at the very least, the expectation that those with whom we exchange things will display some concern for our good, as long as it does not make it impossible for them to benefit from our interactions as well. For confirmation of this expectation, consider how we react to being cheated in an exchange as opposed to how we react to being robbed by a stranger. We certainly get angry with thieves and seek to have them punished. But we do not normally experience when robbed the disappointed expectations we experience when we are cheated unless we share something with the thief, such as a family, a workplace, or a country, that leads us to expect that the thief would show some concern for our welfare.

We share with our exchange partners an activity that is supposed to be mutually advantageous. When someone cheats us by taking more than we agreed to exchange, we are hurt not only by the injustice of the action but also by the fact that an individual has chosen to harm us despite our agreement to engage in mutually advantageous behavior. That individual has treated us as if we shared nothing at all. The more we share with the individual who cheats us, the greater our displeasure will be. The family member, colleague, or compatriot who cheats us adds greater insult to the injury we suffer. It is "reasonable," Aristotle notes, to react in this way since "in addition to the injury" we also consider ourselves robbed of the expected pleasures and benefits of our friendship with such individuals (*Pol.* 1328a10). But even if all that we share with others is the act of exchanging goods for mutual profit, we still seem to develop the expectation our exchange partners will display at least a minimal concern for our good as long as it does not rule out their own.

Aristotle is not, of course, suggesting that we are normally disposed to sacrifice ourselves for the sake of someone who sells us a stick of gum. Exchange friendship, especially when it is based on a single and relatively unimportant action, will be rather superficial and transitory.[34] It will persist only as long as both participants continue to be-

---

by a computer program. But when you transfer stocks through a broker, Aristotelian exchange friendship would develop between you and the broker and the broker and the buyer, if not between you and the buyer of your stock.

34. That does not mean, as John Cooper argues, that Aristotle limits exchange friendship to relationships between individuals who regularly and repeatedly interact. Cooper insists, contrary to the interpretation I have presented, that "Aristotle does not make the mistake, which a superficial reading would seem to convict him of, of counting as *philia*" the bonds between all participants in exchange communities. Cooper is certainly correct when he suggests "that it would be a mistake to call in English all such relationships

lieve that they gain some advantage from their interaction. Aristotle's major point seems to be that our natural sympathy for others grows out of and is shaped by the kinds of ends and activities we share with them.[35] Even such minimal sharing as an exchange of goods leads us to distinguish, to a certain extent, the individuals with whom we exchange things as objects of our concern. Our selective concern for these individuals may not lead us to sacrifice our lives for them, but it might help explain why most of us, to the consternation of rational choice theorists, avoid cheating on them in our exchanges when we can easily get away with it.[36]

Aristotle also argues that some form of justice develops in every human community, even in communities, such as families, that are bound by an intense and intimate form of friendship.[37] Accordingly, he suggests that there are a variety of different forms of justice, such as domestic, despotic, and political justice (NE 1134b), corresponding to the different forms of communal life.

But justice, as Aristotle conceives of it, functions as a communal bond in a considerably more complex way than friendship does. Friendship maintains communities by disposing their members to concern themselves, to some extent, in each other's well-being. This disposition to mutual concern, Aristotle argues, develops naturally among individuals who share goods and activities. But no parallel disposition to act justly emerges naturally out of ordinary social interactions. Like the other Aristotelian moral virtues, justice is a socially acquired "characteristic" rather than a natural disposition. Dispositions toward friendly behavior, like other natural capacities, develop prior to and then express themselves in acts of friendship. In contrast, the disposition to act justly, like all the other moral virtues, emerges only after we have repeatedly performed just actions. It requires extensive training and moral education (NE 1103a).

---

friendships; ... a businessman is no friend to all of his regular customers": J. Cooper, "Aristotle on Friendship," 316. But that hardly settles any questions about the way in which Aristotle uses Greek.

35. It is thus the different forms of social interaction, rather than (as in Adam Smith's *The Theory of the Moral Sentiments*) sympathetic observation, that inspires concern for the welfare of others, according to Aristotle.

36. See Robert Frank's discussion of the failure of the self-interest model of behavior to explain our general avoidance of cheating in *Passions Within Reason*.

37. This point about the existence of a sense of justice among family members has been made recently in critiques of contemporary communitarianism by S. Okin, *Justice, the Family, and Gender*, and I. Shapiro, *Political Criticism*, 215–16.

But if the disposition to act justly does not develop naturally, then what does Aristotle have in mind when he insists that some form of justice develops naturally among members of every community? He seems to be saying that even if our natural capacities do not dispose us to act justly, they do dispose us to seek to establish standards of justice in our communities. Aristotle argues that *logos,* the distinctively human capacity for reason and speech, "is designed to indicate the advantageous and the harmful and *therefore also* the just and unjust, . . . and it is community in these things that makes a household or a polis" (*Pol.* 1253a; my emphasis). Acting justly may not be natural for human beings, but talking about acting justly apparently is.

Justice, Aristotle suggests, develops out of our ability to communicate with each other about the mutual and shared advantages or disadvantages of a particular course of action. Discussion of the advantages and disadvantages of alternative actions naturally leads to assertions of standards of mutual obligation. We do not simply say to others, "Give us this; we want it." We say instead, "Give us this; you owe it to us (given the shared or mutual advantages that bring us together)." "Community in these things [i.e., the just and unjust] makes a household or a polis" (*Pol.* 1253a), or any other form of human community, because a demand for just behavior emerges naturally in the communities formed by social animals who can speak and reason with each other.[38] It is this concern about justice that most distinguishes human communities—*all* human communities, not just the polis—from the communities formed by other animals: although many animals surpass human beings in social friendship and mutual concern, only human beings hold each other accountable to standards of justice.

Moreover, human beings hold each other accountable to such standards in very different ways in different kinds of communities, according to Aristotle. Political justice, a form of justice characterized by public legislation, courts, adjudication, and physical compulsion, is the most

---

38. It would be a mistake, however, to think of our disposition to demand justice from others as a purely rational or calculating state of mind. This disposition is manifested, as well, in the passion Aristotle calls anger (*orgē*). Anger, Aristotle suggests, manifests our desire for revenge against individuals who dishonor us when, according to our own judgment, we do not deserve to be dishonored. He cites, as an illustration, Achilles's complaint that Agamemnon has treated him "Like an alien honored by none" (*Rhet.* 1378b31–34; Aristotle is quoting Homer, *Iliad,* book 9, l. 648.) We express anger, Aristotle implies, when community members treat us as aliens, as individuals with whom they share no mutual obligations because they share no actions and ends with us. Anger is the passion that arises in us when individuals fail to meet the obligations we believe are entailed by their sharing with us communal ends and activities.

familiar form of justice, at least to members of political communities. But as Aristotle makes clear in his discussion of political justice in the *Nicomachean Ethics* (1134a), it is far from the only form of justice. Very different forms of justice develop in the family and other communities.

Unfortunately, Aristotle passes over the nonpolitical forms of justice too quickly in the *Nicomachean Ethics* to provide us with any systematic comparisons of the various forms of justice. It is not entirely clear even what he means by speaking of different forms of justice in different communities. I suggest that he is speaking about different ways in which human beings hold each other accountable to shared standards of obligation or, in more contemporary terms, of different forms of the practice of social justice.[39] The way in which Aristotle distinguishes political from nonpolitical forms of justice implies that we hold each other accountable to standards of justice in a variety of different ways in different communities.[40] The most important of these variations concern the ways in which standards of mutual obligation are determined and imposed in different communities.

Because the practice of justice grows out of our efforts to hold others accountable to standards of mutual obligation that they are not naturally disposed to follow, it is bound to involve the compulsion of some individuals by others. Unlike friendship, which involves other-regarding actions we are ourselves disposed to perform, justice primarily concerns other-regarding actions that we are disposed to demand from others. As a result, standards of justice, as Aristotle conceives of them, inevitably reflect a choice that some individuals make and impose on others.[41] The ways in which different kinds of community construct and distribute the power to impose these standards will largely constitute the specific forms of justice that develop within them. What most distinguishes political from domestic justice, for example, is the public legislation and alternation in positions of authority that domestic justice lacks (*NE* 1134a).

Given this understanding of justice, however, it is not immediately

---

39. "Practice," admittedly, is not a concept that Aristotle explicitly employs. But we need some concept to explain what Aristotle means by the different forms of justice that develop in different forms of community, as opposed to either the virtue of justice or the just acts and states of affairs that such a virtue disposes us to choose. I try to integrate these different ways of talking about justice in chapter 5.

40. I elaborate on the specific character of political justice in the second section of chapter 2 and in chapter 5.

41. I elaborate on these arguments in chapter 5.

clear why Aristotle thinks of justice as a bond rather than a solvent of community. Friendship binds us together by disposing us to help those with whom we share goods and activities. But the only natural disposition that Aristotle associates with justice is a disposition to demand that others conform to what we believe are appropriate standards of behavior. If the practice of social justice consists primarily of angry complaints about each others' behavior, then justice could easily be more of a threat to community than a way of maintaining it.[42]

Why, then, does justice function as a bond rather than a solvent? Again, we have to reconstruct his answer to this question, since he never explicitly addresses it. First, to the extent that community members accept the authority of standards of social justice or of those who establish them, they share important ends, activities, and sources of identity. But even if, as is most often the case, such acceptance does not fully exist among community members, sharing the various forms of the practice of social justice can still reinforce communal ties. Aristotle believes that nature disposes us to develop different ways of holding each other accountable in the different kinds of community that we form, even if it does not dispose us to behave justly or agree on shared standards of justice.

Practicing justice in these different ways establishes links among individuals that would otherwise be missing. We react very differently to those whom we hold accountable for behaving according to shared standards than we do to those who simply fail to treat us well. We get angry at the former group of individuals. We charge them with injustice and seek to enlist the aid of other community members to correct their behavior. Their behavior brings to mind and reinforces the notion that there is some special link between us, that we share with other com-

---

42. Aristotle, moreover, avoids one obvious solution to this problem, a solution dear to the hearts of many modern social and political philosophers: the notion that this disposition serves to integrate communities by inspiring a fear of punishment that can help coordinate our behavior and reinforce social order. Even Adam Smith, whose notion of social sympathy has attracted numerous contemporary critics of individualism, argues that our disposition to resent perceived insults serves to integrate our communities by means of the fear that it inspires. The "terrors of merited punishment" are, he suggests, "the great safeguards of the association of mankind." Without this fear of punishment by the resentful to "overawe" them, human beings "would, like wild beasts, be at all times ready to fly upon him [the innocent man]; and a man would enter an assembly of men as he enters a den of lions." See A. Smith, *The Theory of Moral Sentiments*, 166–68. Aristotle, in contrast, has little to say at all about fear of punishment. He briefly mentions fear of punishment in the *Nicomachean Ethics* (1179b11) and has a more extended discussion of fear as a passion in the *Rhetoric* (1382a–83b). But in neither place does he treat fear of punishment as the cement of social order.

munity members a practice of holding each other accountable to standards of obligation. Even if that link structures nothing more than the way we engage in conflict with each other, it still reinforces the sense that we participate with others in a community. Our disposition to raise and enforce standards of mutual obligation among community members need not promote social order and peace, but it does give rise to the kinds of shared activity and identity that reinforce our sense of living in a community.

Friendship and justice thus support communal life in very different ways, according to Aristotle. Our natural disposition to act in a friendly way toward people with whom we share ends and actions leads us to single out community members as objects of special sympathy and concern. Our natural disposition to hold individuals to standards of mutual obligation also leads us to single out community members as objects of special, though not as benevolent, attention. Both dispositions lead us to distinguish and devote special attention to the individuals with whom we share ends and activities.

## ARISTOTELIAN COMMUNITY AND MODERN SOCIAL THEORY

The Aristotelian social theory reconstructed in this chapter differs from the most influential modern social theories in that it begins with a single concept, community (*koinōnia*), rather than a conceptual dichotomy. Aristotle assumes that what all social groups have in common is significant enough to provide the basis for a generic concept covering all social groups. He explains the great variety of social groups by referring to the variety of goods and activities that individuals share in their communities. In contrast, the classic modern social theorists, such as Ferdinand Tönnies, Emile Durkheim, and Max Weber, build their social theories on dichotomies between fundamentally different forms of social order, dichotomies such as community versus society, mechanical versus organic solidarity, or communal versus associative groups.[43] They begin their explanations of the variety of social behavior by determining to which of the two categories a given social group belongs.

Aristotle's understanding of community cuts right across these familiar modern dichotomies. When we look at his famous claim about

---

43. As formulated, respectively, by Ferdinand Tönnies in *Community and Society*, Emile Durkheim in *The Division of Labor*, and Max Weber in *Economy and Society*, 41–42.

our political nature with these dichotomies in mind, it appears as if Aristotle is suggesting that human beings are, by nature, altruistic sharers in something like the small, highly integrated social group that Tönnies describes as community (*Gemeinschaft*). But Aristotle also repeatedly insists that the bond between members of political communities belongs to the same general category, instrumental or advantage friendship, as the bond between partners to any exchange or contract (*NE* 1160a11; *EE* 1242a6).⁴⁴ These claims, when read through the lens provided by modern social theory, seem to suggest that, on the contrary, political communities belong to the category of voluntary, self-interested social interactions that Tönnies calls "society" or "association" (*Gesellschaft*).⁴⁵

As long as we continue to apply the basic dichotomies of modern social theory to Aristotle's work, his understanding of community cannot help but seem confused and contradictory.⁴⁶ But once we recognize that his concept of community rests on a very different understanding of social interaction than that manifested in the basic dichotomies of modern social theory, this sense of confusion and contradiction disappears.

One reason that modern social theorists favor conceptual dichotomies is their interest in identifying and explaining the novelty of characteristically modern forms of social order. Modern social theorists are heirs to the polemical debates between liberal individualists and their communitarian critics of the Left (Rousseau and the socialists) and the Right (Burke, de Maistre, Bonald, and others). These critics, like their contemporary followers, argue that the increasing acceptance of individualistic political theories and practices threatens the very possibility of social order. The classic modern social theorists agree with these critics that individualistic theories provide inadequate explanations of

---

44. As I argue in chapter 4, few commentators notice Aristotle's explicit description of political friendship as an instrumental or shared advantage friendship. Moreover, most of those who do see this point try to explain it away so it will not contradict their association of Aristotelian political community with altruism and collective identity.

45. Indeed, Enrico Berti recommends translating *koinōnia politike* as "*société politique*" (political society) precisely in order to bring the concept into line with Tönnies's distinction between community and society; E. Berti, "La notion de société politique," 80.

46. As Pawel Rybicki (*Aristote et la pensée*, 40–41) has suggested, modern social theorists, whether they lean to communitarian or individualist explanations of social behavior, usually fail to appreciate Aristotle's understanding of our social nature because they reduce it to "a question of knowing whether human beings come into the world with selfish dispositions or are, on the contrary, born with a strong drive to sociability and altruistic dispositions."

social order. But they also note that new forms of social order seemed to be developing in the modern societies, the nations of Western Europe and North America, that were most closely associated with these theories. The problem that they set for themselves is to identify and explain these new forms and sources of social order. Tönnies's concept of *Gesellschaft*, Durkheim's concept of "organic solidarity," Weber's concept of rationalization,[47] even Marx's concept of the capitalist mode of production—all are inspired by the need to identify and explain the unprecedented forms of social order that develop in a modern, increasingly individualistic world. The great conceptual dichotomies on which they build their social theories thus represent, more than anything else, an attempt to distinguish a novel modern form of social order from its predecessors.

Aristotle, needless to say, does not share these concerns and challenges. Accordingly, he has far less reason to begin his analysis of community, as modern social theorists do, with a dichotomy between two basic forms of social interaction. As a result, his analysis of community can help us gain some critical distance on the advantages and disadvantages of the dichotomous vocabulary of modern social theory.

Viewed from the perspective of Aristotle's understanding of community, the great value of modern approaches to social theory lies in the special insights into the peculiar structures of modern society that they make possible. But these approaches have accompanying disadvantages, such as the tendency to construct overly simplistic conceptions of premodern forms of social order. Oversimplification is probably inevitable when premodern forms of social order are constructed as negative images of peculiarly modern forms. (In the context of my reconstruction of Aristotelian social and political thought, the most important example of such oversimplification is the portrayal of the ancient polis as an "undifferentiated," "face-to-face society" bound by the overwhelming moral consensus characteristic of Durkheim's "mechanical solidarity." I challenge this portrayal of the polis in the final section of chapter 2.) Modern social theorists also pay for their insights into peculiarly modern forms of social order with a certain degree of abstractness in their analyses. When examined closely, the actual forms of social order they study fall more readily along a continuum than into the dichotomous categories that they erect. As a result, modern social

---

47. As noted above, Weber also follows Tönnies by distinguishing between "associative" (*gesellschaftliche*) and "communal" (*gemeinschaftliche*) groups; M. Weber, *Economy and Society*, 41–42.

theorists must abstract from a large part of social reality in order to sustain the "ideal types" that support their conceptual dichotomies.

Weber, among others, concedes that the great majority of relationships he describes as "associative" or instrumental have some of the features of the "communal" relationships from which he distinguishes them. "No matter how calculating and hard-headed the ruling considerations in such a social relationship—as that of a merchant to his customers—may be, it is quite possible for it to involve emotional values which transcend its utilitarian significance."[48] But once we recognize the degree of abstraction from social reality required by the dichotomy between community and society, then we must acknowledge that, valuable as these dichotomies may be for highlighting the contrasts between particular forms of community, we need to correct the distortions that they create by employing alternative approaches to social theory as well.[49] The Aristotelian approach to social theory helps correct this abstraction by treating all social groups as variations on the theme of community. The greater concreteness of its classification of different kinds of communal life greatly compensates for the relative imprecision of its conceptual categories.

The lack of a widely accepted generic concept, such as Aristotle's concept of *koinōnia,* also introduces considerable confusion into the recurring debate about the value of community that has been raging among social and political theorists since the end of the eighteenth century. Aristotle is often drawn into this controversy as a partisan of communitarian political theories and practices. But, as we have seen, Aristotle's understanding of community strongly diverges from most modern understandings of the concept. Once we recognize this divergence, we can use his understanding of community to help us gain some critical distance on the recurrent modern debates between communitarians and liberal individualists.

Modern communitarianism is in large measure a reaction against the limitations of contractarianism and the other liberal political theories that gained popularity in the seventeenth and eighteenth centuries. As a result, it is not surprising that a revival of communitarianism has followed hard on the heels of the recent revival of social contract theory

---

48. M. Weber, *Economy and Society,* 41, 346.
49. One certainly cannot continue to assert, as some do, that this dichotomy "has undergone the rigors of scientific investigation and been found valid"; G. Simpson, *Conflict and Community,* 31.

associated with the work of John Rawls.⁵⁰ Modern communitarianism also grows out of dissatisfaction with the new kinds of injustice, selfishness, and dislocation that have emerged alongside the relatively impersonal social and political institutions that have put liberal theories into practice in the modern world.

As a result, most modern communitarians, from Rousseau to Alisdair MacIntyre, raise both theoretical and practical objections against liberal individualism. They tend to argue, first of all, that liberal theories are inadequate because they ignore the ways in which communities constitute the identity and character of individuals. They then usually go on to argue that liberal practices and institutions are inadequate because they undermine the communal attachments that are essential to individual and social health.⁵¹

The first of these two arguments is considerably sounder than the second. Communitarian critiques of contractarianism and other individualistic social theories rest on relatively uncontroversial assumptions about the influence of communal life on individuals. Like Aristotle, I accept these assumptions and acknowledge the weakness of theories that abstract from the social sources of individual character and identity. Many liberal theories, especially those associated with contractarianism, are built on myths about the possibility of self-constituting individuals, individuals who can somehow free themselves from social influences on their character in order to determine which institutions a purely rational individual should choose.

But most modern communitarians usually go much further. They often argue that the devaluation of community in individualist social and political practices turns modern individuals into alienated and "unencumbered selves,"⁵² thereby dissociating them in a way that threatens both individual integrity and a healthy social order. In doing so, they attempt to ground their critiques of the injustice and dislocation created by liberal practices and institutions in their understanding of the failings of individualistic explanations of social and political life. Because this critique of liberal practices sounds like it rests on the same uncontroversial assumption that supports communitarian critiques of

---

50. For example, see R. Bellah et al., *Habits of the Heart*; A. MacIntyre, *After Virtue*; M. Sandel, *Liberalism*; W. Sullivan, *Reconstructing Public Philosophy*.
51. I develop the following argument more fully in "Liberalism and Its Communitarian Critics"; see esp. 156–59.
52. The "unencumbered self" is Michael Sandel's metaphor for the dissociated condition of modern individuals; see "The Procedural Republic and the Unencumbered Self."

liberal theories, many find it equally plausible. After all, if individualistic theories dissociate individuals, should not the practices that realize these theories do the same?

On closer examination, however, a tension emerges between these two claims. If individualistic theories fail because they abstract from the social constitution of individual character and identity, then whatever their corresponding practices may do to us, these practices cannot dissociate us in the way imagined by individualistic theories. For it is the central premise of the communitarian critique of these theories that self-constituting or dissociated individuals exist only in the fevered imaginations of liberal theorists. It follows from this premise that even if modern individuals *feel* less associated with each other, they still must, like all other individuals, draw a large part of their character and identity from their shared life. Modern individuals may experience a relatively large degree of alienation from each other, but such alienation is no less a social phenomenon, a shared culture, than patriotism or the celebration of tradition.

In fact, the communitarian critique of liberal practices and institutions rests on a highly controversial assumption about the *value* of community rather than a relatively uncontroversial assumption about its existence. Communitarians generally assume that social and political health requires the strong sense of belonging to a community that they believe is characteristic of the specific form of social life that Tönnies and others call "community."[53] This assumption is controversial for a number of reasons. First, it is very hard to prove. Communitarians have been making vain predictions about the upcoming dissolution of liberal and individualistic societies since the end of the French Revolution. Their favorite examples of dissolution, such as the collapse of the Weimar Republic,[54] are not very convincing since they occur in societies in which the individualistic practices that are supposed to bring about social collapse were generally quite weak and bitterly opposed by a large and powerful segment of the population. According to communitarian arguments, it should be precisely the communities in which liberal individualism is most firmly entrenched, such as the United States and Great Britain, that experience a dissolution of social order. Thus, the relative

---

53. For a clear and extended example of such an argument, see S. de Grazia, *The Political Community*.

54. The dissociation of individuals into an inarticulate mass is an important precondition of totalitarianism according to Hannah Arendt (among others); see her influential work *The Origins of Totalitarianism*.

success of the most liberal and individualistic communities in the twentieth century poses a very powerful objection to assumptions that political communities will self-destruct without a strong shared sense of community.[55]

These assumptions are also controversial because it is not at all clear that communities, as conceptualized by Tönnies and those who follow him, actually do generate a strong sense of belonging to a community among its members. We can assume that they do generate this sense only if, like many modern social theorists, we conflate community with communion. But, as we have seen, there are good reasons for doubting that communion always arises out of community and that the sense of belonging that communitarians seek can be anything more than a temporary social phenomenon. And once we question the connection between community and communion, the reasons for preferring forms of social life that resemble Tönnies's community also come into question for without communion, there is little reason to believe that premodern "communities" are any more harmonious or less conflictual than modern "societies" are.

These problems in communitarian arguments are difficult to discern because contemporary communitarians and their liberal opponents both tend to blur the distinction between generic and specific uses of the term *community*. The blurring of this distinction allows communitarians to base their critique of liberal practices and institutions on the relatively uncontroversial premise that grounds their critique of individualistic theories. In effect, they argue that because we are largely constituted by our social experience as a whole, we should live in a very *specific* form of society, usually designated as "community." In other words, because we cannot live without some form of social interaction, we require a particular form of society, unlike our present one, in which individuals express a very strong sense of mutual association.

But as Michael Oakeshott notes, no particular species of society or community corresponds to the adjective *social* in claims about the social constitution of human character and identity.[56] The defense of community in its specific sense requires additional and much more con-

---

55. Some communitarians, such as Robert Bellah and his associates in *Habits of the Heart,* explain the surprising political health of individualistic societies, such as the American republic, by suggesting that they are living off the moral capital of older, more communal traditions associated with religion and civic republicanism. Once this moral capital is exhausted, the breakdown of political and psychic health that they predict for individualistic societies will proceed apace.

56. M. Oakeshott, *On Human Conduct,* 88, 98.

troversial arguments. The validity of communitarian critiques of modern practices and institutions rests primarily on the validity of such arguments. An insistence on the generic social constitution of individuals does nothing to justify them.

Nevertheless, it is very difficult to detect the frequent blurring of the distinction between generic and specific uses of terms such as *community, society,* and *association* in these arguments as long as we lack a generally recognized term for the genus of all social interactions. Lacking a suitable term,[57] we make terms such as *community, society,* and *association* do double duty as generic and specific categories and suffer the consequences in conceptual confusion and repetitious intellectual controversies.

Aristotle's concept of community, or something like it, could help us eliminate some of this confusion. Aristotle's understanding of community captures the most sensible and uncontroversial part of communitarian arguments, the insistence on the way in which all forms of social interactions help shape individual character and identity. But it also leaves open questions about the nature and value of any particular form of communal life that one might advocate. It allows us to give full weight to the social constitution of individual character and actions without suggesting the necessity of any specific form of communal life.

Because Aristotle is so often drawn into contemporary debates between individualists and communitarians as a partisan of communitarianism, it might seem rather strange that I suggest using his concepts to referee their disputes. But one of my aims in this chapter and in the book as a whole is to disentangle Aristotelian insights from these and other modern debates. Aristotle undoubtedly rejects explanations of human behavior that rely solely on examination of individual choice and calculation. But his embrace of communal explanations of human behavior does not blind him to the communal aspects of instrumental associations and other everyday social phenomena. His account of community encourages us instead to identify and explore all the forms of communal behavior created by human beings sharing pleasure, profit, and goodness.

---

57. Georg Simmel used the term *Vergesellschaftung,* usually translated by the coinage "sociation," for this purpose; see *The Sociology of Georg Simmel,* lxiii. Despite the efforts of some of his English-speaking followers, "sociation" has not become generally accepted as a term for the genus covering all social groups.

CHAPTER TWO
# Political Community

What "sort of community" (*Pol.* 1252a1) is political community as Aristotle conceives of it? Because Aristotle offers two different definitions of the term *political animal* in his works, each of which suggests in turn a different understanding of political community, his answer to this question is a little confusing. According to the first of these definitions, found in his *History of Animals,* devotion to the common good is the special mark of political community. According to the second (*Pol.* 1253a)—on which, I argue, we should build our interpretations of Aristotelian politics—political community is a much more complex and exclusively human phenomenon.

In the *History of Animals* human beings are presented as merely one of a large group of species described as political animals. Political animals are, in turn, classified as a subclass of gregarious animals. Gregarious animals live together in herds, swarms, and other forms of community. Some, like bees and ants, work toward a common end in their communities. They are the political animals. Others, like cows, pursue relatively individual ends and are unlikely to sacrifice themselves for the common good of the herd. Human beings, like some other animals, "dualize," according to Aristotle: they use their communities to pursue both common and individual ends (*History of Animals* 488a).

This passage in the *History of Animals* implies that political community is best characterized by the subordination of individual to common ends. It is this understanding of political community that modern partisans of ancient politics, such as Rousseau, usually invoke in their arguments against the individualism of modern political theory and practice. The ancients, they argue, knew what citizenship meant: a life in which individuals derive their value from the success of their political community, just as fractions derive their value from the quantity of their denominators. Modern individuals, in contrast, see citizenship as a necessary evil at best, a means of pursuing and securing individual needs and interests.[1]

But this is not the understanding of political community that guides Aristotle's study of human political life. As we have seen, Aristotle refuses to identify community among human beings—and especially political community—with simple identity of ends. Aristotle insists in the *Politics* that "man is *much more* a political animal than any kind of bee or other gregarious animal" (*Pol.* 1253a8; my emphasis). If he were working with the *History of Animals* definition of political community, then he would have to conclude the opposite, since bees and ants subordinate themselves much more completely to the common good of their community. If human beings are "more political" than bees and ants, then *political community* must have some other meaning than devotion to a common end. In other words, there must be some other kind of sharing, which Aristotle describes as "political," in which human beings naturally surpass all other species.

In the *Politics* Aristotle associates political community with the uniquely human capacity for reasoned speech and argument (*logos*). "Man is much more a political animal than any . . . other gregarious animal" because "man alone among the animals has *logos*" (*Pol.* 1253a8). This capacity for reasoned speech supports a specifically human form of political community, a form that centers, I argue, on a particular way of seeking justice, rather than on simple devotion to the common good.

It is thus unfortunate that Aristotle uses the term *political animal* to characterize both the human species and a larger group of species that includes human beings. (The awkward term *dualize,* which Aristotle uses to describe human sociality in *History of Animals* [488a], suggests that he is running into some terminological difficulties when trying to classify human beings among the gregarious and political animals.) I reserve the term *political* for the interactions of human beings rather than describe them, following Aristotle, as "more political" than bees

---

1. See J.-J. Rousseau, *Emile,* 40, and G. W. F. Hegel's early essay, *Natural Law,* 112–13.

and ants. I leave it to others to come up with an acceptable term to classify a subgroup of social animals that includes both human beings and social insects, such as bees and ants.²

## THE DEFINING CHARACTERISTICS OF POLITICAL COMMUNITY

Because he knows of no examples of political communities apart from the polis, Aristotle tends to use *polis* and *political community* interchangeably, as when he notes that the most authoritative community is "what is called the polis or the political community" (*Pol.* 1253a7). Nevertheless, the two terms are not synonyms. As discussed in the preceding chapter, *community* signifies for Aristotle a group created when heterogeneous individuals share things. The polis gives Aristotle the name for the political "sort of community," the community formed by sharing political things (*ta politika*), which are the kinds of things that citizens share. In this section I try to identify the form of sharing peculiar to Aristotelian political community, devoting special attention to its characteristic forms of friendship and justice.

The individuals who form political communities are, according to Aristotle, the free adult males who head household communities. Unlike the individuals who form many other communities, such as the family, the members of political communities are relatively equal in their natural capacities. Aristotle sees no evidence among them of the clear natural hierarchy that he believes exists between men and women, parents and children, and natural masters and slaves (*Pol.* 1259b–60a, 1332b). In this sense the individual members of political communities are more homogeneous than are the members of families and many other natural communities.

The individuals who form political communities differ primarily in the skills and goods that they possess. These differences in goods and skills in turn endow them with a variety of special interests and standpoints. It is precisely the existence of these differences, Aristotle argues, that bring unrelated individuals from different households and villages

---

2. Larry Arnhart, among others, tries to use the biological definition of politics in the *History of Animals* to explain the arguments in the *Politics*. But when it comes to the passage in which Aristotle insists that human beings are "more political" than other animals, he acknowledges that it is our greater capacity for communication about justice and other cultural matters that Aristotle is talking about rather than a greater capacity for devotion to a common good ("Aristotle, Chimpanzees," 481, 506, 516), as would be demanded if we use the *History of Animals* passage to define political community.

together into a larger community. The heterogeneity of their skills, goods, and interests supplement those possessed by particular individuals and their households. If they can join together in a larger community, these individuals can live a more comfortable and secure life in a relatively self-sufficient community (*Pol.* 1252b28, 1260a24).

These free and relatively equal individuals aim at a self-sufficiency that their more limited household and village communities could not provide. In doing so, they somehow also come to aim at enabling human beings to lead the good life described in detail in Aristotle's ethical writings, a life spent in the active exercise of the moral and intellectual virtues. Accordingly, Aristotle insists that though the political community "comes into being for the sake of living, it exists for the sake of living well" (*Pol.* 1252b29, 1278b21, 1281a1).

I suggested in the preceding chapter that the most important features of any community are the forms of friendship and justice that develop among its members. In the chapters that follow I devote much of my attention to working out the implications of Aristotle's understanding of political friendship and political justice. Here I offer only a brief characterization of them to help define Aristotelian political community.

Let me begin with political friendship. Unlike the members of families and, to a lesser extent, villages, the individuals who make up a political community do not have personal ties of attachment to each other. In other words, they lack the bonds of natural affection that keep husbands, wives, and children together. Nor do they possess the bonds of affection created by extended kinship and neighborly proximity. Whatever friendship bonds they do possess, they lack the personal familiarity that characterizes family and village relations.[3] Even in the small political communities that Aristotle discusses, Aristotelian citizens thus live in "imagined communities," communities that are built around somewhat abstract ideas of mutual and common advantage rather than on personal ties and affection.[4] From this Aristotelian point of view, only a lie, noble or ignoble, could turn the political community into a community of shared origin and personal attachment like the family.[5]

---

3. As noted by Bradfield in his adaptation of Aristotle's distinction between political and nonpolitical communities; see R. Bradfield, *The Natural History of Associations* 1:1–2, 2:442–43.
4. As Josiah Ober pointedly notes in *Mass and Elite*, 33. Ober takes the expression "imagined communities" from Benedict Anderson, *Imagined Communities*.
5. Plato's "noble lie" (*Republic* 315a–e) is "noble" because it is designed to promote

Because the ancient polis is so much smaller than our own political communities, and because Aristotle argues that the best political community should be even smaller than Athens, modern scholars tend to assume that ancient and Aristotelian citizens lived in what they call "face-to-face" communities, communities in which personal familiarity establishes bonds of friendship among citizens. Even so astute an observer as Moses Finley suggests that "ancient Athens was the model of a face-to-face society."[6] But as Robin Osborne points out, this is an "absurd model" for a city of forty thousand male citizens, most of whom were scattered over hundreds of square miles of farming territory.[7] It would be a mistake to identify even the smaller Greek *poleis*—which were closer to the Greek norm than Athens was—with face-to-face communities based on the model of village life. Although ancient Greek citizens were far more familiar with each other than modern citizens are, they were still too numerous and scattered to develop the personal ties that bind individuals together in face-to-face communities.[8]

Aristotle makes clear that the friendship between citizens is not based on personal ties of affection and familiarity. What brings individuals together into political communities is their mutual interest in making use of the various goods and skills they possess. Accordingly, Aristotle insists that "political friendship has been established mainly in accordance with advantage" (*EE* 1242a6; cf. *NE* 1160a11).[9]

Members of political communities come together because they have different skills and goods, not because they share virtues or affection. As a result, they are unlikely, as a rule, to behave like either loving kin or virtuous individuals. Human beings do not form political communities by rounding up all the virtuous individuals that they can bring together. Moreover, even if they could do so, a collection of highly virtuous individuals lacking a variety of skills and goods would not make

---

a truly just order within the community, in part by spreading the lie that its members are all born of the local earth and thus naturally differentiated from all other peoples. The "ignoble" lie I refer to is that spread by extreme versions of nationalism.

6. M. Finley, *Democracy, Ancient and Modern*, 17. Finley uses the same description with a few qualifications in M. Finley, "Introduction," 11–12. The concept of a "face-to-face" society was popularized by C. Cooley in *Human Nature and the Social Order* and *Social Organization*. See also R. Redfield, *The Little Community*, 10.

7. R. Osborne, *Demos*, 64–65. For a discussion of the peasant character of the average Athenian citizen, see E. M. Wood, *Peasant-Citizen and Slave*.

8. Such ties probably did develop, however, in the numerous "demes" into which classical Athens was subdivided; see esp. D. Whitehead, *The Demes of Attica*.

9. Moreover, as I argue in chapter 4, Aristotle's higher, noninstrumental form of friendship, the shared virtue friendship, cannot be stretched beyond a few individuals. It thus cannot provide a model for political friendship, even in the most ideal conditions.

up a political community, according to Aristotle. In contrast, a group of relatively unvirtuous individuals who possessed a diverse range of skills and goods could form political communities. I do not mean to dismiss Aristotle's claim that the political community, which comes into existence for the sake of comfort and security, exists ultimately for the sake of living a good life. My point, instead, is that it is precisely this kind of group of individuals, selected for a variety of skills and goods rather than for any disposition toward virtuous action, which, according to Aristotle, forms a community that exists for the sake of the good life.

Political justice plays an even larger role in Aristotle's understanding of political community than political friendship does. Human beings are the political animals par excellence because of the capacity for reasoned speech, which leads them to make claims about justice and injustice. As we have seen, Aristotle insists that some form of justice develops in every community; community in the just and unjust "makes a household" as well as "a polis" and every other form of human community (*Pol.* 1253a18). But the specific form of justice that develops among citizens is tied much more closely to speech and public deliberation than is any other form.

Aristotle defines political justice most clearly in book 5 of the *Nicomachean Ethics*.

> We must not forget that we are looking for both unqualified [*haplōs*] justice and political justice. This is found among men who share a common life seeking self-sufficiency and who are free and equal, either proportionately or arithmetically. Hence, in a community where this is not the case, there is no political justice in the mutual relations of its members, but only something that bears a resemblance to the just. For the just exists only among those regulated by law.
> ... Despotic and paternal justice are not the same as this [political form of] justice, though they are like it; for there can be no injustice in the unqualified sense toward things that are one's own. ... Political justice is not manifested in these relations; for political justice, as we saw, depends on law and develops among people naturally subject to law, and these are, as we saw, people who have an equal share in ruling and being ruled. Hence justice can more truly be manifested toward one's wife than toward children and possessions, for the former is household justice; but even this is different from political justice.
>
> (*NE* 1134a24–b17)

When we use the term *justice* without any qualifying term—to indicate justice among members of a particular community—what we mean,

Aristotle is suggesting, is political justice.[10] Individuals in every community develop a sense of mutual obligation created by their shared ends and actions. In political communities the standards that define this sense of mutual obligation are expressed in laws, that is, in public rules open to discussion and revision. Moreover, these standards are made, maintained, and enforced by members of the political community who regularly take turns in positions of authority. *Political* standards of mutual obligation are expressed primarily in publicly debated decisions about general rules that citizens take turns in interpreting and enforcing. The Greeks, Moses Finley suggests, "invented" politics by introducing a form of communal life "in which binding decisions are reached by discussion and argument and ultimately by voting."[11] Aristotle's concept of political justice is designed to capture the most unique and important features of this Greek invention.

Politics, for Aristotle, concerns the actions of individuals who hold each other accountable in this way and, especially, their competition for the power to determine, interpret, and enforce the standards of political justice. These individuals are bound to each other in unique ways, even if these bonds lead to as much conflict and competition as cooperation. Indeed, the political form of justice especially encourages conflict and competition since it opens the determination of the community's standards of mutual obligation to public debate and deliberation. In most other communities—families, for example—these standards are not nearly as much a subject of debate and deliberation, since they are either dictated by a particular individual or drawn without public discussion from custom and convention. Given the intensely particularistic interests of families, family members are disinclined to lay down their mutual obligations in general rules. Moreover, given the manifest inequalities in intellectual and emotional capacities between parents and children (if not between men and women and masters and slaves, as Aristotle asserts), they do not establish the kind of regular alternation of positions of authority that characterizes political justice.

Forms of justice, as discussed in chapter 1, develop for Aristotle even in much less permanent and important forms of community than the polis and the family, as we can see if we supplement Aristotle's examples with some of our own. Consider the community of players in a card game. They clearly develop a sense of mutual obligation based on

---

10. I defend this interpretation in the second section of chapter 5.
11. M. Finley, *Politics in the Ancient World*, 52–53. See also M. Gagarin, *Early Greek Law*, 143–46.

their shared activity: they expect each other to play by the rules of the game. Like citizens and unlike family members, game players tend to rely on general rules to establish their mutual obligations.

But the difference between the rules of the game and the rules of political justice is, contrary to influential legal theorists such as H. L. A. Hart,[12] quite significant. Given the very specific and limited purpose of their association, game players require merely that they all follow some set of rules so that they can get on with the pleasure—or profit—that comes from playing the game. No demand for intrinsically valuable or correct standards, apart from the formal obligation to play by the rules of the game, follows from their communal activities. As a result, game players spend relatively little time debating the best rules for their game, let alone competing for the power to determine and interpret these rules. If they cannot interpret and enforce these rules themselves (as most game players do who play for pleasure rather than profit),[13] they are inclined to delegate these powers to a third party, that is, an umpire or referee. Umpires hold their power simply by virtue of their being a third party who understands the rules of the game, not because they possess any substantive knowledge of what the best rules might be.

Members of political communities, in contrast, devote a great deal of attention to determining what they think are the intrinsically correct standards of mutual obligation. Consequently, they are disinclined simply to delegate the power to make, interpret, and enforce these standards to a neutral third party. Instead, they compete for this power or look for individuals with the appropriate substantive qualifications for exercising it.

Given the breadth and importance of the ends and actions that human beings share in political communities, it is inevitable that unless their reasoning powers are violently suppressed they will develop substantive senses of what others owe them. Even with a much more limited understanding of the purpose of political community than Aristotle's—say, the protection of individual security and comfort—we are faced with such an extraordinarily broad range of possible means to

---

12. H. L. A. Hart, *The Concept of Law*, 138–41.
13. From an Aristotelian perspective, whether individuals seek profit or pleasure from their games makes a great deal of difference in the forms of friendship and justice that develop among them. For example, the need for an umpire to interpret rules is obviously far more pressing in profit-seeking games, such as all professional sports, than in a friendly game of cards. Umpires allow one to eliminate the need for the shoot-outs or the mob enforcers whom we associate with high-stakes card games.

that end that individual members of the community will inevitably develop a sense of the intrinsic correctness of some over others. Moreover, even if, like Thomas Hobbes, we think that others owe us obedience to purely conventional determinations of our mutual obligations, we still make a claim about the intrinsic nature of the obligations that community members owe each other. This claim is no less controversial than any other claim about our intrinsic obligations. To the extent that we try to persuade—or, for that matter, gain the power to compel—other individuals to accept this claim, we are competing to determine the standards of political justice.

It is such reasoning, I suggest, that leads Aristotle to insist that the rules of political justice cannot be limited to conventional standards, standards that, like the rules of a game, we agree to follow as a convenient means to a particular end. Political justice, Aristotle notes in the section of the *Nicomachean Ethics* that immediately follows the definition of political justice quoted above, consists of both natural and conventional right (*NE* 1134b18). By "conventional right," he means judgments that are important not because they have any intrinsic merit or worth but because they settle matters in one way or the other. Judgments about these matters—for example, about whether to drive on the left or the right side of the road or to sacrifice "one goat or two sheep"—make up the sphere of conventional right. With judgments of conventional right, all that matters is that citizens come to agree on a binding standard, whatever that standard may be (*NE* 1134b20). By "natural right," Aristotle means judgments about matters in which citizens are concerned to determine intrinsically correct standards of obligation.[14]

By dividing political justice into natural and conventional right, Aristotle emphasizes his conviction that deliberation about political justice will inspire attempts to establish both conventionally and intrinsically correct standards of mutual obligation. As I argue in the next section, Aristotle insists that it is natural for rational beings such as ourselves to form communities in which we argue about the intrinsically correct standards of political justice. Moreover, he makes clear that our capacity for reasoned speech prevents us from limiting our judgments about justice to the establishment of conventional standards.

For another example of a nonpolitical form of justice, an example

14. This is a relatively unorthodox interpretation of the famous passage (*NE* 1134b) in which Aristotle distinguishes between natural and conventional right. I elaborate on and defend this interpretation in chapter 5 and in "Natural Right."

that helps us highlight the characteristic features of political justice, consider the sense of justice that develops among travelers on a ship. There are certain obligations that we come to expect of each other when we travel together. When we confront danger these obligations can be extremely demanding. They may even demand self-sacrifice, as when we expect men to follow the rule "Women and children first."[15] Moreover, we expect that in danger, and sometimes even in relative calm, others will treat the orders of the captain of a ship as binding obligations. These obligations, unlike the obligations characteristic of games and political communities, rarely take the form of general rules, since they arise out of the very specific situations that threaten the safety of a ship. We recognize the captain's authority to determine and interpret these obligations, presumably because we defer to his or her superior knowledge about how to secure the ship against danger. Likewise, we have relatively little patience with individuals who start a debate about standards of obligation in the midst of a shipboard emergency.

Political justice contrasts with shipboard justice for Aristotle both in the form its obligations take and the way it structures the authority to interpret and enforce them. Political justice, unlike shipboard justice, expresses standards of mutual obligation primarily in terms of general rules or, in other words, laws. Members of political communities are, in some way, "naturally subject to law" (*NE* 1134a14), according to Aristotle.[16]

Aristotle also denies that the authority of a captain is an appropriate model for political authority because he denies that there is an art and knowledge of what is good for members of a political community comparable to the captain's art. Analogies to the arts in determining the distribution of political power are flawed because political authority decides the best way for us to live, not just the best means to a particular end. We defer to the carpenter and architect on questions of the best way to build a house, but we remain, to a certain extent, the best judges of whether a particular kind of house suits us (*Pol.* 1282a20). Very few free and relatively equal individuals are inclined to affirm the irrelevance of their judgments about the intrinsically correct standards for

---

15. "Women and children first" is a customary rule that reflects a rarely debated substantive judgment about the best rules to follow in times of danger. As such, it differs from the conventional judgments, the intrinsic merit of which does not concern us, that make up Aristotle's category of conventional right.

16. Given the complexity of his argument, I postpone explaining why he believes this to be the case until my discussion of "the rule of law" in chapter 6.

organizing their lives. Aristotle thus concludes that regular alternation of the positions of authority to establish, interpret, and enforce the mutual obligations of citizens is a necessary component of political justice.[17]

Political and legal theorists have for centuries used metaphors such as paternalism, the rules of the game, and the ship of state to model their conceptions of political justice. Aristotle rejects all of these metaphors because they derive their understanding of political justice from the communal relationships of individuals whose identities, ends, and activities differ substantially from those shared by members of political communities. The family provides an inadequate model for political justice because it consists of manifestly unequal individuals tied by personal familiarity and affection. The "rules of the game" model fails to capture the unavoidable interest in—and competition to shape—the intrinsic correctness of standards of justice in political communities because it extrapolates from the relatively limited concerns of game players. Finally, the "ship of state" metaphor exaggerates the extent and significance of political knowledge and ignores the extent to which all free individuals are, at least in part, experts on their own welfare. We are bound, Aristotle would suggest, to misunderstand the ways in which citizens establish mutual obligations and hold each other accountable as long as we continue to turn to other, nonpolitical forms of communal life to make sense of political justice.

It is this emphasis on political justice that makes Aristotle's understanding of political community so much more exclusive than those offered by most modern political scientists. His understanding of political community effectively restricts the term to republics, that is, to those communities that develop the institutions of public accountability and the sharing of power that are part of the practice of political justice.[13] Nevertheless, the Aristotelian political community is much less exclusive than some of his contemporary partisans—who deny that modern liberal democracies meet its requirements—believe it to be.[19] These promoters of Aristotle's understanding of political community usually associate it with the "civic republican" view that "patriotism is the no-

17. Aristotle is arguing here against Plato, who presented a classic version of the "ship of state" metaphor in *Republic*, 488a–89b. See M. Walzer, *Spheres of Justice*, 285–87, for a similar argument against Plato's "ship of state" metaphor.
18. On the problematic place of monarchy in Aristotle's understanding of political community, see the Appendix to this chapter.
19. For references, see the second section of the Introduction.

blest of moral sentiments" and that the "individual cannot be privately happy when the state is afflicted."[20] Such an understanding of political community would exclude not only most modern liberal democracies but most of the ancient *poleis* Aristotle himself discusses, with the possible exception of Sparta.

Aristotle's concept of political community is more inclusive than is the civic republican view because it does not treat communion, the active submergence of individual identity in a collective identity, as the defining feature of political community. We need not, like Rousseauian citizens, submerge our identities in a "common me" nor even share the same substantive standards of justice in order to participate in Aristotelian political community. Aristotelian political community requires neither the superiority to biological nature nor the moral consensus that Hannah Arendt and Alisdair MacIntyre, respectively, associate with it.[21] To participate in it, we need only share in the practice of holding each other accountable to standards of mutual obligation that Aristotle associates with political justice.

## THE POLITICAL ANIMAL

When Aristotle insists that "there is in everyone by nature an impulse toward this kind of community" (*Pol.* 1253a29), he is arguing that the members of the human species are, for the most part, disposed in the course of following their natural inclinations and exercising their specific natural capacities to form self-sufficient communities based on sharing the practices of political justice. For Aristotle the political community has both a natural origin, in specifically human inclinations and capacities, and a natural end, the development and completion of the human capacity to lead what he calls the good life. Nature disposes us to participate in political communities, and this participation, in turn, somehow completes human development in such a way as to make the good life possible.

This teleological account of the nature of political community raises a number of troubling questions, the most important of which is, How does one get from the existence of natural capacities to the existence of a particular kind of community among us? The teleological reasoning

---

20. A. Black, *State, Community, and Human Desires*, 113–17, summarizing what he calls the "civic view" of political community shared from "Aristotle and Plato to Rousseau and Hegel."

21. H. Arendt, *The Human Condition*, 29–33; A. MacIntyre, *After Virtue*, 222, 263.

usually attributed to Aristotle in response to this question—that since the human capacity for a just and virtuous life can be perfected only in a community, there must exist, by nature, a community devoted to the good life—is especially unsatisfying for most modern readers since it requires us to treat the political community as if it were a living organism. If we were to accept this reasoning as an explanation of the existence of political communities, we would have to think of the political community as an organism that grows out of our natural capacities in the same way that an oak grows out of an acorn. Unless we take the analogy to organic growth literally, the organic analogy merely tells us that whatever process takes us from our capacity for reasoned speech into political communities is, in some way, *like* organic growth.[22] Aristotle's organic analogy does not tell us how we are to identify and account for how that process actually takes us from our capacity for reasoned speech into political community.

I argue here and in the following chapter that Aristotle can answer these troubling questions without portraying the polis as a living, organic whole. Aristotle makes use of organic analogies in the opening pages of the *Politics*, but he does not let those analogies take the place of an explanation of the nature of political community. Instead, he suggests that when human beings come together in particular circumstances, their natural needs and capacities dispose them to form political communities. Much of Aristotle's reasoning here is not fully explicit and can be brought to light only by referring to his discussions of political community and justice in other places. But that reasoning is sufficient to explain the natural inclination among human beings to form political communities. Once formed, Aristotle believes, these communities shape individuals to serve a higher natural end, the completion of human development in a good life.[23] I reserve my discussion of that higher end for chapter 3, in which I offer a reinterpretation of Aristotelian political teleology. In this chapter I focus only on the natural origins of the political community.

Aristotle begins his defense of the naturalness of the political com-

22. Not to mention the problem raised by the fact that for the polis, unlike all other natural species, a completed form is the almost impossible exception rather than the rule. I present a reinterpretation of Aristotle's political teleology in chapter 3, the key point of which is that Aristotle does not treat the polis as a natural substance, like an acorn, with its own internal principle of motion and final end as a completed form.

23. This connection with the good life distinguishes the political community from other, equally natural, communities for Aristotle. It leads him to emphasize the fact that human beings are "political animals," even though he also thinks of them as 'household' and "communal" animals (*EE* 1242a15).

munity by deriving it from family and village life. He assumes that few would doubt the naturalness of these forms of communal life, based as they are on the affection and preference that family members have for each other. (I am assuming here that the villages Aristotle discusses develop around extended family and kinship groups.)[24] "Between man and woman friendship seems to exist by nature; for man is naturally inclined to form couples—even more than to form cities, inasmuch as the household is earlier and more necessary than the city" (*NE* 1162a16). "A natural striving to leave behind another that is like oneself" brings these first communities together (*Pol.* 1252a29). "The friendship of kinsmen" grows out of "parental friendship," that is, the love parents feel for children "as being a part of themselves" (*NE* 1161b18). If the political community arises out of the family and village communities, and everyone admits that these are the earliest communities, then it will be hard to deny, so Aristotle seems to reason, the naturalness of the political community.

But it is not immediately clear why natural needs and capacities should drive human beings beyond the village community, let alone into the political community. In his own account of the origins of the political community Aristotle jumps quickly at this point to the teleological level, noting that the final end for which political community, the self-sufficient community that unites several villages, is the good life, even if this community comes into existence at first merely "for the sake of living" (*Pol.* 1252b29). He does not, however, devote much effort here to explaining how so distinctive a form of communal life as the political community might develop simply "for the sake of living." I try to reconstruct his reasoning in the pages that follow.

What makes it natural for human beings to form communities with individuals other than their kin and their immediate neighbors? The answer to this question seems to require, for Aristotle, reference to the distinctive human capacity for reasoned speech.

> That man is much more a political animal than any kind of bee or other gregarious animal is clear. For, as we assert, nature does nothing in vain; and man alone among the animals has reasoned speech [*logos*]. The mere voice [which other animals possess], it is true, expresses pain and pleasure ... but speech is designed to indicate the advantageous and the harmful, and therefore also the just and unjust; for it is the special property of man that he alone has perception of good and bad, just and unjust, and all other things, and it is community in these things that makes a household or a polis.
> (*Pol.* 1253a)

24. See R. Bradfield, *The Natural History of Associations* 1:1–2, 2:442–43.

Human beings are political animals primarily because they are also rational animals. They possess a capacity for *logos*, which, as is well-known, refers in Greek to speech and argument as well as to reasoning itself. Human beings are unique not only in their reasoning capacities but in their ability to communicate their reasoning to each other (which is why I translate *logos* in the above quotation as "reasoned speech"). This capacity allows human beings "to indicate the advantageous and the harmful" to each other. Many other animals have the capacity to communicate pain and pleasure to each other. But logos gives to human beings the capacity to calculate and communicate advantage and harm—the ability to indicate the consequences that may follow from any given action, as well as to communicate pain and pleasure.[25] This capacity makes possible the development of argument among human beings. Although we can all offer plausible arguments about the consequences of an action, the only person who can offer a final judgment about the existence of pleasure and pain is the individual who experiences it. The rational animal is therefore an argumentative animal, a conclusion implicit in the Greek expression, "animal possessing logos."

Animals possessing logos can calculate the advantages to be gained by interaction with a greater variety of individuals than can be found in the family and the village. They can, moreover, communicate and argue about the best ways of pursuing these advantages, including the formation of communities beyond kinship ties, forms of community not found among other animals. One of these forms of community, according to Aristotle, is the political community. The political community comes into being for the sake of the greater security, comfort, and self-sufficiency to be gained by bringing a relatively heterogeneous group of unrelated individuals, with their different goods and skills, into one community. And it is natural, according to Aristotle, for human beings to form such a community because it is natural for them to reason about and communicate the advantages and disadvantages of various forms of communal living.

As mentioned in the preceding chapter, Aristotle believes that our capacity to communicate and argue about conceptions of advantage and harm disposes us to develop and communicate demands about justice and injustice. (Reasoned speech, he claims, "is designed to indicate the advantageous and the harmful and, therefore also, the just and un-

---

25. In *On the Soul* (433b6) Aristotle notes that whereas desire, which we share with animals, "is influenced by what is just at hand," human rationality "bids us hold back because of what is future."

just" [*Pol.* 1253a15].) Our rational capacities thus dispose us toward expressing concerns about justice, even if they do not dispose us to act justly.

But why does Aristotle believe that discussion of shared advantage among individuals seeking a self-sufficient community naturally leads to the establishment of political community and its characteristic form of justice? The most important reason seems to be the relative equality in reasoning ability of the members of political communities. Political justice "is found among men who share a common life seeking self-sufficiency and who are free and equal, either proportionately or arithmetically" (*NE* 1134a25). Where there is no clear natural hierarchy in reasoning ability among individuals, taking turns in office "accords with nature" (*Pol.* 1279a10, 1259b1). Free adult males, according to Aristotle, are naturally equal enough in their rational capacities to share in these activities. There is the possibility of an extraordinarily gifted individual whose ethical and intellectual excellence completely overshadows the abilities of all other adult males, but that is likely only among relatively uncivilized peoples, such as the Greeks were in earlier times (*Pol.* 1286b).

Political justice is thus natural, according to Aristotle, because any other form of justice would demand the establishment of a conventional hierarchy to restrict argument and participation among members of the community. Within families and many other forms of community these hierarchies exist and are often accepted by all. But that is either because we acknowledge some natural superiority in reasoning abilities that supports hierarchy—as most of us acknowledge in justifying the hierarchy of parents over children, as Aristotle accepts in justifying the hierarchy of husbands over wives, and as many peoples have attributed to their absolute rulers—or because we are uninterested in the intrinsic merits of any particular definition of the standards of justice and are thus satisfied with purely conventional standards, as we are when playing games. Whatever their differences in skills and goods, Aristotle denies that there is a natural difference in kind in deliberative abilities among the free male heads of households who form political communities. As a result, only the imposition of conventional hierarchies—usually backed up by force—will keep them from developing ties of political justice.

Of course, as I have noted, Aristotle restricts this relative equality in reasoning ability to free adult males. Women, Aristotle argues in book 1 of the *Politics,* possess the capacity to reason and deliberate and are thus superior to natural slaves, who lack this capacity altogether. But in women this capacity somehow "lacks authority" (*Pol.* 1260a12). Some commentators have suggested that this passage implies that Aristotle, like most modern social and political theorists, believes that the weakness of female deliberative powers is conventional rather than natural, that female deliberation lacks "authority" because male-dominated popular opinion fails to recognize claims made by women.[26] But the context in which Aristotle makes this argument—a discussion of the natural distinctions of age, gender, and capacity for freedom—makes this interpretation unlikely. Moreover, Aristotle does not even raise the question of whether the subordination of women is purely conventional, a question he discusses at length with regard to the subordination of slaves.[27]

I do not, however, see any reason that this Aristotelian conception of relative political equality cannot be expanded to include women, once one rejects his argument about their natural inferiority in deliberation. Some feminist theorists have suggested that Aristotle's conception of political activity derives much of its character from the subordination of women to a private sphere of activity bound to purely natural functions. Aristotle would not have conceived of politics as the conquest of bodily nature by freedom and reason, they suggest, if he did not identify women with natural functions. Wendy Brown, for example, writes that for Aristotle "man's political nature is rooted in self-repudiation, a drive toward alienation, toward forgetting of his desirous and mortal self." Men thus strive in politics to get beyond the condition of women, who are "enslaved to the body."[28]

Brown's claims make sense only if we accept her assumption about the opposition between humanity and nature in ancient Greek theory and practice, an assumption that she takes from Arendt.[29] But such assumptions, as I argued in the Introduction, are incorrect. They rest on the conceptual dichotomies between humanity and nature that Arendt derives from a post-Kantian German philosophic tradition and imposes on Aristotelian theory and Greek practice.[30] Aristotle certainly subor-

26. See A. Saxonhouse, *Women in the History of Political Thought*, 74–75; S. Salkever, *Finding the Mean*, 184–85.
27. Not to mention Aristotle's infamous characterization of women as deformed males in his biological writings; *Generation of Animals* 731b–732a, 765b–767b.
28. Wendy Brown, *Manhood and Politics*, 37, 51n28.
29. Indeed, Brown backs her interpretation of Aristotle's understanding of women as "enslaved to the body" with a reference to Arendt rather than to Aristotle; ibid., 51n28.
30. See the second section of the Introduction.

dinates women to men, but he does not do so because he associates women with nature and men with freedom and superiority to nature. For Aristotle, politics is a natural activity, an activity that he denies that women are naturally equipped to share. If, however, we acknowledge that women possess the deliberative capacities that Aristotle attributes to adult men, then I see no reason why we cannot expand his conception of political community to include them.[31]

With regard to adult males, Aristotle qualifies his claims about relative political equality by insisting on the existence of individuals whose limited natural capacities make it appropriate for them to be slaves. Among natural slaves, the capacity for reasoning and deliberation is "wholly lacking" (*Pol.* 1260a11). Those who differ from other human beings in the same way and to the same extent that "the body differs from the soul or beast from man . . . are slaves by nature" (*Pol.* 1254b16).

The theoretical and practical significance of this qualification of political equality depends on what percentage of human beings fit into this category of natural slave. If, as Aristotle sometimes implies, the vast majority of human beings, those who live in tribes and empires, are slaves by nature, then that raises serious questions about his claims about the naturalness of political community. In book 7 of the *Politics* Aristotle suggests that the peoples of Northern Europe

> are filled with spiritedness but are relatively lacking in thought and art; hence they remain freer but lack political rule and are incapable of ruling their neighbors. Those in Asia, in contrast, have souls endowed with thought and art but are lacking in spiritedness; hence they remain ruled and enslaved. But the stock of the Greeks shares in both—just as it holds the middle in terms of location. For it is both spirited and endowed with thought and hence both remains free and governs itself in the best manner and at the same time is capable of ruling all, should it obtain a single regime.
>
> (*Pol.* 1327b24–32)

Does this mean that Aristotle believes that the majority of human beings are in some way disposed to slavery by their racial nature? I think not. Aristotle clearly states that some non-Greek races, such as the Carthaginians and the Egyptians, have succeeded in establishing political institutions (*Pol.* 1272b24–1273b, 1329b32).[32] But this passage does suggest that Aristotle relies, at least implicitly, on a more developmental or evolutionary understanding of human nature than is commonly recog-

---

31. For an argument supporting this conclusion, see M. Nussbaum, "Nature, Function, and Capability," 165–66.
32. See G. Huxley, *On Aristotle and Greek Society*, 8.

nized.³³ Northerners lack the thought and art that might lead them to form political communities, though their spiritedness keeps them from being enslaved to emperors and priests. Apparently, Aristotle believes they have not yet fully developed their reasoning and deliberative capacities. They are like the earlier Greeks, who had not yet developed to a point where all adult males shared in a relative equality in reasoning abilities and who, accordingly, submitted control of their affairs to monarchs and heroes (*Pol.* 1261a, 1286b).³⁴

Asian peoples, in contrast, seem to lack the spiritedness or self-assertion needed to form political communities, but given their highly developed civilization, they clearly do not meet the criteria of natural slavery laid down in book 1 of the *Politics*. How, if at all, could Aristotle possibly explain why these people do not now assert their obviously well-developed rational development? In order to maintain his claim about the naturalness of political community, Aristotle would need some account of the possible obstructions to the exercise of our deliberative capacities. With such an account he could then argue that fully civilized human adults, not prevented by some contingent natural or human constraints from using and developing their natural powers of deliberation and speech, will form political communities.³⁵

As I stress in the preceding chapter, the capacity for reasoned speech promotes some form of justice in every kind of Aristotelian community, but political justice develops that capacity more fully than any other form of justice does. With political justice, unlike many other forms of justice, the standards of mutual obligation are explicit rules, open to public debate and revision; the actions of the individuals who make and enforce those rules are also public and open to challenge, especially since they do not regularly turn over their temporary positions of authority to other individuals. If human beings are rational and argumentative animals, then it is in their debates about political justice that they make the fullest use of these capacities—which may be one reason that Aristotle emphasizes so strongly that they are also political animals.

But one might ask, with Hobbes, What makes this naturally argu-

33. See M. Defourny, *Études sur la Politique d'Aristote*, 363–449, and R. Weil, *Aristote et l'histoire*, 327–38, 367–403, for attempts to fill in this Aristotelian account of social evolution.
34. On this point, see P. Rybicki, *Aristote et la pensée*, 75.
35. As I note in the Appendix to chapter 7, a major weakness in Aristotle's account of political life is his failure to develop a clearer understanding of the nonpolitical forms of large-scale social organizations that existed beyond the Greek world. Without such an understanding it is much harder to identify the necessary preconditions and distinctive features of political life.

mentative animal a political animal? In other words, in what way do our natural capacities for argument about justice lead us into community rather than into battle?

Hobbes, like Aristotle, defines human uniqueness in terms of the capacity to calculate and communicate notions of advantage and justice, but he sees in this capacity the source of the unique disorder of human life rather than the natural basis for a particular kind of communal living. The establishment of political society, Hobbes argues, requires the stifling of our inclination to make claims about the intrinsic justice or injustice of different distributions of advantage and power. In any case, such debate would be pointless since claims about justice and injustice make sense only with reference to preceding agreements or conventions. The notion of intrinsically or substantively just states of affairs is merely another species of nonsense for Hobbes.[36] Thus, unlike Aristotle, who suggests that the capacity for reasoned speech makes us political animals, Hobbes insists that "the tongue of man is the trumpet of war and sedition."[37] Without a convention limiting our natural tendency to argue about substantive standards of justice and injustice—a convention that limits the meaning of justice to the performance of contracts and the enforcement of the law by a common authority—Hobbes believes that there can be no political society. An agreement *not* to argue about political justice is for Hobbes a necessary condition of the existence of political society.

Aristotle would probably respond to this criticism by arguing that the establishment of a common authority establishes, willy-nilly, substantive and controversial standards of justice within a community by honoring, implicitly or explicitly, the qualities possessed by the sovereign as especially appropriate to ruling. Where individuals are free to use their reasoning abilities and see themselves as at least relatively equal—as, of course, Hobbes insists that they are[38]—a community of argument about substantive standards of justice will grow up around the standards established by honoring the sovereign's claim to power. One can, like Hobbes, seek to suppress public arguments about the value of these standards as a danger to social peace and order, but that will not eliminate the human disposition to make judgments about what their mutual obligations should be, judgments that will continue to interfere

---

36. T. Hobbes, *Leviathan*, 96, 100, 189–90.
37. T. Hobbes, *Of the Citizen*, 168–69.
38. T. Hobbes, *Leviathan*, 183.

with the sovereign's attempt to maintain order, even if they are denied a public hearing.

Of course, Hobbes believes that the sovereign can count on the natural drive for self-preservation to override whatever natural disposition individuals have to make and express judgments about justice and injustice. But the very power that he expects will so overawe human beings—the power of the sovereign—is threatened by these judgments, since the assignment of absolute political power to a particular individual or group of individuals itself suggests controversial standards of political justice. Hobbes does not want the subjects of his state to think of the sovereign as having a substantively just claim to authority, but only if they do come to think that way will they be likely to accept the sovereign's authority. And if they do, that will raise questions about the substantive standards of justice implied by the sovereign's claim to power, unless one goes much further in suppressing human reason than Hobbes wants to go.[39]

A certain amount of social conflict and distrust is unavoidable among individuals who share in argument about political justice. This distrust and conflict is part of the price, Aristotle would suggest, that we pay for political community. Hobbes is unwilling to pay that price and seeks to eliminate these sources of social conflict and distrust by suppressing our tendency to argue about substantive standards of justice. Aristotle is willing to pay that price not only because of the great value that he places on the capacities that Hobbes wants to suppress but also because he believes that any attempt to suppress these capacities will ultimately be self-defeating.

## THE ANCIENT POLIS AND MODERN POLITICAL COMMUNITIES

Many contemporary social and political theorists believe that the manifest differences in size and social structure between the polis and mod-

---

39. Hobbes cannot go very far in suppressing human reasoning powers since he relies on reason, as opposed to the passions, to lead us to obey the sovereign. If citizens come to think of themselves as intrinsically inferior in their reasoning power to the sovereign, why should they trust the line of reasoning that Hobbes suggests that rational individuals would follow? One might ask what does that matter as long as they obey the sovereign? But it does matter for Hobbes what incentive leads individuals to obey the sovereign. If they obey the sovereign because they think of the sovereign as the best-qualified judge of substantive standards of justice, then they develop a sense of nonconventional standards of justice according to which they can hold each other and later sovereigns accountable, precisely the result that Hobbes is trying to avoid.

ern political communities compel us to reject any attempt to use Aristotle's conception of political community in the analysis of modern political life. Aristotle, after all, derived his conception of political community from the study of tiny city-states, states that relied on slave labor and lacked the high degree of social differentiation and complexity characteristic of modern liberal democracies. The bloated giant among them, Athens, reached only forty thousand citizens at its height. How could an understanding of political life derived from these communities be appropriate for modern political communities?[40]

Moreover, if the most familiar interpretations of Aristotle's political teleology are correct, Aristotelian political communities are compelled by an internal principle of growth toward completion of their natural form in the best regime outlined in book 7 of the *Politics*—a tiny polis of fewer than five thousand leisured gentlemen supported by the labor of slaves, serfs, and totally disenfranchised workers.[41] Because, to state the obvious, we have no reason to believe that we are moving in this direction, it seems clear that we cannot apply Aristotle's conception of political community to modern political communities, at least so long as that conception is interpreted in this way.

I have, however, already indicated that there are good reasons to doubt this familiar interpretation of Aristotle's political teleology, reasons developed at length in the following chapter. Once we clear away misunderstandings of Aristotle's political teleology, many of the objections to using his conception of political community in the analysis of modern political regimes also diminish in importance. For much of what is taken to distinguish Aristotelian from modern political communities, such as their tiny size and extremely limited franchise, are actually preconditions of Aristotle's best regime. Political community, as Aristotle understands it, has far less demanding preconditions than does the ideal regime "established according to our prayers [*kat' euxein*]" for good fortune (*Pol.* 1325b35–39).

The most obvious difference between ancient and modern political communities is, of course, their size. In a famous passage from his discussion of the best regime in the *Politics,* Aristotle insists that a well-constituted political community will not have more citizens than can assemble and deliberate in one place.

40. This critique of the modern use of Aristotle's political philosophy—and of ancient Greek politics in general—as a guide to modern political theory and practice is made most clearly and forcefully by S. Holmes, "Aristippus," 113–28.
41. Aristotle considers even five thousand citizens too large a population for his best regime (*Pol.* 1265a14).

But this too, in any case, is evident from the facts: that it is difficult—perhaps impossible—for a city that is too populous to be well-ordered.... A ship that is a foot long, for example, will not be a ship at all, nor one of twelve hundred feet, and as it approaches a certain size it will make for a bad voyage, in the one case because of smallness, in the other because of excess. Similarly with the city as well, the one that is made up of too few persons is not self-sufficient, though the city is a self-sufficient thing, while the one that is made up of too many persons is with respect to the necessary things self-sufficient like a nation, but is not a city; for it is not easy for it to be ruled in a political way.

(*Pol.* 1326a25–b6)

Does Aristotle believe that such a small size is a necessary component of the less well managed political communities that actually exist in the world? If one identifies actual ancient poleis with what modern social theorists call a "face-to-face society,"[42] then one is likely to answer yes. But as I have already argued, it is a mistake to conceive of actual ancient poleis as small-town societies in which everyone knew everyone else.[43] The question here is whether *Aristotle* believes this sort of familiarity to be a necessary component of political community per se.

Clearly, Aristotle believes personal familiarity to be a necessary component of the best political community. Accordingly, the well-ordered polis should not exceed the number of citizens that can be "readily surveyed" and spoken to at one time (*Pol.* 1326b15–25). In the best regime, "citizens must necessarily be familiar with one another's qualities; otherwise, matters connected with offices and judging must necessarily be carried on poorly." As a result, "it is difficult—perhaps impossible—for a city that is too populous to be well-ordered" (*Pol.* 1326b15, 1325a26). Nevertheless, Aristotle does not deny that larger poleis such as Athens are political communities, nor does he say that it is impossible for a very large city, one more the size of the nations of Asia and Northern Europe, to form a political community. He merely says that "it is not easy" for so large a group "to be ruled in a political way" (*Pol.* 1326b5).[44] Given the kinds of communities that Aristotle knew, it is not surprising that he would come to this conclusion. The great nations of Asia all lived under the control of bureaucratic despotisms. Only the members of the poleis established by the Greeks and other communities escaped such despotism and formed political communities.

42. As do M. Finley (*Democracy, Ancient and Modern,* 17) and S. Holmes ("Aristippus," 121), following Finley.
43. See R. Osborne, *Demos,* 64–65.
44. "Not easy to rule in a political way" translates "*politeian gar ou radion huparxein.*"

Aristotle does note, however, at least one exception to this generalization. The Egyptians, clearly a nation rather than a polis, "are held to be the most ancient people, yet they have obtained laws and political order [*taxeōs politikēes*]" (*Pol.* 1329b33).[45] This exception suggests the possibility of overcoming the difficulties in establishing a "political order" in a large territory with a large population. Perhaps other nations Aristotle has not seen, like those that established modern liberal democracies, could succeed as well in overcoming these difficulties. A large population is an obstacle to Aristotelian political community, but it does not render that community impossible. The large political communities of the modern world could never, according to Aristotle, establish the best regime within their political communities; nevertheless, that failure would not distinguish them very much from actual Greek political communities, which themselves never came close to doing so.

Indeed, Aristotle goes so far as to suggest that larger political communities, because they better support the emergence of a large middle class and the mixed regime, are less prone to factional conflict (*stasis*) than smaller ones are (*Pol.* 1296a9).[46] Large political communities thus have an advantage over small poleis in realizing the regime that Aristotle advises the vast majority of political communities, large and small, to aim at: the mixed regime supported by a large middle class (*Pol.* 1293b–96b). This advantage effectively offsets the disadvantages that prevent large political communities from realizing the best regime of book 7, a regime "according to prayer" for unlikely good fortune and ideal initial conditions (*Pol.* 1325b35–40).

Of course, as Benjamin Constant forcefully argues, the growth in "the size of a country causes a corresponding decrease of the political importance allotted to each individual. The most obscure republican of Sparta or Rome had power. The same is not true of the simple citizen of Britain or of the United States."[47] A small size and population increases the importance of individual participation in politics. The diminished opportunity and importance of individual political participation afforded by large modern political communities is another reason

---

45. Note that Aristotle treats only the first part of the statement, about the great antiquity of the Egyptians, as an opinion held by others, although he presents the description of the Egyptian political order in his own name.
46. This neglected suggestion by Aristotle indicates that he would be far less opposed to Madison's famous argument, in *Federalist* no. 10, about the "extended republic" as a means of moderating the effects of factional conflict than is ordinarily supposed; see Hamilton, Jay, and Madison, *The Federalist Papers*.
47. B. Constant, "The Liberty of the Ancients," *Political Writings*, 314.

that leads modern social theorists to restrict the application of Aristotle's concept of political community to the ancient polis. "Everyone [in the ancient Greek poleis] acquired a certain stature in relation to whatever happened in the world, an ability to influence the course of events that is scarcely conceivable today. They had a fairly direct, concrete, and existential share in the making and execution of decisions (and could identify themselves with the decision makers—and not just in an abstract manner)."[48] But Aristotle demands this degree of participation in political affairs only from the citizens of the best regime. There can be no political community if individuals have no part in ruling, judging, or debating legislation; but that participation can take a variety of more or less intense forms. Intense general participation in civic life is the mark of democratic citizenship—and only one form of democratic citizenship at that—according to Aristotle.

Indeed, the best form of democracy, Aristotle argues, is one in which most citizens are farmers living in scattered settlements too far from the city center to participate regularly in the assembly (*Pol.* 1292b25, 1318b–19a). Athens, as Robin Osborne notes, "is generally accused of being Aristotle's model of the worst form of democracy," but a more careful look at the widely scattered population of Attica suggests "that Athens in fact had elements, at least, of [Aristotle's] 'best democracy.' "[49] Athenian democracy as actually practiced corresponds much better to this model of agrarian democracy than to the urban-based mob rule with which it is usually identified.

Many modern readers mistakenly think of Athens as a city dominated by its urban masses. As a result, most readers assume that Aristotle has Athens in mind when he describes the mob rule that characterizes the worst form of democracy (*Pol.* 1292a, 1293a). But Aristotle himself never explicitly identifies Athens with his worst form of democracy. In assuming that he does so, modern readers impose their misrepresentation of Athens on Aristotle and assume that he shares Plato's violent antipathy to the Athenian form of government.[50] The Athenian regime is certainly imperfect according to Aristotelian standards, but it may be quite appropriate to a large political community.

Aristotelian political community exists where individuals hold each

---

48. C. Meier, *The Greek Discovery of the Political*, 23.
49. R. Osborne, *Demos*, 71–72. See also L B. Carter, *The Quiet Athenian*, 94–95; E. M. Wood, *Peasant-Citizen and Slave*.
50. That antipathy is most vividly presented in Plato's caricature of the democratic individual and city in book 8 of the *Republic*.

other accountable to standards of political justice. These standards require publicly debated general rules and some regular alternation in the positions of authority to make, enforce, and interpret these rules. I suggest that such standards do indeed emerge and bind citizens together in the large liberal democratic republics of the modern world, even if their average citizen's participation in making and interpreting these standards is limited to voting and the occasional stint of jury duty. Modern political communities cannot, given their size, meet the requirements of Aristotle's conception of either the best regime or extreme democracy. But they can develop within them the distinctive sense of political justice that Aristotle associates with political community.

Similarly, although the citizens of Aristotle's best regime rely on enslaved or otherwise disenfranchised labor for the leisure that allows them to lead a good life, there is no indication that Aristotle believes that political community per se is impossible without this leisure. When Aristotle asks in the *Politics* about the nature of the best regime, he is asking about the regime that makes possible the most desirable life. In other words, he is looking for the political conditions of happiness—or human "flourishing," as *eudaimonia* is often translated. We should not be surprised that he discovers that human beings flourish best when freed from the need to engage in self-sustaining labor. When they can rely on others to do that labor, they can devote their entire attention to more interesting and intrinsically valuable activities: for Aristotle, the exercise of the intellectual and ethical virtues. It is hard to deny that these conditions could make for extremely happy lives.

That Aristotle countenances the subordination and disenfranchisement of the great majority of individuals in his best regime appears surprising and shocking only because we are used to utopias, such as Plato's, that are constructed to maximize justice rather than happiness. The justice of disenfranchising, let alone enslaving, the majority of individuals in Aristotle's best regime is, indeed, highly questionable, even by Aristotle's own standards. After all, a natural slave, according to Aristotle, is someone who lacks reasoning skills, someone who is as inferior to a master as body is to soul (*Pol.* 1254b17). It is hard to imagine such an individual performing the variety of complex economic activities required of the subordinated classes in the best regime.[51] Since, however, in book 7 of the *Politics* he is examining the necessary condi-

---

51. See W. Ambler, "Aristotle on Nature and Politics"; D. Charles, "Perfectionism in Aristotle's Political Theory."

tions for happiness rather than the principles of perfect justice, Aristotle never asks whether these individuals are justly subordinated or not.

In contrast, Aristotle does not hesitate to examine the various claims to political power made by different kinds of individuals when he discusses actual political communities. He argues that a variety of claims are made by individuals in actual political communities—birth, wealth, virtue, freedom. None of these claims can be simply ignored in actual political life (*Pol.* 1283b), as he ignores them in his utopian speculations. Within ordinary conditions the best regime available is a mixed regime in which the poor participate to some extent (*Pol.*, book 4).

One might think that even in a mixed regime Aristotle expects all citizens to be free from the need of the work, an idle mob if not a club of leisured gentlemen. But Aristotle never describes the poor citizens of the Greek poleis in this way, nor, despite a widespread myth, is it appropriate to do so.[52] There can be little doubt that the majority of the poor citizens in an Aristotelian mixed regime work for a living. Aristotle would disenfranchise them in his best regime, but he does not recommend doing so in ordinary political communities. His concept of political community thus does not require general dependence on slave labor.[53]

One final reason for rejecting the relevance of Aristotelian political community to the analysis of modern politics has been offered by a number of modern critics. Aristotelian political community, these critics argue, endorses and conceptualizes the almost total subordination of private to public life characteristic of ancient Greek politics. Leaving aside normative considerations, such a subordination cannot be reproduced, they conclude, in the much larger, more complex, and more highly differentiated communities of the modern world.

Like Benjamin Constant, these critics argue that the ancient Greek individual, "almost always sovereign in public affairs, was a slave in all his private relations."[54] Although this subordination of private to public life "may have made sense in a small city-state or *Gemeinschaft*, it is thoroughly out of step with the structural realities of a large modern

---

52. See Ellen Meiksins Wood's explosion of the "myth of the idle mob" in Athens in *Peasant-Citizen and Slave*, 5–41.
53. I am not, of course, denying either that slavery played a historical role in the development of political community in ancient Greece or that the practices of slaveholding and non-slaveholding political communities are likely to differ in significant ways. Here I am arguing only that slaveholding is not a necessary condition for political community as Aristotle understands it.
54. B. Constant, "The Liberty of the Ancients," 311.

society or *Gesellschaft*."⁵⁵ Because "modern societies are not political in the way in which Greek or Italian city-states were political," any "attempt to find in politics the unifying bond that holds modern states together is bound to lead to terror, as the French Revolution demonstrated."⁵⁶ These critics suggest that Aristotle's political philosophy conceptualizes the total supremacy of political over private life by treating the political community as the "whole" in which individuals and groups are parts. And although this premise "was rendered plausible by the relatively undifferentiated character of the Greek city-state," it is totally inappropriate for the analysis of the complex, highly differentiated societies of the modern world, societies that lack a central form of social interaction that structures all others.⁵⁷

In response to these criticisms, let me begin by noting their exaggeration of the "relatively undifferentiated" character of ancient political life. Is it really the case that "the polis provided the only significant link between citizens beyond the home"?⁵⁸ I think not. The contrast with the greater size and complexity of modern societies obscures the forms of social differentiation and nonpolitical activity that developed within the ancient poleis. As Sally Humphreys notes:

> Athens had a much less rigid social structure in which a considerable number of social settings with well-defined norms of behaviour were neither regulated by the State, corporation-based, or explicitly integrated into a comprehensive scheme of values: the market-place, the gymnasium, the symposium, the philosophical discussion, the workshop, the bank. The corresponding occupational roles—trader and shopkeeper, athlete trainer, entertainer, pimp, courtesan and parasite, philosopher, craftsman, banker—were not linked to any organized corporate units.⁵⁹

Indeed, as Oswyn Murray argues, "the amazing creativity and freedom of thought of Classical Athens" owes much to "the fact that the same man belongs" to a variety of communities. "Living in this world of conflicting groups and social duties, he possesses the freedom to choose

---

55. S. Holmes, "Aristippus," 113. See also S. Holmes, *Benjamin Constant*, 56–57; C. Meier, *The Greek Discovery of the Political*, 22–23.
56. F. Jonas, *Die Institutionenlehre Arnold Gehlens*, 30. See also B. Constant, "The Liberty of the Ancients," 318–19; S. Holmes, "Aristippus," 116–17; S. Holmes, *Benjamin Constant*, 46–62.
57. S. Holmes, "Aristippus," 126–27. See also N. Luhmann, *Soziologische Aufklärung*, 138; M. Riedel, *Metaphysik und Metapolitik*, 39; M. Riedel, "Gesellschaft, Gemeinschaft," 2:804.
58. C. Meier, *The Greek Discovery of the Political*, 13.
59. S. C. Humphreys, *Anthropology and the Greeks*, 250. See also J. Ober, "Aristotle's Political Sociology"; J. Ober, *Mass and Elite*, 115.

between their demands, and so to escape any particular form of dominant social patterning."⁶⁰ The growth of Athenian democracy in the fifth and fourth centuries coincided with a growth of a variety of communal activities that were distinguished from both the public and private realms of the political community and the household.⁶¹ The development of a strong differentiation in Athens of a political sphere of activity from kinship and other private family ties opened up a greater freedom of action for religious, economic, family, and intellectual activities that were defined as nonpolitical in character.

> Except in Sparta, the individual was only required to subordinate his own interests to those of the community in specifically political contexts. The dichotomy between public and private life, though it admitted little question of the primacy of the former (while the polis retained its independence), left considerable freedom in the private sphere. The attempt to maintain a clearcut distinction between political and non-political activity carried with it a laissez faire attitude to the latter and so set up the balance which would later tip to support the individual's claim to non-interference as a right.⁶²

N. D. Fustel de Coulanges argued that all modern attempts to imitate ancient models were misguided because of the complete lack of differentiation between state and religion in ancient political communities. "[In] Sparta and Athens, the state was enslaved by its religion; or, rather, the state and religion were so completely confounded, that it was impossible even to distinguish the one from the other."⁶³ But in most of Greece, and especially in Athens, the growth of political community coincided with the increasing *privatization* of religion. "Religion was increasingly regarded as a part of private life" as the Greeks developed "something approaching a personal religion, alongside the public rituals of the city."⁶⁴ The Greeks' political communities did require participation in certain public cults, but where religious practice did not directly interfere with these cults, there was a wide range of latitude for the development of personal forms of religion.

In economic affairs as well, the classical Greeks did not simply subordinate private interests to the public. It is true, of course, that the ancient Greeks did not advocate anything like the inalienable rights to the control of one's property that modern individuals and states often

60. O. Murray, "Life and Society," 209–10.
61. P. Schmitt-Pantel, "Collective Activity."
62. S. C. Humphreys, *Anthropology and the Greeks*, 260–61; see also S. C. Humphreys, "Public and Private Interests," esp. 24.
63. N. D. Fustel de Coulanges, *The Ancient City*, 166–67.
64. S. C. Humphreys, *Anthropology and the Greeks*, 256.

advocate—and just as often transgress. But that should not blind us to the ways in which they did mark off a boundary between public and private control of economic resources. "In the Greek cities where, as modern writers sometimes claim, the citizens were wholly devoted to the city, a permanent direct tax would have been considered an intolerable act of tyranny."[65] "Any form of direct taxes on citizens was condemned as tyrannical (except in war emergencies), and the *metoikion* [the direct tax imposed on resident aliens] was thus the degrading mark of the outsider."[66] Public expenses were, for the most part, financed through liturgies and other more or less mandatory contributions by the wealthy. Because these contributions "could not be seen as a tax," they were "considered as an honour exclusive to an elite."[67] To the Greeks, permanent direct taxation suggested

> the subjugation of one people to another, a mark of slavery. The city, like every citizen, had to live by its own income, obtained from indirect taxes, plus tribute paid by subjects, the tax levied on residents who were not citizens, and the produce of its estates. The absence of direct taxation, strange to our eyes ... should suffice to warn us against the notion, still too commonly believed, that the citizen owed everything to his city. Let us say, instead, that the limits of his devotion and of intrusion by the community upon the individual sphere were not fixed in advance and for ever, any more than they are among us today.[68]

One of the most striking illustrations of Athenian respect for private-public boundaries occurs in the reaction to Pericles' relationship with the courtesan Aspasia. Despite his promotion of nativist legislation restricting citizenship to children of two native Athenians, it apparently did not harm his political career when he left his Athenian wife to live

---

65. P. Veyne, *Bread and Circuses*, 76–77.
66. M. Finley, *The Ancient Economy*, 164.
67. P. Veyne, *Bread and Circuses*, 76. Moses Finley notes that while no modern taxpayer "boasts in a persuasive way of the size of his income tax," in Athens "it was standard practice to boast about one's own liturgies." Even though liturgies were almost compulsory for wealthy citizens, they carried with them an "honourific element" wholly missing from the act of paying our taxes. See M. Finley, *The Ancient Economy*, 151–52; M. Finley, *Politics in the Ancient World*, 36–39.
68. P. Veyne, *Bread and Circuses*, 77. Moreover, when indirect or temporary taxes were imposed on Athenian citizens, those taxes were collected by private citizens, "tax farmers," who made a profit in doing so. As Ernest Badian points out, we moderns, who tend to react in horror to the subordination of private to public life in ancient republics, recoil with equal amazement at the ancients' privatization of tax collection. But the "very spirit of democracy—in the ancient sense—distrusts and excludes the impersonal continuity of power that is inherent in a bureaucratic state machine" required for public tax collection. See E. Badian, *Publicans and Sinners*, 13–14.

with this foreign-born courtesan.[69] Imagine the outcry if an American presidential candidate, such as Gary Hart in 1988, had moved in with a foreign—say, Russian—prostitute at precisely the time he was promoting himself as the defender of nativist and family values! American commitments to defending boundaries between public and private behavior did not prevent the collapse of Hart's career when a simple extramarital fling was exposed in the midst of the campaign. Apparently the Athenians, at least in the case of Pericles and Aspasia, supported a much stronger boundary between public and private spheres of behavior than modern Americans do.

Finally, Socrates' fate notwithstanding, intellectuals developed considerable freedom, at least in Athens, to speak their minds, but only to the extent they differentiated the form of their speech from the political idioms of the assembly and the courts. In effect, "philosophers and poets were offered a choice between a political role as sages and avoidance of politics." To the extent that they tried to influence political decisions their speech was subject to public control. The majority, however, "chose to make their comment on society outside the political arena, and by this choice acquired the freedom to say what they like—at the price of having their remarks considered irrelevant to political decision-making."[70] Perhaps the most striking illustration of the Athenians' acceptance of a clear boundary between political and less constrained nonpolitical speech is the freedom accorded to the wild libels, blasphemies, and calumnies presented on stage by Aristophanes and the other comic playwrights.

The shadow of the twentieth-century totalitarianism and the Jacobin terror lies heavily over the image of the polis as a relatively undifferentiated and politically dominated whole.[71] That shadow obscures the particular forms of social differentiation that developed within the ancient polis and, especially, the kinds of private-public boundaries that it shares, to some extent, with modern political communities. The Greeks discovered something that was rediscovered by modern social and po-

69. S. C. Humphreys, "Public and Private Interests," 24.
70. S. C. Humphreys, *Anthropology and the Greeks*, 264.
71. All of the critics of ancient political models who are discussed in this section, from Constant and Fustel de Coulanges to Stephen Holmes and Christian Meier, directly associate the desire to recover ancient forms of political life with the Jacobin terror or twentieth-century totalitarianism. Robin Osborne makes, in contrast, the interesting suggestion that the striking degree of Athenian solidarity was achieved, in part, through the imitation of political institutions and organizational structures by many different subpolitical communities, rather than through their direct control, totalitarian style, by the political community. See R. Osborne, "The Demos and Its Divisions," 275–76, 285–86.

litical theorists in the eighteenth and nineteenth centuries: public and private spheres of activity need not compete for the same space; they can both expand together. By clearly distinguishing a kind of behavior that is expected in public life, one lessens public interest in forms of behavior that seem to have little to do with public goals, a point, ironically, defended most persuasively by Stephen Holmes.[72] (Of course, how one distinguishes the public from the private depends on a whole range of social and historical contingencies that vary among different political communities.)

In comparing ancient and modern political communities, too many social theorists have had in mind a continuum between two social poles: complete absorption of the individual in public activity and rigid separation of the public and private. The attachment to these two poles grows out of the polemical battles between modern admirers and opponents of ancient republican politics, such as Rousseau and Constant. We would, however, do much better to focus on the different ways in which private-public boundaries are drawn wherever political community emerges.[73]

I am not arguing that the Athenians, let alone Aristotle, advocated anything like the modern notion of inalienable, state-enforced individual rights. As Moses Finley notes, although "Classical Greeks and Republican Romans possessed a considerable measure of freedom, in speech, in political debate, in their business activity and even in religion, . . . they lacked, and would have been appalled by, inalienable rights."[74] Nevertheless, state-enforced rights merely represent one way of guarding private-public boundaries. Without them, modern citizens would probably feel considerable insecurity about the strength of these boundaries. But the lack of these rights as barriers to public encroachment on private life does not necessarily eliminate important and deeply felt boundaries between the demands of public and private life.

Even if ancient Greek poleis possessed a greater differentiation between public and private life than is ordinarily acknowledged, one might still argue that this differentiation is something Aristotle, if not the Athenians, rejects. After all, the Greek polis that he rates most highly, Sparta, stands out as the one that went the furthest in minimizing private-public

---

72. See S. Holmes, *Benjamin Constant*, 254–55. Holmes, unfortunately, applies this brilliant insight only to modern political communities.
73. S. C. Humphreys, *The Family, Women, and Death*, xii.
74. M. Finley, *The Ancient Economy*, 154–55.

distinctions among citizens. But Aristotle criticizes the Spartans as well unlike most political communities, they consciously tried to promote the virtues among the citizens, but they had a limited and incorrect understanding of the virtues. The Spartans focused exclusively on virtues that would improve the strength and military prowess of the community as a whole. They did not consciously promote the virtues that would allow individuals to lead flourishing lives at home, in peace (*Pol.* 1333b). Indeed, one might say that for Aristotle the problem with Sparta is that it devoted too much attention to the success of the city as a whole and too little to the development and happiness of its individual members. The worthiest goal of the city is its contribution to the good life of its individual members. Unlike Plato in the *Republic,* Aristotle does not demand the sacrifice of the individual's happiness in the name of the "happiness of the city."[75]

Even in his best regime Aristotle never demands the complete control of family, economic, and religious life demanded by Plato in the *Republic*. In book 2 of the *Politics,* as is well known, he criticizes Plato's abolition of private families as a threat to the heterogeneity that is a necessary component of any human community. He also criticizes Plato's abolition of private property because it eliminates the opportunity for individuals to develop virtues, such as liberality, associated with the exchange of privately owned goods (*Pol.* 1261a–64b). Aristotle gives very little indication that he wants to move economic activity very much at all out of the private household, which is precisely where, etymologically at least, it belongs for any speaker of Greek.

Aristotle does require publicly appointed religious officials in his best regime, but these positions seem to have little importance in his political community. Religious offices merely give an honored status to citizens "worn out with age" (*Pol.* 1329a31). Again, very much unlike Plato, Aristotle expresses little concern about the actual practice of religion in his best regime. For example, he says nothing about restricting the family worship that was a prominent feature of ancient Greek religious life. Fustel de Coulanges suggests that "if we wished to give an exact definition of a[n ancient] citizen, we should say that it was a man who had the religion of the city."[76] Contrast this definition of citizenship with Aristotle's and the relatively secular character of Aristotelian political

---

75. Plato, *Republic,* 420b, in response to Adeimantus's objection that Plato's imaginary city sacrifices the happiness of its citizens in the name of justice.
76. N. D. Fustel de Coulanges, *The Ancient City,* 194–95.

life becomes clear. Even if Fustel de Coulanges's definition of ancient citizenship were historically accurate, it would seem that here is an instance in which Aristotle departs from ordinary Greek practice.

Cynthia Farrar, among others, notices that Aristotle opens up considerable space for a life not directly controlled by politics. Indeed, she goes so far as to accuse Aristotle of a "retreat from politics." Aristotle, she claims, advocates against Greek practice an "implicit distinction between society and the polis," a distinction that foreshadows modern attempts to constrain political activity.[77] Farrar's critique of Aristotle neatly reverses the critique we have been considering. According to Farrar, we should reject Aristotelian political philosophy precisely because it introduces and defends something like modern liberal distinctions between state and society and public and private, the very distinctions whose absence is the major flaw in Aristotelian political philosophy for Constant, Holmes, Luhmann, and other modern social theorists.

We need not go as far as Farrar in reversing claims about the subordination of private to public life by the classical Greek philosophers. But we should be aware of the exaggerated character of claims, like that made by Fustel de Coulanges, that the ancients are "absolutely inimitable; *nothing* in modern times resembles them; nothing in the future can resemble them." The polemical purpose of such exaggerations is patent. "The last eighty years," Fustel complains, "have clearly shown that one of the great difficulties which impede the march of modern society is the habit which it has of always keeping Greek and Roman antiquity before its eyes."[78] Exaggerated claims about the lack of social differentiation in ancient communities grow, in part, out of the desire to counter this bad habit.

Aristotle's concept of political community has been obscured by the polemical debates that surround the invocation of the ancient Greeks by modern social critics and their opponents. Rousseau and his followers invoke ancient theory and practice in order to defend a romanticized and totalistic conception of political identity—a conception that departs substantially from political community as Aristotle and the Greeks conceived of it.[79] Many of Rousseau's opponents, such as Constant,

---

77. C. Farrar, *The Origins of Democratic Thinking*, 270–72.
78. N. D. Fustel de Coulanges, *The Ancient City*, 11–12. Fustel complains (223) that "it is, a singular error, therefore, among all human errors, to believe that in the ancient cities men enjoyed liberty. They had not even the idea of it. . . . The ancients, especially the Greeks, always exaggerated the importance, and above all, the rights of society; this was largely due, doubtless, to the sacred religious character with which society was clothed in the beginning."
79. See B. Yack, *The Longing for Total Revolution*, 61–72.

Fustel de Coulanges, and their contemporary followers, attack his idea of citizenship by trying to show that whatever its value in ancient times, it is impossible and dangerous to reproduce that idea now. Modern attempts to reproduce ancient devotion to the community, they argue will lead only to political hypocrisy, violence, and terror.[80]

These arguments depend, just as much as the Rousseauian arguments that they are designed to counter, on an exaggeration of the self-abnegation of ancient citizens. As long as this exaggeration continues to color the way in which we read Aristotle's account of ordinary political life, we will find it very difficult to see its relevance to the analysis of modern political communities. But once we disengage the Aristotelian understanding of political community from communitarian polemics and counterpolemics, a whole range of insights into the structure of political life, both ancient and modern, emerge into view.

## *APPENDIX.* MONARCHY AND POLITICAL COMMUNITY

In this chapter I have, for the most part, identified Aristotelian political community with what we would call republican forms of government. Unfortunately, there is one major problem with this interpretation of Aristotle's understanding of political community: Aristotle includes monarchic as well as republican forms of government in his famous sixfold classification of political regimes.

Ordinarily, such a clear and explicit statement would be sufficient to undermine an interpretation that contradicts it. But the place of monarchy in Aristotle's political thought is considerably more ambiguous than this statement seems to suggest. Aristotle also argues that political justice and political community develop "among people naturally subject to law, . . . people who have an [proportionately] equal share in ruling and being ruled" (*NE* 1134b15). These arguments make it very hard to see how any but republican forms of communal organization could qualify as political communities for Aristotle.

Both kingship and tyranny, Aristotle's public-spirited and self-serving versions of monarchy, diverge in important ways from these criteria of political community, most obviously in their monopolization of political rule by a single individual. One-person rule is justified according to Aristotle when one individual or dynastic family so surpasses

---

80. Ibid., 78–79.

other community members in virtue that we cannot establish any reasonable proportion between their claims to political office (*Pol.* 1288a). Any community that included such an individual or family would clearly lack the proportionate equality that Aristotle considers a necessary foundation of political community.[81] Aristotle insists strongly at the beginning of the *Politics* that political rule qualitatively differs from rule over slaves and household since it involves rule over individuals who are competent to judge one's performance and to take turns in positions of authority (*Pol.* 1252a). The rule of kings, in contrast, lacks this distinction from mastery of a household since those legitimately subject to the rule of kings lack the competence to judge or share in their ruling activities.

Tyranny, in contrast, involves one-person rule over individuals who possess at least some of the capacities to participate in political activities. If kingship entails the justifiable elimination of political community, then tyranny entails the unjustifiable elimination of political community. A practical definition of tyranny would be one-person rule over individuals who deserve and are naturally disposed to expect something more than one-person rule.

Kingships and tyrannies also defy the reliance on law that Aristotle sees as a characteristic of political justice. An individual who is so superior in virtue as to deserve royal power should not be constrained by laws in the exercise of that power. If kings rely on laws to govern, then that is a sign that they lack the superior virtue that provides the only justification of their authority. A people that "is naturally subject to a law" is not naturally subject to a single individual. In effect, lawful kings would be tyrants, since they would not deserve to rule alone over a community.

Aristotle recognizes that people often think of kings as monarchs who, unlike tyrants, are constrained by law (which may be why he uses lawfulness and lawlessness in the *Rhetoric* [1365b29] to distinguish between kingship and tyranny). But that opinion conceals an important feature of kingship for Aristotle: kingship, unlike the other two "correct" political regimes, aristocracy and polity, is best understood as a lawless regime.[82] Such a regime is not justifiable among a people, who,

---

81. For a clear account of the ways in which Aristotle's understanding of kingship departs from his understanding of political community, see W. R. Newell, "Superlative Virtue."

82. This ambiguity can be found in Plato's *Statesman* (301b), where it is admitted that the same term, *kingship,* refers both to the absolute and lawless rule of a single

like those who form political communities, "is naturally subject to law."

I conclude that one cannot make room for monarchy in Aristotle's conception of political community without undermining its coherence and consistency. As far as I can see, Aristotle never resolves the difficulties raised by his account of monarchy.[83] A more comprehensive account of Aristotle's political philosophy would devote considerably more space than I do to an exploration of these difficulties. But the aim of my account of Aristotle is theoretical insight rather than comprehensiveness. And I believe that my republican reconstruction of Aristotle's understanding of political community represents, despite the problems created by his account of monarchy, the most coherent and theoretically interesting interpretation of Aristotle's arguments about specifically political practices and institutions.

---

individual with genuine political knowledge and virtue and to the "second-best" rule of a single individual constrained by law.

83. See W. R. Newell, "Superlative Virtue," 208–11, for one attempt at resolving these ambiguities.

CHAPTER THREE
# Political Teleology

The explanation of political community presented in the preceding chapter might seem to many readers to contradict Aristotle's teleological approach to the analysis of human societies. Indeed, apart from anything I have said about political community, there appears to be a glaring contradiction between Aristotle's teleological and empirical approaches to the analysis of political life. The teleological approach seems to demand that Aristotle analyze the polis, like all other natural things, with reference to its completion in a healthy, well-functioning form. The empirical approach, however, leads him to insist that no actual political community exists in a well-ordered form (*Pol.* 1260b35). How can Aristotle use teleological arguments that compare the development of the polis to the development of natural species toward a mature adult form, when no polis reaches the natural form that supposedly moves its development? When it comes to the polis, there certainly "seems to be a pronounced tension between Aristotle's role as descriptive biologist and his role as teleological biologist."[1]

One way of resolving this tension is to argue that the actual regimes that Aristotle examines in the *Politics* resemble the freaks and monstrosities that nature occasionally throws up in every natural species (*Generation of Animals* 770b9). But Aristotle himself never describes actual political regimes in this way—and with good reason. Were he to

---

1. J. Lear, *Aristotle*, 203.

do so, he would have to claim that, with regard to the polis, nature almost always fails to reach its ends, a claim that flatly contradicts his definition of nature as something that happens "always or for the most part" (*Physics* 197a32, 198b35). In all other natural species that Aristotle examines the individual members that fail to realize their complete natural form are the exceptions. If the polis almost always fails to complete its development, it seems impossible to justify Aristotle's description of it as natural.

The implications of this apparent contradiction extend well beyond Aristotle's understanding of the character of political institutions to his theory of the good life itself. Aristotle argues that good habits follow from good laws and political institutions and that good habits "make all the difference" in whether we can develop the virtuous dispositions essential to the good life (*NE* 1103b24). But if it is highly unlikely that we grow up in good regimes, let alone in the best regime, how can we develop those dispositions? If nature almost never brings forth well-constructed regimes, how can any human beings achieve the good life specific to their nature? "Humans tend to live in flawed societies, . . . the only species in nature which tends to live in an unhealthy environment. . . . Why are there not more good states? This ought to have been an urgent and troubling question for Aristotle."[2]

Yet Aristotle never even raises these questions. "There is no sign that Aristotle deduced from the *Politics* the lesson which it would seem clearly to imply, as to man's chance of attaining full virtue and happiness' outside of the best regime.[3] Why did he not find such questions "urgent and troubling?" How could he ignore such a glaring contradiction at the heart of his political philosophy?[4] In this chapter I attempt to answer these questions by means of a reinterpretation of Aristotle's political teleology. I try to show that once we gain a more satisfactory conception of the nature and function of the polis as Aristotle understands it, the contradictions we have been considering disappear.

The key to my reinterpretation of Aristotle's political teleology is my denial that Aristotle treats the polis as a natural substance with its own internal principle of motion. The Aristotelian polis takes its natural

---

2. Ibid., 207–8.
3. W. L. Newmann, *The Politics of Aristotle* 2:400.
4. One might be tempted to revive Jaeger's genetic account of Aristotle's development to explain so glaring a contradiction, were it not for the fact that Jaeger describes both the biological teleology of book 1 and the empirical analyses of books 4–6 of the *Politics* as manifestations of Aristotle's later, less Platonic period. See W. Jaeger, *Aristotle*, 270–74.

character, I argue, from human attributes and ends, not from some inherent potentiality for a complete and perfected form of its own. As a result, it achieves its natural form and fulfills its natural function when it makes the good life possible for particular individuals, rather than when it meets the standards of the best regime. And it begins to do that, I suggest, as soon as it brings free and relatively equal individuals into a community ordered by general rules and political justice. Even deviant regimes, the oligarchies and democracies that exist in most places, can, to a certain degree, serve the good life in this way.

My reinterpretation of Aristotle's political teleology makes it compatible with his analysis of actual political life and the understanding of political community developed in the preceding chapter. It also helps us understand why Aristotle devoted so much attention to the imperfect regimes of ordinary political life. These regimes provide insight into the way in which political communities naturally function; they are not mere pathologies of disease and deformation. Moreover, because we need political communities to develop the virtues necessary to a good life, and because imperfect regimes are the only ones that human beings are likely to know, these imperfect political communities provide the only available means for achieving the Aristotelian good life.

## THE NATURALNESS OF THE POLIS

Aristotle insists that the polis is natural, but does he insist that it is natural in the same way that animal species are natural? Most commentators seem to assume that he does, since they treat the polis as an entity, like an animal species, that possesses its own internal principle of motion propelling it toward its mature and well-functioning form. But once they have made this assumption, they have to choose between abandoning Aristotle's teleological theory of politics or characterizing all actual political communities as "freaks" (*Generation of Animals* 770b), since Aristotle denies that any existing polis is well-ordered.

In the end, however, even the latter option brings Aristotle's teleological approach to politics into question. As David Keyt, who relies on this theory of freaks, notes: "A polis with a deviant constitution differs from a freak of nature in the animal kingdom in one important respect. A freak of nature in the animal kingdom is an anomaly.... In Aristotle's political philosophy this situation is reversed. The best polis ... occurs rarely, if ever, whereas polises that deviate from this norm and are contrary to nature are the rule."[5] How can the same concept of nature be operating in the polis and in the animal kingdom if in the former nature almost never completes the motions it begins, and in the latter it almost always completes those motions?

These considerations should lead us to question the assumption that political communities and animal species are natural in the same way, unless we are willing to admit that Aristotle's political teleology is hopelessly confused and inconsistent. Most commentators, however, proceed as if Aristotle's insistence on the naturalness of the polis in itself justifies this assumption. To be natural, they suggest, implies for Aristotle the behavior characteristic of living organisms. J. H. Day and M Chambers, for example, assert that although "Aristotle did not, indeed, explicitly class the state among biological organisms . . . he needed only to set it beside them, as an entity subject to the same laws used also in biological observation."[6] And Ernest Barker writes that natural things, according to Aristotle, "develop from within, as the result of an immanent force. As such a natural thing, the State has its own life, and it has grown."[7]

But Aristotle himself does not limit the term *natural* to those things that, like living organisms, have an internal principle of motion directing their growth. In the *Physics* he clearly distinguishes between things that "have a nature" and things that exist "by nature or according to nature."

> Things have a nature which have a principle [of their own production] of this kind. Each of them is a substance; for it is a subject, and nature is applied to all these things and also to the attributes that belong to them in virtue of what they are, for instance the property of fire to be carried upwards—which is not a nature nor has a nature but is by nature or according to nature [*kata phusin*].
> 
> (*Physics* 192b30–36)[3]

---

5. D. Keyt, "Distributive Justice," 32. Keyt notes the way in which Aristotle's political teleology, so understood, radically departs from his usual understanding of nature, but he does not ask whether such a departure undermines the consistency and plausibility of Aristotle's attempt to develop a naturalistic explanation of the polis and political phenomena. See also P. Simpson, "Making the Citizens Good," 150. Simpson clearly shows that if the active pursuit of virtue defines the nature of the Aristotelian political community, then no actual political communities, even among the ancient Greek cities, have ever existed. Simpson accepts this as being Aristotle's own conclusion without considering the extent to which such a conclusion contradicts Aristotle's ordinary understanding of nature as what comes about "always or for the most part."

6. J. H. Day and M. Chambers, *Aristotle's History of Athenian Democracy*, 42.

7. E. Barker, *The Political Thought*, 281n1.

8. See S. Waterlow, *Nature, Change, and Agency*, 50, 50n2, for a discussion of this passage.

The things that "have a nature" are "substances." Each has an internal principle of motion guiding its own production. The things that exist "according to nature" constitute a more inclusive category than do the things that possess natures. They include the attributes and the effects of the attributes of things that possess natures. Fire possesses a nature: it always moves in the same way and direction. In contrast, the burning of things by fire exists "according to nature": it follows from a natural attribute of fire.

Are there adequate grounds for concluding that Aristotle thinks of the polis as a substance with its own nature? I think not, although a fair number of scholars argue otherwise.[9] Apart from Aristotle's general claim that the polis exists by nature, the primary evidence that these scholars use to support their arguments is his repeated claim about the priority of the polis's form over its matter. This claim receives its most dramatic expression at the beginning of the *Politics,* when Aristotle insists that the polis is prior to the individual in the same way in which a living human being is prior to its parts. "For if the whole [body] is destroyed there will not be a foot or a hand except in some analogous sense, as when one speaks of a hand made of stone, but the thing itself will be defective" (*Pol.* 1253a20; cf. *Parts of Animals* 640b35). The organic analogies that Aristotle frequently uses to illustrate his claim about the priority of the polis seem to confirm the arguments of these commentators.

But it is clear from Aristotle's other works that form precedes matter in many constructed as well as natural wholes (*Metaphysics* 1016b15, 1041b13).[10] The polis is undoubtedly a whole, a compound of many parts, in which a form organizes the matter of its individual parts (*Pol.* 1252a17, 1253a20). The question is whether or not it is a *natural* whole with its own internal principle of motion and organization. Aristotle's frequent organic analogies do not by themselves answer this question,

9. For example, see E. Barker, *The Political Thought,* 221, 276–77; S. Clark, *Aristotle's Man,* 102–4; M. Riedel, *Metaphysik und Metapolitik,* 76–77. For arguments against this position, see W. Kullmann, "Der Mensch," 435–36; O. Höffe, *Politische Gerechtigkeit,* 269–70. Andreas Kamp has recently presented a much subtler version of the argument that the Aristotelian polis is a natural substance. He argues that the polis is a natural substance with its own internal principle of motion but that its nature is rooted in the nature of human beings. "In the polis a natural entity, man, reaches the complete actualization of his being. 'Polis' refers to the completed condition of a natural being," man. But "it is not an entity apart from man, but rather the actualized essence and ground of his being." A. Kamp, *Die Politische Philosophie,* 116, 106–17.

10. The first of these two passages describes artifacts, such as shoes, as wholes of this sort.

for they may merely seek to illustrate similarities between the structure of the polis and that of organic forms.

Some commentators are clearly uncomfortable with the strange metaphysics implied by calling the polis a living organism and suggest that Aristotle merely "considers the polis *as if* it were a biological organism and tries to discover its nature by examining the pattern of its growth and development" (my emphasis).[11] In this way they avoid the thorny problems created by treating a political community as a living organism. But if the polis is *not* a living organism, what reason can Aristotle have to expect it to behave according "to the same laws used in biological observation?"[12] The behavior of a nonorganic polis may *resemble* the behavior of living substances in many ways, but there is no reason to assume that the two forms of behavior would follow "the same laws." Organic analogies are not sufficient proof that Aristotle thought of the polis as a living substance with its own nature to perfect.

An individual without a city may be analogous to a hand without a body, but he or she is not "dead" in the same way that a severed hand clearly is. The severed hand has lost the source of its life, its internal source of motion. It continues to exist only as decaying matter. Cityless citizens, in contrast, are "dead" only as citizens. Because they retain their own internal source of motion, they continue to live after the disappearance of the cities that gave their lives a political character. We can say a severed hand and a cityless citizen are dead according "to the same laws" only if we are willing to equivocate about the use of terms such as *death* and *life*. Aristotle does not equivocate in this way, despite his use of organic analogies.

Indeed, Aristotle sometimes reverses the organic analogy and uses a political analogy to illustrate the internal structure of animals. The most striking example of this reversal occurs in the following passage from *The Motion of Animals:*

> We should consider the organization of an animal to resemble that of a city well-governed by laws. For once order is established in a city, there is no need of a separate monarch to preside over every activity; each man does his own work as assigned, and one thing follows another because of habit. In animals this same thing happens because of nature: specifically because each part of them, since they are so ordered, is naturally disposed to do its own task. There is, then, no need of soul in each part: it is in some governing

11. R. Mulgan, *Aristotle's Political Theory*, 21.
12. J. H. Day and M. Chambers, *Aristotle's History of Athenian Democracy*, 42.

origin of the body, and other parts live because they are naturally attached, and do their tasks because of nature.

(*Motion of Animals* 703a28–703b2)

As at the beginning of the *Politics,* Aristotle elaborates here on an analogy between the internal organization of a polis and that of an animal, but he also makes clear what distinguishes the internal organization of the polis from that of animals. In the polis, "one thing follows another because of *habit*. In animals this same thing happens because of *nature:* because each part of them, since they are so ordered, is naturally disposed to do its own task." In contrast, *habit* creates for the polis the internal organization of parts into a whole that nature creates for animals. Although the polis may come into being "by nature," it needs habit to function as an organized whole. Animals do not need habit to function as a whole, since each of their parts "is naturally disposed to do its own task." In animals, "as in all the things that come to us by nature," internal organization exists first as a natural potentiality and only later as an activity (*NE* 1103a26). In the polis, in contrast, the organization of the whole exists first in activity, as the repeated performance of actions set down by law and custom. Only after repeated actions produce regular habits among the citizens and families that make up the political community does the polis come to possess an internal organization similar in structure to that of natural organisms. This passage suggests that although the polis does exist by nature, it does not have its own internal principle of production and thus does not possess a nature of its own to develop and perfect.

This interpretation of Aristotle's analogies between the polis and natural organisms is confirmed by his brief comment on the origin of the polis at the beginning of the *Politics*. "The impulse [*hormē*] toward this kind of community exists in all men by nature; but the first man to put it together [*sustēsas*] is the cause of the greatest of goods" (*Pol.* 1253a30).

For Aristotle the "impulse" to form political communities exists in *human* nature. It is the human being that is a substance and "has a nature"; the polis exists "according to nature," a consequence of the natural behavior of human beings. As discussed in the preceding chapters, Aristotle believes that human nature, especially our expansive needs and capacity for reasoned speech, disposes us to form self-sufficient communities in which we hold each other accountable to shared standards of obligation. But nature does not dispose us to accept or follow any particular set of shared standards. Thus, the polis does not come into existence until some individual or group of individuals "puts it together" by establishing means by which its shared standards can be determined. Only then will we see develop the structure of habits that allows the political community to function as an organized whole. Natural impulse disposes us to form political communities, but it does not provide these communities with their internal principles of organization.[13]

I conclude then that the polis, though it is a whole and exists according to nature, is not a natural whole. Like most wholes, natural or artificial, the polis is "prior by nature" to its parts. But it is not itself a natural substance with its own internal principle of motion. It derives its naturalness from natural attributes of human beings, from what we might call their "political" property. The polis is natural to the extent that it owes its end and existence to these attributes.[14] But it does not possess its own nature and therefore does not possess its own internal principle of production and motion toward a perfected form.

Because the polis does not have its own nature, it is a mistake to treat Aristotle's best regime as the completed and mature form of the polis and to portray all other regimes as immature and deformed freaks of nature. The polis is natural in that it develops out of human impulses and plays a role in the development and perfection of human capacities. There are grounds, according to Aristotle's teleological principles, to describe individual human beings as fully developed or freakish members of their species. There is no basis for attaching similar descriptions to the polis, since there is no natural, internally generated pattern of growth that guides the development of the polis.

The "natural" form of the polis, for Aristotle, is that which helps individuals to develop the virtues that perfect human nature, rather than the form that perfects what we would call "polis nature," if the polis possessed its own nature. As a result, there is no reason to assume that an imperfect polis, the only kind of polis we find in the world, cannot perform its natural function. If it can, however imperfectly, perform that function, then we can bring Aristotle's political teleology into line with both his general theory of nature and his arguments about the

---

13. Barker suggests that there is nothing strange about suggesting that art has to finish a motion that nature starts; *The Political Thought*, 222–23. But the contrast that Aristotle draws here between a natural impulse drawing individuals toward the formation of political communities and the human actions necessary to compound individuals into such a community is rather sharp and purposeful. It suggests that he wants to distinguish the establishment of the polis from the motions that manifest the completion of natural impulses alone.

14. For a similar conclusion, see S. Everson, "Aristotle on the Foundations of the State," 95.

imperfections of all existing political communities. Then the polis would, like all other natural things, "always or for the most part" function in a particular way and serve a natural end.

## POLITICS AND THE GOOD LIFE

To determine whether the imperfect political communities of the actual world can fulfill the natural function Aristotle allots to the polis, we must first clearly characterize that function. Although the polis comes into being at first "for the sake of living," Aristotle insists that "it exists for the sake of living well" (*Pol.* 1252b29). In a later reformulation of this claim, he replaces "for the sake of living well" with "for the sake of noble actions" (*Pol.* 1281a2). The polis thus exists in order to make possible the noble "activity of soul in accordance with complete virtue" (*NE* 1102a5) that he argues in his ethical writings comprises the good life for human beings. Almost all commentators accept this interpretation of Aristotle's understanding of the polis's natural function. Few notice, however, that this understanding of the polis implies that the polis, unlike natural organisms, is a means to an end beyond itself rather than an end in itself.[15]

The only passage in which Aristotle describes the polis as an end occurs at the beginning of the *Politics*. He argues there that if the family and the villages that grow out of it exist according to nature, then the polis must also exist by nature. "For the polis is their end, and nature is an end: what each thing is—for example, a human being, a horse, or a household—when its coming into being is complete is, we assert, the nature of the thing" (*Pol.* 1252b31). In this famous argument Aristotle insists that we cannot understand something until we see the final end to which it contributes. In relation to the family, the polis is an end; but in relation to the good life, the polis itself is a means. "That for the sake of which," he continues, a thing exists "is what is best" (*Pol.* 1252b35). The family exists for the sake of the polis; but the polis exists for the sake of the good human life. It is the good life that provides the

---

15. Ernest Barker (*The Political Thought*, 276), for example, insists that Aristotle's polis "is not an instrument for a purpose beyond itself," even though he repeatedly notes that Aristotle argues that it exists for the sake of the human good life. R. G. Mulgan (*Aristotle's Political Theory*, 31) notes, with reference to the polis, that "any process of natural growth and development is directed towards some goal or end," an end that represents "the realization of a thing's nature"; but he fails to notice that the purpose of the polis is the realization of something beyond itself, namely, the human capacity for a good life.

final end within which we can make sense of these forms of human community.

The polis exists for the sake of *human* flourishing (*eudaimonia*) according to Aristotle; human beings do not exist for the sake of the polis's own flourishing. Although the polis is prior to the individual, according to Aristotle, it still exists for the sake of the good life led by individuals.[16] The polis is thus the natural instrument rather than the natural end of human development. A political community is not "truly called" a polis when it lacks any "power to make citizens good and just" (*Pol.* 1280b10), that is, when it completely lacks the ability to contribute to the development of noble activities among its citizens. An imperfect political community might still be truly called a polis if it can make such a contribution despite its imperfections. Whether it can do so, however, depends on both the nature of that contribution and the imperfections of ordinary political communities.

How is the polis instrumental to the development and perfection of human capacities? First and most obviously, it supplies the self-sufficiency and superfluity of goods necessary to a good life. More important and complex, however, is its contribution to the development of the virtues. Aristotle defines the good life, the life of human "flourishing" (*eudaimonia*), as "activity of soul in accordance with complete virtue" (*NE* 1102a5). Such a life represents the completion and perfection of human nature; it exemplifies the characteristic activity or natural work (*ergon*) of human beings. It is, however, rather surprising to learn that the virtues through which the natural work of human beings manifests itself are not themselves natural according to Aristotle. Unlike the polis, the virtues do not even exist according to nature, let alone possess their own natures. They are not contrary to anything in nature; but no natural impulse leads to their development (*NE* 1103a15–35). Nonetheless, there is a natural instrument that makes the virtues and, as a result, the good life, possible: the polis.

The moral virtues are, according to Aristotle, characteristics of the soul that dispose us toward certain activities and away from others. We are not born with these characteristics, nor do they develop naturally along with the growth of our physical capacities. "In all the things that

---

16. In the *Categories* (14a26) Aristotle lays out four senses in which it is appropriate to speak of the priority of one thing to another. The second of these senses refers to cases where something, though appearing later in time, is still essential to the completion of something else that appears before it. This is the sense in which the polis is prior to the individual.

come to us by nature we first acquire the potentiality and later exhibit the activity" (*NE* 1103a25). We have the potential for an adult's physical strength even while still children; but we do not perform deeds that require such strength until that potential has been realized. "The virtues, on the other hand, we acquire by first having put them into action" (*NE* 1103a30). We perform the acts demanded by virtue first and then by repeated performance develop the habit that makes them pleasant to us and gives us an inner capacity to act virtuously. The impulse to act virtuously comes from outside of us, from the lawgivers, educators, and parents who act as our moral trainers, rather than from some inner, natural potentiality. Through the development of habits, moral training creates in us new capacities, capacities that grow out of extranatural dispositions to gain pleasure from virtuous actions and feel pain when indulging the vices.

Being virtuous is, to use one of Aristotle's favorite examples, like being ambidextrous: we are not given this capacity by nature, but all healthy individuals have by nature the capacity to produce it with the proper training. "We are adapted by nature with the capacity to receive" the capacities associated with the virtues (*NE* 1103a24). If we were not so adapted, we could have no more success in training ourselves to be virtuous than we would in training a stone to rise instead of fall (*NE* 1103a21). Nevertheless, since they are brought into existence only by means of active intervention into the natural course of things, the virtues themselves are not natural.

When Aristotle insists that the polis exists for the sake of the good life, he is claiming, I suggest, that the polis provides the active intervention in nature's course that allows human beings to develop the virtues and thus complete themselves. "Just as man is the best of animals when completed, so he is the worst of all when separated from law and adjudication [*dikē*]" (*Pol.* 1253a31). Thus, when Aristotle goes on to suggest that whoever first constituted the polis "is the cause of the greatest of goods" (*Pol.* 1253a30), he is not engaging in rhetorical exaggeration. The establishment of the polis makes possible the greatest good for human beings: the flourishing that Aristotle associates with virtuous activity.

In general, the virtue of a thing represents the completion of its nature (*Metaphysics* 1021b10). The good life of virtue-based activity represents the "work" (*ergon*) specific to completed human beings. But human beings require the intervention and compulsion of laws in order to complete themselves. The general rules contained in laws, Aristotle argues, are the best means that nature provides us for establishing the regular habits that are necessary to promote virtuous dispositions; "for legislators make the citizens good by forming habits in them, and this is the wish of every legislator" (NE 1103b3).[17]

The individual who has no need of the polis and its laws "is either a beast or a god" (Pol. 1253a29), but not a human being. These individuals have no need of the polis to complete themselves because they stand either above or below human nature. But for a flourishing *human* life, the moral training the polis offers "makes all the difference," since that training is essential to the development of the virtuous dispositions that anchor such a life (NE 1103b24). "The man who is to be good must be well trained and habituated, ... and this can be brought about if men live in accordance with a sort of intellect and right order, provided this has force." "Law," Aristotle suggests, "has this compulsive power, while it is at the same time an account proceeding from a sort of practical wisdom and intellect." Moreover, "while people hate men who oppose their impulses, even if they oppose them rightly, the law's compulsion towards what is good is not so burdensome" (NE 1180a14–24).

Law has the requirements needed for the training of virtuous dispositions. It imposes a general, repeatable order on behavior, and it is backed by force. One needs force to nurture virtuous dispositions because ethical training, like "all acts of concentration, strong effort, and strain, [is] necessarily painful; they all involve compulsion and force, unless we are accustomed to them, in which case it is habit that makes them pleasant" (Rhet. 1370a12). Law is also a less burdensome form of compulsion to most human beings, presumably because the general, repeatable activity it commands assimilates itself more easily to habit, which Aristotle suggests is pleasant because of its quasi-natural regularity (Rhet. 1370a5).

Laws, according to Aristotle, are written or unwritten general rules embodying judgments of practical reason. They are not themselves natural, but they do represent part of the "natural" way in which free and relatively equal individuals relate to each other in political communities.[18] Those individuals "who have an equal share in ruling and being ruled" are "naturally subject to law" (NE 1134a29, 1134b14). Where free and relatively equal individuals form a community, they expect to take turns in ruling, "as is natural." "We thus arrive at law; for an

---

17. I discuss the role of law and the political community in moral education at much greater length in chapter 8.
18. See J. Lear, *Aristotle,* 200. See also B. Yack, "Natural Right."

order of succession implies law" (*Pol.* 1279a10, 1287a18). We can thus conclude that, for Aristotle, the polis represents nature's way of providing for the laws—that is, the active and forceful interventions in the natural course of things—required to produce a complete human being.

## AN ANTHROPOCENTRIC UNIVERSE?

Interpreted in this way, Aristotle's political teleology might appear to rest on an assumption that the cosmos is designed to serve the good of human beings by providing us with the external means of perfecting ourselves. If so, one would be justified in concluding that my reinterpretation of Aristotle's political teleology merely replaces one highly implausible idea, the image of the polis as a natural organism, with another, equally implausible idea: an anthropocentric universe. To forestall this conclusion, I shall try to show that we need not burden Aristotle's political teleology with this anthropocentric and un-Aristotelian assumption.

Most recent commentators agree that the idea that the universe is ordered by conscious design to satisfy human needs plays no role in Aristotelian teleology.[19] If they are right, what could Aristotle mean when he claims that the polis exists for the sake of the good life? Because we are dealing here with the relation between an instrumental community (the polis) and organisms (human beings), we are clearly going beyond the realm of organic growth that provides the primary focus of Aristotle's teleology. If we deny that the polis itself is an organism with its own end and internal principle of motion, and if we deny conscious design as the principle ordering relations among species and their environments, then there seems little room for anything but a metaphorical sort of political teleology.

We need not, however, reject or qualify Aristotle's political teleology in this way. Although Aristotle does not suggest that there is a conscious design ordering the nature of all things, he does sometimes suggest that some things, other than parts of organisms, exist for the sake of others. The most famous of these suggestions occurs in the first book of the *Politics*. He suggests there that "plants exist for the sake of animals

---

19. See, for example, M. Nussbaum, *Aristotle's "De Motu Animalium,"* 60, 95–96; J. Lear, *Aristotle,* 41; W. Wieland, "The Problem of Teleology"; S. Waterlow, *Nature, Change, and Agency,* 74; J. Cooper, "Aristotle on Natural Teleology." For an argument against this narrowing of the scope of Aristotelian teleology, see S. Clark, *Aristotle's Man,* ix, 59–60.

and that the other animals exist for the sake of human beings—the tame animals for both use and nourishment, and most if not all of the wild animals, for nourishment and other forms of assistance, in order that clothing and other instruments may be got from them" (*Pol.* 1256b16). Because this passage seems to contradict Aristotle's denial that a conscious design orders the relations among natural things, some commentators treat it as a rhetorical exaggeration addressed to a more popular audience. Wolfgang Wieland, for example, views all such passages "as concessions to popular notions," since "things have no need of man." "It would be strange," he suggests, "if Aristotle in his treatises had championed the idea of a universal teleology, and in his speculative theology had made no use of it."[20] Similarly, Martha Nussbaum dismisses this passage as "a preliminary *phainomenon*, from the human-practical viewpoint, not a serious theoretical statement."[21]

But as John Cooper has persuasively argued, this passage need not imply a universal teleology or conscious design in nature, the interpretation that leads commentators to discount it.[22] The good that Aristotle speaks of in this passage is the good of each species. When he suggests that plants and animals exist for the sake of human beings, he is referring to the means of sustenance naturally available to human beings. In similar fashion, nonhuman species exist for the sake of each other in that they provide each other with their natural source of food. The only difference between human and other species in this regard is that almost all species of plant and animal life can in some way serve to support human existence. From this point of view, whatever natural means serve the existence and growth of a species can be said to exist for its sake. Aristotle is suggesting here that nature provides different species with different means of existence; he is not suggesting that it establishes a rational moral order among them.[23]

The polis, I suggest, is something nature provides for the growth and completion of one of its species. It is something that develops naturally from human needs and capacities and serves to complete a higher set of human capacities. Aristotle is thus willing to say that the polis exists for the sake of the good human life, just as plants and animals exist for the sake of mere human life. Without the needs and capacities that lead to

20. W. Wieland, "The Problem of Teleology," 158.
21. M. Nussbaum, *Aristotle's "De Motu Animalium,"* 95–96.
22. J. Cooper, "Aristotle on Natural Teleology," 218–21.
23. Cooper (ibid.) correctly notes that Aristotle must assume the permanence of species in order to treat the natural means of their survival as existing for their sake.

the establishment of the polis, human beings would lack natural means of perfecting their highest capacities. Perhaps they could find or invent some other means to take the place of the polis. But it makes an important difference to the way we live, or might live, that our nature promotes the creation of *political* means to our completion. Just as a natural inability to digest animal protein would fundamentally alter the way we seek to sustain our lives, so the lack of our natural political characteristics would alter our attempts to sustain the good life. Without imputing any conscious design to nature, Aristotle can suggest that we are fortunate in being provided a natural means to attaining the good life, just as we are fortunate in our natural ability to make use of almost all plant and animal species for food.

## THE GOOD LIFE IN IMPERFECT POLITICAL COMMUNITIES

According to the interpretation I have been developing, the polis exists "for the sake of the good life" as the instrument provided by nature for producing the ethical dispositions essential to human flourishing. What distinguishes the polis from other communities is the particular end that it aims at: human flourishing, "the highest of all goods achievable by action." "We stated the end of political science to be the best end, and political science spends most of its pains on making citizens to be a certain character, that is, good and capable of noble acts" (*Pol.* 1252a1–6; *NE* 1095a15, 1099b29).

In the political community, Aristotle insists, we share the most important interest that human beings possess: concern about developing the ethical characteristics that make a flourishing human life possible. Nevertheless, no matter how high this interest reaches, it is still a shared interest that brings individuals together into the political community. That is why Aristotle treats the polis as a community of shared interest throughout his writings even while insisting that the polis exists for the sake of the good life. What we share in the polis, according to Aristotle, is an interest in making the good life possible, not the good life itself.

The way in which Aristotle uses the adjective *political* confirms this interpretation. For Aristotle, the specifically "political good" is justice or the "common advantage" of the polis rather than shared happiness (*Pol.* 1282b16). The "political good" is the interest that all members of the political community share in promoting the conditions that make virtuous activity possible, rather than that activity itself. "Political courage" is the disposition to show the bravery that serves the needs of one's polis, rather than the genuine virtue of courage (*NE* 1116a17). The "political disposition" is the disposition to perform all of the virtuous actions that the common advantage of the city requires of one, rather than a disposition toward the kind of activities that makes for a flourishing human life (*EE* 1248b37). In short, political action, unlike virtuous action per se, always "attempts to gain advantages beyond political action [itself], advantages such as political power, prestige, or at least happiness for the statesman himself and his fellow citizens, that is, something other than political activity" (*NE* 1177b13).[24]

The most powerful confirmation that Aristotle sees the polis as a means to, rather than as an expression of, the good life comes from his treatment of political friendship. The highest and most complete friendship, according to Aristotle, is the intimate friendship between virtuous individuals. In this friendship individuals share the good life of virtuous activity. Friendships that fail to measure up to that standard are founded on the sharing of interest or of pleasure rather than the sharing of virtue (*NE* 1155b–57a). As discussed in the following chapter, Aristotle clearly states that political friendship is a form of shared advantage friendship, not a form of shared virtue friendship (*EE* 1242a6; *NE* 1160a12, 1161b11). Not even the friendship among citizens in Aristotle's best regime, where all citizens are virtuous, goes beyond shared interest friendship: "one cannot be a friend to many people in sharing with them the complete [shared virtue] type of friendship, just as one cannot be in love with many people at once; ... but with a view to utility or pleasure it is possible that many people should please one" (*NE* 1158a11–17). Because Aristotle further argues that among human beings "the extent of their community is the extent of their friendship" (*NE* 1159b30), we can conclude that the political community is, for him, a community defined by shared interest rather than by shared virtue, despite its existence "for the sake of the good life."[25]

The implications of Aristotle's treatment of political friendship, like the subject itself, have received little attention. Nevertheless, they are

---

24. It is this failure of political action to be desirable wholly for its own sake that makes it inferior to contemplation, according to Aristotle (*NE* 1177b). See B. Yack, "How Good Is the Aristotelian Good Life?" 618–26.

25. As I argue below, a number of commentators find this conclusion hard to accept and, as a result, exert considerable effort to find an interpretation that would allow us to describe political friendship in a good regime as a friendship of shared virtue. I discuss their efforts in chapter 4.

especially important for a proper understanding of his political teleology. Even Aristotle's best regime, the utopian polis he builds at the end of the *Politics*, is an instrumental community. Its citizens share with each other an interest in promoting the good life of virtuous activity, *not* virtuous activity itself. The community in which the good life is manifested is the community that exists between virtuous friends, not the political community.[26] The political community exists to make possible such a life and such communities. It is not an end in itself.

What distinguishes Aristotle's best regime from the imperfect regimes of ordinary life is that it possesses ideal initial conditions that ensure that *all* of its citizens can develop and perfect their virtues. It performs the natural function Aristotle ascribes to the polis better than would a regime in which only a few individuals develop and perfect their virtues. Nevertheless, even imperfect regimes can still perform the same function.

It is only because commentators tend to identify the end of the polis with living the good life that they so often conclude that Aristotle's political teleology implies that the best regime is the only true or natural polis. A polis in which most citizens flourish in their virtues is indeed a better polis than one in which few do so. But as long as a polis makes the good life possible for some of its members, it still serves the natural function Aristotle ascribes to it and deserves to be called a polis according to nature. The polis fulfills its natural function when it lays down laws that can promote the habits on which virtuous dispositions depend. It does not fail to fulfill its natural function simply because the good life is not shared by all of its citizens.

It might, however, still seem unlikely that the imperfect regimes that dominate everyday political life could act to promote the Aristotelian good life. How can Aristotle insist that the polis naturally, which means "for the most part," aims at producing the conditions that promote the possibility of the good life, when actual political communities almost never consciously do so?[27] If the polis naturally promotes the good life, then nature must display some cunning in its organization of political life. If ordinary, imperfect regimes make the good life possible, they must do so indirectly and unintentionally.

---

26. For a similar argument, see D. Winthrop, "Aristotle and Theories of Justice," 1215.

27. Only the Spartans, Aristotle complains, consciously devote their attention to the promotion of virtue among its citizens—and they promote the wrong virtues (*NE* 1180a25; *Pol.* 1271b, 1233b).

Aristotle would argue, I suggest, that indirect and unintentional moral training goes on in all political communities. Nature has given human beings the attributes that lead to this result. The expansive needs that nature gives us lead us to seek larger and more self-sufficient communities than those that center on the family. But when we leave extended family communities behind, we also leave behind the natural hierarchies of age and gender that establish without much controversy the organization of power in these communities. The individuals who establish political communities see each other as free and relatively equal individuals. Nature provides human beings no natural hierarchies of the sort that it provides social animals such as bees, according to which to structure the distribution of power within the polis. It does, however, provide us with the capacity for reasoned speech, a capacity that, as we have seen, makes the human being "much more a political animal than any kind of bee or other gregarious animal" (*Pol.* 1253a8). This capacity allows us to establish structures of authority among free and relatively equal individuals by giving us the means to make laws and the arguments to justify them. Without this capacity, it is unlikely that creatures such as ourselves, possessing expansive needs but few significant—to Aristotle—inequalities beyond those associated with age and gender, could form the kind of complex communities we see in the polis or, for that matter, in a beehive.

The complex forms of social organization found among, for example, social insects depend on the hierarchies created by the natural differentiation between members of the species such as queens, workers, and drones. The forms of social organization we find among other nonhuman animals, such as apes and herding mammals, lack the extensiveness and complexity of that found in those that are so differentiated. As students of human evolution have noted, it is the step beyond small tribal and family societies that puts the greatest strain on human nature and is most difficult to explain from an evolutionary perspective.[28] Prior to that step, human society, for the most part, resembles the societies of other primates. Only human beings develop very complex and extensive forms of social hierarchy and differentiation without the natural differentiation characteristic of the social insects. Aristotle would suggest we owe these complex and extensive forms of communal life to our capacity for reasoned speech.

Our natural capacities thus bring into being the structures of rule

---

28. See R. Masters, *The Nature of Politics*, 151.

and arguments about justice that characterize the political community. No particular law or argument about justice is the natural one, according to Aristotle, but establishing laws and arguing about justice are for him natural activities. Laws are, as we have seen, Aristotle's preferred means of establishing the habits that promote the moral virtues. Nature thus indirectly provides us with the means of promoting the moral virtues by giving us the natural capacities we possess.

Do laws in imperfect regimes promote the development of the moral virtues and the good life? We can exclude tyrannies from consideration, since Aristotle defines them as communities in which rulers totally lack respect for the general rules established by laws.[29] But oligarchies and democracies, the commonest species of regime, often exist in law-abiding forms. Do their laws make possible the good life for at least some of their members?

I think that they do. Aristotle insists that all laws, all general rules made by those who rule the political community, are at least partially just (*NE* 1129b12). "There seems to be some justice between any man and any other who can share in law or be party to an agreement.... Therefore, while in tyrannies friendship and justice hardly exist, in democracies [a deviant form of regime] they exist more fully" (*NE* 1161b5). The laws established by oligarchies and democracies will inevitably promote character-forming habits, even if they are not designed to do so. These habits will not necessarily be the best to establish the dispositions of virtuous individuals; they will, nevertheless, promote them to some extent, for every regime wants its citizens to be moderate, lawful, and courageous in at least some circumstances. They thus provide the means by which individuals can develop virtuous dispositions, even if they do not treat the virtuous life as an end in itself. Aristotle suggests that "it is *difficult* to get from youth onwards a right training for virtue if one has not been brought up under correct laws" (*NE* 1180a31; my emphasis). He never suggests that it is impossible or even improbable.[30]

The proof that Aristotle believes that even deviant regimes can provide the means of developing virtuous dispositions lies in his willingness to teach about the good life in Athens. In a famous passage near the beginning of the *Nicomachean Ethics,* Aristotle states that the appro-

---

29. Aristotle does not restrict the term *tyranny,* at least in this sense, to rule by a single individual. He also describes extreme democracies and oligarchies that continually overturn legislated and customary rules, that is, the written and unwritten laws, as tyrannies (*Pol.* 1292b6).

30. Richard Bodéüs presents a similar picture of the role of imperfect regimes in Aristotelian moral education in "Law and the Regime."

priate listeners for "lectures about what is noble and just" are those "brought up in good habits," rather than those who seek to be persuaded to follow the virtuous life (*NE* 1095b4). "The soul of the student must first have been prepared by the cultivation of habits for noble pleasures and aversions, just as the land is prepared to nourish the seed" (*NE* 1179b24). Without cultivation, the teaching of ethics is a waste of effort. Yet Aristotle makes these claims in the midst of lecturing on the good life to students who come from Athens and other regimes that he himself would unhesitatingly describe as deviant and imperfect. He proceeds to teach them about ethics as if he assumed that their souls were properly "cultivated by means of habits."[31] Either Aristotle believes that deviant regimes can indirectly cultivate the dispositions essential to the good life, or he contradicts himself in assuming the existence of students appropriately prepared for the study of ethics.

One might suspect that Aristotle would be willing to contradict himself in this case, since if he does not assume that one could develop good dispositions in deviant regimes there would be no proper audience for his ethical teaching. I suggest, instead, that Aristotle assumes all along that the deviant regimes play a crucial role in moral training. This assumption would explain why, despite his harsh criticisms of actual political regimes, he shows little fear for the continued existence of the moral virtues and noble actions.

Nature does *not* provide human beings with sufficient conditions to produce the good life, according to Aristotle. It provides, instead, sufficient conditions to produce the *possibility* of a good life. Human beings, for the most part, have the capacities to receive the training that produces virtuous dispositions. Moreover, they have by nature the capacities that bring into being the community that provides that training, the polis. Whether they become virtuous and lead a good life, however, cannot be predicted with any certainty, for the good life necessarily involves choice and the virtues are among the things that can be "otherwise." All Aristotle claims is that the capacities for ethical training and choice that allow us to become virtuous do exist for the most part among free and relatively equal human beings, as do the means of training those capacities, the laws of the polis.

Aristotle can thus still claim that, even though all political commu-

---

31. Aristotle's preferred student of ethics "is someone who already loves what is noble and takes pleasure in it"; M. Burnyeat, "Aristotle on Learning," 75. Yet not even Sparta, the actual regime that Aristotle believes devotes the most attention to moral education, educates its young to love virtue for its own sake.

nities come into being originally to serve mere life and the vast majority of them take no direct interest in the promotion of virtue, the polis exists by nature for the sake of the good life. The polis fulfills its natural function when it provides the habits that make the development of virtuous dispositions possible. It performs its function *better* when, as in Sparta and Aristotle's best regime, it makes ethical training its primary concern. But it still performs its natural function and serves its natural end even when it provides that training imperfectly and indirectly. We thus have no reason to describe the deviant political regimes that rule in almost all actual political communities as "freaks" of nature. They all—excepting the tyrannies among them—serve their natural end, though not nearly as well as Aristotle's best regime would. There is thus no contradiction between Aristotle's political teleology and his analysis of ordinary political life.

It would, in the end, be rather strange if a philosopher who found the innards of insects and reptiles fascinating expressed disdain and distaste for the ordinary political life of what he thought to be nature's most complex and interesting species. Fearing disdain for the study of nature's lower creatures, Aristotle ends the first book of his *Parts of Animals* with his famous edifying story about how Heraclitus told his visitors that "there were divinities present" even in the mundane kitchen where they found him, warming himself over a fire. "Every realm of nature is marvelous," Aristotle concludes; "we should venture on the study of every kind of animal without distaste; for each and all will reveal to us something natural and something beautiful" (*Parts of Animals* 645a15–25).

Because it is far more likely that his students have too high rather than too low an opinion of the subject's importance, Aristotle does not offer similar encouragement to persuade them to study politics. But that does not mean that he gazed with any less wonder at political phenomena. Like every other realm that nature touches, politics reveals "something beautiful" to those who study it. Even amid the cruelty, hypocrisy, and banality that he saw in everyday political life, "there were divinities present" for Aristotle.

CHAPTER FOUR
# Political Friendship

"Friendship also seems to hold cities together, and lawgivers seem to be more concerned about it than about justice. . . . [For] when people are friends justice is unnecessary, but when they are just they need friendship as well" (*NE* 1155a22–27). These famous words from the *Nicomachean Ethics* have inspired numerous critics of modern political theory and practice. Aristotle, they say, helps us see what is lacking in our political life: a bond of empathy that goes beyond mutual interest. He demonstrates "the difference between contract and friendship or between an incorporated economic association (limited liability) and civil community."[1] Modern citizens and political theorists, it is said, have forgotten this difference and thus treat political community as a kind of contract motivated by self-interest rather than a friendship inspired by empathy. The citizens of modern liberal states merely "bond together for their common protection. They possess at best that inferior form of friendship which is founded upon mutual advantage." Aristotle demonstrates, in contrast to modern political theory and practice, that a healthy political life "presupposes a wide range of agreement in that community of goods and virtues and it is this agreement which makes possible the kind of bond between citizens which, on Aristotle's view, constitutes the polis."[2]

1. B. Barber, *Strong Democracy*, 188–89. See also M. Sandel, *Liberalism*, 33, 176; J. Abramson, *Liberation and Its Limits*, 183.
2. A. MacIntrye, *After Virtue*, 155–56. One Irish scholar (G. Huxley, *On Aristotle*

The modern partisans of Aristotelian political friendship rarely notice, however, that Aristotle himself classifies political friendship as a kind of shared advantage friendship. As such, it is one of the two inferior forms of friendship that fall short of the best form of friendship: the friendship shared by virtuous individuals (NE 1160a11; EE 1242a6). In this chapter I try to show that for Aristotle political friendship is a fact of ordinary political life rather than a moral ideal, a source of conflict as well as a means of promoting greater cooperation.

## NEITHER BROTHERS NOR COMRADES

Friendship rarely ranks among the central topics—justice, freedom, equality, domination, social welfare, and so on—discussed by modern political philosophers. Yet if we think of friendship as Aristotle does, as a bond of mutual concern found in some form in every social interaction, then we can discern its importance to the issues explicitly discussed by modern political philosophers. Understood in this way, political friendship involves the kind of mutual concern that we expect or hope to find among citizens. Those who dream of either greater fraternity among citizens or more rational calculation of self-interest among them are taking a stand on the question of political friendship, at least as Aristotle understands it. The former, like Rousseau and his followers, encourage citizens to behave with the intense degree of mutual concern we expect of brothers and sisters. The latter, like Hobbes, tell them that they would be better off if they behaved toward each other with the cool calculation we expect of bankers and accountants.

Aristotle would respond to both of these groups of political reformers by arguing that we cannot simply redesign friendship ties to fit our political goals. Each kind of community, he insists, disposes us toward a form of friendship that reflects the nature and degree of the goods shared by its members. Aristotle recommends something like friendliness as a general virtue (NE 1108a27, 1126b15). But friendly individuals, he argues, should behave in different ways toward different people, depending on the kind of things that they share with others. Although they should try to be amiable to acquaintances and strangers alike, they should "also behave as is appropriate toward each group, since it is not fitting to show the same concern toward acquaintances and strangers,

---

*and Greek Society,* 71), alluding to the troubles in Belfast, laments with touching sincerity that "if we would but heed Aristotle's teaching in our private and public lives today, friendship would enable us to be not only happy, but also good."

nor to pain them in the same ways" (*NE* 1125b25). To behave toward everyone with the friendliness one would show to an intimate is, for Aristotle, a vice. "Those who [claim to] have many friends and mix intimately with them all are thought to be no one's friend, except in the way proper to fellow-citizens, and such people are called obsequious" (*NE* 1171a16). To determine what kind of friendliness one should show to particular individuals, we must ask first about what kind of goods we share with them.

The good that friends promote for each other is thus not, according to Aristotle, the good per se, but rather the particular good that they share. "For the useful friend, one wishes what is advantageous; . . . for the friend who shares in pleasure, sympathy in joy and grief is the proper gift. All of these definitions are appropriate for some friendship, but none fit the single thing, friendship" (*EE* 1244a21–27). It is through the differences between the goods shared in different communities that Aristotle identifies and explains the different kinds of friendship ties.

Aristotle argues that friends share three general kinds of goods: advantage or utility, pleasure, and virtue. Accordingly, shared advantage, shared pleasure, and shared virtue shape the three major species of Aristotelian friendship. Because "it is for the sake of advantage that the political community too seems both to have come together originally and to endure" (*NE* 1160a11), Aristotle classifies political friendship as a shared advantage friendship.

> Political friendship has been established mainly in accordance with advantage; for men seem to have come together because each is not sufficient for himself, though they would have come together anyhow for the sake of living in company. . . . The justice belonging to the friendship of those useful to one another is preeminently justice, for it is political justice.
> 
> (*EE* 1242a6–13)[3]

Given these explicit definitions of political friendship, we must abandon the widely held view that for Aristotle "the properly human friendship—the one that constitutes the political bond—is specified as being based on virtue."[4] Far from associating political friendship with the

---

3. Note that Aristotle uses *political friendship* to describe the bond between *all* members of a political community. He does not use it, as we often do, to describe the friendship that develops among individuals—for instance, members of a political party—who band together to pursue a particular political goal, such as political power or a change in public policy. Greek politics did not develop anything like our highly institutionalized political parties, but there did emerge in Athens and other poleis clubs of like-minded aristocrats known as *hetaireiai*, which I discuss in chapter 7.

4. J.-L. Labarrière, "The Political Animal's Knowledge," 38. For similar characterizations of Aristotle's understanding of political friendship, see A. Kronman, "Aristotle's Idea of Political Fraternity," 128–30; J. Casey, *Pagan Virtue*, 191–94.

trust and intimacy characteristic of virtuous friends, Aristotle associates it with the behavior of international allies. "Just as cities are friends to one another, so in the like way are citizens." When Megara ceases to help Athens, " 'the Athenians no longer know the Megarians'; nor do citizens know one another, when they are no longer useful to one another" (*EE* 1242b23). The Aristotelian author of the *Magna Moralia* goes so far as to suggest that virtue friendships are firmest with foreigners, "for they have no common aim about which to dispute, as is the case with citizens" (*Magna Moralia* 1211a11).[5]

This classification of political friendship as a shared advantage friendship leads Aristotle to qualify in very important ways the opinions about the effects of political friendship that he cites at the beginning of book 8 of the *Nicomachean Ethics*. However necessary political friendship is to holding cities together, it does *not*, he concludes, eliminate the need for justice. "The friendship of advantage is full of complaints; as these friends use each other for their own interests they always want to get the better of the bargain, and think they have got less than they should, and blame their friends because they do not get all they want and deserve" (*NE* 1162b16). For friends such as these, legal justice is absolutely necessary. Reference to a law or contract stating what they owe each other lessens the dissension among them (*EE* 1242b37). As a result, Aristotle concludes that we need political justice to resolve the problems that arise within political friendships. The political form of justice, with its legal standards and public deliberation, grows out of the political form of friendship (*EE* 1242b37).

Aristotle's shared *virtue* friendships do minimize the need for legal justice by minimizing the sources of complaints and quarrels (*NE* 1162b7). But nowhere in his discussion of friendship does Aristotle suggest that political friendship, even when perfected, can turn into a shared virtue friendship. He insists, instead, that we should distinguish "the friendships of fellow citizens, deme members, voyagers, and the like" from the friendships of "kin and comrades," for the former all "seem to rest [unlike the latter] on a sort of agreement" (*NE* 1161a11). ("Comrades" [*hetairoi*] is the term Aristotle uses to describe intimate friends who share in a virtuous life.) Indeed, Aristotle explicitly rules

---

5. Gabriel Herman explains this suggestion by pointing out the persistence of "ritual friendships," personal alliances between members of the elites of different, often opposing cities. These "ritual friendships" often challenged and overwhelmed the weaker, less personal, and often contested ties of political friendship among the citizens of Greek cities. See G. Herman, *Ritualised Friendship*, esp. 30.

out the transformation of political friendship into a virtue friendship when he argues that virtue friendship cannot develop among large numbers of people, even though "with a view to advantage or pleasure it is possible that many people should please one" (*NE* 1158a11). "In the way proper to fellow citizens it is possible to be the friend of many and yet remain a genuinely good man and not be obsequious; but one cannot have with many people the friendship based on virtue and on the character of our friends themselves" (*NE* 1171a18). Political friends may be *like* brothers and comrades in their relative equality (*NE* 1161a25–29), but they do not share the nature and degree of mutual concern we expect to find among brothers and comrades.

Some commentators, remembering that Aristotle repeatedly insists in the *Politics* that the polis exists for the sake of the good life as well as mere life, find it difficult to accept this characterization of political friendship as his final word on the subject. René Gauthier and Jean Jolif, for example, suggest that Aristotle is merely reporting a commonly held opinion when he describes the political community as a community devoted to shared advantage, an opinion that he corrects in the *Politics*.[6] Horst Hutter argues that although the Aristotelian citizen cannot actually share in a virtue friendship with all of his compatriots, "he will nevertheless approach everyone of his fellow citizens as though he were a friend, as having the potential of being a close friend."[7] Terence Irwin suggests that political friendship is "an extension of the best type of friendship."[8] And Hannah Arendt argues that although "the Aristotelian *philia politikē*" lacks the warmth we associate with intimate personal friendships, it resembles "respect," which she defines as "a regard for the person from the distance which the space of the world puts between us."[9]

Unfortunately, none of these glosses on Aristotle's description of political friendship is based on anything Aristotle actually writes about the subject. They rest, instead, on the expectation that a community that exists for the sake of the good life must promote a higher form of friendship than the shared advantage friendship that Aristotle explicitly associates with it. This expectation, however, is based on a misinterpre-

6. R. Gauthier and J. Jolif, *L'Éthique à Nicomaque* 2:698.
7. H. Hutter, *Politics as Friendship*, 116.
8. T. Irwin, *Aristotle's First Principles*, 421, 398–99.
9. H. Arendt, *The Human Condition*, 218. Arendt views Aristotelian political friendship as a form of mutual respect owed each other by citizens. Ronald Beiner notes, correctly, that this understanding of political friendship is, contrary to Arendt's opinion, more Kantian than Aristotelian; R. Beiner, *Political Judgment*, 119.

tation of Aristotle's conception of political community. When Aristotle insists that the political community exists for the sake of the good life as well as mere life, that does not necessarily imply, as it is so often taken to imply, that sharing in political community amounts to sharing in the good life. It merely implies that the political community is a necessary means to the end of good living or human flourishing (*eudaimonia*).

For this reason, political friendship remains a shared advantage friendship even in Aristotle's best regime, the regime in which all citizens lead the good life. Aristotle's best regime perfects political friendship as *homonoia*, that is, as agreement about what constitutes and serves the common advantage, rather than as a kind of virtue friendship. It is "like-mindedness" or "concord," as *homonoia* is often translated, that lawgivers seek "most of all" in order to "hold cities together" (*NE* 1155a21–24). "Concord seems," Aristotle suggests, "to be political friendship, as indeed it is commonly said to be." But concord does not refer to any sharing of virtuous activities, "for it is concerned with things that are in our interest and have an influence on our lives" (*NE* 1167b2). It "is found among good men" because they are like-minded in seeking to establish and preserve institutions that promote the good life (*NE* 1167b5), not because they are sharing the good life. Aristotle's identification of political friendship with concord thus fits neatly with his description of political friendship as a form of advantage friendship.

In the end, Aristotle not only denies that political friendship is or can be transformed into a shared virtue friendship but goes so far as to suggest that this sort of transformation would be undesirable. He makes this point clearly in his little-noticed discussions of the difference between what he calls the "ethical" (*ethikon*) and "conventional" (*nomikon*) forms of shared advantage friendship. When the parties to a shared advantage friendship "proceed by agreement, it is a 'conventional' advantage friendship; when each of the two parties leaves the return for his services to be fixed by the other, we have an 'ethical' advantage friendship, that of comrades [*hetairoi*]" (*EE* 1242b35; cf. *NE* 1162b21–35). Conventional advantage friendships rely on relatively fixed terms to determine the kind of return each party will make to each other. There is, nonetheless, an element of trust and friendliness in this arrangement, since the parties do not demand immediate payment. There can be no contracting unless each party has some trust that the other will do what is required by their agreement at some later time (*NE*

1162b28). But that element of trust is much smaller than it is in the ethical type of advantage friendship, where it is left to the other individual to decide what constitutes an appropriate return for the good received. Conventional advantage friends use laws and agreements to define their expectations of each other, whereas ethical advantage friends seek "a truer and friendlier justice" (*NE* 1243a32).

Ethical advantage friendship certainly seems closer to shared virtue friendship (*EE* 1242b37). One might thus expect that Aristotle would prefer it to its more limited and less trusting counterpart. Accordingly, at least one commentator suggests that "civic friendship is this latter, moral type" and that a "society infused by civic friendship [of this sort] has little need of right" and legal justice.[10]

There are two problems with this interpretation of Aristotle's argument. First, Aristotle explicitly identifies "political friendship" with the *conventional* rather than the ethical form of advantage friendship. "Political friendship," like conventional advantage friendship, "looks to the agreement and the thing, ethical friendship to the choice" (*EE* 1243a42). Second, Aristotle strongly disapproves of the ethical form of advantage friendship:[11] "Recrimination is very frequent in this sort of friendship and the reason is that it is *contrary to nature;* for friendships based on advantage and on virtue are different, but these people wish to have both together, associating together for the sake of advantage but representing their friendship as ethical, like that of good men; pretending to trust one another, they make out their friendship to be not merely conventional" (*EE* 1242b37; my emphasis).

Parties to the ethical form of advantage friendship act, Aristotle suggests, in contradictory ways. They come together because they believe that their association will be to each other's advantage. But they then act as if they are not interested in any return for their actions, a pretense that explodes as soon as they receive none. The participant in such a friendship "makes a gift, . . . as to a [close] friend, but expects to receive as much or more, as having not given but lent; and if a man is worse off when the relation is dissolved than he was when it began he will complain. . . . This happens," Aristotle explains, "because all or most men, while they wish for what is noble, choose what is advantageous;

---

10. J. Kekes, "Civility and Society," 431–32.
11. In my article "Community and Conflict in Aristotle's Political Philosophy" (107–10), I mistakenly described Aristotelian political friendship itself as a contradictory mix of interest and virtue friendship exemplified by the ethical form of the shared virtue friendship. I correct that description here.

now it is noble to do well by another without a view to repayment, but it is the receiving of benefits that is advantageous" (*NE* 1162b31–37).

Participants in mutual advantage friendships seek some advantage to themselves from their friendships. There is nothing wrong or unnatural about that. Human beings, by nature, establish many forms of community in pursuit of their mutual advantage, the most important of which is the polis. But Aristotle insists that it is contrary to nature (or is self-deceiving) to treat activities established for the sake of mutual advantage as if they were being performed for their own sake. Those who share in citizenship, just like those who share in an economic association or voyage, share in an attempt to promote an end that will be to their mutual advantage. Citizens perform their characteristic activities with mutually advantageous ends in view, rather than for their own sake. When they treat each other as "ethical" friends, they are merely fooling themselves into thinking that they are performing these activities for their own sake. In doing so, they create expectations of each other's behavior that are sure to be disappointed.[12]

Most contemporary commentators find it hard to accept Aristotle's unequivocal characterization of political friendship as an instrumental friendship as his last word on the subject, for this notion threatens the overly moralistic conception of political community they impose on his writings. But, as he makes clear in his discussions of reciprocity, Aristotle himself views the instrumental character of political friendship as the foundation, rather than the solvent, of political community. Reciprocity is the sense of justice that leads us to expect good in return for good and evil in return for evil. "[In all] communities of exchange, this sort of justice holds men together." In particular, "reciprocity preserves cities" (*NE* 1132b31; *Pol.* 1261a32). Like partners to an exchange of goods, citizens are brought and held together by the expectation of a return of some good for the good they do for another citizen. To act as if they do not expect a return is to act as dishonestly as individuals who deny any interest in the delivery of the goods that they have bought.[13]

Even in the best regime, which Aristotle assumes is composed of vir-

---

12. Some commentators suggest that political friendship improves as it moves toward the ethical form of shared interest friendship. See J. Cooper, "Aristotle on Friendship," 337n16; K. D. Alpern, "Aristotle on the Friendships," 311–15; A. W. Price, *Love and Friendship*, 195–99. In making this suggestion, they ignore the problems intrinsic to the ethical form of shared interest friendship, problems that Aristotle spells out clearly in the *Eudemian Ethics* (1242a–b).

13. I discuss Aristotle's political conception of reciprocity as a form of justice in the second section of chapter 5.

tuous individuals, it would be inappropriate for citizens to treat each other as "ethical" advantage friends. As virtuous individuals they will probably all seek the common good, but that does not mean that they are not interested in the advantages that will accrue to them from pursuing a particular course of action.[14] It is only in their intimate relations with each other, relations that take place in small groups, that they will express no interest in receiving some return for their actions. The need for justice and law will diminish within these small groups but not within the political community as a whole.[15]

I would go further and suggest that it is precisely in Aristotle's best regime that political friendship least resembles the ethical form of advantage friendship. Virtuous individuals, unlike youths, do not turn every action into an occasion for the display of nobility, Aristotle notes in the *Rhetoric*. The elderly make the opposite mistake, treating the demands of expediency as if they almost always make noble action inappropriate. The mature individual of good character avoids each of these extremes, distinguishing the occasions that concern expedient actions from those that call forth noble or inherently valuable actions (*Rhet.* 1389a–b). The citizens of the ordinary, imperfect regimes of everyday life consist not of mature, virtuous individuals but of people who "wish for what is noble, but choose what is advantageous" (*NE* 1162b35). Such individuals are more likely than genuinely virtuous individuals to portray expedient actions as disinterested and demand similar disinterestedness from others. As a result, we should expect to find more of this pretense of ethical friendship in the deviant regimes of ordinary political life than in the best regime composed of virtuous individuals.

I conclude then that Aristotelian political friendship, far from perfecting itself in a shared virtue friendship, is best practiced when it eliminates any element of the so-called ethical advantage friendship. A move in the direction of the ethical form of shared advantage friendship would only exacerbate the already potent sources of conflict and disagreement in any political friendship. The best political regime is best, at least in part, precisely because it steers away from this pretense of greater friendliness in the political community. Aristotle does not abandon the common opinion that friendship "seems to hold cities together." But he

---

14. See *Rhetoric* 1354b35, where Aristotle suggests that deliberation about the common good should take place in assemblies rather than courts, since in the former, unlike the latter, citizens are discussing matters in which they have a direct interest.

15. As can be seen by the presence and importance of laws in Aristotle's best regime, as presented in books 7 and 8 of the *Politics*.

severely qualifies that opinion by suggesting that it is a far less exalted and harmonious form of friendship that ordinarily binds citizens together.

## THE DANGERS OF POLITICAL INTIMACY

Even if we accept Aristotle's description of political friendship as accurate, what keeps us from trying to transform it into something more exalted and beneficial? Why not try to turn it into something closer to the shared virtue friendship of comrades or the fraternity of brothers? If large communities ordinarily lack the degree of integration characteristic of more intimate groups, why not try to find ways of "personalizing" them?[16] In order to do so, we may have to transform the character of ordinary political life, but if we succeed, might we not succeed in eliminating its worst features?

Political reformers and revolutionaries have repeatedly answered these questions by drawing up inspiring visions of a more fraternal or comradely form of political friendship as a goal for political action. In book 2 of the *Politics* Aristotle examines one of the first of these proposals: Plato's attempt, in book 5 of the *Republic,* to transform the citizenry of his utopian community into one large family. Aristotle's critique of this proposal presents powerful objections not only to Plato's vision of political friendship but to the entire idea of political fraternity or comradeship as well.

In proposing that property, women, and children be held in common, Plato, Aristotle suggests, starts from the common opinion that "friendship is the greatest good for cities, since it minimizes factional conflict; Socrates praises above all the city's being one, which appears to be and is said by him to be the work of friendship" (*Pol.* 1262b8). From this point of view, we experience dissension and conflict within political communities because the political bonds of friendship are too limited and weak. " 'Friends,' as the proverb says, 'hold things in common.' " If we eliminated private property and the family, perhaps citizens would begin to behave toward each other like true friends. When we hear complaints about "lawsuits over contracts, trials for perjury, and flattery of the rich," we are inclined, Aristotle suggests, to accept the Platonic proposal, "thinking that it will produce a wondrous kind

---

16. Robert Frank has recently suggested this approach as a solution to some of the difficulties associated with large, impersonal associations; *Passions Within Reason,* 248.

of friendship in all for each other" (*Pol.* 1263a30, 1263b15–21). If citizens had common families, like brothers, and shared all their property, as intimate comrades do, then we might see the end of the dissensions that plague ordinary political life. Even if, like Plato, we are aware that we will always fall short of completely transforming political friendship into fraternity and comradeship, should we not strive to achieve as much of this transformation as we can?

Aristotle argues that we should reject this proposal, even though it "might seem attractive and humane [*philanthropos*]" (*Pol.* 1263b15). In his view, it establishes an inappropriate, as well as an unreachable, standard against which to measure political friendship. He provides two major arguments to support this conclusion.

First, Aristotle argues that the depth and intensity of fraternal and comradely friendship reflect conditions peculiar to those friendships as they have developed in our experience. "Of the two qualities that most inspire regard and friendly feeling [*to philein*], being one's own and being precious, neither will be available to those who govern themselves in this [Plato's] way" (*Pol.* 1262b21). The friendship of comrades grows out of the intimate familiarity that a few individuals can have with each other's virtues; comrades come together because their intimacy allows them to see something distinctive and precious in each other. Citizens, in contrast, come together because they can help each other achieve their goals. Even if we could make all citizens virtuous, as Aristotle assumes we can in outlining his best regime, they still would need each other and thus would treat each other as means rather than as something precious in themselves. The intimacy of comrades simply cannot be extended to a large number of individuals.

The friendship between brothers, and between family members in general, develops out of a combination of intimacy and a sense that a member of our family is in some sense our own. The friendships among family members are the most natural friendships (*NE* 1162a16) precisely because they are rooted in a common natural origin. Expanding this friendship beyond its natural origins to include the whole political community is, Aristotle suggests, like "adding a lot of water to a small amount of wine": one loses the taste of the original. "In the city, friendship necessarily becomes diluted through this sort of community, and the fact that a father least of all says 'mine' of his son, or the son of his father" (*Pol.* 1262b14–18). Plato's goal was to use the depth and intensity of family relations to overcome dissensions among citizens. But when we eliminate the sense of our "own" attached to natural families, we also eliminate that depth and intensity. "Better to be to someone's own [*idion*] cousin," Aristotle concludes, "than a son in this [Platonic] sense" (*Pol.* 1262a13).

Aristotle's second argument against modeling political friendship on the fraternity and comradeship is less familiar, but it is in some ways more interesting. Sharing something, he argues, does not in itself lessen dissension among those who share it. "For it is precisely those who possess things in common and share whom we see quarreling most" (*Pol.* 1263b22–26). "Living together and sharing any human concern is difficult, and particularly with things [common property] of this sort. This is clear in the communities of fellow travelers; most of them are always quarreling as a result of friction over ordinary and trifling matters" (*Pol.* 1263a15).

When people propose greater sharing as a means of eliminating disagreement and conflict, they seem to forget that living together has its own difficulties. People quarrel over the most trifling matters when they engage in as limited a form of sharing as traveling together. Broader and more intense forms of sharing merely multiply and deepen the possible sources of recrimination. Our expectations of each other increase with our degree of sharing. The depth and intensity of our indignation when these expectations are disappointed grows accordingly as we expand the range and importance of the things we share. "Injustice increases by being exhibited toward those who are friends in a fuller sense. It is a more terrible thing to defraud a comrade than a fellow citizen, more terrible not to help a brother than a stranger, and more terrible to wound a father than anyone else. In addition, the demands of justice also increase naturally with the friendship" (*NE* 1160a3; cf. *Rhet.* 1379b2). We expect more from those we call our comrades and brothers and get angrier when they fail to meet these expectations than when others behave in a similar way. The proposal to turn citizens into brothers and comrades by giving them families and property in common merely appears humane. In reality, it threatens to increase the number and intensity of our conflicts. As noted already, Aristotle believes that "our spirit is more aroused against companions and friends than against unknown persons when it consider itself slighted, . . . as indeed is reasonable; for, besides the actual injury, they also consider themselves robbed of this [companionship or friendship]. Hence the sayings 'Cruel are the wars of brothers' and 'Those who love extravagantly will hate extravagantly as well' " (*Pol.* 1328a1–15).

By treating fraternity and comradeship as the ideal of political friendship, we introduce higher expectations into our interactions, expectations that are bound to be disappointed because citizens cannot view each other as related or precious in the way that brothers and comrades do. To train citizens to see themselves as comrades or brothers would institutionalize the "ethical" sort of mutual advantage friendship discussed in the previous section (*EE* 1242b37). Citizens trained in this way would expect the kind of disinterested concern from each other that we ordinarily expect from our family members and intimate friends. At the same time, however, they will, as members of a political community, have come together for the sake of mutual advantage. They will thus treat laws and other restrictions that require each other to return good for good as beneath their dignity but will still expect to get some advantage from their interactions with each other. When they do not receive such a return—and why should it be provided if the original good was offered as if a gift?—they will complain not only about a failure to return advantage for advantage but about betrayal and treason.

The dissensions among citizens who thought of themselves as friends in this way would resemble those we associate with family businesses, a form of enterprise noted for both highly successful collaboration and especially intense conflicts.[17] As in family businesses, these citizens would think of their interactions as disinterested and, at the same time, expect always to receive some advantage from these interactions. If that expectation is not met, then, like partners in a family business, they will tend to complain not only about cheating but about betrayal, a far more terrible crime. The increased breadth and depth of such a friendship might suppress many of the common sources of political conflict and competition, but only by increasing the risk of much more intense and dangerous conflicts.

Fraternity and comradeship are thus dangerous, as well as impractical, models for the reform of political friendship, according to Aristotle. Devised to bring relief from the inconveniences of ordinary political life, the intensification of political friendship would, he suggests, merely increase their violence.

17. B. Yack, "Community and Conflict," 92, 109. Indeed, W. L. Newmann (*The Politics of Aristotle* 2:254) and C. Lord (Aristotle, *The Politics* 241n12) suggest that when Aristotle is speaking of living together while sharing property (*Pol.* 1263a15), he has in mind the accepted Athenian practice of brothers holding property in common.

## POLITICAL FRIENDSHIP AND THE INCONVENIENCES OF POLITICAL LIFE

To rid political life of these inconveniences has been the aim of some of the most influential modern political philosophers, such as Rousseau and Hobbes. If only a spirit of genuine fraternity or comradeship beat in the breast of every citizen, Rousseau argues, then "government would become so easy, it needs none of that art of darkness whose blackness is its only mystery."[18] In contrast, if we treated each other with the same cool calculation characteristic of parties to a contract, as Hobbes encourages us to do, then perhaps we would have far fewer and less explosive sources of mutual recrimination.

Many modern revolutionaries have followed Rousseau in pinning their hopes for change on efforts to inspire a sense of political fraternity and comradeship among modern individuals. Aristotle would probably subject these efforts to the same criticisms he directed at Plato's attempts to turn political friendship into fraternity and comradeship. To the extent that these efforts merely seek to reinforce demands for equal political status—as does the revolutionary term of address, "comrade," by eliminating status distinctions from names—Aristotle would have little reason to object to them; as we have seen, he considers citizens to be like brothers and comrades by virtue of their relatively equal political status (*NE* 1161a25). But modern revolutionaries also try to educate citizens who will resemble brothers and comrades in the depth and intensity of their mutual concern. Aristotle would surely denounce these efforts as dangerous and doomed to failure.

We can create political fraternity only by taking brotherly affection out of the context of family identity and intimacy and expanding its range to cover all citizens. But by doing so, we would, as Aristotle puts it in his critique of Plato's proposal for fraternity, have to water those feelings down to a point of relative insignificance (*Pol.* 1262b14).

Revolutionary comradeship, in contrast, resembles Aristotle's understanding of virtue friendship in that it involves the intense mutual concern felt by individuals who share in the supposed virtues of the new revolutionary order. In a perceptive critique of Jacobin efforts to create this comradeship, Benjamin Constant argues that "since the public interest does not exert over us the empire it held over the ancients, it was a hypocritical and violent egoism," rather than genuine comradeship,

---

18. J.-J. Rousseau, "Discourse on Political Economy," in *On the Social Contract*, 218.

to which private interest "was sacrificed" by the Jacobins.[19] Aristotle would probably agree with Constant's analysis, adding only that modern individuals have no monopoly on this kind of hypocrisy.[20] As argued above, Aristotle believes that his contemporaries—even the virtuous few who constitute his best regime—are drawn together into their political communities by their shared and mutual advantage. To demand that they treat all other citizens as comrades, that is, as individuals with whom they choose to associate apart from all considerations of their needs and interests, is to demand that they act dishonestly and hypocritically.

Aristotle's concept of an "ethical" form of shared advantage friendship (*EE* 1242b) provides an appropriate model for the bond between citizens who try to live up to these demands. The "comrades" of the new revolutionary order,[21] like the participants in ethical advantage friendships, "wish to have both [advantage and virtue friendships] together; associating together for the sake of advantage but representing their friendship as ethical, like that of good men; pretending to trust one another they make out their friendship to be not merely conventional" (*EE* 1242b37).

Revolutionary rhetoric encourages citizens to behave as if they are not interested in repayment for their devotion to the good of their compatriots and to distrust the motives of the individuals who seem to expect repayment. But because convenience and interest lead the citizens of a revolutionary order, like all participants in political communities, to associate with any particular group of individuals as compatriots, this rhetoric merely increases their mutual resentment and fear of betrayal. Like the participant in Aristotle's ethical advantage friendship, the revolutionary comrade "makes a gift, . . . as to a [close] friend, but expects to receive as much or more, as if having lent rather than given" (*NE* 1162a31). Every time revolutionary comrades act to help their compatriots, they will expect, even though they are unlikely to say so,

---

19. B. Constant, *Les "Principes de Politique*," 438. See also S. Holmes, *Benjamin Constant*, 79–127.

20. In other words, Aristotle would deny that the "ancients" were any more capable than the "moderns" of the moral rigors that Constant associated with "ancient liberty' in his famous essay "On the Liberty of the Ancients."

21. Note that I am using the term *comrade* here to refer to the citizen of the postrevolutionary polity rather than to the "comrades' who shared in the struggle to make and direct a revolution. In doing so, I am following Aristotle, who uses the term *political friendship* to refer to the bond between all members of a political community rather than to the bond between those, like revolutionaries, who share in the pursuit of a particular political goal. Committed revolutionaries resemble the members of the ancient Greek *hetaireiai* rather than Aristotelian political friends.

some return for their efforts. Not only will that expectation be disappointed by compatriots who expect selfless devotion to their interests from each other, thereby generating resentment on the part of the actors against these compatriots, but it will also become, to the extent that it is detected by these compatriots, a source of suspicion about their comrades' devotion to the new revolutionary order. These suspicions are ubiquitous and unavoidable among friends of this sort. It is thus not surprising that the reign of terror lurks so closely behind the reign of virtue whenever revolutionaries have attempted to turn political friendship into revolutionary comradeship.[22]

Must we conclude then that Aristotle agrees with Hobbes that we would be far better off if we based the bond between citizens solely on the kind of self-interested calculation we expect of parties to a business contract? It might appear so, given Aristotle's severe critique of political fraternity and comradeship. But this appearance is deceiving, since Aristotle, unlike Hobbes, does not think of contractual relations, let alone political relations, as based purely on calculations of self-interest.

As argued in chapter 1, Aristotle believes that all social interactions, even the mere exchange of goods, generate some sense of friendship, some disposition toward mutual concern, among its participants. Consequently, he would argue that Hobbes is chasing an illusion when he urges us to remodel our political relations on the cool calculation characteristic of economic interactions. Even if, as Hobbes believes, we would be better off if we eliminated from social life expectations of friendship and the recriminations they often inspire—something Aristotle would clearly deny—human nature, Aristotle would insist, prevents us from ever achieving that goal. And if this is the case with regard to exchange relations, then it is all the more so with regard to political relations.

Political relations are both broader and much more permanent than exchange relations. As a result, they dispose us to a much greater sense of mutual concern than we derive from exchange relations. Although, as we have seen, the "ship of state" metaphor is misleading as a guide to the structure of obligation and authority within a political community, it does shed some light on political friendship. As I noted in chapter 1, when we travel together, our experience of sharing the same ob-

22. The obsession with conspiracy and betrayal in the Jacobin republic has long been a theme for historians of the French Revolution. See, for example, F. Furet, *Interpreting the Revolution*, 47–53; L. Hunt, *Politics, Culture, and Class*, 38–44. The Aristotelian concept of "ethical" advantage friendship could help explain this obsession.

stacles and dangers, of being "all in the same boat," disposes us to help each other far more than we would once we reach our destination.

Citizens, I suggest here, share something of that experience of floating in the same boat and consequently share something similar to that heightened mutual concern characteristic of fellow travelers. Because the goals of political action are not nearly as clear as the destination of a ship, the sense of sharing obstacles and dangers is not as certain to develop among citizens as it is among fellow travelers. Moreover, because these goals, unlike fellow travelers' destination, are always in the distance, this sense often dies as the result of resentment and disappointment. Nevertheless, however fragile it may be, participation in political community, Aristotle would argue, does dispose us to developing a fairly extensive and powerful sense of mutual concern.

Moreover, that sense of mutual concern would be reinforced by the sense of friendship that should develop out of citizens' sharing in the practices of political justice. Aristotle himself never directly associates political friendship with this form of friendship. But it follows from his general account of friendship, and in particular from his insistence that whenever we share ends and actions we develop some sense of mutual concern, that a sense of friendship should grow out of sharing in the practices of political justice. Sharing in these practices should promote what modern political theorists call a political culture, and that political culture should reinforce and expand citizens' sense of mutual concern. Such a notion of political friendship would not rest on shared beliefs and principles, since we so often express conflicting beliefs and principles in attempting to hold each other accountable for our actions.[23] It would grow, instead, out of sharing in the particular kinds of processes and interactions that particular communities establish as forms of political justice.

How far would political friendship, understood in this way, dispose citizens to sacrifice their immediate self-interest? Clearly, ancient and modern experience teaches us that it does not dispose citizens to give their poorest compatriots all the money necessary to raise them to the average standard of living. But does political friendship dispose citizens to other forms of self-sacrifice, such as the risk of their lives in defense of their political communities? Communitarians since Rousseau have

23. In this respect Aristotle's understanding of political community bears considerable resemblance to Michael Oakeshott's understanding of "civil association"; see M. Oakeshott, *On Human Conduct*.

worried that it would not do so. After all, did Hobbes not demonstrate that it was illogical for self-interested social contractors to risk their lives, even in a defensive war, unless a gun was pointed at their backs?[24] Modern communitarians' emphasis on the need for a greater sense of political fraternity, comradeship, and collective identity grows, in part, out of the assumption that only passions capable of overwhelming our sense of self-interest can effectively induce individuals to take risks for each other.

Aristotle's understanding of political friendship suggests an alternative motivation for risk taking, a motivation that grows out of, rather than combats, the pursuit of self-interest. As discussed above, Aristotle suggests that we develop dispositions to aid those with whom we engage in mutually advantageous interactions. Where those interactions are as extensive and permanent as they are within political communities, they might dispose us to risk our lives in defense of the community, just as individuals undertake potentially self-sacrificing risks at sea that they would not take once they reach their destination.

Confirmation of this possibility comes from the fact that the citizens of nineteenth- and twentieth-century liberal democracies, the very individuals whose self-serving egoism modern communitarians lament, have shown themselves quite willing, as both volunteers and conscripts, to risk their lives as citizen-soldiers in defensive wars. As Michael Walzer notes, modern individuals have if anything shown themselves "all-too-willing to sacrifice their lives for the state."[25] This fact is often ignored in communitarian laments about the corrupting influence of modern individualism. But such willingness to engage in citizen-soldiery is hardly universal. Indeed, there has been a tremendous revival of the willingness to sacrifice one's life for one's country in the last two centuries, a revival that, interestingly, coincides with the growth in influence of individualist political theories and practices.

The growth of nationalistic passions and the persistence of dying communitarian traditions are the commonest explanations of this fact offered by the few communitarian theorists who take notice of it.[26] Both explanations, especially the former, have considerable power.

---

24. T. Hobbes, *Leviathan*, 269–70. In the "Review, and Conclusion" that he eventually added to *Leviathan*, Hobbes modified this unpopular position with some rather unconvincing arguments denying the clear implications of his arguments in chapter 21 that no individual has a duty to put his or her life at risk if such an end can be avoided.

25. M. Walzer, *Obligations*, 77.

26. On the problems with the second of these two explanations, see B. Yack, "Liberalism and Its Communitarian Critics," 159–61.

Nevertheless, I believe that the Aristotelian understanding of political friendship developed in this chapter provides us with an interesting additional explanation. Like contemporary communitarians, the eighteenth-century prophets of commercial republicanism, such as Montesquieu and Smith, did not expect liberal individualists to serve as citizen-soldiers.[27] To that extent, it seems, they misunderstood the dynamics of the commercial republicanism they advocated. In order to understand these dynamics, I suggest, it would be best to turn to an approach that, like Aristotle's, allows us to explain the ways in which self-interested and self-sacrificing behavior can grow out of the same social interactions.[28]

Faced with a choice between the cold calculation of Hobbesian political association and the hyperintense warmth of Rousseauian community, Aristotle would offer the lukewarm comforts of his understanding of political friendship. In doing so, however, he would not merely be indulging his well-known penchant for moderation. He would, instead, be offering a model of political friendship that seems to fit best the experience of political communities from ancient Greece to twentieth-century America.

27. See C. S. de Montesquieu, *Considerations*, 155; A. Smith, *The Wealth of Nations*, 659–60. On Smith's arguments, see E. Cohen, *Citizens and Soldiers*, 119–20.
28. On the tensions created for American liberal democracy by demands for military service, see E. Cohen, *Citizens and Soldiers*; J. W. Chambers, *To Raise an Army*.

CHAPTER FIVE
# Political Justice

Political arguments about justice and injustice ordinarily refer to two kinds of standards: the relatively determinate standards embodied in the fund of norms familiar to members of a political community and the much vaguer and more indeterminate standards by which the justice of these norms is measured. The interplay between these two kinds of claims about justice gives political argument much of its characteristic liveliness and lack of finality.

The great majority of moral and political philosophers, however, express considerable discomfort with the indeterminate nature of the standards by which we measure the justice of familiar norms and institutions in political life. Because they most often think of justice as a body of primary rules and principles capable of ordering the basic distribution of benefits and burdens within a community, a way of thinking that Judith Shklar aptly describes as "the normal model of justice,"[1] they tend to see indeterminate standards of judgment as a threat to justice itself. Philosophers who subscribe to this "normal model" of justice usually assume, as does John Rawls, that their task is to identify the body of general but determinate rules and principles that a community can or should use to judge the justice of familiar practices and institutions.[2] It is precisely to eliminate the indeterminacy of ordinary

---

1. J. Shklar, *The Faces of Injustice*, 17–20.
2. J. Rawls, *A Theory of Justice*, 5.

political judgments about justice that Hobbes, to take an extreme example, demands that we limit the meaning of justice to performance of the obligations established by the sovereign's authority. But positivism's opponents among moral and political philosophers also seek, for the most part, to eliminate indeterminacy in our standards of justice. They do so by trying to identify the determinate standards of justice dictated by nature, God, human reason, our shared experiences, our implicit consensus, or any combination thereof.

Even though most contemporary moral and political philosophers disdain any appeal to natural or divine standards of justice, they usually try to eliminate the characteristic indeterminacy of extralegal standards of justice. Rawls identifies determinate standards against which to measure the justice of our social and political institutions by asking which principles of justice rational individuals would choose if they were constrained to reason fairly by a "veil of ignorance" that concealed from them their personal identity and characteristics. Ronald Dworkin offers a path to "right answers" about questions of justice when he insists that our legal and political institutions, when viewed as a coherent whole, contain implicit principles of justice that allow us to resolve even the most difficult legal cases.[3] Even Michael Walzer, who firmly rejects the kind of appeal to trans-historical standards of justice that he finds lurking in Rawls's and Dworkin's arguments,[4] still insists that we can identify a determinate standard against which to measure the justice of our various social institutions. He bases this standard on the "shared understandings" of the goods that we distribute in different spheres of social interaction. These understandings may change from one historical period to another, but, Walzer assumes, they are sufficiently clear, distinct, and shared at any particular time to yield citizens determinate standards against which to measure their judgments about justice.[5]

All three of these philosophers deny that justice is waiting to be discovered out "there" in the nature of the world or of human reason. Nevertheless, they all still insist that we can discover determinate extralegal standards of justice if we reason properly—whether, as with Rawls, by a process of hypothetical reasoning based on assumptions about fairness, or, as with Dworkin and Walzer, by empirical reasoning

---

3. R. Dworkin, *Taking Rights Seriously*, 47, 100. Dworkin modifies this position in *Law's Empire* by quietly dropping his "right answer" thesis.
4. See M. Walzer, "Philosophy and Democracy."
5. M. Walzer, *Spheres of Justice*, xiv, 6–10.

about the determinate standards implicit in "our" cultural, legal, and political systems.

The great majority of Aristotle's interpreters assume that Aristotle shares his successors' discomfort with the indeterminacy of the extralegal standards of justice that ordinarily emerge from political debate. Likewise, they set out to establish the precise nature of the determinate rules and principles that shape Aristotle's understanding of justice—whether, for example, he derives these standards from legal enactments, the spirit of political regimes, human nature, or human reason. The debate surrounding these efforts has been quite lively, not least of all because Aristotle never provides us with a systematic account of the determinate rules and principles that should guide distributive justice in political communities. In the absence of such an account, participants in this debate find it necessary to build their arguments on hints of determinacy that they find in what Aristotle does explicitly say about distributive justice. Nevertheless, few of them dispute the general assumption that Aristotle accepts the philosophers' "normal model" of justice and its intolerance for the indeterminacy of ordinary political justice.[6]

In this chapter I challenge that assumption. The normal model of justice, I argue, is grounded in a legalist or adjudicatory understanding of justice that Aristotle finds inadequate. This understanding conceives of justice, on the model of legal adjudication, primarily as a matter of applying general norms to particular cases.[7] Normal models of justice answer questions about the justice of laws and other familiar norms by seeking to identify a body of extralegal norms against which to measure them. They are offered as guides through the thicket of conflicting standards of judgment to a clearly recognizable and appropriate body of norms to apply in our moral and political judgments about justice. As such, they extend a legalist or adjudicatory understanding of justice beyond the sphere of legal judgment by encouraging us to treat competing claims about the justice of established norms and practices as if they could be adjudicated, like competing legal claims, with reference to a body of shared and commonly recognized norms.

When one conceives of justice in this way, the indeterminate and

---

6. Shklar herself describes Aristotle as the great codifier of the normal model of justice; *The Faces of Injustice,* 17.
7. For this general understanding of "legalism" in politics and morality, see J. Shklar, *Legalism.* I discuss the legalist character of "normal models" of justice in "Injustice and the Victim's Voice."

conflicting standards of judgment that usually emerge in political life appear to be a threat to justice itself, since one cannot make a judgment about justice without a clear and widely recognized body of norms to apply to particular cases. For this reason, among others, moral and political philosophers usually seek some way of identifying a closed coherent, and determinate body of norms to guide our judgments about justice, even if doing so requires them to make highly unrealistic assumptions about our beliefs and practices.

This drive toward unrealistic assumptions is no less evident in contemporary theories of justice than it is in older theories about the standards dictated by God, nature, or reason, even if it is less often noted. When Rawls assumes that a rational and fair person would reason in one and only one manner (maximizing minimum returns); when Dworkin assumes that our political and legal institutions do in fact form a coherent whole that can give us explicit answers to hard and controversial cases; when Walzer assumes that there is at any particular time only one correct interpretation of the shared meaning of goods—they all are imposing single, closed meanings on things, such as reasoning or the interpretation of institutions and shared opinion, that we ordinarily think of as consistent with a variety of meanings. They do so in order to provide us with general standards of justice that possess the kind of determinacy that we find in legal rules and principles.

Aristotle's account of justice in book 5 of the *Nicomachean Ethics*—as even a relatively casual reading confirms—displays little of this urgent quest to define determinate general norms of justice. But since most readers assume that Aristotle, like the majority of philosophers, strives to produce a normal model of justice, they also assume that he also strives to identify such norms. In this chapter I argue, in contrast, that it is no accident that Aristotle's account of justice is not explicitly geared to producing determinate general standards of judgment about justice. I suggest that Aristotle's discussions of justice do not generate standards of this sort because Aristotle rejects the legalist understanding of justice that drives philosophers to seek them. In its place he develops a much more explicitly *political* understanding of justice than we find in most philosophic theories.

Aristotle treats the characteristic indeterminacy of standards of justice in political communities as the foundation of a proper account of justice, rather than, as in more familiar theories of justice, as an obstacle to be overcome. In these theories, politics is at best a means of *implementing* the norms devised for our guidance by philosophers. In Aristotle's understanding of justice, in contrast, politics is the means by which we *identify* the changing and often conflicting standards of justice that guide us in political life.

Viewed as one more attempt to devise a normal model against which to measure the justice of our political judgments, book 5 of the *Nicomachean Ethics* strikes many readers as muddled and incoherent. Much of it is devoted to the analysis of conceptual categories, such as "general," "reciprocal," and "political justice," that have little role to play in normal models of justice. These categories—along with Aristotle's characterization of justice as a virtue of character rather than a state of affairs or set of social relationships—undermine the clarity and determinacy that normal models of justice try to introduce into our judgments.

Commentators can fit Aristotle's account of justice into the contours of the normal model only by dismissing or downplaying the importance of conceptual categories such as general and political justice. After doing so, they are free to focus their attention on other Aristotelian categories—distributive justice, natural versus conventional right, and equity—that are familiar elements of normal models of justice. The most familiar interpretations of Aristotle's understanding of justice are built almost exclusively on these categories. According to these interpretations, Aristotle's formal analysis of distributive justice (*NE* 1130) provides us with the basic concept of justice as proportional equality; his contrast between natural and conventional right (*NE* 1134b) allows us to distinguish intrinsically correct norms of proportionality from our opinions and agreements about such norms; and his concept of equity (*NE* 1137b) guides us in applying these norms to difficult cases. But the coherence of these interpretations is achieved only by ignoring the more unfamiliar categories that Aristotle introduces into his account of justice and by distorting the others.

We can avoid this distortion if we are willing to abandon the search for Aristotle's version of the normal model of justice and construct instead a more political interpretation of Aristotle's understanding of justice. I offer such an interpretation in this chapter. I discuss, in turn, the various conceptual categories introduced by Aristotle in the *Nicomachean Ethics*—political justice and reciprocity, natural and conventional right, justice as a character virtue, general and distributive justice—and attempt to show how they fit together as a coherent and distinctly political understanding of justice. My interpretation of Aristotle's understanding of justice thus both focuses greater attention on unfamiliar Aristotelian categories and returns the more familiar categories, such as distributive justice and conventional right, to the conceptual context in which Aristotle introduces them.

By reinterpreting Aristotle in this way I hope to stimulate critical reflection on familiar theories of justice as well as offer a more satisfactory account of the theory contained in Aristotelian texts. Moral and political philosophers have long appropriated specific Aristotelian categories for their own theories of justice, but they have generally done so in a way that has effectively depoliticized the Aristotelian understanding of justice. By reconstructing that understanding I hope to contribute to efforts to develop less legalistic and more realistic theories of justice than the "normal models" that currently prevail among most moral and political philosophers.

## POLITICAL JUSTICE AND RECIPROCITY

Aristotle introduces the concept of "political justice" in the middle of the *Nicomachean Ethics,* book 5, immediately following his discussion of reciprocity and immediately preceding his discussion of natural and conventional right.[8] He introduces the concept with a reminder that we "must not forget that what we are seeking is both unqualified [*haplōs*] justice and political justice" (*NE* 1134a25).

At first glance, this reminder might seem designed to emphasize the difference between inherently correct standards of justice and those fallible and changing standards established by political communities, especially when we read it in the light of normal models of justice.[9] But when we read on, it becomes clear that Aristotle is associating rather than distinguishing unqualified and political justice. In the sentence following his reminder that we are seeking "both unqualified and political justice," Aristotle states that "this [*tauto*] is found among men who share a common life," clearly suggesting that he thinks of them as a single rather than multiple subject. This suggestion is confirmed in the following paragraph when he clearly identifies political and unqualified

---

8. The concept of political justice has been generally ignored by most of Aristotle's commentators. For exceptions that present interesting ideas about the concept, see F Rosen, "The Political Context"; W. Mathie, "Political and Distributive Justice"; M. Salomon, *Der Begriff der Gerechtigkeit*; E. Voegelin, *Anamnesis,* 58.
9. For examples of this interpretation, see P. Trude, *Der Begriff der Gerechtigkeit* 156; M. Hamburger, *Morals and Law,* 57. See also the translations, listed in note 11 that build this interpretation into their translations of the term "unqualified justice" by rendering that term as "absolute justice."

justice by contrasting political justice with the domestic and despotic relations in which there can be no "injustice in the unqualified (*haplōs*) sense" (*NE* 1134b9). As discussed in chapters 1 and 2, Aristotle believes that every form of communal life develops some form of justice. When he reminds us that we are seeking both unqualified and political justice, he is reminding us that we will not find unqualified justice, whatever it may be, outside of the form of justice characteristic of political communities.[10]

What is the point of identifying "unqualified justice" with "political justice"? Clearly, Aristotle does not mean to suggest that political standards of justice are inherently or unqualifiedly correct standards. After all, in the section that immediately follows these remarks he insists that conventional right, which is made up of standards of justice founded on social agreement rather than correct judgment (*NE* 1134b18), makes up a large part of political justice. If Aristotle identifies unqualified justice with political justice, then the term must mean to him something other than absolute or unqualifiedly correct standards.

I suggest, instead, that when Aristotle identifies the two concepts, he is reminding us that when we citizens speak of justice without qualifying the term by referring to the form of communal justice we have in mind, we are referring to the form of mutual accountability that develops among members of political communities or, in other words, to political justice. Rather than a reminder of the difference between political and inherently correct standards of justice, Aristotle's remarks are a reminder about the specific kind of communal ties that citizens assume when they speak about justice.

The construal of Aristotle's phrase "unqualified [*haplōs*] justice" as "inherently correct justice," a construal encouraged by translators who render the phrase as "absolute justice,"[11] seriously distorts Aristotle's meaning here. Indeed, it is a mistake to speak at all of a distinct Aristotelian concept of "*haplōs* justice." *Haplōs*, as Aristotle makes clear in his *Refutations of the Sophists* (167a), is a term we employ to indicate

---

10. As Max Salomon (*Der Begriff der Gerechtigkeit*, 45) and Eric Voegelin (*Anamnesis*, 58) point out, had Aristotle devoted more attention to the qualified forms of justice that develop among members of domestic and despotic communities, it would be much harder to miss this identification of political with unqualified justice.

11. For example, Horace Rackham in his translation of the *Nicomachean Ethics* for the Loeb Classical Library series (291). Translators of the *Politics* have been particularly inclined to translate *haplōs* as "absolute." See the translations by Ernest Barker for Oxford (112), Rackham for the Loeb Library (247), and Sinclair and Saunders for Penguin (189). Carnes Lord's translation of the *Politics* for Chicago is a rare exception.

Political Justice 135

what we mean by a term when we use it without qualifying it in any way. The meaning of *haplōs* in any particular expression is, accordingly, highly contextual, since it is derived from the particular qualifications it excludes in any particular context. The meaning of the expression "unqualified justice" will, accordingly, vary with reference to the kinds of qualifications it is used to exclude.

Arguments, Aristotle notes, often "turn on whether an expression is used in a certain respect or used 'without qualification' [*haplōs*]" (*Refutations* 167a). He suggests, for example, that we would ordinarily describe an Ethiopian as black without qualifying our description by noting that his teeth are white. The sophist can take advantage of this ambiguity between our qualified and unqualified use of key terms, at least in less obvious cases, to lead us into contradiction, to prove that we are claiming that something is both black and white. Because there is no sense in which an Ethiopian is "absolutely" black, it is clear that Aristotle uses the term *haplōs* to characterize the way in which we describe things without specific qualifications. The Ethiopian is *haplōs* or unqualifiedly black because when we describe the color of people without any qualification, we are ordinarily referring to the color of their skin, not the color of their teeth (*Refutations* 167a).

Similarly, when we describe justice without any qualification, we are referring to justice as we ordinarily talk about it without making any further qualifications. The relevant context of qualification in the passage we have been discussing concerns the differences among various communal forms of justice, as Aristotle makes clear by immediately contrasting political justice with the forms of justice found in domestic and other nonpolitical communities. Thus, when Aristotle reminds that we are seeking both unqualified and political justice, he is reminding us that when we speak of justice without qualifying the term by a reference to the kind of community we have in mind, we are assuming the form of mutual accountability characteristic of political communities. The ideas about justice developed before this reminder—the concepts of general, distributive, and corrective justice, for example—all assume the communal ties characteristic of the practice of political justice.

As discussed in chapter 2, Aristotle's concept of political justice refers both to a particular way of determining and enforcing the mutual obligations that bind citizens and to the particular forms these obligations take. Political justice develops among "people who have an equal [i.e., proportionately equal] share in ruling and being ruled" (*NE*

1134b10). It involves, among other things, public deliberation about correct standards of justice and the establishment of general rules governing the regular alternation of positions of power.

Once we recognize that political justice represents the form of mutual accountability that is appropriate to govern the relations of free and relatively equal individuals, we are faced with an important question. What makes political justice the appropriate or just form of the practice of social justice in these circumstances? I suggest that we look to Aristotle's concept of reciprocity for an answer, since Aristotle does explicitly describe reciprocity as the ground of political justice.[12]

> In communities of exchange this sort of justice [reciprocity] does hold men together.... For it is the reciprocal return of what is proportional that holds cities together.... Men seek to return either evil for evil—and if they cannot do so, think their position mere slavery—or good for good, and if they cannot do so there is no exchange.
>
> (NE 1132b31–40)

In what way does reciprocity "hold cities together?" Aristotle suggests an answer to this question in book 2 of the *Politics*, where he repeats and elaborates on this claim about reciprocity. "It is thus reciprocal equality that preserves cities, as was already noted in the *Ethics*.... For all cannot rule at the same time, but each rules for a year or according to some other arrangement or period of time. In this way, then, it results that all rule, just as if shoemakers and carpenters were to exchange places rather than the same persons always being shoemakers and carpenters" (*Pol.* 1261a 30). Reciprocity, it seems, "holds cities together" by disposing us to take turns in ruling and thereby to engage in the practices associated with political justice. Likewise, it disposes us, in general, to return, and expect the return of, a good for a good and an evil for an evil. Aristotle notes that in popular opinion, as well as according to Pythagorean philosophers, justice as a whole is often identified with reciprocity (*NE* 1132b21). (The same general idea is expressed in our culture by the biblical injunction to take an eye for an eye.) He then proceeds to reduce the scope of reciprocity, suggesting that it provides the necessary foundation for the exchange of goods and for political community.

One reason that commentators have neglected the political impor-

---

12. Few commentators notice this description of reciprocity as the foundation of political justice. For an interesting exception, see F. Rosen, "The Political Context," 237–39.

tance of Aristotle's concept of reciprocity is that he devotes most of his attention here to its role in grounding the exchange of goods. Another reason, a reason that we have considered extensively in earlier chapters, is that commentators tend to exalt Aristotle's view of political community to the point where they cannot recognize the common ground shared by Aristotle's concepts of political and exchange community. But as argued in chapters 1 and 2, economic exchanges and political community belong for Aristotle to the same form of communal life: instrumental or mutual advantage community. It is thus not so surprising that he develops the legitimating ground of political justice in the course of examining the sense of justice that supports the exchange of goods.

When Aristotle argues that a sense of reciprocity holds together mutual advantage communities (such as exchange or political communities), he is suggesting that these communities cannot be maintained if its members do not share a sense that the good that they provide for others will be returned in some form or that the evil that others do them can be returned in some way. He is not, of course, suggesting that members of exchange or political communities must be disinclined to fool each other about what constitutes an appropriate return of good or evil. He is merely suggesting that without a sense that the good we offer others will in some way be returned by them, we are unlikely to form with them instrumental or mutual advantage communities.[13]

Defined in this way, reciprocity represents the form of justice that corresponds to the instrumental or mutual advantage form of friendship discussed in chapter 1. As with that form of friendship, it is a concept that cuts across familiar dichotomies between self-serving and other-regarding actions. By insisting that a sense of reciprocity is necessary even to the exchange of goods, Aristotle is reminding us of the ways in which even the most self-serving forms of social interaction depend on shared moral sentiments. Even those who seek to cheat their partners in the exchange of goods are compelled by the shared sense of reciprocity that grounds exchange to portray their efforts, however falsely, as a "good deal" for their partners. To do otherwise would be to act as

13. Although Aristotle introduces reciprocity immediately following his discussion of fairness in distributive and corrective justice, it is important to distinguish his concept of reciprocity from his concept of fairness. As I argue below, fairness, for Aristotle, involves a disposition to adhere to or restore determinate standards of proportionate merit. Reciprocity, in contrast, requires no determinate standard of proportionate merit; it merely requires a disposition to make a return for a good received. See D. G. Ritchie, "Aristotle's Subdivisions of 'Particular Justice,'" 189, for conclusive arguments against treating reciprocity as a part of fairness.

if their partners could return no evil for the evil done to them, a situation that, Aristotle notes, most individuals identify with "mere slavery" (*NE* 1132b40).

This remark about reciprocity and slavery clearly indicates how Aristotle answers questions about when a sense of reciprocity is an appropriate disposition. We owe reciprocity, according to Aristotle, to the individuals who are by nature our relative equals and with whom we interact in order to seek our mutual advantage. Reciprocity is not the appropriate disposition to guide our interactions with natural unequals—as we implicitly acknowledge in our treatment of animals—or with individuals with whom we associate for purposes other than mutual advantage. Political community, as a mutual advantage community of free and relatively equal individuals, clearly rests on this sense of reciprocal justice. Nonpolitical communities (such as the family), which are based for Aristotle on natural inequalities or motives other than mutual advantage, are not held together in the same way by a sense of reciprocity.

Among free and relatively equal individuals, taking turns in ruling and being ruled, as well as political justice in general, "accords with nature" (*Pol.* 1279a10, 1259b1) because any other arrangement treats individuals as mere slaves, completely incapable of requiting evil to the powerful individuals who harm them (*NE* 1132b40). This is not to suggest that reciprocity requires any particular set of constitutional rules governing the proportionate distribution of power. Nor am I suggesting that, for Aristotle, a shared sense of reciprocity keeps people from developing and acting on exaggerated expectations of the political good they have coming to them. As with the exchange of goods, political reciprocity does not set the standards or proportions by which goods are distributed. It determines only that *some* proportion must be established and justified before citizens can share the pursuit of mutual advantage made possible by the political community. Citizens may disagree about the correctness of these standards. A sense of reciprocity merely ensures that some standard of proportionate merit must be offered, a standard that will claim, at least, to prove that relatively disempowered individuals are receiving an important good in return for a smaller share in political rule. Such standards, like the offers of a "good deal" made in economic exchanges, may often amount to something of a swindle. Nevertheless, the fact that even swindles have to be proposed in the language of a reciprocal return of goods points to an important sense of justice that grounds both political and exchange communities.

Although Aristotle relies on a sense of reciprocity rather than a sense of natural right to justify the practice of political justice, the standards he invokes to guide our judgments about reciprocity are couched in the language of nature. Indeed, all of the passages in which Aristotle refers unambiguously to nature as a standard for assessing the justice of social relationships refer to the standards of inclusion in the practices of political justice rather than to the standards chosen by citizens themselves.

Aristotle describes four basic relationships among human beings as just by nature: the despotic rule of masters over slaves; the superiority of human males over human females; the rule of mature individuals over the young; and the sharing of political rule, regulated by laws, among free and relatively equal males. Slavery is just by nature rather than merely by law or force wherever there exists between individuals "such a difference as that between soul and body, or between men and animals.... [H]e who participates in reason enough to apprehend it, but does not have it, is a slave by nature" (*Pol.* 1254b15–25).[14] Aristotle argues that the domination of women by men—though in a less complete form than the rule of slaves by masters—is also natural because women lack the natural capacities for rational deliberation possessed by men (*Pol.* 1260a). He makes little effort to justify the rule of adults over children, since he assumes that everyone readily accepts the relevance of physical and mental maturity to the distribution of power. Finally, Aristotle claims that among free and relatively equal males, taking turns in ruling and being ruled "accords with nature" (*Pol.* 1279a10, 1259b1). This claim further implies that it is also natural for these individuals to live in political communities and share the bonds created by political justice.

Most of us continue to make similar judgments about natural qualifications for political life, even if we choose different boundaries of inclusion and exclusion. Almost all of us accept the relevance to participation in political deliberation of Aristotle's distinction between the natural capacities of young and mature individuals. Most of us reject his claims about women's lack of capacity to participate in political community, but we do so only because most of us reject his claim that women are by nature deformed or imperfectly developed males. Most

---

14 This does not mean, however, that Aristotle is condemning as unjust the bulk of the Greek practice of slavery. The Greek debate about the naturalness of slavery concerned whether nature or convention justified slavery, not whether or not it was justifiable. Those who described slavery as contrary to nature had no trouble in justifying the practice by convention. See Y. Garlan, *Slavery in Ancient Greece,* 126; R. Mulgan, *Aristotle's Political Theory,* 23–24.

of us also reject Aristotle's claims that there exist large numbers of individuals naturally suited to enslavement (although we do withhold full political rights from those we deem mentally incompetent). But we do so precisely because most of us insist that the natural differences among healthy human beings fall well short of the tremendous gap Aristotle requires as a justification for natural slavery.[15]

Although reciprocity provides Aristotle with a natural standard for inclusion in the political community and the practice of political justice, it does not provide him with a natural standard for measuring the justice of the decisions made by the individuals who participate in political justice. Aristotle's natural standard of reciprocity merely determines that some form of political justice be established among the group of individuals naturally capable of fully engaging in personal and public deliberation. It does not tell us what choices these individuals should make.

Because Aristotle both grounds political justice in a natural standard of reciprocity and insists on dividing political justice into natural and conventional right, it is not surprising that most commentators conclude that he is looking for natural standards against which to measure the choices made by individuals who participate in political justice. But, as I argue in the following section, this conclusion is based on a misreading of Aristotle's distinction between natural and conventional right.

## NATURAL AND CONVENTIONAL RIGHT

Compared to the weighty tomes on natural law produced by his successors, Aristotle's discussion of natural and conventional right—which occupies little more than a page of the *Nicomachean Ethics*—seems amazingly brief and compressed. Nevertheless, these few sentences have inspired commentators to celebrate Aristotle as "the philosophic founder of authentic natural law," for whom natural right represents "the eternal laws of morality" and an "immutable" standard of justice whose

---

15. We tend to draw the natural line of inclusion in political community at the boundary of our species. It is easy for us to do so since there is a relatively sharp—though not nearly as sharp as once believed—distinction between our capacities and the capacities of the species closest to us. But, as Stephen Jay Gould reminds us, there is no natural necessity for that distinction to be so clear. It is easy to imagine an evolutionary scenario in which there developed numerous species that would possess capacities midway between ours and the apes'. Had such an evolutionary scenario unfolded, judgment about the natural capacities appropriate for participation in political community, a judgment we now make easily without much conscious reflection, would become much more complex and difficult to make. See S. J. Gould, *The Mismeasure of Man*, 322–23; S. J. Gould, "Human Equality," 197–98.

superiority to all mere opinion and positive law is "self-evident" and "absolute."[16]

In chapter 2 I offered a very different interpretation of Aristotle's concept of natural right. I suggested there that Aristotle views natural and conventional right as two *kinds* of judgment about justice that normally emerge in political life, rather than as two competing *standards* against which to measure the justice of our judgments. In this section I defend and elaborate on this relatively unfamiliar interpretation of Aristotle's concept of natural right.[17] I try to show that far from providing a higher standard against which to measure the justice of political choices, this concept forcefully expresses Aristotle's understanding of the indeterminate and open-ended nature of the standards of justice invoked by members of political communities.

Aristotle makes three general claims about natural right in this short section of the *Nicomachean Ethics*. First, he describes natural right as part of political justice. Second, he insists that contrary to what "some people" believe, justice exists "by nature" (*phusei*) as well as "by convention and agreement" (*nomikon kai sunthēkē*) (*NE* 1134b24–32). Finally, he suggests that natural right is as mutable as conventional right (*NE* 1134b33). By admitting the mutability of natural right, Aristotle defuses his predecessors' strongest objection to the naturalness of justice: the fact that standards of justice, unlike natural things, differ from place to place and time to time. But this admission makes it much more difficult to determine exactly what Aristotle means by "natural right."

Our interpretation of Aristotle's concept of natural right depends on how we put together these three claims. The most common interpretation identifies Aristotelian natural right with the Stoic, Scholastic, and rationalist conceptions of natural law, all of which treat natural law as an eternal, universal, and unchanging standard of justice. But to maintain this interpretation, one must either ignore Aristotle's claim about the mutability of natural right or gloss it in some way to make it compatible with an unchanging standard of justice. Thomas Aquinas, who identifies Aristotle's conception of natural right with his own concep-

---

16. The quotations are taken from P. Trude, *Der Begriff der Gerechtigkeit*, 177; E. Barker, *The Political Thought*, 326; W. von Leyden, *Aristotle on Equality and Justice*, 74; W. Siegfried, *Der Rechtsgedanke bei Aristoteles*, 57, 62. A much smaller number of commentators have denied that this brief passage of the *Nicomachean Ethics* develops the idea of a final, inherently correct standard of justice. See, for example, F. Wormuth, "Aristotle on Law"; M. Salomon, *Der Begriff der Gerechtigkeit*, 50–72; J. Ritter, "Naturrecht bei Aristoteles," in *Metaphysik und Politik*, 133–79.

17. I develop this interpretation of Aristotelian natural right at greater length in "Natural Right and Aristotle's Understanding of Justice."

tion of an eternal and immutable natural law, provides the most familiar example of such a gloss. He suggests that Aristotle meant only to say that the particular rules through which human beings apply the unchanging fundamental principles of natural right may vary.[18]

These glosses on Aristotle's explicit argument become especially hard to accept when we recognize that Aristotle insists not only that natural right is changeable but that natural and conventional right are "both *equally* changeable" (*amphō kinēta homoios*) (NE 1134b33; my emphasis).[19] Mutability does not refer merely to exceptions or qualifications added to an ordinarily unchanging standard of natural right. It characterizes natural right as a whole and thus plays *no* role in distinguishing natural from conventional right in the *Nicomachean Ethics*.

To make sense of Aristotle's description of a wholly mutable natural right, I suggest that we turn our attention, momentarily, to its counterpart, conventional right. Few commentators devote much attention to the way in which Aristotle defines conventional right. They seem to assume that he means by it much the same thing that we usually mean by conventional justice: the body of commonly recognized agreements and opinions about appropriate standards of justice. Given this understanding of conventional right, it seems logical to treat the concept of natural right that Aristotle opposes to it as the body of intrinsically correct standards against which we measure the justice of the standards asserted by common agreement and opinion.

But conventional right, as Aristotle defines it here, does not refer to the *whole* range of opinions and agreements that individuals and communities use to define legal standards of justice. It represents a far narrower and more specific set of standards: "Conventional right, however, concerns that which is originally indifferent, but once it has been laid down is not indifferent, for example, that a prisoner's ransom shall be one mina, or that a goat and not two sheep should be sacrificed" (NE 1134b18–23).

18. T. Aquinas, *Commentary on the Nicomachean Ethics*, pars. 1017–18. Harry Jaffa clearly demonstrates the extent to which Aquinas's interpretation goes beyond Aristotle's understanding of natural right; see H. Jaffa, *Thomism and Aristotelianism*, 174–82. See also W. von Leyden, *Aristotle on Justice and Equality*, 72, and A. MacIntyre, *Whose Justice? Which Rationality?*, 120, for interpretations similar to Aquinas's. Other commentators have suggested that Aristotle's best regime, which Aristotle does describe here as "the best everywhere by nature" (NE 1135a5), provides us with an unchanging standard of natural right, but one that must be applied in different ways to different situations. For example, see D. Keyt, "Distributive Justice," 32; M. Hamburger, *Morals and Law*, 62; and the works discussed in the last section of this chapter.

19. One might alternatively translate the transliterated passage "*amphō kinēta homoios*" as "both changeable in a similar way."

Aristotelian conventional right refers only to the justice of actions about which we would be indifferent were it not for a prior agreement. We see no intrinsic merit in, say, sacrificing one goat to the gods rather than two sheep, or driving on the left rather than the right side of the road. But once we agree to fix the rules of sacrifices and driving, then we speak of the injustice of those who make the wrong sacrifice or drive on the wrong side of the road. Aristotle uses conventional right to designate a kind of standard of mutual obligation that reflects no judgment about the intrinsic merits of the actions it requires. Conventional right thus concerns those actions whose justice or injustice it is appropriate to determine by the mere fact of social agreement rather than by an exercise of political judgment.

Because conventional right, defined in this way, clearly excludes the majority of the opinions, laws, and customs we use to establish positive standards of justice, it cannot possibly represent the standards of justice asserted by positive law and opinion. We are hardly indifferent about the kinds of actions prescribed and proscribed, for example, by criminal law. Nor are we indifferent about the political questions settled by constitutional law. Because Aristotle divides political justice into natural and conventional right, and our judgments on these matters do not fit into the category of conventional right, it seems that we must treat them as part of natural right. Accordingly, we must conclude that Aristotelian natural right includes all of our judgments about the justice of the actions about which mature and relatively reasonable individuals would not be indifferent. And if it includes *all* of these judgments, then it cannot possibly represent the inherently correct standard against which we measure the justice of particular actions and states of affairs. Ironically, Aristotle's distinction between natural and conventional right "is the strongest evidence that he had no conception of a natural law that annuls positive law."[20]

Aristotle himself never suggests in this passage that natural and conventional right represent two competing *standards* of adjudication. He provides us with no examples of cases where conventional and natural standards of justice conflict, which we would expect him to do if he thought of them as higher and lower standards. He does not say, for example, that no matter what people do or believe, it is by nature right to return prisoners for ransom. Instead, he merely says that the amount

---

20. F. Wormuth, "Aristotle on Law," 24. See also M. Salomon, *Der Begriff der Gerechtigkeit*, 52–54.

of a ransom is, in itself, a matter of indifference to be settled by prior agreement or custom, and thus a matter of conventional right (*NE* 1134b21). We find no challenge of conventional right by the standards of natural right in the *Nicomachean Ethics,* let alone advice about how we might "raise" conventional standards toward natural standards.[21]

Indeed, in *Refutations of the Sophists* (173a6–19) Aristotle goes so far as to condemn the use of nature-convention antitheses as a means of evaluating arguments. Such antitheses, he suggests, generate merely the kind of self-serving paradoxes that sophists manipulate to win arguments. That is, in fact, precisely how Aristotle treats appeals to higher natural standards of justice in the *Rhetoric.* "If the written law tells against our case, clearly we must appeal," he advises us, "to the universal law and equity as most just. . . . We must urge that the principles of equity are eternal and unchanging, while written laws frequently change." We should refer to "the lines in Sophocles' *Antigone* about the eternal, unwritten law" and argue that "the better man will follow and abide by the unwritten law in preference to the written." "If, however, the written law supports our case, we must urge" the judges against "trying to be cleverer than the laws" by referring to some unwritten, superior standard of justice (*Rhet.* 1375a26–1375b25).[22]

For these reasons, I suggest that it is better to think of Aristotelian natural and conventional right as two *kinds* of justice found in the political community rather than as higher and lower *standards* of adjudication. According to this interpretation, Aristotle tells us in the *Nicomachean Ethics* that we will find two different kinds of justice in political communities. One, conventional right, derives its justice from agreements to designate as just or unjust actions about which we would otherwise be indifferent. The other, natural right, derives its justice from judgments about the appropriate obligations to impose on members of political communities in particular situations. In the issues that involve natural right, we reflect on the merits of different standards, for we are concerned to see these issues resolved correctly. In the issues that involve conventional right, we look only to social agreement, for we are merely concerned to see that everyone follow the same standard, whatever it may be.

My interpretation is confirmed by Aristotle's suggestion that "it is

---

21. M. Salomon, *Der Begriff der Gerechtigkeit,* 52; J. Ritter, "Naturrecht bei Aristoteles," 149.
22. Aristotle offers no advice to jurors about how to judge such arguments, although he is quite free with advice to jurors on other topics. In one instance Aristotle tells them, interestingly enough, to stick very close to the letter of the law (*Rhetoric* 1354b).

clear [*dēlon*] what things are just by nature and what by convention and agreement" (*NE* 1134b32). This would be a very strange claim for him to make if he conceived of natural right as the inherently correct measure of justice,[23] for it would imply that it is easy to distinguish inherently correct standards of judgment from the innumerable incorrect and only partly correct standards we come across in our lives. But Aristotle insists, on the contrary, that knowing how to act justly is very difficult (*NE* 1137a10). It is easy, according to Aristotle, to distinguish between naturally and conventionally just things because in order to do so we need merely distinguish issues whose intrinsic merits do not concern us. It takes little skill or experience to distinguish issues such as the number of animals to sacrifice or the proper side of the road for driving from issues whose intrinsic merits do concern us, such as whether and how to punish theft or distribute political power.

This comment about how easy it is to distinguish between natural and conventional right would be especially strange if, as Leo Strauss and other commentators have argued, natural right represents for Aristotle the one inherently correct judgment in a particular situation, rather than a general norm or rule.[24] In that case Aristotle would be suggesting that the correct exercise of practical reason in particular situations would be easy, something he clearly denies (*NE* 1109a28). Moreover, the difficulty of discerning the correct action in any particular situation is something that Strauss and other supporters of this interpretation strongly emphasize.[25]

Among the other passages that commentators have used to support the traditional interpretation of Aristotelian natural right as an intrinsically correct standard of judgment, the most striking are the passages in the *Rhetoric* that mention a "common," "unwritten," "unchanging" standard of right called "natural law" (*Rhet.* 1373b6, 1375b31).[26] Ac-

---

23. So strange, indeed, that at least one translator suggests that Aristotle must have meant to say "though it is *not* easy [*ou dēlon*]" to distinguish the naturally and conventionally just things. See Aristotle, *Nicomachean Ethics*, translated by H. Rackham, 296 note a.
24. See L. Strauss, *Natural Right and History*, 156–63; for a similar view, see D. Schroeder, "Aristotle on Law." Martha Nussbaum also argues that natural right is not grounded in general rules, but she severs its direct connection to nature by grounding its judgments in "some conditions of broad reflective equilibrium"; M. Nussbaum, *Aristotle's "De Motu Animalium,"* 212. Such interpretations appear to offer a much more promising means of reconciling Aristotle's major claims about natural right in that they make room for its inherent mutability.
25. L. Strauss, *Natural Right and History*, 160–61.
26. René Gauthier and Jean Jolif, for example, list the following Aristotelian expressions as synonyms for natural right: "primary [*to proton*] justice" (*NE* 1136b34); "pure and simple [*to haplōs*] justice" (*Refutations of the Sophists* 180b34); "the universal, un-

cording to many commentators, the *Rhetoric* "leaves no doubt" that Aristotle believes in the existence of a natural and absolutely correct standard of justice.[27] I suggest, on the contrary, that Aristotle's reference to natural law in the *Rhetoric* should raise many questions and doubts—most of all because it plainly contradicts his account of natural right in the *Nicomachean Ethics*. That account leaves no room for an "unchanging" law of nature, since, as we have seen, it treats natural and conventional right as "equally changeable."

Moreover, the *Rhetoric* is a work about means of persuasion rather than an inquiry into the good for human beings. It "is not an *Ethics*," as Max Salomon reminds us; "it strives for universal comprehension" rather than knowledge of the good.[28] Aristotle defines rhetoric as "the capacity of observing in any case the available means of persuasion" (*Rhet.* 1355b26; cf. *Topics* 101b8). As such, it "must rest its modes of persuasion and argument on common opinions [*ton koinon*], as we observed in the *Topics*" (*Rhet.* 1355a27). In the *Topics* Aristotle explains that the starting points for dialectic and rhetorical argument are "reputable opinions," which include those opinions advanced "by everyone, or by the majority, or by the wise" (*Topics* 100b20). We learn how to argue and persuade others by learning how to make use of the principles embedded in the opinions that people generally respect. The notion that there is an unchanging "natural law" common to all human beings is something that "everyone to some extent divines" and is confirmed by wise men such as Sophocles and Empedocles (*Rhet.* 1373b6). It is thus very much available as a basis on which to build persuasive arguments. In the context of the *Rhetoric* that is all we need conclude that Aristotle is saying about natural law.

I am not suggesting, however, that Aristotle simply dismisses the notion of natural law because it is a mere opinion. As we have seen, Aristotle has great respect for the reputable opinions of the many and wise. All of these opinions contain a certain element of truth, for "the truth seems to be like the proverbial door, which no one can fail to hit" (*Metaphysics* 993b1). But since Aristotle is teaching the art of persua-

---

written [*koinon, agraphon*] law" (*Rhet.* 1368b7); and "the universal law based on nature" (*Rhet.* 1373b6). See R. Gauthier and J. Jolif, *L'Éthique à Nicomaque* 2:391. I reserve comment on Aristotle's account of equity and "unwritten law" for chapter 6.

27. E. Michelkakis, "Das Naturrecht bei Aristoteles," 146. In addition to Gauthier and Jolif, others who draw similar conclusions from the *Rhetoric*'s reference to natural law include W. von Leyden, *Aristotle on Justice and Equality*, 84; M. Hamburger, *Morals and Law*, 65; P. Trude, *Der Begriff der Gerechtigkeit*, 155n121.

28. M. Salomon, *Der Begriff der Gerechtigkeit*, 61–62.

Political Justice 147

sion rather than seeking truth in the *Rhetoric* and the *Topics,* he makes no effort to sift and refine the reputable opinions with which these works begin; indeed, to do so would be counterproductive. In the *Nicomachean Ethics,* as in most of his other works, Aristotle makes this effort.[29] Consequently, we should take Aristotle's statements in the *Rhetoric* about natural law and the unchanging common standard of justice it contains as unrefined opinions of the many and of some wise men. The account of natural right in the *Nicomachean Ethics* book 5, chapter 7 shows us how Aristotle refines the familiar opinions about natural law quoted in the *Rhetoric.*

What then is "natural" about Aristotelian natural right if not the existence of intrinsically just states of affairs defined by the nature of things? Natural right is natural in the same way that the political community is natural. Nature neither provides us with determinate standards of political justice nor disposes us to act justly. But it does dispose us to form political communities and to hold each other accountable to the kind of standards of obligation that Aristotle associates with judgments of natural right.

"Natural things either always or for the most part come about in a particular way" (*Physics* 198b35). When Aristotle insists that a part of political justice exists by nature, he is suggesting that when free and relatively equal individuals come together to form a political community, they will, "for the most part," have recourse to the particular kind of judgment that Aristotle calls natural right. Moreover, judgments about natural right, like the political community itself, reflect and develop the highest practical capacity nature gives to human beings: their capacity to receive the training that promotes moral virtue and practical wisdom.[30] Natural right is thus natural for Aristotle both in its origin and end.

Aristotle uses this argument about natural right to refute the claim, associated with the Sophists, that "fine and just actions possess so much variety and irregularity that they ... exist by convention only, and not by nature" (*NE* 1094b14).[31] But he does so, as we have seen, only by altering the familiar understanding—in his time as well as ours—of natural and conventional right as competing standards of adjudication.

29. For a discussion of this aspect of Aristotelian method, see G. E. L. Owen, "Tithēnai ta phenomena"; M. Nussbaum, *The Fragility of Goodness,* 240–63.
30. In book 2 of the *Nicomachean Ethics* Aristotle denies that the virtues are natural capacities of human beings. They require training and moral education in order to develop. Human beings, however, do have by nature the capacity to provide and receive the training that promotes the development of the virtues. See *NE* 1103a14–25.
31. On these claims, see F. Heinimann, *Nomos und Phusis.*

It might seem strange that Aristotle reformulates the nature-convention distinction in a manner that differs so sharply from the way in which it was popularized by Greek philosophers and orators. But, as we have seen, it is Aristotle's normal practice to acknowledge and then refine the opinions of the many and the wise on any particular subject. Every reputable opinion, he suggests, "says something true about the nature of things, and while individually they contribute little or nothing to the truth, by the union of all a considerable amount is amassed" (*Metaphysics* 993b1). Aristotle amasses truth in book 5 of the *Nicomachean Ethics* by distinguishing the partial truth from the errors contained in a great number of conflicting opinions about justice.

His discussion of reciprocity represents a good example of his methodological approach to truth and opinion. Aristotle severely curtails the popular and philosophic opinion that identifies reciprocity as the foundation of all acts of justice. As discussed above, he reduces it to the disposition that makes possible the exchange of material goods and political office (*NE* 1132b21). Such a reduction of the scope of reciprocity revises familiar Greek opinions in as severe a manner as would a contemporary theory of justice that suggested that the real meaning of the biblical injunction to seek "an eye for an eye" is "seek ye a good price for your goods."

Aristotle's revision of familiar opinions about natural right is no greater than this revision of widely shared opinions about reciprocity. But since few contemporary philosophers or political theorists continue to be as beholden to Pythagorean conceptions of justice as they are to the idea of an intrinsically correct standard of justice, Aristotle's reformulation of reciprocity does not strike them as odd as does this reformulation of the distinction between natural and conventional right.

According to the view held by most scholars, Aristotelian legislators should aim at a particular naturally just state of affairs when choosing laws. In the *Topics* Aristotle insists, on the contrary, that the common opinion that "law is the measure or image of the things that are by nature just" is neither literally nor metaphorically true. "Such phrases," he suggests, "are worse than metaphor." A metaphor makes use of a similarity between an object of description and something else to make the object familiar and comprehensible to us. But "there is no likeness in virtue of which the law is a measure or image. An image is something produced by imitation, and this is not found in the case of the law" (*Topics* 140a7–15). If we describe law as an image or imitation of natural right, we are seriously misrepresenting it, Aristotle suggests here.

Aristotle recognizes no determinate standard or state of affairs, in the natural order or anywhere else, for law to imitate.[32]

In the end, Aristotle offers two important arguments about the relationship between nature and political justice. In the first, he claims that nature has equipped the human species with capacities that dispose us to form political communities in which we hold each other accountable to the kind of standards Aristotle calls natural right. In the second, he claims that natural distinctions of gender, age, and mental capacity allow us to determine that free adult males are the members of the human species so equipped to engage in these judgments. Nothing, however, in this natural standard provides us with the means to measure the justice of the judgments about political justice made by members of political communities (except, perhaps, those judgments that might violate the natural standards of reciprocity governing inclusion in the practice of political justice). Nature thus tells Aristotle *who* can participate in deliberation about political justice but *not what* they should choose. There are natural standards governing the framework of political justice and membership in the political community, but no natural standards against which to measure the justice of members' decisions and actions.[33]

## THE SUBJECT OF JUSTICE

Aristotle's discussions of political and reciprocal justice do not occur until the middle of his general account of justice in *Nicomachean Ethics* book 5. I have dealt with them before considering the opening sections of the book because Aristotle introduces the concept of political justice in a way that suggests that the concepts discussed in those sections are associated with the political form of justice rather than some abstract and hypothetical generic form of justice among dissociated individuals. In other words, his opening distinction between a general and particular virtue of justice (lawfulness and fairness) reflects, in some way, the bonds of political community and the practice of political justice.

---

32. Moreover, Aristotle is not suggesting here that law *should be,* but usually is not, an image of what is naturally just. If this were his meaning, then it would make no sense to denounce the claim as "worse than metaphor," for the metaphor would be quite accurate with regard to well-framed laws, if not with regard to all laws. Aristotle would then merely have to qualify the statement in order to make it useful. Instead, Aristotle uses the statement to illustrate the kind of misrepresentation that goes beyond that found in a bad or unrefined metaphor.

33. Charles Taylor makes a similar distinction in his account of an Aristotelian understanding of justice in "The Nature and Scope of Distributive Justice."

Once we recognize the political foundation of Aristotle's account of justice, it becomes much easier to integrate his more unfamiliar concepts into a coherent understanding of justice. I have begun to do so with his usually ignored concepts of political and reciprocal justice. In the following sections I continue to reconstruct this understanding by returning to the beginning of book 5 in order to consider Aristotle's general characterization of justice as a virtue of character and his concept of "general" as opposed to distributive justice.

Although Aristotle presents his most systematic discussion of justice as part of his account of the character virtues that support a good life, few scholars see much importance in his decision to associate justice primarily with a state of character rather than with some state of affairs, such as a body of institutions or social relations.[34] Because most modern moral and political philosophers think of justice and injustice primarily as descriptions of states of affairs, they tend to attribute this opinion to Aristotle as well. Moreover, this understanding of justice fits much better with the normal model's portrayal of justice as a body of fundamental norms ordering the affairs of a community than does a character-centered understanding of justice. As a result, to the extent that modern commentators think that Aristotle, like themselves, strives to build a normal model of justice, they tend to disregard his emphasis on justice as a virtue of character in favor of an understanding of justice as, primarily, a state of social affairs.

John Rawls, for example, admits that his understanding of the subject of justice as a set of principles defining basic social institutions seems to conflict with an older philosophic tradition, going back to Aristotle, that identifies justice with "permanent elements of . . . character." But he immediately denies the importance of this difference by asserting that, strictly speaking, the Aristotelian subject of justice is no different from his own.

> Aristotle's definition clearly presupposes, however, an account of what properly belongs to a person and of what is due to him. Now such entitlements are, I believe, very often derived from social institutions and the legitimate expectations to which they give rise. There is no reason to think that Aristotle would disagree with this, and certainly he has a conception of social justice to account for these claims. The definition I adopt is designed to

---

34. For exceptions, see M. W. Jackson, *Matters of Justice*; D. O'Connor, "Aristotelian Justice as a Personal Virtue." Jackson offers an extended critique of modern philosophers' tendency to ignore "personal justice," that is, just character.

apply directly to the most important case, the justice of the basic structure. There is no conflict with the traditional notion.[35]

Unfortunately, as Hugo Bedau notes, Rawls "cites virtually nothing from Aristotle to support this claim" about the Aristotelian understanding of justice.[36] In effect, Rawls, like the majority of contemporary philosophers, assumes that the nature of the primary subject of justice is either self-evident or can easily be settled by reference to ordinary usage. If Aristotle speaks of both a character virtue and states of affairs as justice, he clearly must mean to derive the former from the latter. This conclusion, however, is neither self-evident nor easily settled by common usage.

Consider the following descriptions of the subject of justice by two English political philosophers—David Miller and J. R. Lucas, respectively—descriptions published within five years of each other by the same English press:

> We talk of just men, just actions, and just states of affairs. But the last of these uses must be regarded as the primary one, for when we describe a man as just we mean that he usually attempts to act in such a way that a just state of affairs results.... If we did not have independent criteria for assuming the justice of states of affairs, we could not describe men as just and unjust.[37]

> Although other things—laws, particular decisions, general economic arrangements and particular payments—can rightly be described as just or unjust, these are derivative uses, deriving from the man in a just frame of mind and the laws he would enact, the decisions he would take, the economic arrangements he would approve of and the particular payments he would make.[38]

Contemporary American analyses of justice reflect the same disagreement about the primary subject of justice, even though the predominant understanding focuses on states of affairs. William Galston, for example, affirms Miller's emphasis on states of affairs the proper "point of departure" for a theory of justice. (Indeed, he attributes this opinion, incorrectly, in my judgment, to Aristotle.) Friedrich Hayek, in contrast, is well known for his claim that "strictly speaking only human conduct can be called just or unjust" and that the designation of states of affairs as just or unjust represents a "category mistake."[39] So much for com-

35. J. Rawls, *A Theory of Justice*, 10–11.
36. H. Bedau, "Social Justice and Social Institutions," 159.
37. D. Miller, *Social Justice*, 17–18.
38. J. R. Lucas, *On Justice*, 6.
39. See W. Galston, *Justice and the Human Good*, 100; F. Hayek, *Law, Legislation and Liberty* 2:31.

mon usage as a means of settling the issue of the primary subject of justice.

Clearly, the designation of the primary subject of justice involves a substantive, if usually ignored, moral problem rather than a mere linguistic or semantic difficulty.[40] Justice differs from the other moral virtues that Aristotle discusses in that we regularly use it to describe states of affairs as well as states of character. We speak of just institutions and communities as well as of just individuals. In doing so, we mean to commend something about the way in which those institutions and communities are arranged. We do not, in contrast, speak of courageous or temperate communities in the same way.[41] We use these expressions only to indicate the prevalence of courageous or temperate individuals within such communities or to describe the behavior of the community as a single collective actor. A courageous or moderate community is one in which either the majority of individuals or the community as a whole acts in a courageous or moderate way. A just community, in contrast, is one that is internally ordered in a just way, as well as one in which a majority of individuals or the community as a whole acts in a just way.

The designation of some state of affairs as the primary subject of justice requires that we measure the justice of actions against some privileged set of relationships. Just individuals, according to this understanding, are those who follow and promote the guidelines established by this set of relationships. There is, of course, a tremendous range of choice in the philosophic tradition about which set of relationships we should designate as truly just. Rawls chooses a society's basic institutional structure; Hobbes, positive law and contracts; the Stoics, the natural and rational law ordering the cosmos; and Plato, the natural order within the soul.

The designation of individual character as the primary subject of justice, in contrast, leads us to measure the justice of actions, institutions, and regimes in terms of what an individual with a specific character would do or approve. This understanding of justice, contrary to Hayek, does not demand that we treat the description of states of affairs as just or unjust as a "category mistake."[42] It merely suggests that such de-

---

40. See H. Bedau, "Social Justice and Social Institutions," 159, and D. L. Philips, *Equality, Justice, and Rectification*, 75–76, for insightful discussions of this relatively neglected problem.
41. See W. Galston, *Justice and the Human Good*, 100–101.
42. F. Hayek, *Law, Legislation, and Liberty* 2:33.

scriptions, however important, are secondary and derivative. If we cannot imagine an individual with the characteristics we think of as just promoting a certain state of affairs, then we have every reason, according to this understanding of justice, to describe this state of affairs as unjust.[43]

This approach to reasoning about extralegal standards of justice is far less unfamiliar than it might at first seem to be. As Martha Nussbaum points out, "Often our idea of a good judge is more broadly shared among us, and less subject to disagreement, than is our view of the subject matter concerning which this judge is to render a verdict." We often are much more likely to agree "about the characteristics of intellect, temper, imagination, and experience that a competent judge must have than we do about the particular practical judgments that we expect him or her to make."[44]

Indeed, it makes sense to interpret even some understandings of justice that are explicitly centered on states of affairs—Rawls's, for instance—as implicitly derived from an understanding of just character. Rawls identifies his two principles of justice by asking himself what principles would be chosen by individuals who were compelled by ignorance about their personal identities and abilities to reason fairly. For this reason he describes his conception of justice as "justice as fairness." Much the largest part of his argument rests on the understanding of fairness that supports hypothetical constraints such as the famous "veil of ignorance" that he imposes on our reasoning about justice.[45] In effect, Rawls asks us to treat the principles chosen by fair individuals—that is, individuals who accept the constraints on partiality imposed by the veil of ignorance—as our basic principles of justice. Rawls's connection between the virtue of fairness and justice precedes any reflection on basic social institutions. It represents an implicit admission of the priority of a just character (understood in this case as a fair or impartial character) to just states of affairs.

---

43. J. R. Lucas (*On Justice*, 5n8) points out the purely ideological character of Hayek's argument about the category mistake involved in claims about social justice.
44. M. Nussbaum, *The Fragility of Goodness*, 248.
45. Rawls openly acknowledges that he constructed the hypothetical constraints of his "original position" in order to represent our "most firmly held convictions" about fairness; see "Justice as Fairness," 238–39, and *A Theory of Justice*, 587. But do these "firmly held convictions" refer to a state of character or a state of affairs? One way of interpreting the original position is as a device that allows us to reconstruct the mind-set of a truly fair individual. If so, then Rawls is deriving his understanding of his basic principles of justice from reflection on what a just—that is, fair and impartial—individual would choose.

Viewed from this perspective, Rawls and Aristotle differ primarily in their different understandings of what constitutes a just character. Rawls focuses almost exclusively on fairness and impartiality, whereas Aristotle, as I argue in the following section, treats fairness as only one part of the just character. It is only because Rawls understands a just character primarily in terms of fairness and impartiality that he insists that a "veil of ignorance" must conceal self-knowledge when we reason about justice. And it is precisely because Aristotle does not treat impartiality as the essential component of a just character that he eschews any such constraints on our reasoning about justice.

It should be clear that an explicitly character-centered conception of justice leads to a much more open and indeterminate sense of what constitutes a just state of affairs. According to this conception, evaluating the justice of states of affairs requires that we imagine what a particular individual would do in a particular situation rather than simply check for conformity with some privileged state of affairs. Character-centered conceptions of justice offer no final answer to our questions about what constitutes a just action. They tell us *how*—that is, in what spirit—to act in order to be just, not exactly *what* to do.

Philosophers who seek to establish normal models of justice in order to settle our debates about which actions to count as just will, accordingly, be drawn to state-of-affairs conceptions of justice. But in order to settle these debates about how to behave, they must justify their designation of a particular state of affairs—whether positive law, custom, the natural order, or the social institutions favored by fair reasoners—as the privileged standard of justice. Attempts at this kind of justification make up the largest part of the philosophic literature on justice. We find no such efforts in Aristotle's treatment of justice because Aristotle works with a character-centered understanding. He appears to Rawls and most other contemporary political philosophers to rely ultimately on a state-of-affairs conception only because they assume that he, like they, seeks to end our uncertainty about which actions are just.

Once we recognize that Aristotle accepts a character-centered conception of justice, his reluctance to describe the actions performed by a truly just individual becomes perfectly understandable. "People think it does not take much wisdom to know what is just and unjust, because it is not hard to understand the matters with which the laws deal." If acting justly requires merely the willingness to learn and follow explicit rules of conduct, then it clearly demands far less skill and wisdom than learning the arts. "But," Aristotle responds to this opinion, "these things [laws and rules] are not just except incidentally. No, to know *how* an act must be performed and *how* a distribution must be made in order to be just is a harder task [than learning the arts]" (*NE* 1137a10; my emphasis).

For Aristotle there is no list of inherently just acts against which we can measure the justice of individuals. "In the case of the virtues an act is not performed justly or with moderation if the act is of a certain kind but only if in addition the agent has a certain character when he performs it" (*NE* 1105a29). Virtuous individuals take pleasure in virtuous actions. Individuals who find virtuous actions painful are not virtuous even if they have the strength to overcome pain and perform these actions. A "man who endures danger with joy, or at least without pain, is courageous; if he endures it with pain, he is a coward" (*NE* 1104b8).

> Actions that conform to virtue are inherently pleasant, and, as a result, such actions are not only pleasant for those who love the noble but also pleasant in themselves. The life of such men has no need of pleasure as an added attraction, since it contains pleasure within itself. We may even go so far as to state that the man who does not enjoy performing noble actions is not a good man at all. Nobody would call a man just who does not enjoy acting justly, nor generous who does not enjoy generous actions, and so on.
> (*NE* 1099a13)

Aristotle's distinction between just deeds and acting justly (*NE* 1135a20) might at first appear to correspond to modern distinctions between legally correct and morally virtuous behavior.[46] But in fact this distinction has very different foundations and implications. For Aristotle unjust acts are those acts that individuals who have unjust dispositions choose to perform. One can perform an unjust act without acting unjustly, when, for example, through ignorance or compulsion one acts in the way that an unjustly disposed individual would act in a particular situation. These actions are only incidentally unjust because they do not reflect an unjust character. But Aristotle is still using the choices of just and unjust individuals to define acts of justice and injustice. He is not distinguishing, as do many modern moral philosophers, between those who intentionally and unintentionally choose to perform inherently unjust acts.

If, like Aristotle, we treat justice primarily as a moral virtue—that is, as a set of dispositions that shape an individual's character—then we

---

46. As suggested by D. J. Allan, "Individual and State," 64. Allen's argument is rightly criticized by R. Polansky, "The Dominance of 'Polis.' "

need not invoke a higher standard of natural right in order to declare properly enacted laws unjust. Consider the following passage in which Aristotle describes properly established oligarchic and democratic laws as unjust:

> If the poor as the majority distribute among themselves the goods of the rich, is this not unjust? "By Zeus [they would say], it was justly resolved by the city's authoritative body!" What, then, ought one to say is the extreme of injustice? Is it just, therefore, for the minority and the wealthy to rule? If they act in the same way and plunder the possessions of the multitude, is this just? If so, the other is as well. That all of these things are bad and unjust, then, is evident.
>
> (*Pol.* 1281a15–25)

Passages such as this suggest to many of Aristotle's interpreters that he distinguishes between a lower, conventional conception of justice and a higher, natural one. According to their interpretations, rapacious democratic and oligarchic laws are unjust because they miss the target of a just state of affairs provided somehow by the nature of things. Although pillaging the rich or exploiting the poor may be just according to the conventional standards enshrined by established oligarchic or democratic laws, it is unjust according to the higher and unqualified standards of natural right.

If, however, we start from the virtue-centered understanding of justice, the following alternative interpretation of Aristotle's argument emerges. The oligarchs' and democrats' acts of expropriation are not unjust in and of themselves. It is not the *act* of expropriating the goods of another class that leads Aristotle to condemn these laws as unjust but rather the character imputed to the actors who made them. We can, after all, imagine circumstances—say, in the midst of war or famine—in which such acts might well be justified. When we denounce these laws as unjust, we are, according to this interpretation, insisting that no just individual, no individual in whom we recognize the character traits associated with justice, could have made such a law at the particular time and place it was made. We are insisting that only unjust individuals—in this case, individuals who are disposed to grab more than their share of communal goods—could make such laws in that situation. It is this assumption of a bad character and will that turns an act of expropriation into an act of pillage or exploitation.

It might seem, however, that this interpretation of Aristotle's understanding of justice merely reintroduces a natural right argument through the back door. The naturally right states of affairs, one might suggest, are those that a perfectly just individual prefers in every particular situation. Judgments about justice, interpreted in this way, would still oblige us to try to hit the inherently correct target provided by nature or reason.

I am arguing, on the contrary, that there are, for Aristotle, *no inherently correct* answers to questions about political justice. Aristotle, I expect, would reject Dworkin's claim that we have a right to expect from judges an attempt to discover the right answers to the questions we put before them.[47] When we seek justice, he would argue, we seek the judgments of justly disposed individuals rather than inherently correct answers.

In relatively simple cases, all just individuals would probably agree about what to do, but in more difficult cases the judgments of these individuals might not be identical. This lack of identity does not necessarily mean that one of these judgments is just and the others are unjust. Because just states of affairs are those chosen by just individuals, a number of different states of affairs in any particular situation may deserve to be described as unqualifiedly just. Aristotle's virtue-centered understanding of justice thus provides no single, determinate, and absolutely correct standard of judgment, not even a particularistic standard that records the correct judgments to be made in every particular situation.

In a famous passage at the beginning of the *Nicomachean Ethics* Aristotle warns us that in questions about "what is noble and just . . . we must be satisfied to indicate the truth with a rough and general sketch . . . for a well-educated individual seeks only the degree of precision in each kind of study appropriate to the nature of the subject' (*NE* 1094b15–25). The imprecision that Aristotle emphasizes here includes, I suggest, the inherent indeterminacy of ethical judgments as well as their inherent particularity. It is the lack of inherently correct answers, not merely the vast variety of ethical situations, that keeps him from spelling out for us the right things to do.

## GENERAL AND DISTRIBUTIVE JUSTICE

If the primary subject of justice is a state of character and if Aristotle is speaking in the *Nicomachean Ethics* about the specifically political form of the practice of justice, then the obvious question to ask is, What kind of virtues do members of political communities expect of each other

47. R. Dworkin, *Taking Rights Seriously*, 49, 100.

and associate with a just character? Aristotle answers this question in the account of the "general" and "particular" virtues of justice that opens book 5. The former is a very broad virtue, one that encompasses in a qualified way all the other moral virtues. The latter is the more familiar virtue of fairness, a character state that Aristotle associates with distributive and corrective justice.

The great majority of contemporary, and especially English-speaking, interpreters dismiss or downplay the importance of Aristotle's concept of general justice. For them, the general virtue of justice is little more than an inconvenience of ancient Greek vocabulary that Aristotle himself quickly discards. Aristotle's real interest, they insist, lies, like their own, in the particular sense of justice with its emphasis on fairness and distributive standards. David Miller speaks for these interpreters when he suggests that "we are perhaps fortunate in losing" from English usage the general sense of justice that Aristotle is compelled by Greek usage to discuss.[48] But since Aristotle himself insists that fairness and distributive justice are only parts of justice, parts that are related to general justice "as part to whole" (*NE* 1130b12), it seems likely that we will seriously misunderstand his account of justice unless we devote some attention to his concept of general justice.

What role, then, does Aristotle's concept of general justice play in his understanding of justice? And how does it relate to his more familiar conception of fairness and distributive justice? Aristotle derives the distinction between the general and particular virtues of justice from reflection on the way in which we ordinarily characterize unjust individuals. He suggests that unjust individuals, as we ordinarily describe them, are unlawful (*paranomon*) or unfair (*anison*), and often both. Sometimes we complain about the injustice of individuals who act against the law. (The law here is understood, as I argue below, in its most general sense as the promoter of a community's common advantage.) At other times we complain about the injustice of those who constantly seek more than their fair portion in any distribution of goods and honors (*NE* 1129b). Aristotle concludes that if injustice refers to unlawful

---

48. D. Miller, *Social Justice*, 17. For similar dismissals of the concept of universal justice by Aristotle's commentators, see J. Burnet, *The Ethics of Aristotle*, 202; P. Shorey, "Universal Justice in Aristotle's Ethics," 279–80; M. Hamburger, *Morals and Law*, 50; W. F. Hardie, *Aristotle's Ethical Theory*, 185; P. Springborg, "Aristotle and the Problem of Needs." Terence Irwin (*Aristotle's First Principles*, 424–25), Frederick Rosen ("The Political Context"), and Eric Voegelin (*Anamnesis*, 57) are among the few English-language commentators who see the importance of general justice for Aristotle's understanding of justice.

and unfair actions, then justice, accordingly, refers to the lawful, the acts chosen by those disposed to promote the common good, and to the fair (or equal [*isos*]), the acts chosen by those disposed to take pleasure in their share of distributed goods and burdens (*NE* 1129a32).

My broad interpretation of general justice and the category of the lawful is justified by a number of passages in Aristotle's *Politics*. In these passages Aristotle clearly identifies justice in general with the acts chosen by individuals disposed to promote the common advantage of the community rather than with a narrower disposition to obey laws: "for the political good is justice and this is the common advantage" (*Pol.* 1282a16). Justice, he suggests, is the "political virtue" that seeks the common advantage, the virtue from which "all the other virtues necessarily follow" (*Pol.* 1283a38), a description that corresponds to his similar characterization of general justice as the "complete virtue" that involves the exercise of all the other moral virtues (*NE* 1129b26). Finally, Aristotle's three "correct" (*orthos*) or "unqualifiedly just" regimes—monarchy, aristocracy, and polity—derive their correctness from their rulers' disposition to promote the common advantage of their community. Regimes whose rulers do not seek to promote the common advantage can be called just only with a qualification (*Pol.* 1279).

Once we acknowledge the breadth of Aristotle's understanding of general justice and the lawful, it becomes easier to understand why he insists that the fair and the lawful "are related to one another as part to the whole; for everything unfair is unlawful, but not everything unlawful is unfair" (*NE* 1130b12). Standards of fairness are part of the mutual obligations that citizens establish in order to promote the common advantage of their communities. They measure the standards of fairness in terms of these obligations rather than the other way round.

Aristotle would agree with Rawls that "justice is the first virtue of social institutions" and that "laws and institutions no matter how efficient and well-arranged must be reformed or abolished if they are unjust."[49] But he would insist, against Rawls, that the justice that deserves this honor is general justice and its disposition to promote the common good rather than distributive justice and its disposition to fairness. Indeed, it makes much less sense to treat distributive justice, as Rawls does, as "the first virtue of social institutions." Contrary to Rawls's assertion, we are quite ready to sacrifice the fairness of social institutions to a whole variety of competing ends, from security and individual

---

49. J. Rawls, *A Theory of Justice*, 3.

freedom to civil peace and mental tranquility. If any form of justice is to represent the sine qua non of social institutions, then it could only be something like Aristotle's universal justice, the virtue that seeks to promote the common advantage of a community.

Fairness is a much narrower virtue for Aristotle than it is for most moral and political philosophers. Unfair individuals, he suggests, are grasping (*pleonektēs*) (*NE* 1130a17–30). It pains them to accept socially limited shares of things. Grasping individuals want more than their share of the good things—and less of the burdens—that communities distribute among their members. Fair individuals, in contrast, feel pain when they or others receive more or less than their share and take pleasure in distributing goods and correcting imbalances according to shared communal standards.

It is important to note here how Aristotle's understanding of unfairness differs in a small but significant way from our familiar understanding of greed. Greedy individuals have unlimited appetites for certain good things. (As such, greed is a vice that corresponds to the virtue of moderation rather than the virtue of fairness.) Grasping individuals, in contrast, may be inspired by greed or any of a number of other motives to grab for more than their share of good things; but it is their distaste for standards of fairness that defines their character. When some good is distributed, such individuals are disposed to ask "Why not me?" or "Why didn't I get it?" prior to any reflection on communal needs or individual desert. It is their discomfort with standards of distribution, rather than their attachment to alternative standards, that defines their vice. I suspect we have all at some time encountered this particular vice.

Those who place distributive justice at the center of their understanding of justice have often expressed dissatisfaction and impatience with this account of injustice and unfairness. Surely, they complain, injustice has a far broader range of motives than the desire for more than one's share.[50] A grasping character, however, is only one small part of injustice as Aristotle understands it. It appears to be the whole of injustice for these critics only because they ignore Aristotle's concept of general justice, a concept that provides him with the larger context into which he places fairness and unfairness.

Fairness is only one part of the virtuous character that Aristotle associates with lawfulness and general justice. As noted above, Aristotle

---

50. See, for example, B. Williams, "Justice as a Virtue," 192–94; J. Shklar, *The Faces of Injustice*, 30–31.

believes that "this kind of justice [general justice] is complete virtue' (*NE* 1129b26). In what way does lawfulness involve all of the other virtues? If Aristotle were merely suggesting that general justice acts as a synonym for moral virtue, then there would be little reason to disagree with those who quickly discard it from their accounts of justice. But Aristotle makes a point of qualifying his description of general justice as complete virtue. Lawful individuals display all of the moral virtues "not in an unqualified sense, but in relation to others." This qualification seems important but has proved difficult to interpret. Perhaps the best way of interpreting it is to return to the *via negativa* and ask how Aristotle might derive this broad conception of justice from our common image of the unjust individual.

Cicero makes a suggestion in his *Offices* that can help us answer that question. He distinguishes there between what he calls "passive" and "active injustice."[51] Active injustice refers to the behavior of those who act directly against a community's shared standards of justice. Passive injustice, a much more unfamiliar concept, refers to the behavior of those "who do not prevent or oppose wrong" when they have it within their power to do so.[52] As Judith Shklar notes, passive injustice "is a notion that has special importance for any theory of republican citizenship, ancient or modern." As citizens, "we are passively unjust ... when we do not report crimes, when we look the other way when we see cheating and minor thefts, when we tolerate political corruption, and when we silently accept laws that we regard as unjust, unwise, or cruel."[53] Moreover, since the more power one has, the more that one can do to prevent wrong, passive injustice is a standard that is especially relevant to claims about the justice and injustice of a political community's officeholders, as Cicero meant to emphasize. Many political officials are actively unjust, using their power to help them break laws and take more than their allotted share of public funds. But, as Shklar emphasizes, passive injustice is the characteristic vice of public officials. Public officials are guilty of passive injustice when they evade responsibility for disasters they could easily have foreseen or prevented and when they do not make full use of their powers and talents to prevent cruelty to those who pass through our system of justice.[54]

---

51. Cicero, *De Officiis*, 24–31. Judith Shklar revives this distinction in her critique of philosophic theories of injustice in *The Faces of Injustice*.
52. Cicero, *De Officiis*, 24–25.
53. J. Shklar, *The Faces of Injustice*, 40, 6.
54. Ibid., 40–42.

What concepts of justice follow from these two concepts of injustice? The injustice of actively unjust individuals stems from their negation of determinate rules and principles of justice. The justice that corresponds to active injustice is thus the justice of shared rules and principles governing the basic obligations of a community—in short, what we have been calling the "normal model" of justice. The normal model advocates what we might call *passive* justice, or mere conformity with established rules and principles, as the basis for the virtue of justice.

The justice that corresponds to passive injustice is much harder to pin down. As argued above, passive injustice is not merely the absence of justice as established in some set of shared rules and principles. Passive injustice arises when someone fails to prevent a wrong that he or she may well have prevented. The justice that corresponds to passive injustice is defined by the efforts of good citizens to prevent wrong rather than by determinate rules and principles. Passive injustice thus bespeaks the absence of a kind of *active* justice, a kind of justice based on inherently disputable estimates of our capacity to prevent wrongs rather than on determinate rules and principles.

It is often said that justice is the coldest of the moral virtues, that just behavior rarely excites our imagination as much as generous or courageous behavior, let alone injustice, usually does.[55] That is certainly true if we are speaking about what I have called passive justice. Few poets sing the praises of individuals who merely obey the law and pay their debts. But we do get very warm about what I have called active justice. Active justice is the virtue that we celebrate in great founders, legislators, judges, and administrators. Given the breadth of character and insight it demands, we are inclined to celebrate those who possess it, just as Aristotle tells us that Greek poets celebrate general justice, "as more wondrous than the morning and evening star" (*NE* 1129b27).

Aristotle's unfair individuals, individuals who grasp after more than their share of goods, are actively unjust. Their injustice is derived from the negation of determinate rules and principles of fairness. Aristotle's fair individuals are, accordingly, passively just. Their justice is measured in terms of their fidelity to determinate standards. Passively unjust individuals, in contrast, are those who fail to make full use of their power, whether through cowardice, laziness, foolishness, misanthropy, or any other vice, to prevent wrong. Judges who are so lazy that they

---

55. As J. R. Lucas notes (*On Justice,* 4), "Justice is a cold virtue which can be manifested without feeling; . . . it is when *in*-justice is in danger of being done that we become agitated. Injustice wears the trousers." See also J. Shklar, *The Faces of Injustice,* 103–4.

pay no attention to the testimony of witnesses, immigration officials who are so unpleasant to their clients that they scare them away from their offices, politicians who are so blind and insensitive that they never see the indirect harm caused by the inflammatory rhetoric they use to get elected—all are passively unjust. They are all unjust even though they do not seek to break the law or grab more than their fair share of the goods. Only those individuals who are disposed to none of these vices will escape passive injustice. In other words, only individuals who possess, in some way, all of the virtues in their relations to others will be actively just—precisely the description of the generally just individual that Aristotle offers in the *Nicomachean Ethics*.

I suggest that Aristotle's general justice corresponds to what I have called active justice, that is, to the set of actions that virtuous individuals would make in particular situations to promote the common advantage of the community. According to this understanding of justice, members of political communities expect each other to use their power to promote the common advantage, a task that if best performed would require the possession and exercise, in different situations, of all the moral virtues. (Indeed, Aristotle agrees with the saying that the activity of "ruling will show the [character of the] man" [*NE* 1130a1].) When they conclude that either the disposition to promote the common good or the relevant moral virtue of character was missing in those responsible for setting public standards, they complain about injustice.

This general or active concept of justice extends justice beyond simply passive obedience or loyalty to relevant general norms, the understanding of justice favored by proponents of normal models of justice. In doing so, one might think that it so stretches the concept of justice beyond familiar ideas and experience that we might as well use a different word to describe the concept. But consider how we react to obviously incompetent judges or obviously cruel and insensitive immigration officials, indeed, to all the obviously vicious individuals who have power over us. We do not wait until we hear their judgments, until we hear whether their rulings invoke and apply our conception of the appropriate norm, to question whether their rulings will be just. Their vices themselves lead us to question the justice of their rulings and even to suspect that there may be some hidden injustice even when they do invoke and apply what we think of as the appropriate norm. Their injustice would be more evident to us if they showed an utter disregard for established norms, an utter lack of the passive justice of fairness. But that may only be because in the particular situations in which we meet them, say a courtroom or an immigration hearing, we believe that it is fairness, with its fidelity to established norms, that best serves the common advantage of the community. When we turn to other situations, such as public deliberation by political representatives about a new law or policy, this fidelity is much less crucial in our judging whether particular choices made by powerful individuals are the just choices.

Normal models of justice suggest that we can judge the justice of these choices only to the extent that we can identify beyond established norms a higher body of norms to which we can and should remain faithful. Such models make fairness the virtue that measures the justice of the standards of mutual obligation chosen members of political communities. To do so, they must either claim to have identified norms that in no way represent controversial judgments about what may be to the common advantage or claim, like Rawls, to generate higher norms out of the virtue of fairness or impartiality itself.

From an Aristotelian point of view, however, using standards of fairness to measure the justice of laws and regimes "is to reverse this relationship, to treat justice as the fair or equal as more fundamental than justice as the lawful."[56] Fairness is a passive virtue for Aristotle; he never suggests that it enables us to distinguish the just standards of fairness from the unjust ones.[57] Fairness involves fidelity to a community's shared norms of distributive and corrective justice. These norms of fairness—indeed, the virtue of fairness itself—can themselves be justified only with reference to inherently contestable claims about what completely virtuous individuals would choose to do to promote the common advantage of the community. If someone claims that they have identified standards of fairness that require us to revise or revoke some already established norm, then the passive virtue of fairness is no help in deciding whether his or her claim is just. We must ask, instead, whether this is a claim that an actively just individual would choose, a question that cannot itself be settled by invoking a duty to be faithful to some higher norm.

Commentators most often assume that Aristotle himself tries to settle debates about competing standards of distributive justice by identifying a higher standard of fairness to which we can remain faithful.[58] They

56. W. Mathie, "Political and Distributive Justice," 67.
57. As noted by C. Taylor, "The Nature and Scope of Distributive Justice," 47.
58. For examples, see E. Barker, *The Political Thought*, 313, 345; R. G. Mulgan, *Aristotle's Political Theory*, 80–81; H. Jaffa, "Aristotle," 111; H. Hantz, "Justice and Equality"; D. Winthrop, "Aristotle and Theories of Justice," 1203; D. Keyt, "Distributive Justice in Aristotle's Ethics and Politics."

have considerable difficulty, however, in identifying that standard, since Aristotle never explicitly offers one. In the *Nicomachean Ethics,* where he sketches distributive justice and fairness, he merely notes that although we all agree that communal goods should be distributed according to merit, we do not all share the same standard of merit (*NE* 1131a25).

In the *Politics,* however, Aristotle explores at some length one particular example of this disagreement: the competing claims of merit raised by oligarchs and democrats in their competition for political power. It is easy to make judgments about distributive justice when we need only ask ourselves how to be faithful to a particular shared standard. But what do we do, Aristotle asks in the *Politics,* when multiple and competing standards claim our fidelity? "What if," as is usually the case in political life, "all should exist in a single city—the good, the rich, the well-born, and a political multitude"—and all make claims to rule? "This involves a question, and political philosophy" (*Pol.* 1283b1, 1282b23).

How does "political philosophy" answer this question? Aristotle makes three claims in his analysis of competing claims to political rule.

1. The only unqualifiedly just claim to power is political virtue or general justice (*Pol.* 1283a).

2. Many claims, such as size and hair color, are irrelevant to the distribution of power (*Pol.* 1283a). (Of course, these claims are rarely advanced in political debate.)

3. The small number of claims that are most often advanced in political argument—wealth, freedom, good birth—are all partially just, though "none of the defining principles on the basis of which they claim they merit rule ... is correct" (*Pol.* 1283b27).

Do these claims provide us with a determinate standard of fairness against which to measure claims about the distribution of political power? I think not. They merely tell us that all the politically relevant claims are partially just, whereas the claims of the virtuous are limited in their political relevance. Aristotle ends his discussion of who should rule in the following way: "All of these considerations appear to show that none of the principles on which men claim to rule and to hold men in subjection to them are right.... [W]hat is equally right is to be considered with reference to the *advantage of the polis and the common good of the citizens*" (*Pol.* 1283b27–42; my emphasis).

I interpret this conclusion to mean that we must decide questions about who rules with reference to our judgment about common advantage of particular communities rather than with reference to a distributive standard of political merit. In effect, Aristotle is insisting that we remove the question of who should rule from the category of distributive justice and "abandon the search for a single set of principles of distributive justice."[59] Aristotle's own judgments about how to distribute political power in ordinary political communities—such as his advocacy of mixed regimes and middle-class rule—illustrate this point. He advocates mixed regimes and middle-class rule not because their distributions of power follow from determinate standards of political desert but because, as I argue in chapter 7, they serve the common advantage by promoting relatively stable and decent standards of justice within the political community.[60]

Aristotle insists that we "need political philosophy" to deal with competing claims to political power because we need to go beyond considerations of merit to draw any conclusions about them. Fairness and its fidelity to determinate standards of merit cannot be our guide in choosing standards of distributive justice. We must be guided, instead, by our much more indeterminate judgments about how an actively just individual would promote the common advantage of the community.

## A POLITICAL CONCEPTION OF THE COMMON GOOD

If Aristotle identifies justice with the common advantage of political communities, then it may seem that he has provided us, after all, a way of identifying determinate standards of extralegal justice. According to this approach, a law or public act would be just only to the extent that it promotes the good life of the members of a political community. Most modern legal and political philosophers reject this route to extralegal standards of justice, but they do so only because they tend to deny that there is a single, determinate, and well-defined human good for us to discover. Because Aristotle, in contrast, does not hesitate to identify the nature of the human good, there seems to be no reason for him to share their reluctance to derive the right from the good.

As a result, it seems reasonable to attribute to Aristotle the follow-

---

59. C. Taylor, "The Nature and Scope," 62. This point is made forcefully by W. Mathie, "Political and Distributive Justice," 64–67, 75. See also F. Wolff, "Justice et Politique."

60. See D. Resnick, "Justice, Compromise, and Constitutional Rules."

ing approach to the identification of extralegal standards of justice (1) identify the nature of the good for human beings; (2) construct an imaginary state of affairs—the utopian regime—that would best promote that good among citizens; (3) judge how close we can bring existing political conditions to this best state of affairs.

This reconstruction of Aristotle's reasoning about justice clearly challenges my interpretation of his understanding of justice, especially in its identification of justice with a determinate state of affairs identified by means of one's knowledge of human nature. Moreover, it has come to be seen by many contemporary philosophers and political theorists as an attractive alternative to the inattention to ideas about the human good characteristic of most liberal and procedural theories of justice such as Rawls's.[61] Despite widespread disagreement about the value of this Aristotelian alternative, there is a growing scholarly consensus that Aristotle shares this approach to reasoning about justice.[62]

I believe, however, that this consensus is mistaken. It suggests that Aristotle thinks of justice as something that can be determined by disinterested analysis of human nature and particular sociopolitical conditions rather than as something that emerges from political argument and competition. It thereby imposes on Aristotle an overly philosophic and depoliticized understanding of justice that is foreign to his works. Although Aristotle does claim genuine knowledge of the human good and does construct a utopian regime in which the human good is best realized, he never suggests that we should measure the justice of laws and public acts by asking how close they come to realizing the states of affairs found in the best regime. Nor does he draw up for the edification of legislators anything like a list of basic human goods and the principles of justice they entail, a list such as we find in the works of his contemporary followers William Galston and Martha Nussbaum.[63]

Galston and Nussbaum treat Aristotle's failure to produce a list of

---

61. The most extensive and insightful attempts at constructing a contemporary Aristotelian theory of justice along these lines appear in recent works by William Galston and Martha Nussbaum: W. Galston, *Justice and the Human Good*; M. Nussbaum, "Aristotelian Social Democracy"; M. Nussbaum, "Nature, Function, and Capability"; M. Nussbaum, "Human Functioning and Social Justice."

62. See, for example, Shklar's recent complaint about the growing popularity of this "Aristotelian" approach to reasoning about justice. Shklar acknowledges in passing, however, that Aristotle's works also contain a "more modest" and more political theory of distributive justice, a theory that "is not much recalled" today; J. Shklar, "Injustice, Injury, and Inequality," 17.

63. See W. Galston, *Justice and the Human Good*; M. Nussbaum, "Aristotelian Social Democracy"; M. Nussbaum, "Nature, Function, and Capability"; M. Nussbaum, "Human Functioning and Social Justice."

human goods as if it were merely an accidental omission or oversight on his part. I believe, on the contrary, that Aristotle's decision not to draw up a guide to authoritative extralegal standards of justice is far from accidental. Although Aristotle seeks determinate and certain knowledge of the human good, he denies the existence of comparable standards of justice. As a result, he rejects a perfectionist understanding of human justice, even while advocating a perfectionist understanding of the human good.[64] Contemporary "Aristotelians," such as Nussbaum and Galston, often complain about the tendency of modern moral philosophers to distinguish the right or just from the human good. But Aristotle himself, I argue, also introduces a disjunction between justice and human goodness. He differs from modern defenders of liberal distinctions between the right and the good in thinking that it is standards of justice, rather than standards of goodness, that must be left indeterminate and open to a variety of interpretations.

There is one major problem with any attempt to use Aristotle's best regime as a source of basic principles of justice: Aristotle seems singularly unconcerned with the justice of its basic structure. The best regime is a political community that contains a small number of citizens, all wealthy enough to support a life of relative leisure, and a large number of individuals who do almost all of the productive labor but have no share in either citizenship or the good life led by the citizens (*Pol.* 1328b35–1329a). This distribution of goods and burdens need not offend Aristotle's standards of justice if he could argue that all of the workers in the best regime were natural slaves. However, Aristotle not only fails to make such an argument but also makes numerous claims that would preclude their being natural slaves. (For example, by suggesting that they are capable of emancipation [*Pol.* 1330a32], he implies that they lack the mental incapacity that defines the natural slave.)[65] Moreover, although Aristotle notes that it would be far better if the subordinate class in the best regime were made up of slaves or alien serfs, he does not make this a necessary precondition for the best regime (*Pol.* 1330a25–30). The only just grounds for exclusion from the political community, according to Aristotle's natural standards of reciprocity, is lack of the natural capacities for political deliberation. We have seen how he uses these grounds to exclude women, children, and natural slaves from a share in citizenship. He cannot use these grounds

---

64. For a similar conclusion, see D. Charles, "Perfectionism in Aristotle's Political Theory," 199–201.
65. Ibid., 191.

to exclude laborers who have these capacities simply because they lack the wealth and leisure that would allow them to best lead the good life.

Aristotle's rather cavalier exclusion of laborers from full citizenship in the best regime poses a serious obstacle for anyone who wants to use that regime as a guide to basic principles of justice. Nussbaum tries to remove this obstacle by arguing that this conception of political distribution, a conception that identifies the common good of the whole community with the best life that can be lived by its wealthy and leisured part, is only one of a number of competing conceptions that shape Aristotle's best regime. She contrasts it with a more "distributive conception" that she finds in his sketch of that regime. This conception of political distribution identifies the common good with the best life that can be led by all members who have the natural capacity to participate in a good life. She argues that this distributive conception fits far better than the "whole/part" conception with the rest of Aristotle's political philosophy, which suggests to her that the latter may represent an older, unrevised strand in the text of the *Politics*.[66]

I have a much simpler explanation of the apparent injustices of Aristotle's best regime. Aristotle is so cavalier about the basic standards of inclusion in his best regime because he never thinks of it as the perfection of political justice. He thinks of it, instead, as a model of the conditions that would be most conducive to leading the good life. Influenced by the example of Plato's *Republic* and its many imitations, we usually think of utopian regimes as descriptions of perfectly just states of affairs that provide us with a standard against which we can measure the justice of our laws and institutions. But Aristotle never presents his utopia in this way. His best regime, unlike Plato's, is preceded by a discussion of happiness and the good life rather than a lengthy investigation of the nature of justice (*Pol.* 1323a–25b). It remains for Aristotle the "one best regime everywhere" (*NE* 1135a5). But what makes it *best* is its role in supporting the most flourishing human lives rather than its justice.

Aristotle's best regime represents a sketch of the political conditions in which a good life can *best* be led. We can best lead the life of active virtue in a community in which all citizens have the leisure and material goods to share in such a life. Aristotle abstracts here from questions about justice and the competing conceptions of the common good that inspire these questions in ordinary political communities. His best re-

66. M. Nussbaum, "Nature, Function, and Capability," 155–60.

gime seeks the good of a part of the community, the part that can best lead the good life, rather than the common good and political justice. As a result, it cannot provide us with a model of justice. It offers us no determinate standards for assessing the competing claims about the common good that arise in ordinary political life.

This disjuncture between justice and the human good would make nonsense of Aristotle's political philosophy if he accepted the understanding of political teleology usually attributed to him. According to that understanding, the best regime is the natural growth and completion of the political community and the forms of justice that develop within it. But as I argue in chapter 3, Aristotle has a very different understanding of political teleology, according to which our natural needs and capacities drive us to form political communities and to seek stable standards of justice and law to order them. By these means even highly imperfect political communities make it possible to lead the good life by giving us the training necessary to the development of the ethical virtues. Political communities continue to serve their role in human development as long as they continue to seek such standards of law and justice, even if they fail to provide us with the optimal conditions—found in the best regime—for living the good life. It may be unfortunate, from Aristotle's point of view, that the political preconditions of the good life, especially the concern for justice and the common advantage, prove to be an obstacle to the optimal conditions for living that life. But that is one of the problems we face as political animals.

Aristotle, I suggest, is using a political conception of the common good, a conception that cannot be derived simply from reflection on human nature, when he speaks of measuring the justice of established laws against "the advantage of the polis and the common good of its citizens" (*Pol.* 1283b41). The "common advantage" he has in mind here is not a determinate state of affairs that can be discovered by applying philosophic knowledge of the human good to particular political situations. It is instead a much less determinate notion that depends to a great degree on the nature and intensity of the claims made by competing groups within the political community itself. The common advantage in ordinary political communities represents something of a compromise between the competing conceptions of the common advantage advanced by different political groups. It depends to a great extent on what different groups are willing to accept and thus cannot be derived simply from philosophic knowledge of the human good. It thus reflects a willingness on the part of a just individual to hear and find ways of accommodating competing conceptions of the common good rather than some privileged philosophic knowledge of the best state of affairs.

When looking for justice in ordinary political communities, torn as they normally are by competing claims, we look, Aristotle would suggest, for individuals disposed to hear and accommodate all relevant claims rather than for individuals who offer us certain knowledge of what is in our own good. Indeed, we have some reason to be suspicious of individuals who claim such knowledge in the midst of political competition. After all, if they are so certain about what constitutes the common good, then they may completely reject our own claims rather than seek to find some place for them in a more compromising understanding of the common good.[67]

Justice thus represents, for Aristotle, a disposition to seek and promote states of affairs in which citizens will find some common advantage rather than a disposition to identify and apply supposedly true knowledge of the common good. Knowledge of the human good is far from irrelevant to identifying these states of affairs, but it does not provide us with a target to hit in our assessments of the justice of laws and public acts. It acts instead as a limiting condition on the choices we should make. We need to know something about the nature of a good life in order to avoid political choices that would make that life impossible—for example, by eliminating the private control of personal property that is a necessary precondition for the virtue of liberality (*Pol.* 1263a–b). But within these limits, knowledge of the human good does not yield us determinate standards of justice.

The disposition to seek and promote the common advantage of competing groups within the political community is the virtue of general or active justice discussed in the preceding section. It includes fairness or particular justice as one of its parts but contrasts sharply with fairness in its overall character. Fairness relies on a disposition to be faithful to a set of determinate shared standards, a disposition that inspires us to apply those standards impartially and consistently. As such, it is modeled on the virtue we expect of adjudicators, that is, of individuals who apply general rules and principles to particular cases. General justice, in contrast, represents a disposition to seek and promote the common advantage of competing groups. Fidelity to some preceding rule or prin-

---

67. By denying that political virtue necessarily trumps other claims to power, despite its being the only unqualifiedly just claim to power (*Pol.* 1283b), Aristotle allows for citizens' acting on such suspicions.

ciple is not its hallmark. Individuals who are generally just neither possess prior determinate standards to apply to particular situations nor apply standards in abstraction from what competing groups are willing to accept.

Aristotle's general conception of justice is thus a much more political conception than the theories of fairness with which it has frequently been identified in the past. It is a distinctly political conception of justice, first of all, in its political understanding of the common good, an understanding that reflects the nature and intensity of the claims made by competing groups within the political community. It is also distinctly political in that it focuses on what people do with the power they gain in political communities to shape the life of other individuals, not just on whether or not they are faithful to basic standards of fairness. Aristotelian justice is not "a pattern laid up in heaven,"[68] or anywhere else for that matter. It is, instead, a disposition to do what we can to promote the common advantage of competing individuals and groups, a disposition that we use to measure the performance of political actors.

The indeterminacy of extralegal standards of political justice introduces considerable instability and tension into political life. It is therefore hardly surprising that most moral and political philosophers set themselves the task of eliminating this indeterminacy. As mentioned above, those who seek to render extralegal standards of justice more determinate often use fairness as a model for political justice as a whole. They try to make impartial fidelity to shared standards the guide to political choice of standards of justice. In this way, they encourage us to treat competing claims about the best standards of political justice as if they can be adjudicated with reference to a set of prior, shared, and authoritative standards, just as the courts adjudicate competing claims about the application of legal standards.

From an Aristotelian point of view, however, these attempts to depoliticize political justice are doomed to failure, since one cannot justify the priority and authority of extralegal standards without invoking controversial and inherently contestable claims about the common good of the community. Political justice, with its public debate and rotation of office, inevitably revolves around such claims. Philosophers have exercised a great deal of ingenuity in order to avoid appearing to base their theories of justice on them; but they cannot construct their extralegal standards of justice without them. Controversial and inherently con-

---

68. Plato, *Republic*, 592b.

testable assessments of what constitutes the common good always come in through the back door in these theories.

Consider, again, John Rawls's *Theory of Justice* and Michael Walzer's *Spheres of Justice,* two of the most influential contemporary attempts to identify and justify determinate extralegal standards of justice. Rawls can generate his two principles of justice only by making highly controversial assumptions about the "primary goods" of citizens and the rational strategy—maximizing one's minimum return—for attaining them. In order to maintain the claim that his principles of justice can adjudicate competing claims about the common advantage of a community, Rawls has to treat these assumptions as if they follow from relatively uncontroversial understandings of individual rationality. But these understandings of primary goods and rational strategies are themselves highly controversial. We can choose among them with reference only to the kind of life and goods we want our community to promote. Similarly, Walzer tries to represent inherently controversial judgments about the best standards to promote the common good as if they necessarily follow from the shared "historical meanings" of goods. His highly implausible claim that economic democracy, the shared control of factories and other large-scale operations, necessarily follows from "our shared understandings" of property and power in modern America shows just how far he is willing to go in using this argument to support inherently controversial claims about the common good.[69]

Clearly, Rawls and Walzer have powerful claims to make about the shape of a just social order. But they seek to persuade us of the justice of their claims by presenting these ideas as if they were necessitated, as in adjudication, by a preceding common standard rather than through direct argument about the common good. This legalistic approach to political argument is completely foreign to Aristotle. Rawls and Walzer pursue it in order to diminish the indeterminacy and controversial character of political justice. But their efforts result merely in introducing new arguments about the common good into political debate, a result that Aristotle would approve of, even if it falls short of their own ambitions.

These arguments, like all other arguments about the common good, are bound to be controversial since they inevitably affect the interests of different groups in different ways. Just individuals, according to the Aristotelian approach presented in this chapter, seek conceptions of the

69. M. Walzer, *Spheres of Justice,* 291–303.

common good that will be acceptable in some way to the most important of these competing groups. Just states of affairs, according to this approach, are the states of affairs chosen by just individuals. This understanding of justice lacks the determinacy and finality that most moral and political philosophers seek in their theories of justice. But finality and determinacy are inappropriate goals for a theory of political justice. One can find relatively determinate standards of political justice only in the laws made by the most powerful groups within a political community. These standards, which often shape the way of life led by all citizens, inevitably reflect the partial interests and knowledge of the powerful. For this reason, we look for judgments that reflect a disposition to seek a common good when we raise questions about the justice of established laws and other official acts.

All political communities, no matter how imperfect, promote the use of these two kinds of judgment about justice. The leaders of every political community try to persuade us to be faithful to the determinate standards established in their laws and to view these laws as a means of promoting the common advantage of the community.[70] In doing so, they promote the development of the two states of character, fairness and love of the common good, that Aristotle associates with justice. These two states of character recommend differing and often conflicting standards of justice. Political life and argument would be far simpler if we could discover some third and final set of standards to guide our judgments about justice, but Aristotle's analysis suggests that no such standards are available to members of political communities.

---

70. In the *Rhetoric* (1358b) Aristotle notes that the one necessary element of every political proposal is an appeal to the common advantage of the community. No matter how self-interested a proposal may be, the structure of political argument compels us to portray it as a means to the common good. One might add that the structure of political argument compels us to portray even selfless and highly moral proposals as serving some common advantage. A good example of this phenomenon would be Diodotus's attempt (Thucydides, *History of the Peloponnesian War*, book 3) to dissuade the Athenians from slaughtering the defeated citizens of Mytilene.

CHAPTER SIX

# The Rule of Law

Although Aristotle makes numerous suggestions about how to improve the quality of life in ordinary political communities, two of these suggestions stand out as the most important for a decent political order: the rule of law and the mixed regime. I discuss the former in this chapter and the latter in chapter 7.

The claim to be governed by laws, rather than by individual men and women, is one of the most popular and enduring boasts of republican rhetoric. Liberal republicans portray the rule of law as a set of hedges that blocks and channels the cruel fury of mobs and monarchs; they celebrate it as a check on the arbitrary exercise of power by capricious monarchs, arrogant aristocrats, and vindictive demagogues. Radical republicans portray the rule of law as the fair and impartial exercise of authority that one expects from a responsible and well-educated citizenry; they celebrate it as an important part of the freedom from personal domination that participatory governments seek to protect.[1] Both groups loudly proclaim the need to ensure that the community's laws rule supreme over the wills of particular individuals.

---

1. Locke presents the most influential theoretical defense of the liberal republican understanding of the rule of law, whereas Rousseau presents the most influential theoretical defense of the radical version. Political rhetoric celebrating the liberal republican version of the rule of law is far too familiar to American audiences to need any reference. For political rhetoric celebrating the more radical republican view, consider Pericles' praise of law in his famous "funeral oration"; Thucydides, *History of the Peloponnesian Wars* book 2, ch. 37.

But republican boasts about the rule of law are very easy to undermine and ridicule. Like Thomas Hobbes, complaining about yet "another error of Aristotle's *Politics,* that in a well ordered commonwealth, not men should govern, but the laws," critics of the rule of law have asked: "What man, that has his natural senses, though he can neither write nor read, does not find himself governed by them he fears, and believes can kill or hurt him when he obeys not? Or that believes the law can hurt him; that is, words, and paper, without the hands, and swords of men?"[2] All that we need to do in order to undermine the popular image of the rule of law is to ask the subversive question that Socrates posed to his accusers more than two millennia ago: Who made these laws?[3] It is a commonplace among defenders of the rule of law that "when we obey laws, in the general sense of abstract rules laid down irrespective of their application, we are not subject to another man's will and are therefore free."[4] But laws are made, interpreted, and enforced by particular individuals, individuals who use their power to impose their understanding of a community's standards of mutual accountability on others. To insist that we are governed by laws, rather than by particular individuals and groups, merely conceals the political power of these individuals and groups by protecting it from direct challenge and criticism.[5]

Although Hobbes singled out Aristotle as a major contributor to this obfuscation of political power, Aristotle is well aware that the rule of law is a form of, rather than a substitute for, the exercise of political power.[6] Laws, according to Aristotle, inevitably express the preferences and passions of the particular individuals who make and interpret them. "One might perhaps assert," Aristotle suggests, "that it is bad for the authoritative element generally to be man instead of law, at any rate if he has the passions that result [from being human] in his soul." But, he continues, "if law may be oligarchic or democratic, what difference will it make with regard to the questions that have been raised? For what was said before [about the rulers' exploitation of the ruled] will result all the same" (*Pol.* 1281a34). In the end, Leo Strauss accurately sums

---

2. T. Hobbes, *Leviathan,* 699.
3. Plato, *Apology of Socrates,* 24d–25c. See also Xenophon, *Memorabilia,* 41–47.
4. F. Hayek, *The Constitution of Liberty,* 153.
5. This point is repeatedly emphasized by contemporary critics of the rule of law. See, for example, R. Unger, *Law in Modern Society,* and the articles collected in D. Kairys, *The Politics of Law,* and A. Hutchinson and P. Monahan, *Critical Legal Studies.*
6. In "The Hobbesian Conception of Sovereignty" Curtis Johnson persuasively refutes Hobbes's criticism of Aristotle.

up Aristotle's position on law and politics when he insists that "no law and hence no constitution, can be a fundamental political fact because all laws depend on human beings. Laws have to be adopted, preserved and administered by men."[7] The rule of law means for Aristotle the rule of the general rules preferred by oligarchs, democrats, or whoever has the power to make and interpret law.[8]

The passages in which Aristotle seems to suggest that laws rule in place of particular individuals and groups represent summaries of the arguments advanced by partisans of the rule of law rather than Aristotle's own conclusions. Those who celebrate Aristotle as a proponent of the rule of law rarely ask whether Aristotle understands the rule of law in the same way that they do, that is, primarily as a barrier that blocks or replaces the exercise of political power by particular individuals.[9] By assimilating Aristotle's view of the rule of law to their own, they obscure an alternative understanding of the rule of law, one that views law as a necessary constituent of political power as well as a constraint on its exercise.

In this chapter I try to show, among other things, that this Aristotelian understanding of the rule of law provides us with a novel perspective on contemporary arguments about the relationship between legal constraints and participatory democracy. Many contemporary proponents of participatory democracy see popular commitments to the rule of law as one of the main obstacles to increased self-government in modern republics. But the Aristotelian understanding of the rule of law developed here suggests that these efforts are bound to be self-defeating. According to this understanding, popular rule itself, like all shared self-government, depends on a widespread disposition to follow general rules. Without such a disposition, it will be impossible to maintain a system in which a large number of individuals take turns in occupying and relinquishing positions of political power.

In the first two sections of this chapter I explore Aristotle's general understanding of law and adjudication, taking particular care to distinguish his notions from the later ideas about these subjects with which

---

7. L. Strauss, *Natural Right and History*, 136.
8. E. F. Miller, "Prudence and the Rule of Law," 204–5.
9. Many commentators clearly identify Aristotle's conception of the rule of law with modern republican rhetoric about law overruling the particular wills of particular individuals. See W. L. Newman, *The Politics of Aristotle* 3:225; R. Robinson, *Aristotle's Politics, Books III and IV*, 35; E. Barker, *The Politics of Aristotle*, 128. In effect, they adopt Hobbes's interpretation of Aristotle's conception of the rule of law while reversing his evaluation of it.

they have often been identified. I then try, in the chapter's final section, to reconstruct Aristotle's understanding of the meaning and purpose of the rule of law.

## WHAT IS LAW?

Unlike Plato, who devoted a separate dialogue (the *Minos*) to the question, Aristotle never explicitly asks, What is law? This omission is somewhat surprising, given both the importance he places on law and his tendency to ask "what is" questions about the major concepts he employs. (In the *Politics*, for example, Aristotle asks such questions about the polis, the citizen, and the regime, among other concepts.) Although there are many places in his political writings where inquiry into the nature of law would be appropriate, Aristotle never pursues this sort of investigation.[10]

Aristotle's apparent lack of interest in developing a precise definition of law is especially striking when contrasted with the tremendous efforts that modern legal theorists devote to this problem. Many of the most intense and enduring debates in modern jurisprudence center on competing definitions of law. Viewed in the light of these debates, Aristotle's ideas about law appear imprecise, haphazard, and incomplete, since Aristotle attempts neither to distinguish legal from moral and conventional rules nor to determine with any precision the nature of legal sanctions or the source of legal authority.[11] Aristotle's implicit definition of law is relatively broad and simple. When contrasted with most contemporary conceptions of law, it is probably most remarkable for how little it tells us. But that may be as it should be, as far as Aristotle is concerned, since he does not seem to think that we can gain very

---

10. Aristotle's lack of interest in this question is all the more surprising in light of his interest in collecting and classifying the fundamental laws of the different Greek cities.

11. Aristotle has had, accordingly, little influence on contemporary discussions about law and legal institutions, despite his considerable influence on the conceptions of justice discussed by contemporary legal philosophers. Even neo-Aristotelians such as John Finnis, let alone legal positivists such as Kelsen and Hart, turn to other authorities when discussing the rule of law and legal institutions; see J. Finnis, *Natural Law and Natural Rights*, 267, 260–91. Ernest Weinrib tries to use Aristotle's analysis of law and justice to support a rather apolitical and formalist account of the rule of law in "The Intelligibility of the Rule of Law." Weinrib's attempt to demonstrate that "law . . . constitutes, as it were, its own ideal, intelligible from within" (63), seems to me to owe more to Kant than to Aristotle, an impression confirmed by his admission that Aristotle's "most striking insights about law received their appropriate elaboration only in the writing of Kant and Hegel" (61). See also E. Weinrib, "Legal Formalism," 977–79.

much political and ethical guidance from a formal definition of law.[12]

The Greek word *nomos,* ordinarily translated as "law," has a long history. Originally—that is, in its earliest recorded uses—it stood in contrast to what we describe as positive law or legislation. *Nomos* referred to the "way" people and things normally behave, to the spontaneous pattern their behavior manifests. Our evidence suggests that it was only at the end of the fifth century that *nomos* came to include among its meanings the legislation enacted by political assemblies.[13]

Aristotle, who is not ordinarily reluctant to raise questions about the ambiguities in the conceptual vocabulary he inherited from the Greek language, seems content with the rather broad and vague range of the Greek term *nomos*. One recent commentator contends that "Aristotle takes pains to distinguish law from custom. The distinction is important because the fact that law is written is [for Aristotle] of its essence."[14] But there is little direct evidence in Aristotle's writings to support this contention. Aristotle repeatedly describes unwritten customs as laws and, indeed, goes so far as to say, with regard to the important laws governing moral education, that "whether the laws are written or unwritten would seem to make no difference" (*NE* 1180b1). He apparently does not consider the use of a common term to refer to statutory, customary, conventional, and moral rules to be a source of ambiguity or confusion about political phenomena.

*Nomos,* as Aristotle uses it, has the general range of our term *norm.*[15] The *nomoi* represent for him the ways in which a community behaves, the general rules and principles it seems to follow. Nomoi are legislated or customary, written or unwritten, sanctioned or unsanctioned, enforced by shame or punishment. Distinctions between statutory, moral, customary, and conventional rules, distinctions that play so large a part in modern definitions of law, play no part in his general conception of law. Even the simplest and least loaded of modern distinctions between moral and legal rules—that laws are norms enforced by the state through

---

12. Huntington Cairns sees important advantages for the study of legal institutions in Aristotle's reluctance to pursue a single definition of law. Aristotle, Cairns suggests, saw "the inherent complexity of legal phenomena, and he found no single description of it could embrace its manifold aspects.... In this approach he was on much sounder ground than Plato, who saw law as a simple unitary phenomenon. All the elements which Aristotle emphasized have been taken separately as the single bases of subsequent systems' ; H. Cairns, *Legal Philosophy,* 95.
13. See M. Gagarin, *Early Greek Law*; S. C. Humphreys, "The Discourse of Law," 473; D. Kelly, *The Human Measure,* 19–20.
14. S. Letwin, "Justice, Law, and Liberty," 230.
15. M. Salomon, *Der Begriff der Gerechtigkeit,* 12.

punitive sanctions, whereas morals are unenforced norms—does not seem to interest him. He does, of course, recognize that the political community has some unique powers when it comes to enforcing norms (*NE* 1180a, *Pol.* 1286b32); but he makes no effort to distinguish between norms that demand enforcement and those that do not.[16]

Aristotle attributes three general characteristics to all laws: laws involve general rules or principles; they are shared by members of communities; and they are derived in some way from the practical reason of particular individuals and groups.

Aristotle associates both the virtues and limitations of law with its generality (*NE* 1137b11–24, *Rhet.* 1354b). The generality of laws gives them a prospective character that distinguishes them from what he calls "decrees" (*psēphismata*). Decrees are actions undertaken by a political community with regard to particular individuals and circumstances already known to the actors (*NE* 1141b28). Laws, in contrast, provide general norms for dealing with a variety of future circumstances.

The second general characteristic of laws, according to Aristotle, is that they are shared by members of communities. In other words, laws are general norms that community members expect each other to follow. It is important to note here that Aristotle does not restrict laws to the rules shared by members of political communities. *All* communities have general norms that their members expect each other to follow. Aristotle describes all of these norms as *nomoi*, regardless of whether they are legislated by the supreme group in the political community or they are associated with some sub- or suprapolitical community.

As discussed above, Aristotle recognizes a tremendous variety of communities. Accordingly, he recognizes a great variety of laws that require adjudication. There are, for example, the unwritten laws he describes as "general" or "common" (*koinon*) laws (*Rhet.* 1368b7, 1373b). They reflect the various forms of community shared by some or all Greeks, or even, in rare cases, by all human beings.[17] All of these communities develop general norms, mostly unwritten, which their members expect will guide each other's behavior. And these norms, even though unwrit-

---

16. The reason for this omission is not a lack of analytic rigor but the simple fact that Aristotle does not share the liberal political goals that inspire modern efforts to demarcate a sphere of behavior within which it is inappropriate to have the state enforce rules and norms. See J. Shklar, *Legalism*, 42, for this interpretation of modern efforts to distinguish legal and moral rules.

17. Aristotle indicates the existence of a universal, albeit not very deep, sense of community among human beings when he speaks of the friendship that "members of the same species, especially human beings, feel for one another"; *NE* 1155a19.

ten, are among the laws that require adjudication within the political community. There are, in addition, unwritten laws that develop within the political community itself that demand adjudication (*Rhet.* 1373b).

The unwritten common law that Aristotle refers to in the *Rhetoric* thus refers merely to one of a variety of laws that demand adjudication rather than to some supremely authoritative form of law, such as natural law has come to represent for many of Aristotle's heirs.[18] He does assert in the *Politics* (1287b5) that "unwritten laws are more supreme and deal with more supreme matters." But this assertion need not be interpreted as a claim that common, unwritten laws stand above and overrule written legislation in some legal hierarchy. As argued above, there are unwritten laws particular (*idios*) to a political community, as well as more universal unwritten rules. Aristotle never asks which should take precedence over the other, even though this would be a very pressing question indeed if he were seeking to establish a systematic hierarchy among the various forms of law.[19]

Aristotle does not address this question because his remarks about the supreme character of unwritten laws refer to their greater impact on individual character and behavior rather than to their position in a legal hierarchy. Law's capacity to shape moral dispositions through the inculcation of certain habits is, as I argue below, one of its greatest contributions to political life. Unwritten laws perform this function better than written laws do, since the habits they shape are more spontaneous and less alien to the individual. They are thus "more supreme" in the way that they shape moral character, and they deal with "more supreme matters" in that they are concerned primarily with the most important political goal: moral education. But Aristotle leaves it to adjudicators to decide for themselves between those who assert, like Antigone, the supremacy of the unwritten law and those who demand the enforcement of written regulations (*Rhet.* 1373b). Although he clearly distinguishes between unwritten suprapolitical laws and the written laws of a particular community, he says nothing here or elsewhere to indicate that one of these sets of law should, by its very nature, overrule the other.

The third common feature of laws, according to Aristotle, is that

18. See F. Miller, "Aristotle on Natural Law and Justice," and L. Arnhart, *Aristotle on Political Reasoning*, 104–5, for thoughtful attempts to link the unwritten common laws of the *Rhetoric* to Aristotle's understanding of natural right.
19. As Martin Ostwald notes in "Was There a Concept of *Agraphos Nomos* in Classical Greece?" for Aristotle and the Greeks in general, unwritten law was a general category whose meaning varies in context rather than a specific type of law to be adjudicated.

they all have their origins in practical reason. In a passage that comes close to suggesting a general definition of law, Aristotle suggests that law is "a rule of reason from some practical reason [*phronēsis*] and intellect [*nous*]" (*NE* 1180a21). This passage, along with his famous description of law as "intellect without desire" (*Pol.* 1287a33), has inspired lyric celebrations of law's rationality. Ernest Barker, for example, is moved by Aristotle's description of legal rationality to proclaim: "In man reason is close neighbour of many passions and can hardly be heard for their clamour: in law it emerges pure, a clear and solitary voice, which calls aloud through a silence in which all passion is hushed. But morality consists in a life according to reason: the words of reason are the moral code. The law, which is one with reason, must therefore also be one with the moral code."[20]

Many aspects of this celebration of legal rationality make it highly dubious as an interpretation of Aristotelian ideas. Where, for example, does Aristotle speak of anything remotely resembling a "moral code," that is, a set of laws that establishes the supremely rational and correct forms of behavior? "Virtuous action" refers, for him, to actions that follow from certain settled dispositions, not to actions that conform to a supremely rational moral code. The very idea of such a code reflects a legalistic conception of morality that is completely foreign to Aristotelian ethics.

Aristotle has a much more modest sense of the inherent rationality of law. When he states that laws have their origins in practical reason or prudence (*phronēsis*), he is merely indicating the human capacity to apply intelligence to a choice of possible actions within a particular set of circumstances. Law thus flows from the same source as decrees (*NE* 1141a25–29)—and no one would suggest that ordinary political decrees represent moral reason's "pure" and "solitary voice." The practical wisdom in law manifests the deliberation and actions of human beings who are in a position to impose their judgments on others. It is no less fallible than the human beings who supply it.

There is also a second, more formal sense in which law is rational according to Aristotle. Laws establish for future actors what for Aristotle is the characteristic pattern for reasoning: the syllogism. Laws, because of their general and prospective character, impose on those who accept them syllogistic reasoning. To judge whether an individual has

---

20. E. Barker, *The Political Thought*, 321.

obeyed or broken a law, we must construct a syllogism with the law as the major premise and the individual's action as the minor premise.

Laws are thus, in Aristotle's view, both substantively and formally rational. But they are not identical with reason per se, as Barker seems to suggest. The exaggerated picture of Aristotle's understanding of legal rationality grows out of two sources. The first is the influence of the biblical and natural law ideal of a final and inherently correct body of moral rules and principles. The second is the misinterpretation of the famous passage in *Politics* book 3 in which Aristotle describes law as "intellect without desire" and suggests that with law "God and intellect rule" without the wild beast that lurks in human appetites (*Pol.* 1287a30).

Few passages from the *Politics* are more frequently quoted or more frequently ripped out of context. Those who quote this passage rarely note that it appears as part of Aristotle's summary of the arguments made by the partisans of rule by law or that Aristotle juxtaposes these arguments with the arguments made by the partisans of absolute monarchy.[21] His suggestion that law is divine in character thus has its counterpart in the claim that lawfulness is not appropriate for the rule of that "God among men" who deserves absolute power (*Pol.* 1284a10–15). Both claims are partisan; they are not meant to represent Aristotle's final judgment.[22] Aristotle frequently approaches controversial questions by identifying the best arguments on each side.[23] His final judgment always makes use of the strongest claims on each side. In this case, Aristotle concludes that most often the rule of law is the appropriate way to rule; but he also recognizes the limitations in legal rationality pointed out by the partisans of absolutism. His conclusion does not repeat the partisan claims about law's divine and pure rationality.

We must then turn to other passages to flesh out Aristotle's picture of legal rationality. These passages both emphasize law's role as an obstacle to reasoning and praise its inherent rationality. Aristotle's exploration of the problems involved in legal innovation (*Pol.* 1268b–69a) illustrates this emphasis well. Here Aristotle notes that law restricts a

---

21. He ends the chapter in which he outlines these arguments by stating that "the arguments of those who dispute against kingship are, then, essentially these"; *Pol.* 1287b35.

22. See R. Robinson, *Aristotle's Politics, Books III and IV*, 31. Robinson notes that Aristotle's juxtaposition of competing arguments has allowed both advocates of absolutism, such as Robert Filmer, and partisans of the rule of law to cite Aristotelian arguments in support of their political opinions.

23. In the *Politics*, for example, he discusses slavery, legal innovation, and the definition of citizenship according to this approach (*Pol.* 1254b, 1268b–69a, 1275).

specific and highly valued kind of reasoning: the reasoning that guides the practical arts and skills. In the arts we change a practice when we find a better way of doing the thing we want to do. We always encourage and welcome the use of reason to discover better ways of producing things and training our skills. Laws, in contrast, restrain this application of reason. Even when a better law is known, it may be unwise to adopt it, since the acceptance of legal limitations rests more on habit than on instrumental rationality (*Pol.* 1269a20).

Laws also limit the rationality we can apply to particular situations that do not exactly fit the standards they establish. This limitation represents one of the strongest objections to the rule of law made by advocates of absolutism. Inflexibility is part of the price we pay for the relatively dispassionate character of legal rationality. Human beings may be uncertain and erratic, but in them reason is alive to changing circumstances. In law, in contrast, reason is dead, an already determined judgment applied to future unknown circumstances. Law thus limits as well as manifests practical reason.

Pointing out the ways in which laws act as an obstacle to human reasoning reminds us that although law and reason intersect, they are not identical. Despite our rationality, we are, Aristotle suggests, "the worst [of animals] when separated from law and adjudication. For injustice is harshest when furnished with arms; and man is born naturally possessing arms for practical reason and virtue which are nevertheless very susceptible to being used for their opposite" (*Pol.* 1253a31). Without the limits created by laws, human beings would make unlimited use of their reasoning capacities, a prospect that Aristotle wisely fears. For Aristotle, then, law is a limit on the exercise of practical reason that is derived from practical reason itself.

## ADJUDICATION

Huntington Cairns has suggested that Aristotle "assigned to jurisprudence what must always be its main task, the establishment of a rational legal order for a given society." By "the establishment of a rational legal order," Cairns, like most modern legal theorists, means the rationalization of a variety of laws into a coherent, consistent, and hierarchically organized system that will guide judges and litigants about what the law demands. "Thus with Aristotle," he concludes, "we are brought face to face for the first time with an effort to deal with legal materials systematically, by justified methods, and as part of a larger whole."[24]

The rationalization of laws, whether through a written code or the systematization of precedent, is certainly a major aim of jurisprudence according to most modern conceptions. But I see no evidence that Aristotle seeks to rework laws and adjudication into anything resembling a "rational legal order." Indeed, the very concept of a legal order or system seems absent from his writings.[25] Aristotle does advise legislators to adapt their laws to the political regime that will adjudicate and enforce them, but he never suggests that the rationalization of laws into a coherent and consistent system is an important task for legislators, adjudicators, or political philosophers.[26] The absence of any interest on Aristotle's part in reshaping the variety of laws into a consistent, hierarchically organized system becomes apparent once we turn from his general statements about law—into which so much can be written—to his account of adjudication.

The adjudicators (*dikastai*) whom Aristotle discusses in the *Rhetoric* face a tremendous variety of laws: local, national, and supranational customs, shared moral principles, as well as written legislation.[27] Some commentators have seen in the classification of types of law in the *Rhetoric* an attempt to outline a consistent and hierarchically organized legal system.[28] In particular, Aristotle's distinction between "particular" (*idion*) and "common or general" (*koinon*) laws, a distinction that brings to mind later distinctions between natural law or the Roman *jus gentium* and positive law, is often treated as if it provides the basis for such a system of laws. But as I have tried to show in the preceding section,

---

24. H. Cairns, *Legal Philosophy*, 79.
25. For this concept, see J. Raz, *The Concept of a Legal System*.
26. See R. Bauman (*Political Trials in Ancient Greece*, 8–9), who notes Aristotle's lack of interest in systematic jurisprudence and suggests that Theophrastus, Aristotle's successor at the Lyceum, was the first to pursue such studies.
27. Throughout this chapter I translate *dikastēs* as "adjudicator" rather than "judge" or "juror," as it is more frequently translated. I do so in order to avoid the anachronistic connotations, reflecting our own highly differentiated legal system, that "judge" and "juror" suggest. Athenian legal institutions did not rely on the specialized roles of judge, juror, lawyer, and so forth that our institutions require; see P. Maio, "*Politeia* and Adjudication." Misinterpretations of Aristotelian legal ideas frequently arise because of the anachronistic reference to these modern legal roles. Even a notable attempt to put "the philosophy of law in historical perspective" speaks of Aristotle's description of the "task for lawyers"; see C. J. Friedrich, *The Philosophy of Law in Historical Perspective*, 24. On the emergence of a legal profession in ancient Rome and its absence in ancient Athens, see B. Frier, *The Rise of the Roman Jurists*, 184–96, 269–87.
28. Max Hamburger (*Morals and Law*, 64–66), for example, suggests that the *Rhetoric* represents "the consummation of Aristotle's legal philosophy" in which "perfect harmony is established among the various legal spheres." See also P. Trude, *Der Begriff der Gerechtigkeit*, 158.

Aristotle does not use this distinction to establish any hierarchical relation among laws. Litigants, he suggests, will argue, as suits their purpose, that either written or unwritten law should prevail. Aristotle leaves it to adjudicators to decide in each case which law is the most relevant and important (*Rhet.* 1373b). In the end, Francis Wormuth is right to warn us against "build[ing] a jurisprudence on the basis of a few sentences in the *Rhetoric.*"[29]

Modern legal theorists seek to rationalize and systematize laws in order, among other reasons, to avoid uncertainty about what the laws demand and prohibit. Such uncertainty was a continuing problem in Athens; the variety of laws made it difficult to ascertain what law adjudicators would or should invoke in a particular case.[30] The Athenians introduced a number of reforms to deal with this problem after the restoration of democracy in 403. The most important of these reforms was the requirement that a large panel of citizens, called the *nomothetai*, review new legislation approved by the assembly for inconsistencies with earlier laws before it could be enacted into law.[31] Athenians also made greater use of the *graphē paranomon*, a criminal charge that could be lodged against anyone who proposed a law that contravened the city's fundamental laws, after these reforms.

Whether or not the Athenians ever did replace popular sovereignty with the sovereignty of law, as some historians have recently argued,[32] we would expect Aristotle to show interest in these Athenian legal innovations and the confusing situation they were designed to improve, if

---

29. F. Wormuth, "Aristotle on Law," 24. See also G. Wright, "Stoic Midwives," 173–75.

30. See D. M. Macdowell, *The Law in Classical Athens*, 46. Richard Bauman (*Political Trials in Ancient Greece*, 4) complains about the "extraordinary resistance of Athenian procedure to all modern attempts to give it coherence and clarity."

31. D. M. Macdowell, *The Law in Classical Athens*, 48–49.

32. Historians disagree about how successful the Athenians were in systematizing their laws. D. M. Macdowell (*The Law in Classical Athens*, 48) and J. W. Jones (*The Law and Legal Theory*, 100) argue that they had relatively little success. More recently, a number of historians have argued otherwise, suggesting that the constitutional reforms that followed the return to a democratic regime in 403 went a long way toward establishing a stable "rule of law" in Athens. See R. Sealey, *The Athenian Republic*, 146–48; M. Ostwald, *From Popular Sovereignty*, 524. R. K. Sinclair (*Democracy and Participation*, 83–84) and Richard Bauman (*Political Trials in Ancient Greece*) argue against this group that these reforms did not fundamentally diminish popular sovereignty in Athens. Mogens Hansen suggests that it would be more appropriate to speak of the sovereignty of the law courts as a political institution than of the rule of law per se. See M. Hansen, *The Athenian Assembly*, 98–113, 129–30; M. Hansen, "The Political Powers." Harvey Yunis argues persuasively that the *graphē paranomon* was used primarily as a political means of controlling the power of popular leaders rather than as a means of maintaining the consistency of laws; H. Yunis, "Law, Politics, and the *Graphē Paranomon*."

he were an advocate of the establishment of a rational legal order. But we never find such interest expressed among Aristotle's numerous complaints about Athens. It is the failure of Athenian laws to promote moral education, rather than their unsystematic profusion, that disturbs Aristotle (*NE* 1180a25, *Pol.* 1310a11–25).[33]

If one believes that the establishment of a rational legal system is "always" the "main task" of legal theory, then we must judge Aristotle a terrible failure as a legal theorist. But there is no need to hold Aristotle to this relatively narrow view of legal theory, a view promoted by the two most influential schools of modern jurisprudence: the legal positivists and the natural lawyers. If one aims, like legal positivists, at the rationalization of laws or, like natural lawyers, at their adaptation to a supreme and unqualifiedly correct set of rules, then the systematization of laws will be a very high priority. If, however, one does not share these goals, then systematization is not necessarily the rational approach to legal materials.

Indeed, one could make a case that there may be considerable advantages in leaving unaltered laws and precedents whose provisions may potentially conflict in adjudication. If, as Aristotle believes, one of the most important benefits of general rules is its contribution to the habits that ground moral dispositions,[34] then one might want to maintain potentially contradictory laws that successfully promote certain characteristics, despite the confusion and uncertainty their provisions may inspire. It would be better, all other things being equal, if we could promote these dispositions by means of more systematic and consistent laws. But, as Aristotle notes, we do not have the luxury in ordinary political life of picking the best and most consistent ways of promoting moral character. The unwritten laws that have the greatest impact on shaping moral character bear the impress of the peculiar and unrepeatable situations in which they arose and were accepted. We can surely conceive of situations in which desirable characteristics could be promoted by more consistent means; but it is most likely that these are not the situations in which we find ourselves. We might conclude then that if we pursue Aristotle's goals, the beneficial effects of potentially inconsistent laws outweigh the confusion and uncertainty they may inspire. The continual revision of laws in the name of order and consistency threatens the settled habits that older laws have promoted (*Pol.* 1269a10).

33. As Barry Strauss ("On Aristotle's Critique of Democracy," 219–23) notes, Aristotle completely ignores the Athenian requirement for annual review of new legislation.
34. I develop this understanding of law's role in political life in the following section.

How then does Aristotle view adjudication and its relationship to laws, if not as part of an effort to establish a rational legal order? His most precise, if overly compact, description of adjudication occurs in the first pages of the *Politics*. "Adjudication [or 'judgment'; *dikē*] is an arrangement [*taxis*] of the political community, and adjudication is the decision [*krisis*] about what is just" (*Pol.* 1253a38).[35] Adjudication is the institutional arrangement or order (*taxis*) by which members of the political community determine the justice or injustice of particular actions.[36] Law and adjudication together prevent our rational capacities from promoting depravity (*Pol.* 1253a31). The improvement of human character requires not only laws, shared general rules limiting the use of practical reason, but also some arrangement for determining which particular actions the political community considers just and unjust.

Note that in this passage Aristotle describes adjudication as the determination of justice or injustice rather than as the determination of whether laws have been broken. If Aristotle simply identified law and justice, then we could ignore this distinction since the determination of injustice and of whether a law had been broken would be identical. But as I argue in the preceding chapter, for Aristotle laws do not, in themselves, define just actions. Just actions are those that individuals with just characters perform. Among the things that just individuals are disposed to do is to act as recommended by the shared rules of communities within which they live. That makes all laws just, in a certain sense, according to Aristotle. But the just action is defined by the action that a justly disposed individual would perform in a particular situation, not the action that laws recommend.

Adjudication thus seeks to determine the justice, not merely the legality, of actions. It seeks to determine whether an unjust action, the action unjustly disposed individuals would undertake in particular situations, has been performed. Adjudicators can no more than individual actors know justice simply by referring to laws, whether written or unwritten. Ideally, adjudicators must be "living [*empsuxon*] justice" (*NE* 1132a20), since they should know what a just individual would do in a particular situation in order to render the best judgment.[37]

35. Cf. the similarly worded passage in *NE* 1134b31.
36. Like Carnes Lord, in his edition of the *Politics,* 248n12, I interpret *taxis* in this passage as an institutional arrangement rather than as the broader order within the political community.
37. In the *Rhetoric* Aristotle does, in passing, identify injustice with "voluntarily causing harm against the law" (*Rhet.* 1368b), but this statement, I suggest, represents a relatively rough definition that Aristotle accepts in order to proceed with the analysis of criminal

Adjudication thus demands something more than the application of general rules to particular cases. It requires prudential rather than technical judgment. Adjudicators must decide what justly disposed individuals would do in particular situations in order to determine whether an individual has acted unjustly or not. The most important qualification for an Aristotelian adjudicator then is a just disposition—that is why an ideal adjudicator is "living justice"—rather than the special knowledge of the law we demand of judges. Here is one case where modern democratic theory and practice are more favorably disposed toward special knowledge as a qualification for an important political position than Aristotle is.

Given this understanding of adjudication, it should not be surprising that Aristotle expresses little interest in modern ideas about the separation of law and politics through the creation of an independent and politically neutral judiciary. Ideas of this sort would clearly be out of place in communities, such as Athens, where most cases were tried before miniature assemblies of five hundred citizens. But Aristotle does not even suggest that an independent judiciary should guide us as an ideal. Adjudication is for him an essentially political activity.[38] Sharing in ruling and adjudicating defines citizenship (*Pol.* 1275a23). In democracies it is entirely appropriate that ordinary citizens without any special training in the law should play a large role in adjudication. In a better regime, with higher standards of citizenship, we might find better—that is, more virtuous—adjudicators, but to deprive the citizens of a democracy, or for that matter of a polity, of some role in adjudication would fundamentally alter the political character of the regime. Accordingly, Aristotle rejects Hippodamus's proposal that one small supreme court review all judicial decisions as inappropriate for all but the most oligarchic regimes (*Pol.* 1267b39). Because he regards the determination of justice and injustice as a prudential rather than a technical de-

---

motives that this passage introduces (*Rhet.* 1368b–1372a). It does not accord with his more fully worked out analysis of justice in *Nicomachean Ethics,* book 5. Besides, Aristotle goes on in the *Rhetoric* to describe laws as one of the "inartificial" (*atechnon*) proofs that rhetoricians offer to demonstrate the justice or injustice of actions, rather than as the definitive measure of justice and injustice. The other forms of proof mentioned here are witnesses, contracts, oaths, and torture (*Rhet.* 1375a). If Aristotle thought of unjust action as identical with illegal action, it would have made much more sense to speak of the proofs that witnesses, contracts, oaths, and torture may offer that a law has been broken than to describe laws as another such proof.

38. *The Constitution of Athens* (36) suggests that Solon's introduction of popular juries gave the Athenian demos the means of gaining control of the city. As R. K. Sinclair (*Democracy and Participation in Athens,* 132–33) argues, the courts provided a much more popular and accessible arena for popular participation than the assembly did.

cision, he insists that all members of a political community must play some role in adjudication.[39]

Despite the tremendous growth of technical legal knowledge and specialized legal institutions since Aristotle's day, we still recognize, to a certain extent, the importance of this imperative, when, for example, we assign the final decision in criminal cases, where punishment is most serious, to juries made up of ordinary citizens without legal training. Our legal institutions and practices create limits to the discretion of modern jurors that did not burden their Athenian counterparts. But by deferring to the judgment of citizen-jurors, we implicitly acknowledge that decisions in criminal cases involve something more than the technical application of special legal knowledge and that ordinary citizens should, in some way, share in the exercise of this discretion.

As for the interpretation of specific laws—as opposed to decisions about whether an injustice has occurred—Aristotle recommends that adjudicators adopt a relatively narrow approach that minimizes interpretive discretion (*Rhet.* 1354b). Although Aristotle insists that adjudication is no less an exercise of political power than legislation is, he still tries to erect a sharp distinction between them as two different kinds of political activity. Recognizing that adjudication frequently presents opportunities to reopen deliberation about the value of particular laws, he introduces a number of arguments against making use of these opportunities.

The first of these arguments rests on the claim that "it is easier to find one or a few men of good sense capable of framing laws" than the large number we would need to apply good laws if we allowed adjudicators great discretion in interpreting the laws (*Rhet.* 1354b1). Although this argument seems especially appropriate for ancient Athenians, among whom adjudication was assigned to large and randomly selected citizen juries, it still has some relevance for modern institutions. We need only one prudent individual to write a valuable law, whatever help that individual may need to get that law enacted. But we need a rather large and indeterminate number of individuals to interpret laws, since we will apply them to many different cases in many different situations. It seems much more reasonable to Aristotle to hope that a rel-

---

39. Aristotle would agree with Martin Shapiro (*Courts*, 20) that "the universal pattern is that judging runs as an integral part of the mainstream of political authority rather than as a separate entity. In those societies in which sovereignty can be located, the sovereign judges. In those in which political authority is not clearly concentrated, those who hold the dispersed authority judge."

atively insightful individual will gain sufficient influence to enact a beneficial law than to hope that all the judges who apply laws to particular situations will possess similar insight.

The second reason Aristotle offers for limiting the discretion of adjudicators in interpreting specific laws is that "legislation is a result of long deliberation, while judgments are delivered on the spur of the moment, so that it is difficult for adjudicators to decide questions of justice or expedience" (*Rhet.* 1354b3). This argument also seems most appropriate to Greek legal systems, in which trials were short and deliberation minimal. Contemporary adjudication, as we know all too well, can drag on for months and years, allowing much greater opportunity for deliberation by both judge and jury. Nevertheless, even in modern circumstances the need to come to a decision in a particular case imposes limits on judicial deliberation that make adjudication an inappropriate forum for considering which is the best form of a particular law. Individuals demand from adjudicators a decision that will settle their conflicting claims. Adjudicators thus do not have the luxury possessed by legislators of redefining or dropping subjects that might better be avoided, deferred, or treated in another context.[40] They must, in the end, issue a decision that will stand as a declaration of approved and disapproved actions. Even if they do not decide "on the spur of the moment," the necessity of deciding and, in effect, affirming some rule makes it less appropriate that we rely on their deliberations to determine what is the best formulation of a law.

Aristotle's third argument for limited discretion in interpreting laws is probably the most familiar to us. Legislation, he argues, seeks to establish general rules for future conduct, whereas adjudication seeks to decide "present and definite issues." As a result, legislators can distance themselves a little more than adjudicators can from the pain and profit for particular individuals that follow from their judgments. This greater distance, Aristotle suggests, provides them with a more suitable environment for deliberation about the best laws (*Rhet.* 1354b5). Aristotle is not suggesting here that legislators are inherently more impartial than adjudicators are. After all, according to Aristotle's view of adjudication and political office, they are the same individuals. He is speaking rather of the conditions conducive for good deliberation about the best formulation of general rules. Adjudicators' greater proximity to actual pain

---

40. I am not, of course, suggesting that appellate court judges are completely without means of avoiding controversial issues, means that are discussed and recommended in A. Bickel, *The Least Dangerous Branch*.

and profit limits, in his view, the effectiveness of judicial deliberation on general questions.

Finally, Aristotle recommends limited discretion in interpreting laws because

> deliberative rhetoric lends itself to trickery less than forensic since it is of more general interest. For in the assembly the judges decide on their own affairs, so that the only thing necessary is to prove the truth of the statement of one who recommends a measure, but in the law courts this is not sufficient; there it is useful to win over the hearers, for the decision concerns other interests than those of the adjudicators, who, having only themselves to consider and listening merely for their own pleasure, surrender to the pleaders but do not give a real decision.
>
> (*Rhet.* 1354b35)

This final argument for limited interpretive discretion might at first seem to contradict the previous argument, since it apparently suggests that distance from a particular issue has negative effects on our deliberation about it, whereas the previous argument seems to suggest the opposite. I would suggest, however, that the two arguments do not contradict each other. The particularity of a trial does expose adjudicators much more directly than legislators to personal interests, to the individual instances of pain and profit that follow from their decisions. But it also makes it easier for adjudicators to separate their own interests from the issues deliberated. It is not, after all, their own fate they are deciding, unless, of course, they have a personal connection with the litigants. One might think that this aspect of adjudication would make it more, rather than less, conducive to deliberation about the value of particular laws, since it seems to promote greater impartiality. Instead, Aristotle argues that the lack of personal interest lessens the seriousness of judicial deliberation, suggesting that adjudicators often accept sophistic and frivolous arguments that they would reject were their own interests involved in the matter at hand. He does not, of course, think that legislators are immune to rhetorical tricks. He is merely noting that their direct involvement in the consequences of their decisions makes them warier of the kind of seductive, sophistic, and theoretically provocative arguments that sometimes sway adjudicators who have no practical stake in the outcome of their deliberations.[41]

Despite all of these arguments, Aristotle does acknowledge, in his

---

41. See L. Arnhart, *Aristotle on Political Reasoning*, 23.

famous and influential discussion of equity, that some cases demand greater interpretive discretion from adjudicators. "The equitable," Aristotle suggests,

> is a corrective of what is legally just. The reason is that all law is universal, but there are some things about which it is not possible to speak correctly in universal terms. Now, in situations where it is necessary to speak in universal terms but impossible to do so correctly, the law takes the majority of cases, fully realizing in what respect it misses the mark. The law itself is none the less correct. For the mistake lies neither in the law nor in the lawgiver, but in the nature of the case. For such is the material of which actions are made. So in a situation in which the laws speak universally, but the case at issue happens to fall outside the universal formula, it is right to correct the shortcoming, in other words, the omission and mistake of the lawgiver due to the generality of his statement. Such a correction corresponds to what the lawgiver himself would have said if he were present, and what he would have enacted if he had known [of the particular case].
> 
> (NE 1137b12–23)

Laws are inherently general; they cannot specify exactly how an adjudicator should apply them in every case and circumstance.[42] "Life would not be long enough to enumerate the infinite number of cases" to which a law may apply (*Rhet.* 1374b30). Consequently, Aristotle suggests that the adjudicator has the responsibility of "correcting" the law when literal application to a particular case would be inappropriate.

According to some commentators, Aristotle's conception of equity requires adjudicators to measure all conventional laws against a more authoritative set of natural laws. For example, René Gauthier and Jean Jolif suggest that Aristotle is asking judges to correct the law by referring to the "law inscribed in the heart of man, the norm of natural right that opposes itself to written laws." Equity, they conclude, reflects a "superior law inscribed in nature" rather than an indulgent, compassionate disposition.[43] By demanding that adjudication correct the law in particular circumstances, Aristotle, they suggest, acknowledges the existence of a higher natural law against which judges must measure the justice of all the laws that come before them.[44]

In the years since Aristotle invented the legal conception of equity,

---

42. Even the best of legislators, such as the Athenian lawgiver Solon, cannot eliminate this kind of generality from their laws. See *The Constitution of Athens*, ch. 9.
43. R. Gauthier and J. Jolif, *L'Éthique à Nicomaque* 2:432–33.
44. P. Trude (*Der Begriff der Gerechtigkeit*, 124–25, 129) and W. Siegfried (*Der Rechtsgedanke bei Aristoteles*, 80) are among the other scholars who identify Aristotelian equity with natural law.

rules of equity have frequently been identified with natural law;[45] but Aristotle himself never mentions nature or natural standards in his discussion of equity. He suggests instead that equity's correction of law "corresponds to what the lawgiver himself would have said were he present" (*NE* 1137b22). Equitable adjudicators look "not to the letter of the law but to the intention of the legislator" (*Rhet.* 1374b10). Aristotle's conception of equity merely requires that adjudicators consider the spirit and purpose, as well as the letter, of a law when applying it to a particular case.

Aristotelian equity is, in the end, a characteristic we expect of just individuals (*NE* 1138a3) rather than a set of rules. One sure sign of an equitable disposition in an individual is "satisfaction with less than his share even though he has the law on his side" (*NE* 1138a2). An equitable disposition moderates and complements just individuals' lawfulness, their preference for applying general rules to particular cases. It allows just individuals to accept the need to put aside rules in particular cases without upsetting their disposition toward following general rules. Untempered by an equitable disposition, a just character tends toward fanaticism. Equity and lawfulness represent for Aristotle two dispositions that we should look for in adjudicators, rather than higher and lower sets of moral standards.

A POLITICAL CONCEPTION OF THE RULE OF LAW

What meaning does the rule of law possess for Aristotle if it does not conform to familiar republican rhetoric about laws ruling over the wills of particular individuals?

Two ideals, which I call "moral rectitude" and "administrative regularity," shape most theoretical accounts of the rule of law as well as most interpretations of Aristotle's understanding of the concept. According to the first of these two ideals, the rule of law seeks to bring our behavior into line with a supreme and morally correct set of rules that have their source in God's will, in the nature of things, in an idealized view of human reason or a community's shared standards, or in any combination thereof. The ideal of administrative regularity, in contrast, merely requires the universal and impartial application of two sets of morally fallible rules: the general rules that empower certain individuals to make and interpret laws for a community and the general rules

---

45. See M. Hamburger, *Morals and Law*, 63–65, 100.

that these individuals establish. Its goal is a regular and predictable social order rather than a morally correct one; its enemy is arbitrariness rather than immorality. These two ideals of the rule of law correspond to two very different conceptions of political rationality. For the advocates of rectitude, the order created by law is rational because it is the right order, that is, the one shaped by substantively correct rules. For the proponents of regularity, the legal order is rational because it is a relatively impersonal order, one in which the arbitrariness inspired by whim and passion has been eliminated or minimized.[46]

Commentators have associated Aristotle's ideas about law with both of these ideals of legal rationality.[47] But as I have argued in the preceding sections on the nature of law and on adjudication, Aristotle himself defends neither rectitude nor regularity.[48] Because Aristotle denies that laws can capture the refinements of good moral judgment, it makes little sense to speak of his rule of law as the rule of morally correct standards. Because he expresses little interest in making sure that laws form a consistent and hierarchically organized system, it makes little sense to speak of his rule of law as the guarantor of a regular and predictable social order.

Does this mean, as some have concluded, that the rule of law has very little significance for Aristotle?[49] Not necessarily. It merely means that Aristotle's understanding of the rule of law does not conform to our most familiar ideals of legal rationality.

Aristotle's understanding of the rule of law is hard to identify because it does not share the legalistic understanding of law and politics that characterizes the most familiar ideals associated with the rule of law. Moral rectitude and administrative regularity, like the "normal models" of justice discussed in the previous chapter, reflect a legalistic

---

46. Between them, these two ideals provide the poles between which all legalist or adjudicatory conceptions of the rule of law develop. At the end of the spectrum identified with the ideal of regularity, we find most positivist accounts of the rule of law. For a particularly clear statement of the virtues that positivists associate with the rule of law, see J. Raz, "The Rule of Law." At the other end of the spectrum we find the most moralistic versions of natural law arguments, such as those in the Old Testament or Aquinas's account of divine, natural, and human laws. Contemporary challenges to positivist accounts to the rule of law, such as Lon Fuller's (*The Inner Morality of Law* and *The Principles of Social Order*) and Dworkin's (*Taking Rights Seriously* and *Law's Empire*), seek to balance regularity and rectitude and thus tend to fall somewhere between these two poles.
47. See, for example, E. Barker, *The Political Thought*, 321–23.
48. See F. Wormuth, "Aristotle on Law," 15, for a similar argument.
49. Francis Wormuth, for example, concludes that the rule of law "although inaccurate is also dispassionate. This is all the rule of law meant to Aristotle"; ibid., 18.

understanding of political morality that is foreign to Aristotle's writings. Both of these ideals extend the model of legal adjudication into the realm of politics by treating the rule of law as a set of standards against which to measure the legitimacy of particular political actions. When informed by the ideal of rectitude, the rule of law measures the legitimacy of political actions against a supreme body of moral rules; when informed by the ideal of regularity, it measures their legitimacy against the requirements of the previously established rules of obligation and empowerment. The difference between the two ideals lies in the nature and extent of the standards of adjudication they erect.

Aristotle, in contrast, does not treat the rule of law as a set of adjudicative standards against which to measure the legitimacy of particular political actions. In recommending the rule of law, Aristotle is merely suggesting that ordinary political communities will fare best when citizens are influenced by a disposition to follow and govern by means of general rules. Rather than a moral ideal or an institutional standard of legitimacy, Aristotle conceives of the rule of law as a general disposition that provides, in ordinary conditions, an important and necessary condition for a decent political life.

In order to reconstruct Aristotle's understanding of the rule of law, let us begin by exploring his distinction between lawless regimes and those regimes in which "law rules" (*Pol.* 1292a1).[50] This distinction is far less familiar than his famous distinction between correct and deviant regimes. But because the set of existing law-respecting regimes, unlike the set of existing correct (*orthos*) regimes, is not empty, it is far more useful in classifying and evaluating actual political regimes. Aristotle distinguishes actual lawful oligarchies and democracies from their more lawless counterparts and recommends their imitation, even though they are unlikely to be ruled by just individuals disposed to promote the common good (*Pol.* 1292a, 1292b1, 1272b5). Laws can rule, apparently, in Aristotle's "deviant" regimes, a political category that includes all the regimes we are ever likely to know.

Aristotle's move from virtue to lawfulness as the measure of acceptable regimes resembles a similar move in Plato's *Statesman*.[51] In that dialogue Plato first distinguishes good regimes from bad by asking whether they are ruled by individuals who possess full knowledge of the

---

50. It would be more appropriate to speak of the rule of *laws* in Aristotle's case than the "rule of *law*," since, as I argue, Aristotle makes no effort to reshape laws into a rational and systematic order. For the sake of recognizability, however, I will continue to speak of the rule of law in reconstructing Aristotle's understanding of lawfulness.

51. Plato, *Statesman*, 300–302.

political art. He then goes on to suggest that because such individuals are unlikely to gain power in actual political communities, we should settle for a "second-best" standard, obedience to laws, as the measure of acceptable regimes. Aristotle's famous sixfold classification of regimes appears first in the *Statesman* as the distinction between the lawful and unlawful rule of the one, the few, and the many.[52]

But Aristotle's move to lawfulness as the measure of acceptable regimes differs from Plato's in important ways. First, Aristotle is far less harsh in his criticisms of the limitations of the rule of law than Plato is. Both philosophers argue that laws necessarily constrain practical reasoning and the social reforms that come from improvements in our knowledge. But Plato suggests that in doing so the laws act "like an obstinate and ignorant tyrant,"[53] whereas Aristotle reserves complaints about tyranny for the extreme oligarchies and democracies that ignore laws (*Pol.* 1292a18, 1292b6).

Lawful regimes are for Aristotle more than the mere "second-best" substitutes for virtuous and knowledgeable regimes that they are for Plato. Indeed, apart from the special case of monarchy,[54] they do not substitute at all for Aristotle's initial class of "correct" regimes. Aristotle's set of lawful regimes includes aristocracies and polities as well as oligarchies and democracies. Correct regimes, no less than deviant ones, must rely on a disposition to follow general rules in order to support the sharing of power characteristic of political community. "To rule and be ruled by turns," Aristotle suggests, is already law, "for the arrangement of succession of ruling is law" (*Pol.* 1287a17). As a result, only those who are "naturally subject to law" tend to participate in the practices of political justice (*NE* 1134b14).

In the end, Aristotle's greater appreciation of lawfulness reflects his insistence, against Plato,[55] on distinguishing political rule from the rule of kings over their subjects and masters over their slaves and households (*Pol.* 1251b). Political rule, unlike these other forms of ruling, involves for Aristotle rule over individuals who take turns in ruling and being ruled. And this practice of ruling and being ruled cannot exist without means that these other forms of ruling do not necessarily require: namely, a widespread disposition to follow laws or general rules. Because Aristotle, unlike Plato, thinks that this practice is natural for

---

52. Ibid., 302.
53. Ibid., 295–96. This argument is made in response to complaints about the "harsh sound" of the idea that a regime without laws could be the best regime.
54. See the Appendix to chapter 2.
55. In Plato, *Statesman*, 259, 267.

the relatively equal individuals that he sees in most Greek cities, he is far more appreciative of lawfulness than Plato is. It is for him a means to something positive, political community, rather than, as it is for Plato,[56] merely a means of constraining human vice and ignorance.

The transition from a lawful to an unlawful regime occurs, Aristotle suggests, "when decrees [*psēphismata*] rather than law become supreme" (*Pol.* 1292a5). A lawless regime is one in which those with power rule by means of decrees rather than by means of the enactment or enforcement of general rules.[57] Aristotle elaborates on the difference between decrees and laws in book 6 of the *Nicomachean Ethics*.

> There are two kinds of practical reason [*phronēsis*] concerning the political community: the one, which acts as practical wisdom supreme and comprehensive, is the art of legislation; the other, which is practical wisdom as dealing with particular facts, . . . is concerned with action and deliberation. For a decree [unlike a law] is a matter for action, inasmuch as it is the last step [in deliberation]. That is why only those who make decrees are said to engage in politics, for they alone, like workmen, "do" things.
> (*NE* 1141b24–28)

A decree deals with a particular situation that demands present action. A law seeks, in contrast, to cover a wide range of future situations with a general rule. As a result, a decree is an action in a sense that a law is not. It is the last step in a deliberative process about the action demanded by a particular situation. The decree performs that action. Laws put off this final step, for the action contemplated by a law is complete only when adjudicators decide to apply it to a particular situation. Laws thus stretch deliberation, as it were, into the future, allowing different generations to share in the same action and deliberation.[58]

Laws and decrees represent for Aristotle the two ways in which citizens impose standards of mutual obligation on members of their communities.[59] While acknowledging the continuing need for decrees (*NE*

---

56. Ibid., 300.
57. On the difference between laws (*nomoi*) and decrees (*psēphismata*) in Athens, see M. Hansen, *The Athenian Assembly*, 129; F. Quass, *Nomos und Psephisma*.
58. Aristotle does not, in the end, agree with those who think that legislators, unlike the authors of decrees, do not " 'do' things" (*NE* 1141b28). Laws themselves, he suggests, are "the products of politics" (*NE* 1181a26). Legislation is itself an action that completes a deliberation; it is only the action recommended by laws that remains, according to Aristotle, incomplete.
59. Aristotle's distinction between laws and decrees is derived from Athenian practice, although occasionally the Athenian Assembly issued decrees that dealt with continuing issues and laws that dealt with very specific circumstances. See R. K. Sinclair, *Democracy and Participation*, 84.

1137b26), Aristotle insists that oligarchies and democracies that rely primarily on them tend toward tyranny, the worst of deviant regimes (*Pol.* 1292a18, 1292b6). In characterizing extreme oligarchy and democracy as near-tyrannies, Aristotle goes beyond his original definition of tyranny as selfish rule by a single individual. He now associates tyranny with disregard for general rules, whether the ruling group contains one, few, or many individuals.

Tyranny, Aristotle suggests, is not properly described as a regime (*politeia*) since it lacks a respected body of constitutional rules governing access to political office and the shared way of life that he believes is promoted by such rules. "Where laws do not rule," Aristotle declares, "there is no regime" (*Pol.* 1292a32). Lawless oligarchies and democracies verge on tyrannies, among other reasons, because their disregard for general rules undermines and threatens to eliminate the regimes (*politeiai*) associated with these forms of government. Government through decrees constantly cancels earlier formulations of a community's mutual obligations. It thereby threatens the authority of those formulations and of their makers since the authority of these standards rests to a great extent on the habit of following familiar standards (*Pol* 1269a20). Continued reliance on decrees thus threatens the regime itself by undermining the respect for the general rules that maintains the political authority of individuals and groups within the political community. Oligarchs and democrats may seek to override long-accepted general rules in the name of the general standards favored by their constituencies, but in doing so they render both their own power and the power of these standards, even among their own constituencies, much more unstable and fragile.[60]

When we examine Aristotle's recommendation of regimes in which "laws rule," it is important that we recall the wide extension that Aristotle gives to the term *laws* (*nomoi*). Laws refer for him to all the general rules and norms that communities develop to measure the mutual obligations of their members, not just to statutes and constitutional rules. Consequently, when Aristotle talks about a regime in which "laws rule," he is talking about a regime in which the legislators and adjudicators are disposed, for the most part, to respect and apply—or at least not directly contradict—the customary, conventional, and religious norms, as well as the constitutional and statutory rules, of their political com-

---

60. For example, *The Constitution of Athens*, ch. 36, discusses the problems created by the Thirty Tyrants' repeated withdrawal of laws defining suffrage and citizenship.

munities. By doing so they will, of course, reinforce their political authority, since many constitutional rules are derived from customary rules and practices. Nevertheless, given his broad definition of rules, it is clear that a lawful regime is one in which there is a disposition among rulers to follow the community's general rules, rather than one in which merely statutory and constitutional forms are respected.[61]

This point is illustrated by the praise of Theramenes' political career in *The Constitution of Athens*. Theramenes was reviled by many Athenians as a disloyal and inconsistent opportunist who supported and then opposed virtually all of the oligarchic and democratic regimes that sprang up in Athens during the turbulent years at the end of the Peloponnesian Wars. *The Constitution of Athens* defends Theramenes by arguing that "he worked for the good of any established government as long as it did not transgress the laws," thereby showing "that he was able to serve the polis in any kind of political order, which is what a good citizen should do, but would rather incur enmity and hatred than yield to lawlessness."[62] Because Theramenes worked to undermine the authority of a number of legally established regimes, including the oligarchy of the Thirty Tyrants, the opposition to lawlessness for which he is praised here must refer to something other than a positivistic commitment to the rules made by legally established authorities. His lawfulness refers instead to his general disposition to follow long-established Athenian laws, including customary and unwritten ones, even as the Athenian regime jumped back and forth between democracy and oligarchy.[63]

Once we take into consideration the broad and vague meaning that Aristotle attaches to the term *laws,* it becomes clear that the rule of law cannot be for him, as it is for most modern legal and political theorists, an adjudicative standard by which to measure the legitimacy of particular exercises of political power. To use the rule of law as an adjudicative standard, one must have a clear and determinate standard to deter-

---

61. Accordingly, Aristotle recommends that tyrants can imitate more acceptable regimes by trying to maintain and follow a community's laws. Tyrants violate constitutional norms by their assumption of political power, so the laws that Aristotle refers to here must go well beyond constitutional rules. The Athenian tyrant Peisistratus was said by many to have respected the customary and statutory laws of Athens during his reign. See *The Constitution of Athens,* ch. 20; Thucydides, *History* 6:54.
62. *The Constitution of Athens,* ch. 28. (There remains doubt whether Aristotle was the author of *The Constitution of Athens.*)
63. As Kurt von Fritz and Ernest Kapp imply by supplying the word "fundamental" in their translation of the passage, "he worked for the good of any established government as long as it did not transgress the [fundamental] laws," quoted above. See *Aristotle's Constitution of Athens,* 99.

mine what counts as a law, something Aristotle never supplies.[64] Because Aristotle neither demands a clear hierarchy nor rational consistency within a political community's laws, he cannot invoke the adjudicative ideal of administrative regularity. Because he raises no body of laws to the status of a supreme and intrinsically moral code, he cannot invoke the alternative adjudicative ideal of moral rectitude.

Instead, the rule of law represents for Aristotle a moral disposition the disposition to follow and apply general rules, rather than an adjudicative ideal. That disposition is probably best characterized in his discussion (*Pol.* 1269a) of the pros and cons of legal innovation. He clearly recognizes there the necessity and rationality of legal innovation Nevertheless, he prefers that rulers be disposed against it, since frequent legal innovation upsets the habits and familiarity that lend authority to general rules. Although he does not encourage us to freeze our political community's general rules at the stage we find them, Aristotle does recommend that we try to promote a disposition among citizens that will make it painful and uncomfortable to change or ignore long-standing general rules. It will, of course, on occasion be necessary in a law-respecting regime for citizens and officeholders to abrogate or contradict long-standing general rules. In a regime of this sort, however, they will come to that conclusion infrequently and only after overcoming considerable internal and external resistance. Moral dispositions rather than political institutions define the Aristotelian rule of law.

In contemporary political theory and practice, the rule of law is usually associated with liberal ideals of individual independence and moral neutrality. As a result, the reliance of the rule of law on particular moral characteristics and the dependence of these characteristics on moral training are subjects that contemporary, especially liberal, theorists usually ignore.[65] But some of these characteristics have become so deeply embedded in our character that we no longer notice that they are part of a particular moral ethos or ideology. For example, most of us view subordination to a general rule as far less burdensome than subordination to the will of a particular individual, at least after (if not before) we have left the parental home. We are thus likely to agree with Aristotle that although "people hate any men who oppose, however rightly, their impulses," the generality of law makes it less "invidious

---

64. It is precisely because of modern efforts to use the rule of law as an adjudicative standard that the definition of law has become so central a question among contemporary legal theorists.

65. See J. Shklar, *Legalism,* for a rare exception among liberal theorists.

when it enjoins what is right" (*NE* 1180a22).⁶⁶ Nevertheless, laws remain for Aristotle constraints on our behavior formulated and applied by particular individuals and groups of individuals. Laws do not replace political power for Aristotle. They merely represent the least offensive form of its exercise among free and relatively equal individuals.

But, as Georg Simmel points out, there is nothing necessary or universal about this preference. "Whether rule by man is considered as something provisional in lieu of rule by perfect law, or, inversely, rule by law is considered a gap-filler or an inferior substitute for government by a personality which is absolutely qualified to rule—this choice depends upon decisions of ultimate, indiscussable feelings concerning sociological values."⁶⁷ In ancient Greece and modern Europe, Simmel notes, personal subordination is experienced as a constraint on one's freedom and spontaneity. But in medieval Europe and elsewhere, in contrast, it is impersonal subordination that is experienced as an affront to one's freedom. "The ruler's order was felt to be something personal; the individual wanted to lend him obedience only from personal devotion; and personal devotion, in spite of its unconditional character, is always in the form of free reciprocity."⁶⁸ In some communities, subordination to law can appear less free and more burdensome because it is demanded of all, whereas personal subordination is given by choice of the particular individual.

The difference between these preferences results from a deep difference in moral ethos. Without the more legalistic ethos of ancient Greeks and modern Europeans the rule of law would have little practical meaning. As noted earlier, the dispositions that Aristotle associates with the virtue of justice in book 5 of the *Nicomachean Ethics* are those appropriate to justice in political communities rather than to justice per se. In regimes in which absolutism is appropriate—that is, regimes in which one individual is so superior to all others as to justify absolute power,

---

66. In this passage Aristotle is contrasting political with paternal power as a means of educating people. Political power is normally exercised by means of laws or general rules that affect a broad range of individuals in present and future circumstance. Paternal power is normally exercised by means of commands directed at a particular individual to perform a particular action. Laws are a less offensive way of opposing the inclinations of adults, according to this argument, because they do not directly oppose one particular individual's will to another's. Constraints seem to be far less of a direct opposition to one's own choices when they are imposed generally. There is less indignity in submitting to them.
67. G. Simmel, *The Sociology of Georg Simmel*, 252–53.
68. Ibid., 251–52.

unconstrained by laws (*Pol.* 1288a)—Aristotle would consider lawfulness a vice rather than a virtue.[69] In such circumstances he would advise us to be careful to promote the characteristics appropriate to justice in the specific community we are considering. Institutions designed to promote the rule of law will likely misfire if community members share the dispositions characteristic of more personal, nonpolitical forms of social interaction.

By focusing on a disposition toward rule following as the defining element of the rule of law, Aristotle avoids the familiar criticism that the rule of law necessarily masks the political power of particular individuals and groups. Aristotle clearly recognizes that laws depend for their enactment, adjudication, and enforcement on the political choices that some individuals and groups impose on others. Despite the partisan rhetoric quoted in book 3 of the *Politics* (1287a), there can be no question for Aristotle of the rule of law replacing politics and political rule. The rule of law constrains politics in Aristotle's account only through the influence it has on the character of the individuals who have the power to make political choices. It is a means of political rule, a particular way of exercising political power that is possible when a disposition to lawfulness is widely shared in a community; it is not a replacement for politics.

Although Aristotle denies that law can replace political choice in any way, the development of a disposition to lawfulness remains a serious internal, if not external, constraint on the choices of political actors. It has, for the most part, a conservative impact on politics, since whatever the regime in which it appears, it provides an internal barrier to social, political, and legal innovation. To the extent that citizens and officeholders are disposed to following existing general rules, they are bound to resist large-scale reforms, even when new ruling groups come into power. Aristotle's rule of law thus imposes considerable limits on political rationality and flexibility.

Why should we seek such constraints on the range of political actions? Aristotle offers three reasons: (1) the value of accustoming citi-

---

69. As I argue in the Appendix to chapter 2, for Aristotle the only correct (*orthos*) monarchy is one in which there is a single individual who deserves to rule absolutely. Monarchies in which laws rule deviate from the unqualifiedly just regime version of one-person rule: a regime in which there is only one individual who displays superior virtue. Lawful monarchies are thus deviant regimes, like lawful oligarchies and democracies, according to Aristotle.

zens to particular, if imperfect, standards of justice; (2) the contribution that a relatively stable legal order makes to the moral education of individuals; and (3) the necessary role that respect for general rules plays in establishing and maintaining the regular alternation of officeholders that constitutes a political community.

The first of these reasons for preferring the rule of law is probably the most familiar: because you cannot count on all citizens to develop and follow a disposition to promote the common good, it is better that they follow some standards of justice rather than none at all—which is what Aristotle fears if citizens and officeholders lose the habit of following general rules.

Aristotle's second reason for preferring the rule of law has to do with moral education.

> To obtain the right training for virtue from youth up is difficult unless one has been brought up under the right laws. To live a life of self-control and tenacity is not pleasant for most people, especially for the young. Therefore, their upbringing and pursuits must be regulated by laws; for once they have become familiar, they will no longer be painful.... Since they must carry on these pursuits and cultivate them by habit when they are grown up, we probably need laws for this, too, and for the whole of life in general.
> (NE 1179b31–1180a4)

Laws are a particularly useful means of promoting the Aristotelian moral virtues. Aristotelian moral training consists primarily in habituation: the repeated performance of particular actions until one develops a disposition toward actions of that sort (NE 1103a15–25, 1179b20). Because laws demand the repeated performance of a particular sort of action in a variety of circumstances, they are a particularly efficacious means of developing moral dispositions. Individuals tend to internalize laws after they become familiar, turning them into the habits that anchor moral dispositions. Laws may originally command actions that cause individuals pain, but "once they become familiar they are no longer painful" (NE 1179b35). Because decrees do not set down general patterns of behavior to cover future circumstances, conformity to them does not become as familiar and habitual. Laws, in contrast, become, with repeated performance, part of our individual character, part of the way we view the world, rather than something we are told to do. This aspect of laws will probably seem pernicious when one is opposed to the requirements demanded by particular laws, since it leads individuals to lose sight of the origin and mutability of laws. According to Aristotle, however, we could not begin to offer moral criticism of laws unless we had already developed certain moral dispositions, and we cannot develop these dispositions without the aid of general norms. On balance, then, the rule of law is to be preferred, he would argue, even if, in promoting moral habits, it protects somewhat unjust laws and promotes somewhat flawed dispositions.[70]

The role played by laws in the development of the moral virtues explains why Aristotle insists that it is specifically the lack of "law and adjudication [*dikē*]," rather than the lack of constraint per se, that makes human beings the most depraved of animals (*Pol.* 1253a32). Human beings do not naturally have virtuous dispositions. Moreover, they need something more than externally imposed constraints if they want to develop these dispositions. They need a special kind of constraint, one that they can internalize as a disposition-forming habit. For Aristotle laws provide that kind of constraint. Decrees may command the same specific action as a law, but unlike a law, they are relatively temporary and specific; hence, they are far less conducive to the development of morally beneficial habits. Human reason may, in Aristotle's view, be more alive to the peculiar demands of specific situations when unconstrained by law. Nevertheless, he sees the "deadness" of legal rationality as a decided advantage in moral education.

Aristotle's final reason for promoting a disposition to lawfulness is the least familiar but probably the most important. As mentioned above, a disposition to lawfulness is for him a necessary and essential condition for the establishment and maintenance of political community. "For political justice, as we saw, depends on law and applies to people who are naturally subject to law, and those are people who have an equal share in ruling and being ruled" (*NE* 1134b13). Where "laws do not rule, there is no regime" (*Pol.* 1292a32) and, consequently, no political community.

Political justice, as opposed to the forms of justice appropriate to other kinds of community, involves a practice in which individuals take turns in exercising the political powers of legislation and adjudication. "It is no more just for equals to rule than to be ruled, and it is therefore just to rule and be ruled by turns. But this is already law; for the arrangement of succession of ruling is law" (*Pol.* 1287a17).

Why does Aristotle suggest that taking turns in ruling and being ruled "is already law?" He does not explicitly answer this question, but it seems that he cannot conceive of regular alternation in positions of po-

---

70. See R. Bodéüs, "Law and the Regime," 235–36, for a similar argument.

litical power without explicit general rules—whether customary, constitutional, or statutory in character—and a disposition to follow them. It is indeed hard to imagine regular alternation of positions of political power in a community whose participants were not disposed to follow general rules. One could perhaps imagine a community in which individuals would take turns ruling by means of decrees; but these individuals would, at the very least, need to respect a general rule about when to trade positions. Moreover, it is hard to believe that citizens could trust officeholders who show no respect for general rules to yield office when required by the rules of political succession.

As noted in the preceding chapter, for Aristotle the exchange of goods and the exchange of political office—and with the latter, political community itself—have their foundation in a sense of reciprocity (*NE* 1132b; *Pol.* 1261a–b). Aristotle notes in his discussion of the exchange of goods that a sense of reciprocity is sustained in communities of exchange by the existence of a conventional good, money, that assures us that we will receive commensurable goods in the future for the ones we have just sold. I would suggest that for Aristotle just as money provides our "surety" of "future exchange" of goods (*NE* 1133b11), so a respect for law acts as our surety that we will in the future receive the good, political office, we give now to our relative equals.[71] Without such a surety, the exchange of office would be just as difficult as the exchange of economic goods without money. In this way, law acts as the conventional means that allows us to realize our political nature—which might explain why Aristotle insists that only individuals "who are naturally subject to law" (*NE* 1134b13) can practice political justice and form political communities. If the practice of establishing and respecting general rules directly countered human nature, it would be difficult for Aristotle to maintain that human beings are by nature political animals.

Although a disposition toward lawfulness clearly constrains the exercise of power, *political* power, the power exercised by individuals who take turns in positions of authority, is impossible without it. Although this assertion might appear contradictory, given the tendency to oppose the exercise of political power and the rule of law against each other, it involves no logical inconsistencies.

The rule of law, as Aristotle understands it, acts as what I would call an "enabling constraint" rather than as a mere barrier or limit to polit-

---

71. Recall here the passages in the *Nicomachean Ethics* (1132b) and the *Politics* (1261a–b) in which Aristotle treats reciprocity as the foundation of both economic exchange and political community.

ical power.[72] An enabling constraint is a limit on our freedom of action that enables us to engage in a whole new range of actions that would otherwise be unavailable to us. Enabling constraints free us to engage in a particular set of actions by constraining us from performing a different set of actions. Take, for example, the rules of spoken and written languages. Early training and habituation dispose us to impose the severe limits of the rules of a language on the sounds we make to each other; but by limiting our sounds in this way, we tremendously expand the range and precision of our communication.

Similarly, a disposition to follow shared general rules will severely limit the way in which we make use of power. People who share this disposition will forego many opportunities to take control of their lives or to transform their institutions. But, if Aristotle is right, then it is only by limiting themselves in such a way that they can exercise *political* power at all. The freedom to exercise political power is, from this point of view, bound up with constraints on its exercise.

The historical experience of republican communities, from the classical republics to modern America, offers some support for Aristotle's view that the rule of law and political power are complementary rather than mutually exclusive commitments. Consider the Athenian democracy. Few regimes have done more to involve so many of its members in the practice of self-government. Nevertheless, it is quite clear that the Athenians maintained as deep an attachment to the notion of the rule of law as to popular sovereignty.[73] Indeed, the reverence for the "ancestral constitution" loomed so large in Athenian minds that almost all political innovations in Athens had to be presented as ways of recovering its letter or spirit.[74] The need for such reverence for laws becomes

---

72. I elaborate on the idea of "enabling constraints" in "Towards a Free Marketplace," 1967–68. Stephen Holmes develops a similar idea in his account of constitutional constraints in "Precommitment," 215–16.

73. Josiah Ober (*Mass and Elite,* 299–304) and Mogens Hansen (*The Athenian Assembly,* 106–7, 112–13) provide interesting accounts of the Athenians' simultaneous attachment to the rule of law and popular sovereignty. Barry Strauss tries to explain why Aristotle ignores this important aspect of Athenian political behavior in "On Aristotle's Critique of Democracy," 219–23, 229–32.

74. See M. Finley, *The Ancestral Constitution*; A. Fuks, *The Ancestral Constitution*. In addition, Athenians, as noted above, set up a legal device, the *graphē paranomon,* for punishing individuals who made proposals that were perceived to counter their received laws. Although it would be a mistake to think that the Athenians used such practices to maintain a systematic and consistent body of fundamental law, the *graphē paranomon* reflected a popular moral disposition among them toward maintaining familiar rules. (On the purely political functions of the popular courts and the *graphē paranomon,* see M. Hansen, "The Political Powers"; H. Yunis, "Law, Politics, and the *Graphē Paranomon.*")

apparent once one begins to look over the daunting list of rules that define and organize the profusion of political offices that Athenians took turns in occupying.[75] Without a disposition to follow this mass of general rules, it is hard to understand how the Athenians could possibly have managed to maintain all of these participatory institutions.

The combination of seemingly contradictory attachments to both the rule of law and popular sovereignty is very familiar to students of republican political rhetoric. Aristotle's understanding of the rule of law can help us explain why they both tend to emerge among members of political communities. These two strands of republican rhetoric will seem contradictory to those who, like the majority of legal theorists, see the rule of law as a final adjudicatory standard against which to measure the legitimacy of political actions. But if, like Aristotle, we see the rule of law as moral disposition toward lawful behavior, it becomes clear that they can work together in important ways.

Aristotle's understanding of the rule of law turns the contradiction between popular sovereignty and the rule of law into an unavoidable but creative tension in the life of a decent and relatively stable political community. Attempts at eliminating this tension in the name of increased democracy and political flexibility are bound to be self-defeating, according to this understanding. Political power depends, according to this view, for its existence on a disposition to follow general rules. Attempts to free political power from the constraints of a preference for lawful behavior are thus bound to undermine the very instrument that political reformers seek to liberate from the shackles of the rule of law.

Aristotle's account of the rule of law suggests that a political community's ability to maintain simultaneous attachments to popular sovereignty and the rule of law is something to be prized rather than eliminated.[76] We need, according to Aristotle, an attachment to general rules in order to establish and maintain political communities, but that attachment severely limits what we can do in the communities it helps us create. This problem introduces considerable tension and discomfort into political life. Nevertheless, Aristotle's analysis suggests that we should seek to bolster our ability to endure this tension and discomfort, rather than engage in vain and self-defeating attempts to eliminate it.

---

75. For a partial list, which in its compact form conveys the daunting organizational requirements of a participatory government, see *The Constitution of Athens*, chs. 42–69.

76. Josiah Ober (*Mass and Elite*, 299–304) makes a similar suggestion in his discussion of the tensions in Athenian political rhetoric.

CHAPTER SEVEN

# Class Conflict and the Mixed Regime

Because Aristotle clearly and repeatedly points to the division between rich and poor as the main source of conflict within political communities, it is somewhat surprising that no one has attempted to develop a distinctly Aristotelian approach to class conflict. Apparently, the long shadow cast by Marx's ideas has obscured older approaches to the study of social classes and their role in promoting social conflict. As Moses Finley notes, the "current bad habit of pinning the Marxist label on any and every political analysis that employs a concept of class . . . ignores the long history of such an approach, in one form or another, in western political analysis ever since Aristotle."[1]

When Aristotle's commentators raise the subject of class, they almost always do so in order to ask whether or not his ideas are compatible with Marx's approach to class conflict. Some, such as G. E. M. de Ste. Croix, find in Aristotle's works a nearly perfect reflection of Marx's ideas about class struggle, a reflection that proves the relevance of Marx's theory for the study of classical antiquity.[2] Others insist that because Aristotle's ideas about social conflict diverge so greatly from Marx's we are seriously distorting Aristotle's social and political thought when we attribute to him a theory of class conflict.[3] Neither group con-

---
1. M. Finley, *Politics in the Ancient World*, 9–10.
2. G. E. M. de Ste. Croix, *The Class Struggle*, 69–80.
3. See M. Wheeler, "Aristotle's Analysis of Political Struggle," 164–66; E. Barker, *The Political Thought*, 488.

siders the third alternative that I develop in this chapter: that Aristotle does indeed present an extensive and interesting account of class conflict, but one that sharply differs from and challenges Marx's.

The distinctive feature of Aristotle's understanding of class conflict is his insistence on treating it as something that develops, for the most part, among members of political communities. Aristotle, unlike Marx, does not treat class conflict as the universal source of social conflict and stratification. His understanding of class antagonism is relevant only for individuals who live in political communities, and only for the citizens among that already small portion of the human species. It is primarily *political friends* who become *class enemies* in Aristotle's account. In other words, it is primarily those who have the mutual expectations characteristic of members of political communities who turn the division between rich and poor into the main source of their social conflict.

As long as we are looking for a universal theory of social stratification from Aristotle, the distinctive features of his understanding of social conflict are bound to remain obscure. Once we put aside this demand, however, the Aristotelian approach to class conflict emerges into view and poses a powerful challenge to theories, such as Marx's, that treat class conflict as the universal source of social stratification and instability.

## CLASS CONFLICT IN ANCIENT GREECE

Questions about the existence and extent of class conflict in the ancient Greek republics have sparked considerable controversy among social theorists and classical historians. The importance of noneconomic forms of social stratification in Greek social life—for instance, distinctions between free and slave, citizen and metic—raises serious questions about the appropriateness of a theory of social conflict based on the place of different groups in the process of production. Metics and even slaves, for example, could gain great wealth, owning and operating large enterprises. But their noncitizen status clearly kept them from fully sharing interests and identities with wealthy citizens.[4] Faced with these difficulties, Marxists have had to exercise considerable effort and ingenuity

---

4. Indeed, in most ancient Greek republics, wealthy metics could not even own land or their own homes within the boundaries of the cities they inhabited; see M. Finley, *The Ancient Economy*, 48, and, in general, D. Whitehead, *The Ideology of the Athenian Metic*.

to justify the relevance of Marxist theories of class conflict for ancient Greek social life.[5]

The opening line of *The Communist Manifesto* announces the central assumption of Marx's social theory: "the history of all hitherto existing society is the history of class struggle."[6] According to Marx, the struggle between classes—that is, groups of individuals who are hierarchically positioned within the process of production—explains the nature and direction of social change and historical development. The social struggles that move history are, accordingly, those that emerge from the relationship between exploited and exploiter, the relationship between those who produce things and those who reap the fruits of others' labor. Marx presents a rather harsh view of social development—harsh because it identifies unrelenting conflict of class interests as the primary agent of social change. Nevertheless, his view is, in some ways, surprisingly optimistic, not least of all in its faith that exploitive productive relations inevitably lead to conflicts that transform and improve the structure of social life.

However we assess the value of Marx's theory for the explanation of the relations between modern workers and capitalists, there are severe difficulties in applying it to social conflicts in ancient Greece. Most significantly, the most exploited ancient Greek class, the slaves, had little or no role in the major social conflicts of most ancient Greek cities.[7] There was nothing in Greek cities to correspond to the alliance of subordinate classes, led by the bourgeoisie, that Marx believed toppled feudalism and the French aristocracy. On the issue of slavery there is little reason to doubt that rich and poor citizens closed ranks tightly. Moreover, although ancient slaves sometimes fought for their own emancipation, the emancipation of slaves as a class never emerged as a theme in the Greek political rhetoric. The exploitation of slaves inspired no dreams of a new, emancipated form of society, such as Marx believes emerged from the oppression of the bourgeois and proletarian classes.

---

5. By far the most elaborate and interesting effort is G. E. M. de Ste. Croix, *The Class Struggle*. See also E. M. and N. Wood, *Class Ideology*, 25–64; P. Anderson, *Passages from Antiquity to Feudalism*.

6. K. Marx, "The Communist Manifesto," in *The Marx-Engels Reader*, 473. Ste Croix rightly emphasizes the universality of Marx's claim about class struggle against other classical historians who, despite their sympathy with Marx, are inclined to deny that Marx was very serious about that universality.

7. I am speaking, of course, of chattel slaves here and not of subject and enslaved peoples like the Spartan helots, who engaged in frequent and violently suppressed rebellions.

and thus cannot play the role in social development that Marx's theory needs to ascribe to it.[8] Clearly, ancient Greek social life depended for many of its most distinctive features on slave labor.[9] Nevertheless, master-slave relations never came close to provoking the kind of social conflict and transformation that Marx's optimistic association of exploitation and social change leads us to expect to develop.

To suggest, as one Marxist has, that we can save Marx's theory by distinguishing between a society's latent "fundamental" contradiction (in this case, the master-slave relation) and its active "principle" contradiction, the contradiction that gives rise to overt social conflict,[10] merely begs the question of why the so-called fundamental contradiction is *not* the actual source of social conflict and change. These distinctions, which are very common in attempts to apply Marx's understanding of class conflict to premodern and non-Western societies, merely point to the difference between a society's actual sources of antagonism and the sources that Marx's theory leads us to expect to find. Similarly, when Marxist historians and social theorists tell us that order or status stratification, as in the citizen-noncitizen dichotomy, merely "masks class-consciousness" and "the objective reality of class,"[11] we rarely receive much evidence to prove the greater "reality" of what lies behind the "mask" than their initial assumption about the primacy of class stratification.

As Ste. Croix insists, a much more thorough rethinking of Marx's social theory is needed to demonstrate its relevance to the study of ancient Greek social life.[12] The great merit of Ste. Croix's attempt to develop a Marxist account of social conflict in ancient Greece lies in his frank acknowledgment of the challenge that Greek social realities pose to Marx's theory. His efforts at adapting Marxist theory to Greek social realities are by far the most sustained and serious attempt to meet this challenge. The failure of these efforts is therefore instructive. It teaches us something important about both the limitations of Marx's theory of

8. See J.-P. Vernant, "Class Struggle," 3.
9. I accept Moses Finley's reasoning here for calling the ancient Greek polis a "slave society" even if, as in the American South, many or even most citizens did not own slaves. See M. Finley, "Was Greek Civilization Based on Slave Labour?" and M. Finley, *Ancient Slavery and Modern Ideology*.
10. See C. Parain, "Les caractères spécifiques." This distinction is repeated uncritically in J.-P. Vernant, "Class Struggle," 1–2.
11. E. M. and N. Wood, *Class Ideology*, 57, following G. Lukács, *History and Class Consciousness*, 55–57.
12. G. E. M. de Ste. Croix, *The Class Struggle*, 57–65.

social conflict and the kind of alternative we need to supplement or replace it.

Ste. Croix clearly recognizes that Marx's social theory stands or falls on his claim about the universality of class struggle. If we limit class struggle to conscious and overt social conflicts, then "it virtually disappears in many situations," such as the relationship between the slave class and their owners. If, however, we follow Marx in asserting the universality of class conflict, then we must assume its existence even in situations where there is "little conscious struggle of any kind." Ste Croix decides that if we are to follow Marx we have to choose the latter option since "the opening sentence [of *The Communist Manifesto*] and the whole type of thinking associated with it have made this inevitable."[13] The "whole type of thinking" that makes this choice inevitable is that derived from Marx's association of society-transforming conflict with the exploitation of subordinate classes. If one cannot find a way of reinterpreting class conflict that makes it relevant to exploitive relationships such as slavery, then the most important and inspiring claim of Marx's social theory disappears.

Ste. Croix saves this claim by so emphasizing Marx's association of class conflict with exploitation that he uses exploitation itself to define class and class struggles. Class, according to his reinterpretation of Marx, refers to a position within a relationship of exploitation rather than merely to one's place within a system of production. Class relationships, accordingly, refer to the relationships between primary producers and those who exploit them by expropriating the surplus value created by their labor. Even if there is no overt social conflict between the two groups, this relationship of exploitation is itself, for Ste. Croix, a form of class struggle, since it centers on the attempts of one group to wrest from another the fruits of its labor.[14]

Wielding this interpretation of class and class conflict, it is easy for Ste. Croix to demonstrate the relevance of Marx's theory of class conflict for the explanation of ancient Greek society, since the wealthy classes of that society clearly drew the bulk of their wealth from the labor of slaves. The problem for Ste. Croix is to connect what he understands as class conflict with the overt social struggles between rich and poor citizens that directly shaped social change in the ancient Greek republics.[15]

13. Ibid., 57.
14. Ibid., 44–57.
15. The great majority of contemporary students of ancient Greece see the tensions between rich and poor citizens as the most important source of conflict within ancient

If we follow Ste. Croix's definitions of class and class conflict strictly, it becomes hard to describe poor citizens, most of whom worked small pieces of land of their own,[16] as a class engaging in class conflict. No one was directly or, for the most part, even indirectly expropriating the labor of these peasant citizens. Ste. Croix can bring them into his theory of class conflict only by emphasizing their fear of falling into the exploited condition of the slaves.[17] His theory of social conflict can thus accommodate the most overt and influential conflicts in the ancient Greek cities only incidentally and with difficulty.

It is thus not surprising to discover that Ste. Croix effectively abandons his revised understanding of exploitation and class conflict when he turns from social theory to an account of historical events. In his historical account he focuses instead on the conflicts between rich and poor citizens that are well attested in his Greek sources.[18] Nor is it surprising to discover that he is citing Aristotle's description of the conflicts between rich and poor citizens, rather than any account of the exploitation of slaves or any other form of dependent labor, when he insists that Aristotle's political analysis reflects a Marxist understanding of class conflict.[19] Ste. Croix's reinterpretation of Marx's social theory saves its relevance for the explanation of ancient society only by making clear its inability to explain the most overt and influential social conflicts in ancient Greece.[20]

In the end Ste. Croix's massive effort to save the universality of Marx's theory of social conflict is a failure.[21] But its failure teaches us about some of the limits of Marx's theory of social conflict. Ste. Croix's effort fails because, however one interprets it, there is a massive gap between the most striking form of exploitation in ancient Greek society, slavery,

---

Greek cities. See, for example, M. M. Austin and P. Vidal-Naquet, *Economic and Social History*, 244; M. Finley, *Politics in the Ancient World*, 11–23; J.-P. Vernant, "Class Struggle"; A. Fuks, *Social Conflict in Ancient Greece*, 12.

16. See E. M. Wood, *Peasant-Citizen and Slaves*.
17. G. E. M. de Ste. Croix, *The Class Struggle*, 96–97. Although such fears were certainly an important source of conflict in the early polis, they grew far less salient in the fifth and fourth centuries.
18. As noticed by E. M. and N. Wood, *Class Ideology*, 121.
19. G. E. M. de Ste. Croix, *The Class Struggle*, 74–77.
20. One way of saving the concept of exploitation pursued by some contemporary Marxists is to reformulate it, by means of rational choice theory, into a general attribute of social systems that limit individual opportunities in important ways. See E. O. Wright, *Classes*; J. Roemer, *A General Theory*. But to do so diminishes the ability of Marxist theory to help identify the specific ways in which exploitation develops within different historical periods, a contribution that Ste. Croix rightly believes to be one of the most important Marx made to social theory.
21. See the similar conclusion in J. Elster, "Three Challenges to Class," 161.

and the most important forms of social conflict. Marx's "optimistic" assumption about the necessary connection between forms of exploitation and society-transforming conflict is refuted by the social structure and experience of the ancient Greek republics. Extensive social exploitation and intensive class conflict clearly existed in these communities, but the latter did not develop directly from the most important examples of the former. Uncomfortable as it may be to admit, classical antiquity's massive forms of slave exploitation developed and passed from the scene without inspiring the kind of social conflict that might wreak vengeance on the exploiters and bring some improvement to the lives of the exploited.

To make sense of class conflict as it emerges in the ancient Greek republics, we thus need a theoretical approach that does not derive class conflict from a general, society-wide account of exploitation. Moreover, we need an approach that directly associates class conflict and participation in political life. We can find such an approach, I argue, in Aristotle's account of political conflict.

A POLITICAL UNDERSTANDING OF CLASS CONFLICT

For Aristotle, as for most students of classical Greece,[22] the most persistent and dangerous source of conflict within political communities is the mutual suspicion between rich and poor citizens. The continuing struggle between oligarchs and democrats, a struggle that occupies the largest part of his account of ordinary political life, is for him primarily a struggle between rich and poor citizens. As Aristotle repeatedly notes, the rule of the few and of the many is better and more precisely understood as the rule of the few rich and the many poor (*Pol.* 1279b, 1290b1).

Given this understanding of political conflict, it is quite reasonable to attribute to Aristotle a theory of class conflict. It is not, however, reasonable to attribute to him *Marx's* theory of class conflict, as Ste. Croix does. Ste. Croix argues that Aristotle's clear reliance on models of class conflict demonstrates the relevance of Marx's theory of social conflict to the study of ancient Greek society.[23] But in order to rescue Marxist interpretations of ancient Greek society from charges of anach-

---

22. See, among others, M. M. Austin and P. Vidal-Naquet, *Economic and Social History*; M. Finley, *Politics in the Ancient World*; J.-P. Vernant, "Class Struggle"; A. Fuks, *Social Conflict in Ancient Greece*.
23. G. E. M. de Ste. Croix, *The Class Struggle*, 79. In response, Josiah Ober ("Aristotle's Political Sociology") rightly points out that Aristotle clearly recognizes the importance of status and order, as well as class, in his account of social and political life.

ronistic irrelevance, Ste. Croix has to present an anachronistic interpretation of Aristotle. As noted in the previous section, the passages that Ste. Croix cites in support of this interpretation all refer to conflict between rich and poor *citizens* rather than conflict between all exploiting and exploited classes, as Ste. Croix's Marxist theory requires. Ste. Croix thus rightly draws our attention to Aristotle's insistence on the importance of class conflict, but he misleads us when he assumes that Aristotle's understanding of class conflict mirrors Marx's.

Aristotle's understanding of class conflict differs from Marx's in that it is an account of social conflict among members of political communities rather than a general and universal account of social conflict. Nowhere does Aristotle suggest, as Marx does, that class conflict provides the key for understanding social conflicts among all inhabitants—women, slaves, metics, as well as citizens—of a political community. Nor does he insist, as Marx does, that it provides the key for understanding social conflict and change among all forms of social organization, that is, the tribes of the north, the empires of the east, and the political communities of the Mediterranean. To the extent that Aristotle presents an understanding of class conflict, that understanding concerns the relations among members of political communities rather than among all individuals in all forms of social life.

Aristotle undertakes a number of analyses of the parts of actual political communities, but he always seems to come back to the division between rich and poor as the division that citizens treat as the most important of all (*Pol.* 1290a1–30, 1291b5, 1296a20). Perhaps, he suggests, the rich and poor are seen as the basic parts of a political community because no one can be *both* rich *and* poor, whereas one can simultaneously occupy many of the different functional positions that are often used to divide up a polis (*Pol.* 1291b5). In any case, Aristotle's emphasis on the division between the wealthy and the poor clearly grows out of popular perceptions of social cleavages rather than out of any theoretical or legal categories.

The lack of precision in Aristotle's language here—he uses the ordinary words for parts or portions (*mere* or *moriai*) rather than a more technical philosophic or sociological vocabulary—has discouraged some scholars from exploring his understanding of class conflict.[24] But the

24. Peter Calvert (*The Concept of Class*, 30), for example, contrasts the vagueness of Aristotle's categorization of rich and poor with the precision of the wealth classifications introduced by Solon into the Athenian constitution and suggests that such vague categories can have little theoretical interest.

lack of a technical theoretical vocabulary to describe class conflict need not be a disadvantage, especially if it helps capture truths that emerge from actual political experience. Our familiarity with Marx's elaborate theory of social conflict leads us to associate the category of class with specific productive locations rather than with the constructions of political rhetoric. Starting with the vague categories that emerge from Greek political rhetoric will not lead to the kind of general and universal theory of social conflict that Marx attempts, but it might open the way to insights into the nature of class conflict that escape these approaches. "Demagogues," Aristotle complains, "are always dividing the polis into two, waging war against rich," whereas oligarchs proclaim, " 'I shall be ill-disposed to the people and plan whatever evil I can against them' " (*Pol.* 1310a3–10). I agree with Moses Finley that such talk "exemplifies class, class consciousness and class conflict sufficiently" to warrant further investigation.[25]

The broader theoretical significance of Aristotle's approach to class conflict emerges only when one situates that account within his general understanding of political community, something scholars, given their tendency to treat conflict as the absence of community, have so far been reluctant to do. But once we recognize, as I have urged us to do, that the form of community shared by individuals will shape the kinds of conflict that arise among them, an interesting theoretical insight emerges from Aristotle's analysis of social conflict: social conflict among individuals who share the mutual expectations characteristic of citizens will, for the most part, develop and persist along the line between the wealthy and the poor.

This theoretical insight is interesting because, contrary to a fairly common opinion, social conflict between rich and poor is not necessarily the primary form of social conflict in every form of society. The evidence cited to demonstrate the universal primacy of class conflict is most often drawn, I suggest, from the history of *political* communities. When, for example, James Madison declares that the "most common and durable source of factions has been the verious [sic] and unequal distribution of property,"[26] he might appear to be making a universal claim about the nature of social conflict. On closer examination, however, it becomes clear that Madison is speaking of the causes of faction within "popular" and "republican" government,[27] forms of social or-

25. M. Finley, *Politics in the Ancient World*, 11.
26. Hamilton, Jay, and Madison, *The Federalist Papers*, no. 10.
27. Ibid.

ganization that map neatly onto Aristotle's concept of political community. In general, the most frequently discussed examples of class conflict are drawn from the histories of city-states, the political communities of ancient, medieval, and Renaissance times, and of republican nation-states, the political communities of the modern world.

But political communities, and the distinctive experience of social conflict within them, are relatively rare over the whole course of human history. The majority of human beings have lived and continue to live within a variety of nonpolitical forms of social organization, from empires and absolute monarchies to feudal communities and military or one-party dictatorships. This fact poses problems for social theorists, such as Marx, who seek to develop a universal theory of class conflict. They need to expend a great deal of energy in order to unearth evidence that class conflict lies concealed beneath the surface of social life of the nonpolitical communities that occupy the larger part of human history. Although evidence of occasional flare-ups of class conflict in nonpolitical communities, such as periodic peasant uprisings, is not hard to come by, it is quite difficult to demonstrate that class conflict is the main source of social conflict and social transformation in nonpolitical communities that it seems to be in political communities.[28]

From an Aristotelian point of view, Marx and his followers appear to have mistaken a particular form of social conflict for a universal one. In doing so, they treat the conflicts that they experience in their own communities, the political communities of modern Europe and North America, as characteristic of all forms of social organization. Marx suggested that Aristotle's emphasis on the universal significance of the polis was due to his failure to consider the particular socioeconomic conditions, such as slavery, that made Greek political life possible.[29] Given the opportunity, however, Aristotle could turn the tables on Marx and his followers. According to Aristotle's understanding of class conflict, one could say that Marx and his followers treat class conflict as the universal cause of social development only because they ignore the underlying *political* conditions that shape social conflict in the modern communities in which they live.

## PERCEIVED INJUSTICE AND CLASS INTERESTS

It might seem at first that all we need to do in order to identify the sources of social conflict within a community is to locate the major

---

28. For debates about the primacy of class conflict in medieval Europe, see the essays collected in T. Ashton and C. Philpin, *The Brenner Debate*.
29. K. Marx, *Capital* 1:69.

competing interests that emerge within it. But we should not assume that competing interests, in themselves, lead to social conflict. Among other reasons, if we do not *expect* that others should take our interests into consideration, then their opposition to our interests need not, and often will not, lead to social conflict. Without these expectations, we are less likely to hold individuals responsible for the harm that their actions do to our interests.[30] We hold our family members far more responsible than our neighbors for the harm that, for example, their economic activity may do to us. Similarly, we expect more consideration from our compatriots than from foreigners and thus are more likely to complain when their economic activity hurts our interests. Both examples suggest that the identification of mutual expectations will make as important a contribution to any account of social conflict as the identification of competing interests.

Mutual expectations reflect the extent and nature of the communities that bind individuals to each other. One way, then, of locating the nature and sources of conflict among individuals is to reflect on their competing interests in the light of the different forms of community that they share with each other. Aristotle, of course, does not make explicit use of the concept of "expectations." Nevertheless, something like this approach seems implicit in his famous analysis of *stasis* (factional conflict),[31] especially when we view this analysis in the light cast by his general understanding of political community.

Aristotelian political community involves shared forms of mutual accountability and mutual concern rather than social unity and shared identity. The citizens who engage in stasis in Aristotelian political communities act within the expectations created by political justice and political friendship. The ways in which they engage in social conflict will reflect something of the bonds that shape their shared life.

For Aristotle, perceived injustice, rather than competing interests, is the "general cause" (*aitia*) or "starting point" (*archē*) of stasis (*Pol.*

---

30. See M. Smiley, *Moral Responsibility,* for an insightful account of how our social expectations lead us to include and exclude individuals from our communities of mutual concern and responsibility.

31. *Stasis* is the Greek word that Aristotle, and the ancient Greeks in general, use to characterize the whole range of political conflict and competition among individuals and groups. It is important to keep in mind that *stasis* refers for Aristotle to a broad range of phenomena from everyday competition between political factions to extraordinary and violent events such as civil wars and other attempts to overthrow established governments. For this reason, I leave *stasis* untranslated.

On the meaning the Greeks gave the term *stasis,* see M. Finley, *Politics in the Ancient World,* 105–6. In general, see D. Loenen, *Stasis;* A. Fuks, *Social Conflict in Ancient Greece;* A. Heuss, "Das Revolutionsproblem." For an exhaustive collection of incidents of social conflict in ancient Greece, see H. J. Gehrke, *Stasis.*

1302a23, 1301a25–40). Competing interests in honor and profit are, in contrast, "the things for which individuals engage in stasis" (*Pol.* 1302a33). The key to Aristotle's understanding of class conflict lies in how he relates this "general cause" of stasis with the object that individuals seek when they engage in it.

Aristotle insists that what motivates people to struggle against each other within the political community is not merely the fact that they want something others will not give them but that they believe they *deserve* something from others that they are not getting. In political communities mutual accountability takes a particularly open form: public deliberation about general rules and other standards by citizens who regularly exchange positions of power. Political justice provides a public forum for debate about competing conceptions of fairness, a forum that is lacking in most other forms of social justice. Moreover, since political justice inevitably involves deliberation about natural right, that is, about decisions whose intrinsic merits concern us,[32] citizens will always have good reason to make use of this public forum. Citizens are thus involved in a practice of mutual accountability that encourages them to assert their own understanding of justice and to expect recognition of the justice of the claims they assert. When some citizens rise up against others in political communities,[33] they do so, according to Aristotle, because they feel that their compatriots have failed to live up to these expectations, especially their expectations about sharing in the power to establish and adjudicate their community's standards of justice.

Aristotle makes two further assumptions that make perceptions of injustice and stasis all but inevitable in ordinary political communities: the heterogeneity of interests and character among citizens (*Pol.* 1261a) and the tendency of citizens to be bad judges of justice in their own cases (*Pol.* 1280a15). Sharing in political community prompts citizens to put forward for public approval their understanding of justice as the basis for the community's standards of mutual accountability. The variety of interests and characters among them, along with an understandable tendency to exaggerate their own deserts, ensures that they will put forward *competing* conceptions of justice. Political decisions about which understanding of justice to enshrine in laws and other public standards are, as a result, bound to inspire the perceptions of injustice and the kind of resentment that lead to stasis.

32. As argued in chapters 2 and 5.
33. *Stasis* is derived from the Greek verb for standing up or rising to one's feet.

Aristotle uses the debate between oligarchs and democrats to illustrate this explanation of social conflict among citizens.

> Popular rule arose as a result of those who are equal in any respect supposing that they are equal simply, for because all alike are free persons, they consider themselves to be equal simply; and oligarchy arose as a result of those who are unequal in some one respect conceiving themselves to be unequal simply. Then the former claim to merit a share in all things equally on the grounds that they are equal, while the latter seek to aggrandize themselves on the grounds that they are unequal, since "greater" is something unequal. All such regimes have, then, some sort of justice, but in an unqualified sense they are in error. And it is for this reason that, when either group does not share in the regime on the basis of the conception it happens to have, they engage in stasis.
> 
> (*Pol.* 1301a28–38; cf. *Pol.* 1282b, *NE* 1131a25)

To what extent are these competing conceptions of justice ideological masks for the pursuit of group and self-aggrandizement? As the example of oligarchic versus democratic claims clearly shows, Aristotle recognizes the deep connection between the "general cause" of stasis in perceived injustice and the pursuit of profit and honor that leads individuals to engage in it. Nevertheless, he does not go so far as to suggest that individual and class interest is the underlying cause that explains the public assertions and social conflicts of oligarchs and democrats.[34]

Although Aristotle's account of class-based views of justice may bring to mind Marx's theory of ideology, it differs from that theory in important ways. Marx argues that the universalization and idealization of the general interest of the ruling class establishes the dominant understanding of justice in any particular society.[35] Justice and injustice thus represent, for him, a means of maintaining class dictatorship, that is, the imposition of the partial interest of the ruling class over the activity of the whole community. For Aristotle, in contrast, the rich and poor tend to universalize their partial conceptions of *justice* rather than their partial conceptions of interest; the claims that they make are not, in themselves, illegitimate impositions of their particular interests on the community. Instead, their claims "each have some element of justice," even if "in an unqualified sense, they are in error" (*Pol.* 1301a36).

---

34. Thus, although Moses Finley (*Politics in the Ancient World*, 2, 134) rightly criticizes commentators for ignoring "Aristotle's 'important truth' that the state is an arena for conflicting interests, conflicting classes," he misses an important element of Aristotle's understanding of that arena when he suggests that "*stasis* was avowedly a clash of interests, nothing more, whether or not it was covered by rhetoric about justice or about 'true' equality."

35. K. Marx, *The German Ideology*, 60.

As a result, Aristotle does not treat oligarchy and democracy as forms of class dictatorship, even though he considers them imperfect regimes in which the good of the ruling group usually takes precedence over the good of the community as a whole. Oligarchies and democracies, unlike class dictatorships or Aristotelian tyrannies, set up some standards of justice, however limited and partial they may be. These standards, embodied in the oligarchic and democratic regimes, most often serve the interests of the ruling group. But they still provide some standards of mutual accountability. Only the most extreme and degenerate forms of oligarchy and democracy, forms that verge on tyranny, are no longer constrained by such standards (*Pol.* 1292a15, 1292b8).

Aristotle argues that oligarchs and democrats universalize one-sided views of justice because "they themselves are concerned in the decision, and perhaps most men are bad judges when their own interests are in question" (*Pol.* 1280a15). Nevertheless, it is still justice that they are concerned about, however much their interests lead them to misjudge its full requirement. And it is the inevitable failure of their compatriots to live up to the one-sided standards of justice they put forward that provides the general cause of factional conflict.

Of course, Aristotle recognizes that each class has good reason to fear the full recognition of each other's claims. The stakes in this argument are very high: the power to make law and set general standards for life within the political community. Accepting the rich's claim to rule seems to grant them the power to oppress and exploit the poor. Accepting the poor's claim to rule seems to grant them the power to despoil the rich (*Pol.* 1281a11–38). Each class suspects, often with good reason, that selfish interests lurk behind the other's claims about justice. Nevertheless, we would be wrong, according to Aristotle, to see class conflict as a mere battle for spoils. Class conflict is driven by the kind of indignation that injustice inspires rather than by unvarnished lust for power and material advantage. Without the expectation that citizens should live up to shared standards of justice and acknowledge each other's right to participate in the formulation of those standards, the competing interests of rich and poor would not inspire the kind of conflict found in most political communities.

Political community is particularly prone to conflicts growing out of competing views of justice and injustice because it encourages people to formulate and put forward for public approval their understandings of justice. By encouraging citizens to participate in determining the standards that will promote the common good, political community in effect encourages individuals to act as judges in their own cases, thereby ensuring the emergence of competing, one-sided standards of justice. Participants in nonpolitical forms of community will be no better judges in their own cases than citizens will be. But they do not get the kinds of opportunities that citizens ordinarily get—or at least expect to get—to be judges in their own cases. Unlike citizens, they do not share a form of mutual accountability that encourages the expectation that they can bring forward and have approved their own view of appropriate standards of justice. As a result, nonpolitical communities are far less likely to suffer from the kind of social conflict, characteristic of political communities, that arises out of the assertion of competing perceptions of justice.[36]

Even if we grant that competing, one-sided perceptions of justice and injustice are bound to clash in Aristotelian political communities, we might still ask why the fundamental contradiction among these perceptions should reflect the gap between the views of rich and poor citizens. Aristotle's answer to this question seems to lie in the way in which he conceives of distributive justice and the claims that rich and poor citizens make about it. Justice, all agree, requires "equal [shares] for equal persons." What people disagree about is what weight to give various equally and unequally held attributes when deciding the distributions of goods and honors (*Pol.* 1282b20). Given their different social situations, the many poor and the few rich are likely to grasp only one side of justice, the importance of either egalitarian or inegalitarian principles. When they raise their claims against each other, they thus raise the most fundamental question about distributive justice: To what extent should equalities or inequalities be recognized as the basis for distribution of goods, honors, and power? Most questions about distributive justice can be recast in these terms, and thus most questions about distributive justice will adapt themselves to the form provided by the debate between the rich and the poor.

There is, for Aristotle, another group in the political community who would much more justifiably defend inegalitarian principles of distribution: the virtuous. But the virtuous always form a far smaller and less powerful group than the wealthy within any political community. "In what city shall we find a hundred persons of good birth and of virtue? The rich, in contrast, are abundant everywhere" (*Pol.* 1302a1; cf

---

36. This is not, of course, to deny that they may be plagued by other forms of social conflict.

1304b1). Moreover, although the virtuous have the greatest justification for rising up to defend inegalitarian principles, "they are the least likely to do so" (*Pol.* 1301a38), since, as just individuals, they are the least likely to grasp after more power and honor. As a result, although the opposition between virtue and vice may, in principle, be the greatest opposition in the community (*Pol.* 1303b15), it is the opposition between the wealthy few and the many free and poor citizens that, in practice, defines the basic lines of social conflict in the political community.

## POLITICAL FRIENDS, CLASS ENEMIES

While we are considering Aristotle's understanding of stasis, it is important to keep in mind that, for Aristotle, participants in factional conflict share the bonds created by political friendship, as well as competing perceptions of injustice. Aristotle, like Plato, insists that stasis, in contrast to war (*polemos*), is a kind of conflict that takes place among friends.[37] Friendship ties may often keep us from complaining about an affront that we would not accept from strangers. But as I have noted in previous chapters, Aristotle believes that friendship ties can also lead us to take offense at actions that would not bother us when performed by strangers, since we bring expectations of special solicitude to our interactions with friends. When friends disappoint these expectations, we feel betrayed as well as hurt, which leads to a more intense anger than we express toward strangers who harm us (*Rhet.* 1379b2; *Pol.* 1328a10).

The individual citizens who engage in stasis begin with the expectations of, and dispositions toward, mutual concern characteristic of political friends. Sometimes these expectations and dispositions will moderate factional conflict. At other times they are bound to heighten social tension and suspicion, especially when one takes into account the unequal and asymmetric nature of the political friendship between rich and poor citizens.

Accordingly, to present a complete Aristotelian account of stasis we need to turn to Aristotle's account of friendship in the *Nicomachean Ethics,* and especially to his discussion of unequal friendships between rich and poor individuals. Aristotle does not directly invoke these discussions in his analysis of stasis in the *Politics.* Nevertheless, their im-

37. See G. Contiourgos, *La théorie des révolutions,* 26, 60; J.-P. Vernant, "City-State Warfare," 20.

plications provide a useful supplement to that analysis, a supplement that is interesting both in its own right and as a means of rendering a fuller picture of Aristotle's understanding of social conflict.

Political friendship, as discussed in the *Nicomachean Ethics,* is a tie that binds *all* members of a political community, not just those who share political viewpoints and goals.[38] The ancient Greeks had considerable experience with small groups of individuals who band together to pursue common political goals. They called these groups *hetaireiai* (from the word for "comrade" or "intimate," *hetairos*), which is usually translated as "club" or, far less accurately, as "party." The hetaireiai were, for the most part, groups of wealthy individuals and their friends and clients who socialized together and worked to advance each other's social and political interests.[39] But, except in *The Constitution of Athens,* Aristotle focuses his attention on the friendship ties that bind all citizens together rather than on these narrower forms of political friendship.[40]

Friends, for Aristotle, do "what they can" to help each other, as opposed to what they are obliged to do according to some mutual standard of obligation (*NE* 1163b15). Aristotle—rightly, in my opinion—seems to take for granted the existence among citizens of at least some minimal disposition toward mutual concern.[41] Exaggerated rhetoric aside, the question that promotes controversy in political life is the extent to which and in what way, not whether, citizens should support each other. Representatives of poorer classes may treat anything less than the level of support that they demand as no support at all, whereas the represen-

38. As emphasized in chapters 2 and 4.
39. See W. R. Connor, *The New Politicians,* 25–87; Calhoun, *Athenian Clubs.* The normal path to a political career, at least in fifth-century Athens, led directly through one or more of the hetaireiai. Thus, Connor (*The New Politicians,* 25–66, 119–51) argues that Cleon initiated a "new style" of politics in Athens by ceremoniously announcing that he would pursue his political career without the help of personal friends and hetaireiai. To highlight the unusual nature of Cleisthenes' political strategy as a democratic reformer, Herodotus (*History,* book 5, chs. 62–63) suggests that after Cleisthenes failed to gain political backing in the usual way, from the hetaireiai, "he introduced the *demos* into his *hetaireia.*" (A similar point is made in *The Constitution of Athens,* 20.) Thucydides (*History,* book 3, chs. 82–83), among others, thought that the hetaireiai were primarily responsible for the internal conflicts that broke out among so many Greek cities during the Peloponnesian War. See also A. Lintott, *Violence, Civil Strife, and Revolution,* 91–92.
40. A comprehensive account of the relationship between stasis and friendship ties, which Aristotle does not provide, would have to include a full discussion of the hetaireiai and, more generally, partial, as opposed to community-wide, bonds of social friendship.
41. See *Pol.* 1320a30, where the question is the form that such support should take. On the Greek practice of social support, see A. Fuks, *Social Conflict in Ancient Greece,* 56; and, more provocatively, P. Veyne, *Bread and Circuses.*

tatives of wealthier classes may offer arguments against mutual support altogether in order to defend themselves against suggestions that they should greatly increase the support that they already give. Nevertheless, this rhetoric merely masks the reality of some, however minimal, level of mutual support, of public beneficence by the rich and public service by the poor, within political communities.

In unequal forms of friendship, such as that between rich and poor citizens, both the needs that friends expect each other to support and the abilities to do what one "can" to help friends are asymmetrical. Wealthy individuals, of course, have fewer needs and far greater abilities to assist their friends than poorer people have. For this reason, Aristotle suggests, it is hard to see how wealthy and poor individuals can be friends rather than patrons and clients. Nevertheless, he concludes, friendship between unequals is possible as long as we do not demand the *same* or symmetrical expressions of mutual concern from rich and poor.

> This then is also the way in which we should associate with unequals; the man who is benefited in respect of wealth or excellence must give honor in return, repaying what he can. For friendship asks a man to do what he can, not what is proportional to the merits of the case; since that cannot always be done, for example, in honors to the gods or to parents; for no one could ever return to them the equivalent of what he gets.
> (NE 1163b12–19)

Because friendship urges us to do for each other "what we can," then it is satisfied when friends support each other with the means at their disposal, the rich with public beneficence, the poor with public honors. In this way Aristotle accounts for "liturgies" (NE 1163a28), the system of expected but noncompulsory expenditures by wealthy individuals that ancient Greek cities, especially Athens, relied on for much of their public finance. The liturgy system treated the great expenditures of wealthy citizens on the city's defense and food supplies as admirable acts of public beneficence rather than the fulfillment of public obligations—no matter how strong the pressure was to perform them.[42] As a result, one could say, with Aristotle, that rich and poor friends both get more of something from the other, "not more of the same thing, however, but the superior more honor and the inferior more gain: for honor

---

42. See P. Veyne, *Bread and Circuses*, 76–77; M. Finley, *The Ancient Economy*, 151–52; M. Finley, *Politics in the Ancient World*, 36–39.

is the prize of excellence and of beneficence, while gain is the assistance required by inferiority" (*NE* 1163b1).

Aristotle supports direct aid to the poorer citizens of a community as well as a system of public liturgies. He ridicules, however, the utility of distributing small regular payments to the poor, which he compares to pouring water into the proverbial "leaky jar." Aristotle prefers, instead, the accumulation and distribution of larger, one-time payments geared to helping poor citizens gain relative economic independence by buying a piece of land or setting themselves up in a trade. By such means, he concludes, the Carthaginian upper classes "have acquired the friendship of the people" (*Pol*. 1320a30–b10).

Aristotle's arguments suggest that as long as we think of political relationships in terms of justice (that is, in terms of standards of mutual obligation), the inequalities of contribution and receipt of benefits in the relationship between rich and poor is bound to create problems. But if we can think of the relationship between rich and poor in terms of friendship (that is, in terms of relative ability to show mutual concern), then we can be more easily satisfied when rich and poor citizens offer each other different and unequal forms of support. Without the dispositions promoted by this kind of unequal friendship between rich and poor citizens, it might be impossible to establish and maintain political communities among rich and poor individuals.

Before moving on to the ways in which this unequal political friendship contributes to class conflict, we need to distinguish it from patron-client relationships, a form of "instrumental friendship" that looms large in contemporary political sociology and cultural anthropology.[43] As students of social patronage frequently point out, patron-client relations tend to cut across class lines and diminish class conflicts. If political friendship between rich and poor citizens turns out to resemble patronage relations, then we would have good reasons to doubt conclusions about how it contributes to class conflict.

There are indeed some striking similarities between patron-client relations and Aristotle's unequal political friendship: the basic inequality of its participants, the instrumental character of their relations, the asymmetric character of their obligations and expectations, and the kind

---

43. See especially E. Wolf ("Kinship, Friendship, and Patron-Client Relations"), who explicitly refers to Aristotle and his concept of instrumental friendship. In general, see the collection of essays in S. Schmidt, J. Scott, et al., *Friends, Followers, and Factions*; C. Clapham, *Private Patronage and Public Power*; S. Eisenstadt and L. Roniger, *Patrons, Clients, and Friends*.

of benefits that its participants receive from each other. Nevertheless, patron-client relations involve a kind of personal dependence on and subordination to a particular patron that is incompatible with Aristotle's understanding of political friendship. "A free man," Aristotle notes in the *Rhetoric* (1367a31), "does not live in dependence on others [*pros allon*]." If you depend on other particular individuals for your livelihood, you are in danger of becoming "slavish" in character (*Pol.* 1337b19), which is one reason why Aristotle happily welcomes poor farmers as citizens but works to exclude laborers in "menial" and vulgar activities. Patron-client relationships are incompatible with the kind of individual character that Aristotle expects of citizens.[44]

The beneficence that poor citizens receive from wealthy ones is, for Aristotle, a *public,* rather than a private, beneficence. In insisting on the public character of beneficence, Aristotle seriously differs from Isocrates, who made similar arguments about support for the poor but wanted to impose a private and ultimately patronizing form of redistribution.[45] Although Aristotle recommends individual honors for wealthy public benefactors, they are to be honored for the public good they have done for their fellow citizens, for their acts of *political* rather than *personal* friendship. As long as such expectations of *public* beneficence are maintained, then it will be difficult to develop the kind of dyadic relations of beneficence and dependence characteristic of systems of patronage.

This is not to suggest that all personal patronage and patron-client relationships disappear in a community bound by ties of political friendship. As long as there remain considerable differences in levels of wealth and status, patronage will persist as an important social relationship. Nevertheless, the existence of ties of political friendship will block the development of the systematic forms of patron-client relations, such as those that political sociologists and anthropologists have identified as the foundation of social stratification in many Mediterranean and other societies. Individual patron-client relationships undoubtedly exist in every form of human society, but systematic structures of patron-client relationships are far rarer.[46]

---

44. See P. Millett, "Patronage and Its Avoidance," 17, 28, 33.
45. See A. Fuks, *Social Conflict in Ancient Greece,* 180, for a discussion of Isocrates and Aristotle on this point. Paul Millett ("Patronage and Its Avoidance," 25–28) notes the "patronizing" implications of Isocrates' arguments.
46. See the insightful defense of this distinction by T. Johnson and C. Daneker, "Patronage," 223. Barry Strauss notes that in classical Athens "clientelism was crucial to elite politics, but it played only limited role in the political community" as a whole; B. Strauss,

Systematic patron-client relationships tend to defuse class conflict since they promote vertical and personal ties of solidarity among chains of patrons and clients in place of horizontal ties of solidarity among the rich and the poor. It is thus not surprising to find both a resistance to systematic patron-client relationships and an emphasis on systematic class conflict between rich and poor in ancient Greek political thought and practice.[47] Some forms of social organization, such as the kind of political community that Aristotle explores, seem both to block the development of systematic structures of patronage and promote class conflict and stratification.

To understand the ways in which political friends are particularly prone to become class enemies, we need to go a little beyond Aristotle's explicit arguments and consider some ways in which his explanation of political conflict and his ideas about unequal political friendship might work together. If friendship involves a disposition to do what one *can* to aid someone with whom one shares things, then it is clear why friendship between unequals might ameliorate the conflicts that arise from their conflicting perceptions of justice: it may lead them to support each other far more than they think they are obliged to do by the community's standards of justice. Conversely, however, friendship ties may also dispose individuals to support each other *less* than even their own standards of justice insist on, since friendship asks them do what they *can* rather than what they are *obliged* to do. Real friends, for example, do not ask each other to impoverish themselves in order to pay back a debt. No friend, they will think, should ask another to do more than he or she can even to avoid an injustice.

By asking us to do what we can for each other, rather than what justice obliges us to do, friendship introduces an essentially subjective component into our judgments about other-regarding behavior. When we do what we *can* for others, we always have to make a judgment about our abilities to help others without seriously harming ourselves, a judgment that cannot, without being turned into a judgment about justice and injustice, be measured against shared public standards. There will, of course, be quite a variety of shared expectations about what

---

*Athens after the Peloponnesian War*, 174–75. This important distinction between individual instances of patronage and *systematic* structures of patronage is ignored by historians, such as Moses Finley (*Politics in the Ancient World*, 40–41, 45), who want to assimilate the Greek practice of liturgies and instrumental friendship to the general concept of patron-client relationships.

47. See P. Millett, "Patronage and Its Avoidance."

friends will do for each other in particular situations. Nevertheless, friendly action, if it is to be *friendly* action at all, must proceed from an individual's disposition to help someone to the extent he or she can and therefore must include subjective judgments about one's ability to help others.

Given our tendency to be bad judges in our own cases when it comes to determining appropriate standards of distributive justice (*Pol.* 1280a15), it would not be surprising to discover that we are also bad judges when it comes to determining the needs of our friends and our ability to help them without seriously harming ourselves. This tendency will likely be especially pronounced among participants in shared advantage friendships, a group that includes members of political communities. Shared advantage friends come together because of the differing skills and goods they possess rather than because of any special moral virtues that might make them good judges of their obligations and ability to help their friends.

Consider the ways in which rich and poor citizens might be bad judges of their needs and of their abilities to support each other. Wealthy citizens may feel disposed to contribute some of their wealth toward the support of their poorer compatriots. But they are likely to expect very great honors for minimal contributions, since they are likely to think, as when they reason about justice, that their "unequal" contribution is so much more important than the support offered them by poor citizens. They are also likely to place the threshold past which expected contributions to the community exceed their ability to provide them at a relatively low level, especially since they are likely to think of any demand for a contribution that might endanger their "unequal" wealth and leisure as the equivalent of asking them to "impoverish" themselves for friends.

Conversely, poor citizens will likely be disposed to expect maximal contributions for relatively minimal honors, given the relatively greater importance that this more "equal" capacity to bestow honor will have for citizens who lack the unequal assets of their wealthy compatriots. They will, not without reason, tend to be suspicious of wealthy citizens' complaints about being impoverished by their expectations of friendly support, since given their more literal notion of impoverishment, it will take the wealthy far longer to reach the limits of their ability to help their poorer compatriots. Moreover, they will also be suspicious of wealthy citizens' demands for maximal honors for services rendered, since the accumulation of honors tends to increase the power and reputation of wealthy citizens to the extent that it threatens the one main honor poor citizens have: their political freedom. As a result, poor citizens will also worry about the threshold past which they cannot honor the rich without risking their own political freedom, a risk that no political friend should ask of another.

Given our tendency to be bad judges in our own cases of the needs of our friends and our abilities to satisfy them, as well as the asymmetric needs and abilities of rich and poor, political friendship ties can thus promote mutual tension, suspicion, and conflict between rich and poor citizens. Because rich and poor citizens think of each other as political friends, they will expect from each other solicitude both for their needs and for the limits of their abilities to support each other's needs without seriously harming themselves. But since they are likely to react to these issues in the ways described in the preceding paragraphs, these expectations of mutual solicitude are bound to be disappointed. And when these expectations are disappointed, or when rich and poor citizens suspect that they will be disappointed, these citizens will likely feel betrayed as well as injured. The harshness and ugliness of civil conflict owes much to this sense of betrayal, a sense of betrayal that we cannot appreciate unless we first identify the bonds of friendship shared by its participants. Strangers may become competitors or hated opponents, but only political friends tend to become class enemies.

## THE MIXED REGIME AND POLITICAL JUSTICE

Aristotle's analysis of stasis suggests that mutual suspicion, competition, and conflict between rich and poor citizens are normal states of affairs in political life. In books 4–6 of the *Politics* Aristotle offers much advice on how to limit and moderate the consequences of this persistent tension between rich and poor citizens. But he offers little hope of simply eliminating the sources of factional conflict from political life, for the sources of stasis lie in the very nature of political community, in the combination of expectations about participation in framing public standards of justice with the social heterogeneity that Aristotle thinks is essential to political life.

Accordingly, I disagree strongly with W. L. Newman when he suggests that Aristotle "hardly realizes how difficult it is to prevent stasis."[48] Aristotle's major means of taming stasis, the "mixed regime," assumes

---

48. W. L. Newman, *The Politics of Aristotle* 4:277.

the persistence of the competing perceptions of injustice that provide the "general cause" and "starting point" of class conflict. Moreover, the mixed regime is never more than a partial means of preventing stasis, a means that must rely on compromise and ad hoc adaptation to changing circumstances if it is to be successful even in moderating factional conflict in the political community. Although Aristotle insists that political philosophers must concern themselves with improving imperfect regimes, he never suggests that legislators and politicians can gain *control* of political contingencies in such a way as to eliminate stasis.

The Aristotelian statesman should not be confused with the Machiavellian political virtuoso. A reading of Aristotle's daunting list of the ways in which regimes can be challenged and overthrown is unlikely to inspire the exhilarating sense of the endless possibilities for political manipulation that one gets from a reading of Machiavelli. It is much more likely to inspire a sense of the enormity of the task that faces anyone who seeks to preserve a political regime, let alone that which faces anyone who seeks to replace an established regime with a new and stable political order.[49] For Aristotle, keeping up with the impact of changing circumstances—let alone manipulating their effects—seems hard enough,[50] which may be another reason for his relatively conservative attitude toward political and legal innovation. Custom and habit often bring people to accept constraints on their behavior that they would be unlikely to accept were they to deliberate openly about the best constraints to choose. Indeed, laws have no better source of authority than the long habit of following their requirements. Accordingly, it is foolish to introduce legal and political innovations except when absolutely necessary (*Pol.* 1260a). But this means that political virtuosity is seriously limited by the vast variety of contingent and often contradictory habits that different peoples develop in response to the changing circumstances of their political life.

The mixed regime is Aristotle's basic recommendation for moderating the effects of stasis because it directly addresses the "general cause" of factional conflict: the differing perceptions of injustice among rich and poor citizens. As long as rich and poor citizens cleave to exclusively inegalitarian or egalitarian principles of justice, both groups will be prone

---

49. Reforming an established regime, Aristotle notes, involves many of the same difficulties, such as countering socialization of individuals by earlier institutions, involved in introducing a revolutionary new regime (*Pol.* 1289a3).

50. As Ronald Polansky ("Aristotle on Political Change," 325) points out, such ordinary events as a good harvest can upset political and constitutional calculations by greatly increasing the number of citizens who meet a property qualification for office.

to suspect each other of the kind of injustice that inspires factional conflict. To tame stasis, one must therefore find a way of moderating these one-sided views of justice and injustice. Aristotle implicitly rejects as ineffective the most direct means of broadening perceptions of justice: public education or other forms of enlightenment. (Public education does have a role to play in limiting stasis, according to Aristotle, but it plays that role by socializing individuals in the spirit of justice characteristic of regimes, such as oligarchy and democracy, rather than by challenging and broadening the regime's partial standards of justice [*Pol.* 1316a].) Instead, he recommends an indirect approach to broadening perceptions of justice: the "mixing" of democratic and oligarchic—and, occasionally, aristocratic—claims to rule. Some political offices should be distributed in accord with equally held qualities, such as political freedom, whereas others should be distributed in accord with unequally held qualities, such as wealth, birth, and virtue.[51]

How will the mixing of claims to rule broaden standards of justice and thereby moderate factional conflict? Alexis de Tocqueville, for one, dismisses the idea of the mixed regime as a "chimera" that usually conceals the predominance of the kind of one-sided views of injustice that Aristotle seeks to moderate. "When a society really does have a mixed government, that is to say, one equally shared between contrary principles, either a revolution breaks out or society breaks up."[52] De Tocqueville argues that what passes for mixed regimes are really nothing but relatively stable and successful democracies, such as the United States, or oligarchies and aristocracies, such as Rome and Venice. Far from being a means of moderating factional conflict, the mixed regime is, he suggests, a recipe for bringing factional conflict into the very structure of government. Mixing the claims of political office merely gives contending factions greater power with which to intensify their struggles.

Aristotle has a compelling response to de Tocqueville's arguments against the mixed regime. But in order to appreciate that response, we must first distinguish Aristotle's understanding of the mixed regime from the more familiar conception of the mixed regime as a balance of power among competing social forces, for de Tocqueville clearly had the latter conception in mind when offering his critique of the mixed regime.

The familiar conception of the mixed regime as a balance of powers owes much to Polybius's influential analysis of the Roman constitution.

---

51. These arguments are developed throughout books 4 and 6 of the *Politics*.
52. A. de Tocqueville, *Democracy in America*, 251.

Polybius reconstructed the constitution of the second-century Roman republic as a mix of monarchical, aristocratic, and democratic institutions whose internal balance checked the usual cycle of decline that plagued most other political regimes.[53] According to this understanding of the mixed regime, the Romans used social hostility as a stabilizing force by giving competing groups institutional powers with which to check and balance their opponents. It is this Polybian view of the mixed regime, rather than the Aristotelian view, that has shaped the most familiar accounts of the mixed regime in Western political thought.[54]

For a particularly ferocious version of this image of a balance of internal powers, consider the following defense of the mixed regime by Gouverneur Morris at the American Constitutional Convention.

> The checking branch [of government] must have a personal interest in checking the other branch. One interest must be opposed to another interest. Vices, as they exist, must be turned against each other. It [the Senate] must have great personal property, it must have the *aristocratic spirit; it must love to lord it thro' pride,* pride is indeed the great principle that actuates both the poor and the rich. . . . To make it independent, it should be for life. It will then do wrong, it will be said. He [Morris] believed so; he hoped so. The Rich will strive to establish their dominion and enslave the rest. They always did. They always will. The proper security against them is to form them into a separate interest. The two forces will then control each other.[55]

Such portrayals of the mixed regime seem to confirm de Tocqueville's arguments against it. If ever a community were so foolish as to establish a mixed regime along these lines, it would soon suffer from either civil war or anarchy. Americans should be grateful that Morris's views did not prevail at the Constitutional Convention.[56]

Were Aristotle to share the Polybian view of the mixed regime as a mere balance of social power, then his arguments would be vulnerable to de Tocqueville's criticism. But "Aristotle in no way seeks the correct mixture [of regimes] . . . in a balance between competing elements of

---

53. Polybius, *Histories,* book 6. On Polybius, see K. von Fritz, *The Theory of the Mixed Constitution*; W. Nippel, *Mischverfassungstheorie und Verfassungsrealität,* 142.
54. G. Aalders, *Die Theorie der Gemischten Verfassung,* 69.
55. In M. Farrand, *The Records of the Federal Convention* 1:512 (July 2); my emphasis.
56. The separation of powers, clearly approved of by the members of the American Constitutional Convention, should not be confused with a mixed regime. The separation of powers requires the division of a single claim to rule, in this case popular consent, into different forms and offices that will check each other, whereas the mixed regime requires public recognition of different claims to rule (for example, wealth as well as popular consent).

the regime."⁵⁷ Indeed, Aristotle suggests that it is a serious mistake to seek to combine the elements of each regime in mixed regimes (*Pol.* 1317a35). Aristotle's mixed regime is tremendously flexible. In some circumstances it should lean toward democracies and will be described as a "polity." In other circumstances it should lean toward oligarchy and will be described as an aristocracy (or, as Aristotle qualifies the description in order to distinguish this regime from genuine aristocracies in which a few virtuous individuals hold power, as a "so-called aristocracy") (*Pol.* 1293b–94a). In all cases, the mixed regime should be constructed and maintained in accordance with the kinds of institutions that local traditions and experience make most acceptable. Aristotle offers no general model of political equilibrium or balance of power as a guide to statesmen. Instead, he encourages them to seek out the most effective contingent and local means of introducing some mixing of egalitarian and inegalitarian claims to power into a community's regime. Success is achieved when citizens find it hard to tell whether the regime is a democracy or an oligarchy (*Pol.* 1299b15), rather than when one approaches a particular institutional model.

But how can the mixed regime moderate factional conflict if not through the kind of balance of internal powers that de Tocqueville criticizes? Aristotelian mixed regimes moderate factional conflict indirectly by broadening the one-sided views of justice that citizens ordinarily appeal to in political life.

The regime (*politeia*) is, for Aristotle, both the institutional ordering of public offices and the general standards or way of life associated with particular, say, democratic or oligarchic, ways of ordering these institutions.⁵⁸ Moreover, it is the "governing body" (*politeuma*) that defines "the regime" (*politeia*) (*Pol.* 1278b11). With this assertion Aristotle suggests that the ruling group sets general standards throughout the political community. It does so, however, not simply by virtue of its power to formulate general standards of justice but, more significantly, through the way in which communal standards and ways of life come to reflect the general standards of justice embodied in publicly recognized claims to political power.⁵⁹

If stasis is usually caused by one-sided views of justice that lead to

---

57. G. Aalders, *Die Theorie der Gemischten Verfassung*, 61.
58. See L. Strauss, *Natural Right and History*,
59. In this respect Aristotle has much the same view of the effect of political regimes on general standards of taste and behavior as that expressed by de Tocqueville in the second book of *Democracy in America*.

perceptions of injustice, and if the claims to power recognized in a constitution shape general standards of justice in a community, one way to moderate stasis would be to introduce both inegalitarian and egalitarian claims to power into the structure of a regime. If one is successful in gaining acceptance for competing principles as claims to power, even if only for less powerful and important offices, then one will accustom citizens to invoking both egalitarian and inegalitarian principles of justice, thereby making them less suspicious and combative when they are faced with fellow citizens who make claims on them on the basis of these principles. Socialization in the standards of a mixed regime would provide the basis for an indirect yet effective form of moral education. Such socialization would not likely eliminate the competing perceptions of justice and injustice that give rise to stasis, but it might, on occasion, help defuse social tensions and make each class more amenable to compromise.

Conceived in this way, the mixed regime is not vulnerable to de Tocqueville's critique since it moderates civil conflict by broadening one-sided conceptions of justice rather than by arming competing groups with the power to check their opponents. Moreover, this Aristotelian model of the mixed regime provides us with a far subtler and more flexible conception of political institution building than the rather mechanical construction of balanced powers associated with the Polybian model. To achieve its desired effects, the Aristotelian mixed regime seeks publicly acceptable means of introducing competing principles of political justice rather than a fine-tuned equilibrium among the powerful groups within a community. The socializing effect of the mixed regime depends on the acceptance of competing claims for specific political offices, claims that members of particular communities will be comfortable, for historical and sociological reasons, in acknowledging, despite the fact that they run counter to the general standards of oligarchic or democratic regimes.

Accordingly, there are as many kinds of mixed regimes as there are particular political opportunities for mixture (*Pol.* 1294a–b). Indeed, Aristotle is quite willing to endorse the use of extreme democratic practices that he ordinarily despises, such as payment for attendance at the assembly, if they provide a means of establishing a mix of political principles (*Pol.* 1297a35). Payments can, for example, be combined with fines for members of the upper classes who do *not* attend the assembly as a means of getting public acceptance for both egalitarian and inegalitarian standards of justice. Success in building a mixed regime depends on finding combinations of practices that will lead otherwise reluctant groups of citizens to recognize the justice of competing claims to political office.[60]

Ellen and Neal Wood have argued that Aristotle uses the mixed regime as a means of pushing democratic regimes in a more oligarchic direction, an effort that follows from what they claim is his general conviction that "the oligarchs' position, while imperfect, is less so than that of the democrats."[61] But far from suggesting that oligarchy is less imperfect than democracy, Aristotle repeatedly insists on the superior moderation and stability of democracy and more democratically inclined mixed regimes (*Pol.* 1289b4, 1296a12, 1302a9). The best mixed regime, Aristotle insists, will be one in which the majority of citizens have political rights (*Pol.* 1297b4). Finally, and most important, Aristotle insists that the *pleonexia*—the "grasping" quality that leads individuals to want more than what is distributed to them—of the wealthy is far more dangerous to the stability and moderation of regimes than is that of the many (*Pol.* 1297a10).

The implication of these passages seems to be that it is far harder to moderate the pleonexia and partiality of the wealthy than the pleonexia and partiality of the many. There is considerable historical evidence to support this contention. Even in the most democratic of ancient Greek regimes, Athens, the great majority of leadership roles continued to be occupied by elites of wealth and birth.[62] The many, it seems, are more likely to accept a mixture of inegalitarian and egalitarian principles than are the few wealthy individuals. The "characteristic mildness" of democracies emerges most clearly in the moderation of their revenge against civic enemies in comparison to that exacted by oligarchs.[63] As long as

---

60. Richard Bodéüs ("Law and the Regime," 237) presents a similar picture of the task of building an Aristotelian mixed regime.

61. E. M. and N. Wood, *Class Ideology*, 249, 239. The Woods seem to base this judgment on Aristotle's clear dissatisfaction with Athenian democracy. Within the context provided by Athenian political debate, a defense of polity and the mixed regime would no doubt be perceived as a somewhat oligarchic move. But Aristotle's audience is considerably broader than the body of Athenian citizens. Aristotle addresses the problem of stasis, which was increasing throughout the fourth-century Greek world (see A. Fuks, *Social Conflict in Ancient Greece*, 12–13; B. Strauss, *Athens after the Peloponnesian War*, 171–72), as it affected all Greek cities, with their wide range of regimes, not just democratic Athens. In that context, his defense of the mixed regime leans, if in any direction, toward democracy.

62. For the best account of this phenomenon, see J. Ober, *Mass and Elite*.

63. *The Constitution of Athens*, 22, 40. After the defeat of the Thirty Tyrants and the restoration of democracy in 403, the Athenian people established a general amnesty for crimes committed in the civil struggle and "even refunded at common expense the money that the Thirty had borrowed from the Spartans for the war." Such behavior,

they receive important forms of political recognition, the many often accept nonegalitarian principles of distribution such as election, wealth, and birth in some offices (as Aristotle recognizes in his account of the argument for democracy in book 3 of the *Politics* [1282a–b]). As a result, one will likely be far more successful in establishing the kind of mixture of political principles that Aristotle seeks if one starts with democratic rather than oligarchic institutions.

But more than the poor, it is the middle class that Aristotle expects to be most favorably disposed toward mixed regimes. The social position of the middle class, where there is one to be found, disposes them toward the broader mix of egalitarian and inegalitarian principles of justice that Aristotle seeks to enshrine in the mixed regime. Middle-class citizens have what we might best describe as "simulated virtue." Without in fact developing the virtues of character that would dispose them toward justice and willingness to promote the common good of the whole community, the social position of "middling" citizens disposes them, more than most other citizens, in the direction that virtues of character would dispose them. Because they have relatively little to fear from the poor, whose envy is directed at the upper classes, and little need to covet the redistribution of the wealth of the rich, they will express less pleonexia than will either their poorer or wealthier compatriots (*Pol.* 1295b30). Because they have less occasion to be either arrogantly superior or vindictively envious, they will be more reasonable and willing to take turns in positions of political power (*Pol.* 1295b5). We should expect the middle class, accordingly, to be much more open to recognizing the relevance of both egalitarian and inegalitarian principles of justice. It is for this reason, I suggest, that Aristotle designates the middle class as the most favorable social foundation for the mixed regime.

If one is fortunate enough to have a large middle class in one's community, then it will be relatively easy to establish the broadened public conception of justice that Aristotle associates with the mixed regime. But Aristotle believes that the existence of a large middle class will be relatively rare and therefore cannot be counted on when drawing up political plans (*Pol.* 1295b38–1296a36). The normal situation for political communities will be one in which legislators will have to deal with the mutual suspicion and hostility created by the differing percep-

---

according to *The Constitution of Athens* (40), "was the most admirable and most statesmanlike that any people have ever shown in such circumstances."

tions of injustice held by the rich and the poor. Without the stabilizing effect of a large middle class, legislators will need much more political subtlety to maintain a mixed regime and use it to defuse the mutual suspicion and hostility associated with class conflict.[64]

## APPENDIX. "POLITICAL REVOLUTION": A MISSING ARISTOTELIAN CATEGORY

Aristotle has a great deal to say about the revolutions (*metabolai*) that occur within political communities, that is, the kind of revolution that leads to the replacement of one kind of political regime with another, democracies with oligarchies, mixed regimes with democracies, and so on. His account of this kind of revolution has been fully explored by other commentators.[65] In this appendix, in contrast, I want to consider a kind of revolution that Aristotle does not discuss: "political" revolutions, that is, the revolutions that lead to the establishment of political communities in place of nonpolitical forms of social organization. Aristotle explicitly discusses only the revolutions of regime that occur *within* already established political communities. Without a supplement that helps explain the establishment (and dissolution) of political communities, his account of revolutionary change is radically incomplete.

It has often been noted that Aristotle's concept of revolution lacks the sense of the singular, extraordinary historical event that the concept conjures up in the minds of most modern individuals.[66] Aristotle never speaks, as we often do, of *the* Revolution (whether we mean by the term the French or the Russian revolution or some continuing process that includes both). One reason he does not speak this way is that he rejects the idea, implicit in such talk, of a political event that gives historical events a particular direction. Although revolutions within political communities occur quite frequently, according to Aristotle, they follow no rational or predictable pattern, not even a cycle of decline, such as Plato describes in the *Republic* (*Pol.* 1316a). Another reason for this difference is Aristotle's unfamiliarity with the phenomenon of revolutionary ideologies. Aristotle was, of course, quite familiar with ideolog-

64. Modern liberal democracies have the advantage of possessing large middle classes, which may be one reason why their citizens are more inclined than were their ancient counterparts to accept political institutions, such as representation and judicial review of legislation, that limit the power of democratic assemblies.
65. See esp. G. Contiourgos, *La théorie des révolutions*; M. Davis, "Aristotle's Reflections on Revolution"; R. Polansky, "Aristotle on Political Change."
66. See, for example, M. Davis, "Aristotle's Reflections on Revolution," 50; R. Polansky, "Aristotle on Political Change," 325.

ical justifications of arguments for oligarchic and democratic revolution. But the construction, by intellectuals, of grand ideologies that involve claims about the direction of human history did not begin until long after the collapse of the classical polis. Marsilius of Padua noted that the one cause of revolution that Aristotle could not possibly have foreseen is the ideological claim to power made by Catholic priests and bishops.[67] We should add to Marsilius's list the ideological claims to power made by intellectuals who claim to have identified and speak in the name of *the* revolutionary direction of human history.

Nevertheless, even when we leave aside self-deluding claims about intellectual vanguards and the direction of history, there is something of importance and grandeur in an event such as the French Revolution that Aristotle's discussion of revolutions fails to capture. I would suggest that Aristotle's discussion of revolutions is inadequate to an event such as the French Revolution because that event involves the creation of a political community where there was none before, rather than the mere replacement of one kind of political regime with another.

This view of the French Revolution has become increasingly popular in recent years. The last decade has seen a widespread effort among historians to replace the "social interpretation" of the Revolution as the story of the bourgeoisie's rise to power with a more "political" interpretation that identifies the development of a new, more inclusive and participatory political culture as the Revolution's central drama.[68] The advocates of this political interpretation of the Revolution usually speak of the birth of "democratic" or "modern political culture" rather than of the birth of political community.[69] But much of what they mean by "democratic political culture" is captured by the concepts of political justice and political friendship that Aristotle associates with political community per se. (Indeed, Aristotle's understanding of political community could help to clarify the conceptual framework of this new interpretation of the Revolution.)

Conversely, Aristotle's account of revolutions also needs to be supplemented with an account of the collapse of political community into

67. Marsilius of Padua, *Defender of the Peace*, 4–5, 89–91.
68. This move toward a more political interpretation of the French Revolution has been led by F. Furet, *Interpreting the French Revolution,* and is the guiding theme of the three large bicentennial volumes edited by Keith Baker, F. Furet, et al., *The French Revolution.* See also K. Baker, *Inventing the French Revolution*; L. Hunt, *Politics, Culture, and Class.* For a critical assessment of what the author describes as the "new orthodoxy" about the Revolution, see J. Censer, "The Coming of a New Interpretation."
69. As in the title of the bicentennial volumes edited by K. Baker, F. Furet, et al., *The French Revolution and the Birth of Modern Political Culture.*

nonpolitical forms of social organization, something the classical Greek world experienced with the final triumph of Macedonian imperialism shortly after Aristotle's death. Aristotle does, of course, speak of revolutions that lead to the establishment of tyrannies within political communities; and, tyrannies, according to Aristotle, barely have the form of regimes and thus seriously diminish political life. But he clearly thinks of tyrannies as temporary interruptions within the life of a political community rather than the dissolution of the bonds that join individuals in a shared political life (*Pol.* 1315b).[70] Tyranny seems, for Aristotle, to be self-seeking, one-person rule over individuals who share the expectations characteristic of political justice and political friendship. In other words, tyranny involves rule over individuals who expect considerably more than the self-aggrandizing rule of a particular individual. Aristotle's concept of tyranny does not provide us with a category with which to conceptualize the social condition that dissolves political community and the mutual expectations political community inspires. Like the category of political revolution, serious consideration of the collapse of political community is missing from Aristotle's analysis of revolution.

Even if Aristotle is unfamiliar with the revolutionary emergence or collapse of political communities, we certainly have experience of such events and thus need to supplement Aristotle's analysis of revolutions with a concept of "political revolution." One of the most significant limitations of Aristotle's account of actual political life is the absence of serious consideration of the relationship between political and nonpolitical forms of large-scale social organization. His account of ordinary political life would be much clearer and more useful if it were accompanied by a sketch of nonpolitical forms of social organization that would help us think about the emergence and disappearance of political communities.

70. Aristotle knows only one tyranny that lasted a century. Most collapse far more quickly, with even a forty- or fifty-year duration being quite remarkable (*Pol.* 1315b).

CHAPTER EIGHT

# The Good Life in Political Context

If the Aristotelian good life of virtuous activity is something that human beings have actually experienced and can continue to experience in the future, it must be able to develop within the constraints of imperfect political conditions. We have no reason to believe that anyone ever has lived or ever will live under the ideal political regime sketched in books 7 and 8 of the *Politics,* given the improbability of its preconditions, preconditions that Aristotle suggests we can only "pray for" (*Pol.* 1325b38, 1330a25). Thus, even though Aristotle argues that the good life is *best* led within his ideal regime, *in practice* it has been and will continue to be led within the confines of the imperfect political communities that have been the subject of this book.

If Aristotle thought that human beings could achieve and sustain a flourishing life on their own, then the imperfect political context of the good life would be relatively unimportant. But Aristotle makes clear that we depend on each other and our political communities for the moral training and external goods essential to human flourishing. Human beings, he insists, are the "worst of animals" when their reasoning capacities are "separated from laws and adjudication" (*Pol.* 1253a32). Moreover, "the right training for virtue is difficult unless one has been brought up under the right laws" (*NE* 1179b32). Consequently, the imperfect political context within which the good life is actually led will impose serious constraints on both the acquisition and exercise of the virtues that anchor human happiness. Accordingly, some commentators go so far as to conclude that "without the ideal city, there will be no good men,"[1] a conclusion that, given Aristotle's opinions about the likelihood of realizing his best regime, implies that there never have been nor likely ever will be any "good men."

Because Aristotle clearly believes that some human beings have achieved the happiness of a good human life, we need not accept such an extreme conclusion.[2] But if good human beings actually have existed, they develop and exercise their virtues within the manifestly imperfect conditions of ordinary political life. Apparently, the "difficulty" of attaining a good character under bad laws is, for Aristotle, a constitutive element of moral education and action for almost all human beings. It is thus one of the most important problems facing political animals such as ourselves. By exploring the political context of the Aristotelian good life, I hope to shed some light on the ways in which flawed political conditions shape the development and exercise of moral virtues, both in Aristotle's theory and our own experience.

## MORAL CHARACTER IN POLITICAL CONTEXT

The recent revival of interest in Aristotelian ethics reflects, among other things, increasing impatience with the unrealistic degree of control over our moral reasoning and character demanded by influential modern moral theories such as Kantianism and utilitarianism.[3] Unlike the most influential modern moral theorists, Aristotle is willing to accept that, as Martha Nussbaum puts it, "much that I did not make goes toward making me whatever I shall be praised or blamed for being." As a result, Aristotelian ethics can help us understand the ways in which both "making and being made" contribute to a good human life.[4]

Two elements of Aristotle's ethical theory make the good human life especially vulnerable to events beyond an individual's control: his claim that the moral virtues require habituation and social training and his

---

1. T. Irwin, *Aristotle's First Principles*, 410.
2. In some cases, such as Priam's, he even speaks of someone losing such happiness; *NE* 1101a.
3. This is true of many of the most influential books in the recent revival of Aristotelian moral philosophy, such as Alisdair MacIntyre's *After Virtue*, Martha Nussbaum's *The Fragility of Goodness*, and Bernard Williams's *Ethics and the Limits of Philosophy*. The other major focus of this revival has been Aristotle's understanding of prudence and the indeterminacy of moral judgment, as in Hans-Georg Gadamer's *Truth and Method*, Ronald Beiner's *Political Judgment*, and Charles Larmore's *Patterns of Moral Complexity*.
4. M. Nussbaum, *The Fragility of Goodness*, 5, 2.

insistence on treating external goods, such as friends, political community, and wealth, as necessary parts of human happiness (*eudaimonia*). If the development of good moral character requires habituation and training, then we are clearly dependent, to some extent, on others for our virtuous dispositions.[5] And if our ability to exercise our virtues in praiseworthy ways depends on our acquiring external goods such as friends, good political institutions, and moderate wealth, then we are clearly dependent on good fortune and the choices of other individuals for our happiness.

Understood in this way, the misfortunes that prevent, diminish, or eliminate human happiness are a regular part of ordinary human experience. Tragic misfortunes, those rare and dramatic disasters that inspire poetry and terror, may gain greater attention than the everyday misfortunes that concern only those directly affected by them. But more mundane and familiar events, from the death or divorce of our parents to periods of political instability or even an untimely teachers' strike, can still seriously stunt our moral development and thereby diminish our happiness.

Clearly, Aristotle recognizes the importance in our lives of the phenomenon that contemporary moral philosophers describe as "moral luck."[6] These philosophers suggest a number of ways in which good and bad fortune shapes the praiseworthiness of our lives and actions. Fortune helps constitute our moral character and identity; it often determines whether our actions have harmful or beneficial consequences; it helps determine whether we can, without moral disapproval, acquire the external goods, such as moderate wealth and friends, that allow us to develop and exercise the full range of virtues; finally, it helps determine whether we will be exposed to the kinds of situations in which it is difficult to avoid blame or easy to win praise.[7]

Nevertheless, I am reluctant to use the term *moral luck* in exploring Aristotle's ideas here. The concept of moral luck lumps together, in a most un-Aristotelian way, sociopolitical contingencies, such as the vices

---

5. Moreover, since Aristotle insists that we need such training even as adults (*NE* 1181a1), then that dependence continues to shape our chances for happiness throughout our entire lives rather than just during our childhood years. See N. Sherman, *The Fabric of Character*, 6; C. Lord, *Education and Culture*.

6. See T. Nagel, "Moral Luck"; B. Williams, "Moral Luck"; J. Andre, "Nagel, Williams, and Moral Luck." One of the great virtues of Martha Nussbaum's *The Fragility of Goodness* is the way in which it recovers this forgotten dimension of Aristotelian ethical philosophy.

7. This list is drawn primarily from Nagel's list of four kinds of moral luck; T. Nagel, "Moral Luck," 28. See also J. Andre, "Nagel, Williams, and Moral Luck," 202–3.

of our parents and compatriots, with natural contingencies, such as earthquakes and tornadoes. In doing so, it minimizes the important differences between our exposure to unavoidable natural misfortunes and to the misfortunes created by the choices and behavior of other individuals.[8]

From the perspective of a single individual faced with a moral dilemma—the viewpoint most often occupied by contemporary moral philosophers—it makes some sense to lump these two kinds of misfortune together since they both refer to unchosen constraints on an individual's choices and moral goodness. But from a broader point of view the differences between these two kinds of misfortune are extremely important. We tend to hold people who have some power over us accountable for the consequences of social contingencies but not for the consequences of what we think of as natural contingencies. Lumping natural and social contingencies together into a single concept of "moral luck" obscures this distinction and the controversies about social accountability it inspires.[9] Accordingly, I try to distinguish between natural and sociopolitical contingencies in my account of the Aristotelian good life, focusing more on the latter in this chapter and the former in the next.

Many modern moral philosophers are quite uncomfortable with Aristotle's understanding of moral development because they find it highly repugnant to hold individuals morally accountable for anything but the choices that are completely in their power to make. Aristotle, it seems to them, ignores the elementary moral principle that "ought implies can." How, they ask, can Aristotle hold individuals morally responsible for their actions if praiseworthy and blameworthy actions require moral dispositions that it is not within these individuals' power to create for themselves? Some contemporary moral philosophers, such as A. W. H. Adkins, treat this feature of Aristotelian ethics as an obvious defect, a remnant of the ancient Greeks' distressing inclination to identify desert with success.[10] Others, such as Terence Irwin, have argued that Aristotle recognizes this problem and corrects it with a more "complex" and adequate theory of moral responsibility.[11]

Irwin admits that Aristotle often suggests that voluntariness, which

---

8. On the importance of this distinction for Aristotle's understanding of moral character, see J. Roberts, "Aristotle on Responsibility," 30.
9. Judith Shklar explores these controversies in *The Faces of Injustice*.
10. A. W. H. Adkins, *Merit and Responsibility*, esp. 328–30.
11. T. Irwin, "Reason and Responsibility in Aristotle." This argument is further elaborated in Irwin's book, *Aristotle's First Principles*, 339–75.

Aristotle defines as lack of coercion and ignorance and attributes to animals and children as well as to mature human beings, is all that we require to hold individuals accountable for their actions. But he insists that Aristotle also presents a more exclusive understanding of moral responsibility in the *Nicomachean Ethics*. This more "complex theory" limits moral responsibility to creatures who can rationally choose and control their actions and states of character. "A person is responsible for her actions and states," according to this theory, only "in so far as they proceed from states that are in her control as a rational agent. . . . A rational person will choose the states of character that involve rational control." Individuals who choose other states of character fail "to realize their nature as a rational agent."[12]

The problem with the "complex theory" of moral responsibility that Irwin attributes to Aristotle (apart from the way in which it directly contradicts what Aristotle explicitly states about voluntariness and how we acquire moral character) is that it implies that a "mysterious shift" in human nature takes place as we move from childhood to maturity.[13] Before we reach adulthood, we seem to be little more than automatons, pushed about mechanically by external forces. Then, at some ill-defined point in our maturation, we are miraculously transformed into autonomous beings capable of complete rational control over our actions and even our character traits.

Irwin's "complex theory" of moral responsibility is the latest in a series of efforts to provide Aristotle with the notion of free will and moral autonomy that his writings seem to lack. Irwin tries to replace Aristotle's explicit discussion of voluntariness with a more "complex" notion of rational self-control because, like most modern moral philosophers, he assumes that only individuals who are in complete control of their choices and character can be held morally accountable for their actions. But there is little indication that Aristotle shares this assumption. His discussion of moral responsibility completely lacks the anxiety about finding a defensible notion of free will that characterizes most modern discussions of the topic. Indeed, he would probably think of this assumption about human autonomy, with its highly unrealistic picture of human development and self-control, as a serious liability to any adequate theory of moral responsibility.[14]

12. T. Irwin, *Aristotle's First Principles*, 373–74; T. Irwin, "Reason and Responsibility in Aristotle."
13. M. Nussbaum, *The Fragility of Goodness*, 285. See also J. Roberts, "Aristotle on Responsibility."
14. For an acute discussion of the ways in which modern philosophers have imposed their own conceptions of responsibility on Aristotle and other premodern thinkers, as

Aristotle is clearly unwilling to characterize either children as unfree or adults as autonomous molders of their own fate and character. It is simply "not consistent with Aristotle's moral psychology" to look for a break in the chain of social and natural dependence, a break that might allow adults to gain complete rational control over their choices and character.[15] Children share with adults the ability to make voluntary choices, even if they lack the fully developed rational faculties and moral character to make the best choices.[16] And adults share with children a certain level of dependence on chance and the efforts of others for the development of the moral virtues, even if we sometimes hold them accountable for the absence of these virtues in a way that we are not willing to impose on children.

Moreover, Aristotle never suggests that in order to hold adults accountable for their lack of moral virtue we have to assume that they are always capable of choosing and creating a good moral character for themselves. Most communities draw a line between childhood and maturity, a line that separates two kinds of praise and blame. But in doing so, they are merely making judgments about at what point youth and immaturity should no longer excuse individuals from the forms of blame and punishment reserved for adults. It is not as if children are not blamed and punished before they reach the legal age of maturity. They are simply allowed to use immaturity as an excuse to avoid the blame and punishment that communities reserve for individuals who have had sufficient time to develop moral and intellectual virtues. The line between childhood and moral adulthood represents a community's decision about how to hold individuals accountable for their actions. It cannot represent an ontological assertion about the existence of a free will unless one is willing to believe that on a conventionally chosen date, such as the twenty-first birthday, individuals suddenly transform themselves from slavish automatons into autonomous deliberators.

Aristotle is not, of course, suggesting that our choices make *no* contribution to the development of our moral character. He states clearly that "we share in causing [*sunaitioi*]" our moral character (*NE* 1114b22). But by doing so he is merely pointing to the important contribution that our choices make in the formation of our moral character; he is not implying that we possess anything like "rational control" over its na-

---

well as a helpful reconstruction of Aristotle's understanding of moral responsibility, see M. Smiley, *Moral Responsibility*, esp. ch. 2.

15. J. Roberts, "Aristotle on Responsibility," 28.
16. M. Nussbaum, *The Fragility of Goodness*, 285–86.

ture and development. Moral character is not, for Aristotle, an unavoidable natural necessity. The way in which we react to moral training will contribute in important ways to the shaping of our moral character, but we never face a moment during which we can subject our lives and character to that favorite figment of modern moral philosophers' imagination, a rational "life plan."[17]

Aristotelian moral education thus combines training in socially approved forms of behavior with frequent practice in exercising choice and deliberation. Recent studies of the subject have rightly emphasized the latter in an effort to eliminate the widespread impression that Aristotelian moral training involves little more than mindless and mechanical responses to external stimuli.[18] Nevertheless, these studies often swing too far in the opposite direction, thereby missing the political and coercive dimension of Aristotelian moral education. In order to gain good moral training, we need to live with people with sufficient force and authority over us to get us to do things that we are, at first, strongly disinclined to do.

Virtuous actions, Aristotle notes, are painful when first undertaken. "To live a life of self-control and tenacity is not pleasant for most people, especially for the young. Therefore, their upbringing and pursuits must be regulated by laws; for once they have become familiar, they will no longer be painful" (*NE* 1179b33). To get individuals to begin to perform virtuous actions, we thus need "the guidance of a kind of intelligence and right order that can be *enforced*." Laws have this "power to compel" and are less resented as the source of a painful action than the will of particular individuals. "While people hate any men who oppose, however rightly, their impulses, the law is not invidious when it enjoins what is right" (*NE* 1180a17–24). Imitation of and persuasion by beloved friends and parents,[19] however important their contribution to moral education, will not provide sufficient incentive to perform virtuous actions and accept moral training. There must also be sufficient force and authority to overcome our initial aversion to the pains that moral actions cause us.

Aristotelian moral education is political in the broadest sense of the term in that it involves the exercise of authority by some individual or

---

17. J. Roberts, "Aristotle on Responsibility," 30.
18. See, for example, N. Sherman, *The Fabric of Character*, vii; M. Burnyeat, "Aristotle on Learning."
19. Laurence Thomas emphasizes the role of friends in Aristotelian moral education in *Living Morally*, 129. Nancy Sherman (*Fabric of Character*, 171) emphasizes persuasion by and imitation of parents.

individuals to compel others to behave in a particular way. This will be the case no matter which social community—a family, a tribe, a club, or a state—provides moral training. In each, some individual or individuals will be determining how others should behave.[20] Unlike many contemporary students of moral education, Aristotle does not sentimentalize "private" as opposed to "public" sources of moral education. However much love and respect may, in some cases, legitimize the authority of parents over children, moral education in the family also rests, to a considerable extent, on the superior force that parents can use to compel their children's behavior.

But Aristotelian moral education is also political in the narrower, specifically Aristotelian sense that we have been using in this study. In other words, it requires, when best designed, active involvement by the political community. As noted above, Aristotle believes that people generally are less resentful when the political community's laws, rather than the wills of particular individuals, oppose their inclinations. If many people are performing, and have in the past performed, the same painful action, it will be far less onerous than it would be if it were picked out especially for us and imposed on us by a particular individual. Even young children soon chafe at the personal authority of their parents, preferring instead to do what "everyone else is doing," even if what everyone else is doing causes as much pain as the actions demanded by parents.[21] Aristotle suggests that things that are generally done are less painful because their regularity resembles that which is naturally done. For this reason, he concludes that the development of habits is the best means of promoting virtuous behavior, and general laws are the best means of promoting moral habits.

Another argument for supporting public moral education also fits in quite well with Aristotle's understanding of political life, even though he does not explicitly advance it. The laws of a political community, unlike the commands of parents, are open for public deliberation by relatively equal individuals.[22] Moral training by means of laws thus

20. For this reason virtuous friendships are not, contra Laurence Thomas (*Living Morally*, 129), an appropriate community for moral education. The equality and mutual respect characteristic of such friendships make them the ideal forum for the exercise of the moral virtues but not for their acquisition.

21. Accordingly, Aristotle recommends parental moral education up to the age of seven, with public education thereafter; *Pol.* 1336b1. Parental guidance still has a role to play in education after that point as a transmitter of the community's rules to children; *NE* 1180b1. Moreover, in the less than ideal political conditions in which most children grow up, parental responsibility for moral education is magnified; *NE* 1180a31.

22. See chapter 5 for a discussion of the differences between political and domestic justice.

prepares individuals for their life as adults by accustoming them to dealing with standards that can be publicly challenged and reconsidered even while they set authoritative guidelines for present behavior. Citizens will not be prepared to participate in the practices associated with political justice if they are trained from youth to think of their duties as unchangeable forces of nature or as the commands of a beloved but unquestionable parental authority.

There is a sense, in any case, in which political education by laws is inevitable for Aristotle, whether laws were consciously designed for that purpose or not. Aristotle would probably agree with Rousseau that "laws make men in their image," whether they intend to do so or not.[23] It is important to remember how broadly Aristotle conceives of the term *laws* (*nomoi*) when speaking of the role of laws in Aristotelian moral education. For Aristotle, vague and unwritten customs are just as much laws as statutes are.[24] Whether or not a political community decides to draw up a design for moral education, a broad range of written and unwritten laws will shape behavior within it.

But the lack of conscious design in moral education undermines the stability of regimes, since the laws that inevitably do shape moral development may promote characteristics unsuited for life in the regime under which they are enforced. At the same time, the fact that we depend to a certain extent on imperfect laws and regimes for the development of good moral character increases the difficulty of acquiring this character and the good life it supports. We will not necessarily develop a tyrannical character if we grow up under a tyranny, but we will face great difficulties in our moral development. We will, for example, have to resist, to some extent, the examples of people in authority while still accepting some of the initial and necessary training in character that they provide. As a result, growing up under a tyranny could easily promote either an overly submissive or an overly rebellious character.

Our partial dependence on imperfect political communities for our moral education is one of the most troubling problems that emerge from our political nature as Aristotle describes it. But if we are drawn, as are increasing numbers of contemporary philosophers and intellectuals, to a virtue- and character-based approach to ethics, then this problem may be, as Amelie Rorty suggests, one of the "somber" truths that we will

23. J.-J. Rousseau, "Discourse on Political Economy," in *On the Social Contract*, 216–17.
24. See the first section of chapter 6.

have to learn to live with. "Reconstructivist moral philosophers who propose to assure virtue by offering either rules for or an imitable model of acting well tend to bracket [such] contingencies. . . . But it is just the strength of practical, descriptively oriented virtue theories that they acknowledge the pervasive presence of moral luck."[25] By clearly identifying the specifically political contingencies that surround the acquisition of good moral character, Aristotle's account of moral education helps us to identify and deal with the "somber" truth about human goodness.

## MISFORTUNE AND THE ASYMMETRY BETWEEN PRAISE AND BLAME

Before exploring some of the moral conflicts that arise in Aristotelian political life, I want to look a little more closely at Aristotle's understanding of the relationship between misfortune and human goodness.[26]

"Those who say that someone who is tortured on the wheel or suffers great misfortunes is happy if he is good," Aristotle complains, "are, willingly or not, saying nothing" (*NE* 1153b19). If happiness merely designated an emotional state for Aristotle, then these remarks would be very easy to understand and accept. But Aristotle thinks of happiness as a praiseworthy way of living rather than as a mere emotional state. As a result, his insistence that misfortune can harm or even destroy happiness shocks many of his modern readers. Priam's life is certainly less satisfying after his terrible misfortunes. But do these misfortunes really make his life any less praiseworthy, as Aristotle seems to suggest when he denies that Priam, despite all of his virtues, can lead a happy and flourishing life after the fall of Troy (*NE* 1100a5)? How can we praise or blame people for things that are completely beyond their control to bring about or prevent? Aristotle, quite sensibly, notes that we reserve praise and blame for states and actions that agents contributed in some way to bringing about (*NE* 1109b30). How can he then describe Priam's life as less praiseworthy merely as a result of his terrible misfortune? Perhaps Adkins is justified after all in his complaint that Aristotle never completely shed himself of the ancient Greeks' tendency to confuse merit with success.[27]

25. A. O. Rorty, "Virtues and Their Vicissitudes," 146–47.
26. I examine this question at greater length in "How Good Is the Aristotelian Good Life?"
27. A. W. H. Adkins, *Merit and Responsibility*, 328.

Aristotle has not lacked for defenders against Adkins's charge. John Cooper, for example, suggests that "Aristotle goes out of his way to avoid the error which some allege is endemic to Greek moral thinking, namely, the glorification of success, however attained." As Cooper interprets him, Aristotle would insist that "if two persons have the same good character but one is thwarted and disappointed at every turn by blows of fate, while the other's life is one dazzling success after another, they would have to be said to flourish in precisely the same degree." Nevertheless, Cooper admits that "it is not easy to see exactly how [Aristotle's] theory of *eudaimonia* could accommodate this insight" about fortune's ability to destroy Priam's happiness.[28]

Other commentators try to supply Aristotle with a distinction that would accommodate this insight without suggesting that an individual can be less praiseworthy because of misfortune. Aristotle, they say, distinguishes between being happy (*eudaimon*), a condition that depends only on a good character, and being blessed (*makarios*), a condition that includes prosperity as well as good character. Bad fortune cannot deprive us of happiness and ethical praiseworthiness, they suggest, even if it can deprive us of the blessedness that includes prosperity.[29] But this argument collapses when we look more closely at Aristotle's words. Aristotle tends to use *happy* and *blessed* interchangeably, both in this and most other important passages.[30] "Blessing [*makarismos*] and felicitation [*eudaimonismos*] are identical with each other" (*Rhet.* 1367b34). *Blessed*, it turns out, is, according to Aristotle, merely the most appropriate adjective with which to praise something like happiness. "No one praises happiness [*eudaimonia*] as he praises justice," Aristotle suggests, "but rather calls it blessed [*makarios*], as something better and more divine" (*NE* 1101b25).

Must we conclude, with Adkins, that Aristotle did succumb in the end to some irrational form of success worship? I think not. Aristotle never blames anyone for the results of misfortunes, even if he believes that the unfortunate lead less praiseworthy lives. As for praising the

---

28. J. Cooper, *Reason and the Human Good,* 124–26. Terence Irwin presents a persuasive critique of Cooper's interpretation of Aristotle's understanding of fortune and the good life in "Permanent Happiness," 94n9, 95–96, 96n12.

29. W. D. Ross, *Aristotle,* 192; H. Joachim, *The Nicomachean Ethics,* 59. Adkins (*From the Many to the One,* 257–58) characteristically suggests that Aristotle tried to use this distinction "to internalize" his conception of moral goodness, thereby freeing that conception from any connection with fortune, but in the end failed to follow the distinction consistently because of the persistent influence of traditional Greek prejudices on his thought.

30. As clearly demonstrated by M. Nussbaum, *The Fragility of Goodness,* 330–34.

more fortunate, it is neither irrational nor foreign to modern sentiments to do so, once we recognize the important asymmetry between blaming and praising.

Aristotle teaches that we should pity rather than blame individuals who suffer undeserved bad fortune. The unfortunate Priam is not blameworthy, according to Aristotle. Just as we do not blame people for being born ugly, we should not blame them for any other bad fortune that they suffer (*NE* 1099b2). Nevertheless, because the absence of the external goods that depend on fortune, such as good looks, wealth, power, good children, friends, and so on, are serious impediments to virtuous actions, we will not be able to perform very many virtuous actions without them. Bad fortune should not make us wretched—that is, capable of vicious acts (*NE* 1101a)—but it can deprive us of the ability to perform the virtuous acts that make up the better part of happiness.

Thus, we do tend to praise the fortunate, at least in part, simply because they are fortunate. But this praise is not, for Aristotle, a morally offensive celebration of success because we do not praise happiness in the same way that we praise the virtuousness of actions. We praise happiness, but we do not—or should not—hold individuals accountable to some standard of blame for not achieving it. Aristotle relies on an important asymmetry between the ways in which we praise and blame, an asymmetry that most modern moral philosophers ignore. We blame only agents and the actions for which they are responsible, but we praise good things, such as happiness, and not just agents and the actions for which they are responsible.

Aristotle draws his distinction between the praiseworthiness of happiness and the praiseworthiness of the virtues directly after his discussion of fortune and happiness.

> Everything that is praised [*epainēton*] seems to be of a certain kind and have some relation to something else: for we praise the just and the brave man and in general both the good man and virtue itself because of their actions and their activities, and we praise the strong man, the good runner, and so on, because he is of a certain kind and is related in a certain way to something good and important.... But if praise is for such things, then clearly it is not praise that the best things deserve, but rather something greater and better, as is indeed manifest; for we call the gods and the most godlike of men blessed and happy. And so too with good things; no one praises happiness as he does justice, but rather calls it blessed as something better and more divine.
>
> (*NE* 1101b12–26)

Hans Joachim suggested many years ago that this passage "has no philosophic interest."[31] Most later readers must agree, since almost none but the line-by-line commentators even mention it.[32] I suspect, however, that later readers have generally ignored this passage because they view the praise that we oppose to blame as the only ethically relevant sense of praise.

Clearly, Aristotle does not share their view. Unfortunate individuals such as Priam lose praiseworthiness of life, according to Aristotle, when they lose the opportunity and capacity to perform many virtuous actions. But they also lose "something greater and better": happiness itself. Happiness itself is praiseworthy, according to Aristotle, but in a different way than actions are. Because happiness is something greater, better, and more divine than virtuous actions, this different sense of praise is still relevant to the ethical evaluation of lives. In honoring or cherishing happy lives we are describing them as praiseworthy, above and beyond the praiseworthiness owing to the virtues of the individuals that lead them. Such lives are the best things for human beings to aim at, but we do not blame someone because they fail to lead a happy life. Although happiness is more praiseworthy than virtue, it is not within our power to achieve; and blame should be ascribed only to states and actions voluntarily initiated by individuals. It is clear from this passage, then, that Aristotle believes that more than one sense of praiseworthiness is relevant to the evaluation of human lives.[33]

One might paraphrase Aristotle in the following way. We praise and blame individuals for the actions they undertake. We praise lives, in contrast, for how cherishable or happy they are. When we praise lives we are praising them for having something good and complete in themselves, something, it turns out, that is not within the power of individuals to achieve merely by their own efforts. When we praise individuals, we are praising agents who do or do not try to behave in the ways that

31. H. Joachim, *The Nicomachean Ethics*, 61.
32. And even these commentators, such as Burnet (*The Ethics of Aristotle*, 56) or Gauthier and Jolif (*L'Éthique à Nicomaque* 2:88) are somewhat dismissive of the passage. Larry Arnhart (*Aristotle on Political Reasoning*, 84–85), in contrast, presents an interesting commentary on this passage and a parallel passage in Aristotle's *Rhetoric* (1367b).
33. A passage from the *Magna Moralia* helps clarify this distinction: "Goods may be divided into the cherishable, the praiseworthy, and capacities. By the cherishable I mean such a thing as the divine, the more excellent (for instance, soul, intellect), the more ancient, the first principle, and so on.... Other goods are praiseworthy, as virtues; for praise is bestowed in consequence of the actions which are prompted by them"; *Magna Moralia* 1183b20–28.

contribute to happiness that are in their power.[34] But the virtues and vices for which we praise and blame individuals are, unlike happiness, relative goods. They are good because they contribute to something cherishable in itself, which is happiness. We praise the virtuous individual "because he is of a certain kind and is related in a certain way to something good and important" (*NE* 1101b6). Accordingly, happiness itself is something better than virtue, deserving of something "greater and better" than the praise we devote to the virtues.

Although it has been ignored by most of Aristotle's commentators, this distinction between different forms of praise is not as foreign to modern sensibilities as it may at first seem. We too rely, I suggest, on a similar asymmetry between praising and blaming in our own moral judgments, an asymmetry that this distinction can help us understand.

Consider the way in which we ordinarily use the terms *praise* and *blame*. We do, of course, praise actions and character. But we also praise things without reference to agents and agency. We praise paintings and sunsets as well as painters and the creator of the heavens. In short, when we offer praise, we do not necessarily think of the agent responsible for the state we are praising. When we offer blame, in contrast, we invariably look for an agent. Blaming requires answers to both "who" and "what" questions. We must identify both something bad and an agent responsible for it in order to blame. Without an agent, we find it difficult to blame anything for our misfortunes.[35] To praise something, in contrast, we need only judge that something is good, whether or not we can identify an agent connected to this goodness.

When Aristotle suggests that our praise for happiness should be "something greater and better" than our praise for virtue, he builds on this asymmetry in our attitudes toward praise and blame. He distinguishes between praising things as cherishable in themselves and praising them as agents responsible for good things. The latter parallels the way we speak about blame; the former does not. Aristotle's praise of happiness, unlike his praise of virtuous actions, makes no reference to

---

34. Accordingly, Aristotle advises orators to exaggerate the degree of control over events possessed by the individuals whom they seek to praise; *Rhet.* 1367b.

35. That is why we are so inclined to invent agents of our misfortunes in moments of anger, as when we strike out at the bringer of bad news or kick the garbage can over which we trip. Without the ascription of responsibility to some agent, divine, human, or inanimate, we cannot express any blame for our misfortunes. When we calm down, we usually recognize our irrationality by recognizing that many of the objects of our anger, such as messengers and garbage cans, do not deserve our blame, since they did not themselves act to bring about our misfortune.

the choices of agents, since no agent is responsible for its existence.³⁶

Modern moral philosophers frequently assume that "our" modern practice of moral appraisal restricts praiseworthiness to actions within the power of an individual, that is, to the kind of praise that is opposed to blame.³⁷ It seems more accurate, however, to say that modern moral philosophers are trying to correct rather than identify "our" practice of moral appraisal. For them, the only sense of praise relevant to the evaluation of an individual's life and actions is that which relates to voluntary decisions. But to maintain this claim, they have to remove the asymmetry between praise and blame in our ordinary judgments. They must bring the way we praise things into line with the way we blame things.

The most important and influential attempt to restrict praiseworthiness in this way is Kant's moral philosophy. When Kant insists that there is nothing that "can be called good without qualification, except the good will,"³⁸ he is, in effect, trying to bring our practice of praising into line with our practice of blaming. Kant is demanding that we should limit unqualified praise to agents responsible for actions, just as we so limit unqualified blame. The other "good" things we often praise are only qualifiedly good, since the only certain source of goodness or evil lies in the will of a responsible agent. But Kant has to distort our ordinary moral judgments in order to limit praise in this way. Most people, I suspect, would be much more likely to agree that there is nothing absolutely bad or blameworthy except a bad will than to agree that there is nothing absolutely good or praiseworthy except a good will.³⁹

John Rawls, like many modern moral philosophers, takes this aspect of Kantian moral philosophy for granted and, as a result, ascribes it to

---

36. Aristotle does not think of God as the creator responsible for the way the world is, nor does he think of nature as an agent that shapes the world. Aristotle's frequent personifications of nature, personifications that might be take to imply that he thinks of nature as an agent, are, in the end, metaphorical. See R. Sorabji, *Necessity, Cause, and Blame*, 167; J. Lear, *Aristotle*, 41.

37. For example, A. W. H. Adkins (*Merit and Responsibility*, 2) insists that "we," unlike the ancient Greeks, "are all Kantians now," at least in this regard. See also J. Macdowell ("The Role of Eudamonia," 374–75n22), who insists that for better or worse "we are stuck with a notion of morality" similar to the Kantian notion defended by Prichard. He suggests further that to the extent that Aristotle may go beyond this notion of morality his "thesis cannot be intellectually satisfying to *us*."

38. I. Kant, *Fundamental Principles*, 11.

39. Susan Wolf makes a similar point about the asymmetry between our judgments of praise and blame in "Asymmetrical Freedom," 155–56. She points out that we do not feel the need to raise questions about whether an agent was free, in the sense of being capable of doing otherwise, when we are about to praise someone, even though such questions almost always arise in our deliberations about blame.

our ordinary "considered judgments." Rawls repeatedly insists that it is among the fixed points of our "considered judgments" that the possession of natural talents is "arbitrary from a moral point of view" and that we must therefore construct "a conception of justice that nullifies the accidents of natural endowment" if we are to follow our most basic judgments.[40] The possession of natural abilities is morally arbitrary, according to Rawls, because no one does anything to deserve them. They represent the outcome of the lottery of birth.

So far, Rawls does not depart very far from common moral judgments. But when he suggests that because the distribution of talents is morally arbitrary, special rewards for their possession and use are improper, he clearly goes well beyond these judgments. Like Kant, he misses the asymmetry in our judgments about praise and blame. Few people would want to see individuals punished because of their misfortunes at birth. But just as few people, at least in our society, would deny that individuals who do things very well, even if it is only because they have natural gifts, deserve greater rewards than those who do not. The great basketball players did not earn their height or leaping ability; yet few would suggest that these abilities are irrelevant to considerations about the rewards that they should receive. We offer praise to those who perform well, regardless of how they gained their abilities, even though we try to be careful not to blame individuals for lacking the natural talents to match the best performances of a certain activity.

Kant and Rawls would probably reply that the asymmetry I am discussing is an inconsistency, one that we should try to correct on reflection. After all, if we insist that no one should be penalized simply because of misfortune at birth and then go ahead and offer greater rewards to those with greater natural endowments, are we not behaving inconsistently? I think not. This behavior would be inconsistent if we were seeking to measure praiseworthiness and blameworthiness according to one uniform principle, which is exactly what Kant and Rawls want us to do. But there may be good reasons for employing different kinds of principles to measure praiseworthiness and blameworthiness, even if doing so somewhat diminishes the clarity of our moral standards.

Human capacities are not chosen or in our control. A good human life, whether we describe it in Aristotelian or Kantian terms, is a life in which we develop and exercise some of these capacities. When we say that such a life is praiseworthy, we are praising something that fortune,

---

40. J. Rawls, *A Theory of Justice*, 12, 15, 72.

so to speak, has given us: the particular way of life that human beings, as a species and as particular individuals, happen to be capable of living. Even when Kant argues that there is nothing absolutely good except the good will, he is arguing that a specifically human way of being is the good way of being. In effect, he is suggesting that we must live up to our highest given capacity: the capacity for a free and rational determination of the will. In doing so, he is assuming that this way of being is *the* good way of being for human beings. The human good, even if defined in Kantian manner, is not something that we choose or make for ourselves. In order to praise moral virtue, even Kant has to praise something beyond the good will: the human or rational way of being.

Similarly, natural talents, such as Rawls considers, are good things even though they are neither willed nor earned. When we praise their achievements, we praise things that are, to a certain extent, beyond our control but enhance our lives. In praising these achievements, we acknowledge that what is good for us is determined, to a great extent, by our contingent make-up as human beings. This form of acknowledgment does not decide, by itself, whether and how much these talents deserve to be rewarded; but it does justify making asymmetric judgments about praise and blame.

A passage from Sophocles' *Ajax* helps us perceive the roots of this asymmetry. Ajax's flaw, as Sophocles presents it, was that he wanted to perform praiseworthy deeds on his own, without help from fortune or the gods.

> Ajax, even when he first set out from home,
> Proved himself foolish, when his father gave him
> His good advice at parting. "Child," he said, "Resolve
> to win, but always with God's help."
> But Ajax answered with a senseless boast:
> "Father, with God's help even a worthless man
> Could triumph. I propose, without that help,
> To win my prize of fame." In such a spirit
> he boasted. And when once Athena stood
> Beside him in the flight, urging him on
> To strike the enemy with his deadly hand,
> He answered then, that second time, with words
> To shudder at, not speak: "Goddess," he said,
> "Go stand beside the other Greeks; help them.
> For where I bid, no enemy will break through."
> These were the graceless words which won for him
> The Goddess' wrath; they kept no measure.[41]

41. Sophocles, *Ajax*, ll. 762–77.

We do not have to believe in the Greek gods in order to appreciate the nature of his Ajax's hubris. Ajax eschews all external help in achieving his noble goals. He believes that if his achievements owe something to fortune or to the gods, they lose their nobility. But can we really believe that everything that Ajax achieves is due to his efforts alone? To do so, we would have to ignore the good fortune that gave him a strong body and good birth, the accident of timing that allowed him to live at the time of the Trojan expedition with its opportunities for glory, the lucky breaks that spared him from an early inglorious death by accident or disease, and so on. Only those who, like Ajax, "forget their merely human nature" and go "beyond human measure" so ignore the limitations of the human condition.[42]

Nevertheless, Ajax's understanding of the form of a good life is quite Kantian in character—even if his understanding of its content, the glorious virtues displayed when slaughtering one's enemies, is not. Kant, like Ajax, disdains heteronomous sources of praiseworthy actions. He too insists that an individual's willed actions and achievements must be the only basis for praise. In doing so, Kant too forgets human nature. He forgets that human capacities and the circumstances that allow for praiseworthy acts are given to human beings rather than made by them.

To confirm the asymmetry in our attitudes toward praise and blame, ask yourself how you would react to Ajax's boast if it referred to blame rather than praise. If he had eschewed the help of fortune and the gods in seeking blame, you would hardly think him hubristic, for blame is something that is always within our power to achieve. We can always pick up a stick and beat the next person we see on a crowded street if we want to do something blameworthy. It is not, in contrast, always in our power to do something that deserves praise. For that we need appropriate opportunities and abilities. Blame, as it were, comes looking for us; we have to strive constantly to avoid it. But praise is something that we have to seek, and may never find.

## MORAL CONFLICT IN POLITICAL CONTEXT

Once we acknowledge the extent to which moral praiseworthiness lies beyond our control, it becomes hard to deny the possibility of moral conflict in our lives. If our goodness depends to a great extent on good fortune and a healthy, well-ordered communal life, bad luck and a dis-

42. Ibid., l. 759.

ordered social environment are bound to throw us into situations in which we cannot satisfy all of our moral expectations. It is thus not surprising that discussion of moral conflict usually follows hard on the heels of most contemporary discussions of moral luck.[43]

Aristotle, as noted above, has a deep appreciation of the role that natural and sociopolitical contingencies play in the development and exercise of the virtues of character. Does he have an equal appreciation of the depth and extent of moral conflict to which misfortune and imperfect communities expose us? I believe that he does, even though the majority of moral philosophers, citing his belief in the essential harmony of the human virtues, disagree.[44] I try to show that the importance of moral conflict in Aristotelian ethics emerges once we return his understanding of the good life to the everyday political context in which it must actually be lived.

Stuart Hampshire rightly notes that for Aristotle there is no *necessary* incompatibility among human virtues, that there is "no feature of human nature" that allows us to realize "some virtues only at the expense of others." In principle, although "only with luck," we should be able to realize them all.[45] Were we fortunate enough to be citizens of Aristotle's best regime, as well as to escape all natural disasters to ourselves, friends, family, and compatriots, then we should, indeed, be in a position to realize completely all of the Aristotelian virtues. But that is not the situation in which actual human beings find themselves. They have to deal with the imperfections of the various communities on which they depend, as well as the problematic situations created by unexpected misfortune. In the actual sociopolitical context within which the good life is led, conflicts among the demands of different virtues not only arise but are an everyday occurrence.

Aristotle gives an extreme example of such conflicts at the beginning of book 3 of the *Nicomachean Ethics* (1110a). A tyrant holds our parents hostage and orders us to do something base if we want to save their lives. Among the noble dispositions of a good moral character is a disposition to support and honor one's parents. It would be base, not just painful, for us to let our parents die when it is in our power to save

---

43. As in T. Nagel, "Moral Luck"; M. Nussbaum, *The Fragility of Goodness*; B. Williams, "Moral Luck."

44. For example, see S. Hampshire, *Morality and Conflict*, 31. Michael Stocker (*Plural and Conflicting Values*) is an important exception, since he builds an original account of moral conflict on Aristotelian foundations, as does Martha Nussbaum in *The Fragility of Goodness*.

45. S. Hampshire, *Morality and Conflict*, 31.

them. Nevertheless, acting as the tyrant demands remains a base action that goes against a good individual's moral dispositions. Whatever choice we make in this situation will conflict with a disposition we expect to find in a good individual.[46]

Moreover, Aristotle does not allow us to ease the moral character of this conflict by denying that a coerced action, such as the one demanded by the tyrant, is truly voluntary and therefore not subject to moral appraisal. These actions are "mixed," according to Aristotle. They are in one sense involuntary, "since nobody [of good character] would choose to do any one of them for its own sake." But they are voluntary in another sense; indeed, Aristotle suggests that "they come closer to being voluntary than to being involuntary actions. For they are desirable at the moment of action; and the end for which an action is performed depends on the time at which it is done" (NE 1110a11–18). We have a choice to make in this situation about whether to initiate a base action or to act basely by failing to come to the aid of our parents.

Aristotle makes clear that some actions, such as murdering one's mother in order to escape danger, are so base that no good individual would perform them in any situation (NE 1110a26). But there is a tremendous variety of base actions, many of which will fall well below that threshold. As a result, in situations such as the one we have been considering, we have to ask ourselves which one of our moral dispositions we will choose to counter. These questions have no straightforward answer, according to Aristotle. Life would be far happier, in the Aristotelian sense, were we lucky enough to avoid all such situations. Prudent individuals deal with them as best they can, knowing that however they decide, they will have something to regret.

Living as we do in imperfectly organized communities, we are bound to face this sort of situation. We may not face moral conflicts as stark and tragic as a choice between our dignity and our parents' lives, but we will almost certainly face less painful and dramatic conflicts among our loyalties and moral dispositions. Take, for example, our reaction to imperfect laws. Although Aristotle does not demand any absolute obligation to obey our community's laws, he does expect good individuals to obey and support many irrational and even offensive laws when resistance to these laws or efforts to change them will undermine the habitual basis of the legal and political authority (Pol. 1268–69a). Given

---

46. See M. Stocker, *Plural and Conflicting Values*, ch. 3, for an excellent discussion of this example.

the imperfect institutions, political conflicts, and historical contingencies that characterize most actual political communities, most political communities will have some relatively irrational and offensive laws. These laws demand base actions, at least from the point of view of individuals of good character. It would be clearly wrong for such individuals to disobey or work to overturn these laws, however irrational they may be, when they cannot do so without undermining the customary authority that the laws gain from longevity and familiarity. As a result, Aristotle asks good individuals to do something base for the common good of their political communities. Even everyday political conditions will thus promote moral conflict and regret in good individuals.

Aristotle sums up the basis for moral conflict in ordinary political life in his famous distinction between the good man and the good citizen (*Pol.* 1276b–78b). Only in the best regime will the good man and the good citizen have exactly the same virtues (*Pol.* 1278b). In ordinary political conditions their characteristic virtues will be in tension with each other. The good citizen's characteristic virtue is love of the common good of a community's members, the virtue described in the *Nicomachean Ethics* as "general justice."[47] The good individual, in contrast, is disposed more generally to noble actions, even if they conflict with the good of a particular community.

One might think of the good individual–good citizen dichotomy as Aristotle's way of representing the conflict between political and moral duties, but Aristotle never makes this distinction. General justice, the love of the common good of one's community and the primary virtue of a good citizen, is also a disposition that Aristotle expects from a good individual. A good individual should be *disposed* to promote the common good of the regime in which he participates as well as to obey its laws. He "should choose lawful acts ... for their own sake, i.e., because they are just and lawful acts."[48] Because a disposition to follow general rules is part of his character, the good man should find it painful to resist, disobey, or evade community standards. Of course, some laws will be so base that good individuals, unlike good citizens, should resist and overcome the pain caused by resisting or evading a community's general rules. But Aristotle offers no greater certainty about how to make that decision than he offers about when a base but coerced action

---

47. See chapter 5.
48. R. Polansky, "The Dominance of 'Polis,' " 44. Polansky is countering D. J. Allan's claim that Aristotle sharply distinguishes moral and political-legal duties from one other; see D. J. Allan, "Individual and State."

should be performed. In any case, even if we are confident about making the right choice in such circumstances, we will still have reason for regretting, to a certain extent, the need to make that choice.

Good individuals will also be disposed to be good citizens. They will, accordingly, be disposed to act justly by promoting the common good of their communities. But the common advantage of a particular political community may require, as when one has to institutionalize base practices in order to promote a mixed regime, actions that virtuous individuals would ordinarily be disinclined to perform. In these circumstances justice comes into conflict with the other moral virtues in the character of good individuals.

International relations also introduce moral conflict into the structure of ordinary political life. Among the improbable preconditions that Aristotle lays down for his best regime is relative isolation from other nations and political communities (*Pol.* 1324b35). The best regime will imitate the very best life, the life devoted to philosophic contemplation, by focusing entirely on its own affairs and by ignoring those of other political communities (*Pol.* 1325b15–30). But it will be able to engage in such self-absorption only if it is relatively isolated from powerful neighbors and the threats that they pose.

Aristotle makes relative isolation a condition for the best regime because he worries about the way in which the need for military virtues, a need that arises whenever a political community has powerful neighbors or gets involved in international affairs, distorts the development and exercise of the moral virtues. He points to Sparta and Crete as examples of this distortion (*Pol.* 1324b, 1333b). Aristotle insists that they have the only Greek regimes that are consciously designed to promote the virtues of their citizens, but these virtues are all directed toward success in war and conquest. By treating military success as the end of moral education, these regimes promote the idea that happiness consists primarily in conquering and dominating others (*Pol.* 1333b), an idea that clearly contradicts Aristotle's understanding of the good life.

Nevertheless, unless we are lucky enough to lack potentially threatening neighbors, it is hard to avoid this exaggeration of the importance of the martial virtues, for the demands of self-defense, as any reader of Hobbes is well aware, are infinitely inflatable. We can never be *completely* certain of our security until all of our present and potential enemies are completely in our power, a condition that we can never fully reach. As a result, those who insist that we need to do more to defend ourselves—for example, to devote more of our budget or moral training to military matters—are never at a loss for arguments to support their demands. Only if we are lucky enough to live in isolation from powerful neighbors will their arguments, and the distortion of the good life these arguments promote, lack justification.

Of course, in the actual political world in which we attempt to lead a good life, arguments for military necessity and the military virtues are unavoidable, since few real regimes lack actual or potential enemies.[49] Moreover, the need to engage in wars, even if they are relatively just wars of self-defense, will involve us in all of the familiar conflicts with ordinary moral standards that arise in the midst of battle: decisions about our willingness to sacrifice the lives of other individuals in place of our own, about how far one is willing to relax moral constraints in the name of military necessity, about conflicts of loyalty, and so on.

Consider, for example, the potential conflict between loyalty to friends and to country. Aristotle would never say, with E. M. Forster, that he hoped he would sacrifice his country for his friends. But he does recognize that the most perfect forms of friendship can exist between members of different political communities.[50] Moreover, there is a sense in which friends share a community of virtue that political communities never can.[51] As a result, a need to choose between friends and political community should, when viewed from an Aristotelian perspective, present us with a deep and painful moral conflict.

Such moral dilemmas and conflicts loom large among the problems of a political animal. Aristotle does not explicitly discuss these conflicts at any length,[52] but he may do so only because he thinks that there is not much to say about how to deal with them. Because the choices we must make in situations of moral conflict are both highly particular and inherently unsatisfying, he may think it more important to emphasize the need to promote healthy moral dispositions in a variety of directions rather than dwell on the problems that arise when these dispositions come into conflict with each other.

Aristotle, unlike most other philosophers who acknowledge the ex-

---

49. Consequently, actual political regimes will almost certainly overvalue the military virtues, a common vice in the history of republics. For a valuable discussion of Aristotle's critique of the ancient Greek's overvaluation of military virtues, see S. Salkever, *Finding the Mean*, 169–74.

50. The *Magna Moralia* (1211a11) goes so far as to suggest that members of different political communities will have a better chance of remaining comrades since they have less to quarrel about.

51. See chapter 4.

52. C. Larmore, *Patterns of Moral Complexity*, 10.

istence of moral conflict, seems very reluctant to place it at the center of his ethical theory. Jean-Paul Sartre, for example, builds his existentialist conception of moral choice as free but irrational commitment on examples of irreconcilable duties.[53] One of these examples, the case of an individual who has to choose between taking care of a sick mother or abandoning her that he might join the French resistance to the Nazi occupation, has become a focus for much of the contemporary literature on moral conflict. It might shed some light on Aristotle's understanding of moral conflict to consider this case from an Aristotelian point of view.

First, Aristotle would acknowledge the existence of extreme moral conflicts such as Sartre describes. Like Sartre's resistance fighter, the individual who must either perform some base action or have his parents slaughtered by a tyrant (*NE* 1110a) cannot perform one duty without abandoning another. But for Aristotle the plight of such individuals exemplifies extreme misfortune rather than ethical decision making in general. These individuals have the deep misfortune to live in circumstances that compel them to abandon completely a deeply felt obligation. Had Sartre's resistance fighter lived under a bad but less absolutely evil occupying power, had his mother been even a little better able to take care of herself, or had the French resistance, like some other resistance movements, moved whole village communities to relatively safe havens, then there would have been much more room for compromise between his conflicting senses of duty, even if they could not both be entirely satisfied.

These less extremely unfortunate situations, are, from an Aristotelian perspective, closer to the normal conditions in which moral conflict arises. They require us to take actions that give us some cause for regret, since they force us to act more basely than we would otherwise choose to act. But they do not force us simply to abandon important ethical commitments, as rare and tragic circumstances do.

From an Aristotelian point of view, Sartre's willingness to place tragic moral conflict at the center of his understanding of ethical decision making expresses the romantic and somewhat irrational reaction of someone who is shocked and shaken by the discovery that human goodness can be undermined by the effects of extreme misfortune. Aristotle treats this discovery as an aid to defining the constraints within which moral choice

---

53. J.-P. Sartre, *Existentialism Is a Humanism*.

and rationality are exercised. Sartre, in contrast, reacts to it by declaring that we have no choice but to embrace with firm but irrational resolution the tragic choices that fate imposes on us.

By using the most extreme and tragic situation as the model of moral conflict and ethical decision making, Sartre encourages us to identify regrettable ethical decisions far too hastily with tragic ones, to take our stand resolutely on one side of an ethical canyon that might yet be partially bridged. If we think of ethical decision making as the determined resolve to pursue one ethical commitment over another, we will be ill prepared and disinclined to reason prudently in the much more common moral conflicts of everyday life, conflicts in which we can pursue competing commitments to a certain extent, even if not as completely as we would like. The extreme cases of moral conflict dwelt on by contemporary moral philosophers may be "morally gripping, even tragic. But precisely because they involve disasters and extreme situations, they may well be less important for ethical theory than is thought."[54] Relax these extreme conditions, and moral conflict becomes recognizable as an everyday experience in which existentialist leaps of irrational commitment appear ridiculous.

Consider an individual who has to decide about whether to attend weekly political meetings on one of the two nights a week that she regularly visits her aging father. Imagine how ridiculous she would appear if she declared that, faced with this tragic conflict of commitments, she must irrevocably abandon either her political principles or filial devotion! Yet she, no less than Sartre's resistance fighter, faces a moral conflict. She simply faces a nontragic moral conflict, a situation in which she is bound to be somewhat dissatisfied by any choice that she makes, but one in which she still has room to reason about how to weigh and balance her conflicting moral sentiments.[55]

Everyone experiences and has to deal with these kinds of moral conflicts, even if few of us ever confront truly tragic situations. Moral phi-

---

54. M. Stocker, *Plural and Conflicting Values*, 125.
55. Moreover, Sartre offers a poor guide even to the rare tragic choices that fortune may thrust on us. See Martha Nussbaum's critique of Sartre's understanding of tragic choice in *The Fragility of Goodness*, 30–50. Using examples drawn from Greek tragedy, Nussbaum makes a persuasive case that individuals (such as Agamemnon in Aeschylus's *Oresteia*) who defiantly and irrationally commit themselves to one side of a tragic dilemma provoke our horror rather than our admiration. Irrational commitment of this sort requires an inhuman dismissal of the pain and regret associated with choosing between unpalatable alternatives even in truly tragic situations, let alone in the much less dramatic and overwhelming moral conflicts to which ordinary political life regularly exposes us.

losophers, as Michael Stocker suggests, often seem to suffer from a kind of "moral blindness, best explained by willful inattention" to the ways in which "the world as we know it gives us grounds for regret and conflict even if we do what is to be done."[56] Exaggerating the tragic and extraordinary character of moral conflict blinds us to its regular appearances in human life just as surely as ignoring the problem as a whole. Returning the Aristotelian good life to the political context in which it must be led helps open our eyes to the everyday, if painful, character of moral conflict as we actually experience it.

56. M. Stocker, *Plural and Conflicting Values*, 125.

CHAPTER NINE

# The Good Life in Extrapolital Context

The ancient Greeks, Hugh Lloyd-Jones once suggested, "were capable of their unique achievements largely because they could bear . . . very much more reality than most human beings."¹ Aristotle's understanding of human goodness, with its emphasis on our deep and unavoidable dependence on natural and political contingencies, represents a fine example of that Greek capacity to value human life without ignoring or sentimentalizing its terrible limitations. Human goodness has a special, aching beauty for Aristotle and the Greek poets precisely because of its vulnerability to misfortune.² Like the flowers that bloom in deserts and on mountainsides, a good human life is all the more cherishable for its appearance in an inhospitable environment.

Nevertheless, Aristotle also understood the irrationality of celebrating an aching kind of beauty as the most desirable end of human activity. Aristotle clearly recognized the limited goodness of a form of life so vulnerable to the vagaries of fortune and so much preoccupied with responding to the vices of others. He never goes so far as Sophocles in the famous ode from *Oedipus at Colonnus*: "Not to be born surpasses thought and speech. / The second best is to have seen the light / and then to go back quickly whence we came."³ But he does, like the Athe-

---

1. H. Lloyd-Jones, *The Justice of Zeus*, 163–64. Like Nietzsche, Lloyd-Jones sees Plato's efforts to discover a rational and lasting order behind appearances as a "failure of nerve."
2. On this point, see M. Nussbaum, *The Fragility of Goodness*, 1–5.
3. Sophocles, *Oedipus at Colonnus*, ll. 1224–26.

nian tragedians, warn us against viewing ourselves as "the best thing in the world" (*NE* 1141a21, 1141b35). For Aristotle, as for tragic Greek culture in general, human goodness is a limited as well as a fragile kind of goodness.

The good life of active virtue remains, for Aristotle, the best life that human beings can *completely* achieve. Nevertheless, he insists that our reasoning abilities allow us to conceive of a better, more divine life, even though we cannot fully achieve it. Such is the conclusion of the famous and highly controversial passage (*Nicomachean Ethics* 1177a–79a) in which he considers the relative merits of the contemplative and practical lives. In this passage Aristotle considers the good life and its political context from an extrapolitical or, for lack of a better word, cosmic perspective. Because he believes that we are capable of at least partially occupying this perspective on our lives, he insists that we take note of the limitations of the good life that political communities are designed to promote.

## HOW GOOD IS THE ARISTOTELIAN GOOD LIFE?

If the *Nicomachean Ethics* were a work of fiction rather than a philosophic treatise, it would most resemble one of those unimaginative mysteries in which the murderer turns out to be some relatively minor character that the plot has given us no reason to suspect. Up to the very last pages of the book, the practical life, the life of virtuous activities shared with friends, appears to represent Aristotle's answer to his initial question about the nature of happiness. But in these final pages (*NE* 1177a–79a) Aristotle surprises us by presenting a new answer to this question: the philosophic life of contemplative activity provides the best model for human happiness.

If Aristotle really believes in the superiority of the contemplative life, then it is hard to understand why he devotes almost all of the *Nicomachean Ethics* to exploring the practical life of active virtue. Our picture of the Aristotelian good life would be considerably clearer—although ultimately less intriguing—if we could find some reason to discount his praise of one of these two lives.

Perhaps Aristotle's praise of the practical life is primarily "apologetic," part of an effort to "make the city safe for philosophy" by defusing the abiding suspicion that philosophers are enemies of conventional morality.[4] But if that is Aristotle's aim, why would he conclude

---

4. As suggested by, among others, A. Tessitore, "Making the City Safe for Philosophy."

his book by explicitly defending the very idea—the superiority of the philosophic to the moral life—that he is trying so hard to conceal? If Aristotle is trying to deflect attention from his belief about the superiority of the philosophic life, then he has a great deal to learn about esoteric writing.[5]

Alternatively, it is tempting to eliminate the importance of Aristotle's celebration of the contemplative life with a convenient wave of the genetic wand. We could then treat the superiority of the contemplative life as a superseded idea from an earlier draft or lecture, an idea that remains in the manuscript of the *Nicomachean Ethics* despite its manifest inconsistency with the rest of the book.[6] But the only reason we have to suspect that the end of the *Nicomachean Ethics* comes from an earlier version of Aristotle's ethical philosophy is the existence of a tension between his accounts of the practical and contemplative lives. Until we have exhausted plausible interpretations that do justice to both sides of this tension, we should refrain from invoking genetic hypotheses to dissolve that tension.

We do not lack such interpretations. Some try to resolve the tension between Aristotle's two forms of the good life by demonstrating how the practical and contemplative lives can be mutually supportive.[7] Others try to show that the practical life is good for Aristotle, but only as means to the contemplative life.[8] Finally, a third group argues that although Aristotle clearly believes in the superiority of the contemplative life, his justification of that belief is manifestly inadequate.[9]

All three groups of interpreters usually focus their arguments on how well the contemplative and practical lives serve as answers to the questions about happiness Aristotle raises in book 1 of the *Nicomachean*

---

5. If Aristotle were interested in undermining public suspicion of philosophers and their arrogant dismissal of conventional morality, it would have made more sense for him to communicate his beliefs about the superiority of the contemplative life subtly and indirectly, which would not be too difficult to do. Instead, he announces that superiority directly and in the concluding pages of the book—rather than hiding it somewhere in the middle—as if he wants to alert all his readers of the importance of a point that, according to the esoteric interpretation, he should be trying to hide or downplay.

6. J. D. Monan, *Moral Knowledge*, 108–11, 133–34, 151–52; M. Nussbaum, *The Fragility of Goodness*, 373–77. Gunther Bien (*Die Grundlagen der Politische Philosophie*, 153–60) combines both approaches to eliminating the problem posed by this passage.

7. See R. Gauthier and J. Jolif, *L'Éthique à Nicomaque*, 860–66, 891–96; A. O. Rorty, "The Place of Contemplation"; N. Sherman, *The Fabric of Character*, 99–100.

8. See R. Kraut, *Aristotle on the Human Good*; T. B. Erikson, *Bios Theoretikos*, 6–8.

9. See T. Nagel, "Aristotle on Eudaimonia," 7–14; M. Nussbaum, *The Fragility of Goodness*, 373–77.

*Ethics*. I take a somewhat different approach to this interpretive problem. Instead of asking what makes the contemplative or practical life the superior answer to Aristotle's earlier questions about happiness, I focus on the limitations of practical happiness that Aristotle chooses to emphasize at the end of the *Nicomachean Ethics*. I do so because I believe that Aristotle has important insights into the limitations of the practical life, insights that should be of interest to us even if we remain suspicious of his arguments for the superiority of the contemplative life. Most contemporary commentators suggest that it is "easy for us" to settle the conflict between the two lives in favor of the practical life, even if they admit that Aristotle thinks otherwise.[10] But they are so confident about the way we should settle this conflict only because they make the issue depend on the "divine" character that Aristotle attributes to contemplative activity. Were they to pay more attention to the limitations that Aristotle finds in the practical life, some of that confidence might disappear.[11]

One reason that contemporary commentators have paid so little attention to these limitations is because, as academics, they are far more familiar with and committed to the contemplative life than the practical life. Lacking the experience of direct and daily immersion in practical affairs, they have little familiarity with the wearisome character of the demands that such a life often places on us. (Ironically, individuals who choose to lead a political life are often far more aware of its limitations than are the academics who study that life from the sidelines.) If Aristotle's commentators would reflect a little more on their reaction to their own everyday experience of practical affairs—the much-despised realm of "academic politics"—they might better appreciate both Aristotle's insights into the limitations of the practical life and their own attraction to the theoretical life.

Aristotle argues at the end of the *Nicomachean Ethics* that ethically virtuous actions are not entirely "desirable for their own sake" (*NE* 1177b17). In making this argument he is qualifying rather than rejecting his earlier insistence that the virtuous individual performs virtuous actions for their own sake. He is not denying here that these individuals take pleasure in performing these actions and never choose them merely

---

10. See, e.g., K. Wilkes, "The Good Man," 352.
11. For a relatively rare acknowledgment of these problems, see N. Sherman, *The Fabric of Character*, 99–100. Neither Richard Kraut nor Trond Erikson, who devote entire books (*Aristotle on the Human Good* and *Bios Theoretikos*, respectively) to the issues raised by the final pages of the *Nicomachean Ethics,* has much to say on the subject.

as a means to another end. He is suggesting, instead, that the occasions for virtuous actions and the particular acts that they demand are not necessarily desirable in themselves. Being courageous, for example, requires us to take pleasure in displaying the proper mean between confidence and fear in battle. But the occasion and expression of that virtue may require us to kill the particular individual who faces us in battle, even if that individual is our moral equal or better. Apart from the social demands on us to display courage in certain circumstances, such an action is clearly not desirable in itself. We would not seek an opportunity to kill the particular individuals whom we face in battle were we not called on to defend the common good of our community.

As with courage, so with the other moral virtues: we would not seek to perform the particular actions associated with them were it not for communal needs. Take justice, for example. The just individual should take pleasure in doing things such as returning deposits, following laws, and distributing goods according to standards of desert. But do we, even if we are just, really *seek* opportunities to pay back the corner grocer, follow traffic rules, or slice up communal pies? I think not, even if we fully agree with the standards that we are following.

Similarly, the exercise of prudence demands that we reflect on the vices of those around us so that we can come up with the most effective political choice in difficult circumstances. Acting prudently should be pleasurable for virtuous individuals; but apart from the needs of communities in particular situations, we would rarely seek to perform many of the particular actions that prudence demands. Even virtues such as liberality and magnificence often dictate particular actions that are not wholly choiceworthy in themselves. These virtues lead us to take pleasure in giving our resources to our friends and to the political community. A magnificent action would be the building of a temple or warship for the community. But often we will not have much respect for the gods honored in such a temple or for the purposes for which our leaders will use a warship. Nevertheless, we will still be expected, as virtuous individuals, to provide these communal goods. As a result, we will often be disinclined to seek out opportunities to perform the particular acts demanded by liberality and magnificence.

Ethically virtuous actions, Aristotle concludes, involve something beyond themselves to make them fully desirable. They attempt "to gain advantages beyond political action itself, advantages such as political power, prestige, or at least happiness for the statesman himself and his fellow citizens, and that is something other than political activity" (*NE*

1177b12). But happiness, at least in its most complete form, should consist of activity that is choiceworthy in itself apart from any by-products, a point Aristotle makes most clearly in the *Metaphysics*.

> Where, then, the result is something apart from the exercise [of an activity], the actuality is in the thing that is being made, for example, the act of building is in the thing that is being built ... and in general the movement is in the thing that is being moved; but when there is no product apart from the actuality, the actuality is in the agents, for example, the act of seeing is in the seeing subject and that of theorizing in the theorizing subject and the life is in the soul, and therefore happiness as well; for it is a certain kind of life.
> (*Metaphysics* 1050a22–37)

When we reflect on the good life as it is actually lived in political context, we can see why Aristotle associates happiness with activities that are desirable regardless of their by-products. Without their communal by-products many acts of ethical virtue are tiresome, unpleasant, and undesirable.

If we thought these specific actions fully desirable in themselves, we would seek them as occasions to display our virtue. Without war, for example, we lack the opportunity to display courage in the manner that Aristotle associates with moral virtue. Nevertheless, Aristotle warns us against the conclusion that wars are therefore desirable, even as means to virtuous acts. "For no one chooses to make war for the sake of being at war, nor aims at provoking such a war; a man would seem absolutely murderous if he were to make enemies of his friends in order to bring about battles and slaughter" (*NE* 1177b9). Yet if acts of courage were wholly choiceworthy for their own sake, and we were not provided with opportunities to perform them, it would be hard to avoid concluding that we should seek to create these opportunities, even if it meant making enemies of friends or neutrals. "The ancients," Montesquieu once complained, "conquered without reason, without utility. They ravaged the earth in order to exercise their virtue and demonstrate their excellence."[12] Whether or not most ancient Greeks approved of such behavior, Aristotle condemns it just as vehemently as Montesquieu does. But he can condemn it only because he recognizes that acts of courage in battle are not wholly choiceworthy in themselves.

Such is the case with the other moral virtues, once we recognize their political context. Most acts of justice and prudence involve establishing and maintaining standards of behavior that support a relatively decent

---

12. C. S. de Montesquieu, *Pensées*, in *Oeuvres complètes* 2:210.

but imperfect political order within a community. Without the sources of civic disorder, there would be relatively little occasion to exercise these virtues. Does that mean we should seek civic disorder when we lack it in order to provide occasions for our virtues to shine? Clearly not. But by answering this question negatively, we implicitly admit that many or most actions of justice and prudence are not wholly choiceworthy for their own sake.

Of course, we are very unlikely to find ourselves in situations that do not demand the exercise of these virtues, given the disordered character of human communities. Yet reflection on the desirability of the circumstances in which we exercise the moral virtues betrays the limited goodness of the practical life. The practical life has, as noted above, a special, aching beauty all its own, a beauty that cannot be separated from its limitations. But for Aristotle this beauty cannot make the pains of cruel and distasteful circumstances fully choiceworthy. Rousseau may advise us to pray for "ignorance, innocence and poverty," since he sees them as necessary preconditions of moral virtue.[13] Nietzsche may advise us to pray for arbitrary discipline and cruelty, since he sees them as a necessary condition of life and growth.[14] But Aristotle is unwilling to endorse war and civic disorder, even if they do provide the opportunities for the display of moral virtue and its fragile, aching beauty.

Aristotle tries to clinch this argument about the limited desirability of the practical life by asking us whether the gods would choose this way of life. If we could live like gods, without the unpleasant constraints that provide occasions for the exercise of the moral virtues, would we choose the practical life? Not at all, Aristotle answers.

> We suppose that the gods are the happiest and most blessed of beings; but what sort of actions can we ascribe to them? Just acts? Won't the gods seems ridiculous making contracts and returning deposits and so on? But what of brave acts, enduring dangers and running risks for the sake of nobility? Or liberal acts? To whom will they give? It would be very odd if they had money or anything like it. And what would their temperate acts be? Wouldn't such praise be rather vulgar, since they have no bad appetites? Were we to go through all the circumstances of actions, they would all seem trivial and unworthy of gods.
>
> (NE 1178b9–19)

The "circumstances of actions" (*ta peri tas praxeis*) would be "unworthy of gods" because they are necessarily bound up with the limitations

---

13. J.-J. Rousseau, "Discourse on the Arts and Sciences," 62.
14. F. Nietzsche, *Beyond Good and Evil*, 101–2, par. 188.

and imperfections of human existence. Our reasoning abilities allow us to imagine a better way of being than that described by the ethical life. Only by suppressing our reason with an irrational act of will, an act such as Nietzsche exhorts us to perform in willing the "eternal return" of the cruel and banal circumstances of ordinary life, can we come to think of these circumstances and the life they shape as wholly desirable in themselves.

I am not suggesting that Aristotle rejects the ethical life as an object of striving. He clearly views it as a noble goal whose achievement provides the largest part of human happiness. Nevertheless, he seems to want us to be aware of the disparity between our praise of virtue and the particular acts that we expect virtuous individuals to perform. A little weariness with a world that compels us to perfect our natures in such inherently undesirable activities as warfare does not seem to be a bad thing for Aristotle.

The question remains, however, whether we have any abilities that would allow us to share with the gods a life activity that is wholly desirable in itself. Aristotle clearly believes that our theoretical capacities allow us to participate, at least partly, in this life. There is no distinction within contemplative activity between the desirable actions and undesirable "circumstances of action." The particular action performed by a contemplator would be choiceworthy no matter what the situation was, whereas an ethical act is desirable only in the particular circumstance in which our social commitments call for it. As a result, "this [contemplative] activity seems to be the only activity that is loved for its own sake; for nothing arises from it apart from the contemplation, while from practical activities we gain more or less apart from the action" (*NE* 1177b1). To the extent that we can act this way, this would be the best and happiest way for us to live (*NE* 1178b5).

Of course, human beings, unlike gods, cannot live entirely in contemplation. "For it is not insofar as he is a man that he will live so, but insofar as something divine exists in him; and to the same extent as this element is superior to that arising from the other virtues" (*NE* 1177b27). Contemplators may be somewhat more self-sufficient than political actors, but that does not remove the elements of social dependence and good fortune underlying their happiness.[15] The happiness of philoso-

---

15. Martha Nussbaum (*The Fragility of Goodness*, 373–77) argues that the self-sufficiency of the contemplative life does do away with its dependency, thereby contradicting Aristotle's prior emphasis in the *Nicomachean Ethics* on our social dependence and vulnerability to fortune. Nussbaum, it seems to me, is assuming that Aristotle envisions the

phers will not be *as* exposed to misfortune or the choices of other individuals, since it requires fewer external goods to support its characteristic activity. Nevertheless, the contemplative and the practical life "both need the necessities, and do so equally, even if the statesman's work is more concerned with the body and things of that sort" (*NE* 1178a25). Aristotle never suggests that philosophers can maintain their happiness in the face of severe misfortune, such as enslavement or extreme pain. Even if it were Socrates himself on the rack, Aristotle still insists that it is nonsense to describe the victim of misfortune as happy (*NE* 1153b19).

Moreover, human nature constrains our ability to engage in contemplation in spiritual as well as physical ways. It is not just that we need food, water, and security in order to stay alive and contemplate. Given our "composite nature," our souls have irrational passions, passions that need moral training if we are to engage in contemplation or any other activity. As Aristotle notes in the *Politics* (1323a29), no one who is so cowardly as to fear the flies that buzz around his head can possibly be happy. But if we need moral training—as well as intellectual training—in order to engage in contemplative activities, then we are dependent on the communities that provide us with this training. Because human beings, unlike the gods, have both mortal bodies and irrational emotions, they cannot dispense with such dependence.

As a result, philosophers are no less "political animals" by nature than are other human beings, even if they seek their greatest happiness in contemplative activities. Thus, they share the problems of political animals. They receive their indispensable moral and intellectual training from a variety of relatively imperfect communities—family, friends, polis—with all the problems and conflicts such an education can create. Moreover, educated in this way, they are bound to develop dispositions to support and defend the communities that nurture them, dispositions that may often clash with a disposition to engage in contemplative activities. For example, young philosophy students may be called on to drop their studies in order to support their aged parents or defend their political communities. If they did not depend on family and polis for their moral and intellectual training, they might simply dismiss these

---

contemplative life along the more familiar lines proposed by the Stoics and Platonists. These philosophers do treat the philosophic life as a way to achieve self-sufficiency and protection against misfortune. Aristotle, however, does not. Aristotelian philosophers have more self-sufficiency and somewhat less vulnerability to misfortune than political actors do; nevertheless, they still depend to a very great extent on good fortune and the choices of other individuals for their happiness. I discuss Nussbaum's critique of this passage more fully in "How Good Is the Aristotelian Good Life?" 621–23.

duties as impediments to the philosophic activities that bring them happiness. But because they have been trained by these communities, they are likely to feel disposed to perform such duties. It will be part of their happiness to engage in them even if it interferes with the more choiceworthy happiness associated with contemplation.

## THE TENSIONS WITHIN A GOOD HUMAN LIFE

Where do we stand, then, with regard to the two kinds of happiness, the practical and contemplative lives, that Aristotle offers us? Aristotle himself says little about how to choose between them if and when they come into conflict with each other. He merely advises us that the contemplative life is more choiceworthy, but not fully attainable, whereas the practical life is less happy, but appropriate to the limitations of our human nature (*NE* 1177b–78b).

It is a mistake, I believe, to try, as most commentators do, to uncover an Aristotelian resolution to the tensions between these two forms of the good life. In discussing the tensions between the practical and the contemplative life, Aristotle is trying to identify problems inherent in our nature rather than "get rid of them."[16] These problems are themselves discoveries about the human condition rather than theoretical inconsistencies crying out for correction. The aching beauty of the practical life is the most appropriate goal for the combination of political predispositions, reasoning capacities, and bodily constraints inherent in human nature. Nevertheless, our reasoning capacities also allow us to imagine and, to a certain extent, lead a somewhat more desirable way of life, a way of life that, in effect, transcends human nature as a whole.[17] We would be fools to think that we could leave behind the bodily and irrational elements of our nature in order to lead a life of continuous contemplation. But we would have to fool ourselves, to will intrinsic worth into circumstances and actions that we know are not intrinsically valuable, in order to treat the practical life as *wholly* desirable in itself. Aristotle teaches us that the contemplative life is better but is not wholly attainable for human beings, whereas the ethical life is not as good but is more fully human. Any choice that we have to make between them should be guided by both of these judgments and cannot be made without some regret.

16. T. Erikson, *Bios Theoretikos*, 11.
17. J. Lear, *Aristotle*, 9–10. As Erikson (*Bios Theoretikos*, 35) notes, there is something of "a break in Aristotle's anthropology."

Consider the following example of a conflict between the demands of the practical and theoretical lives.[18] A gifted prince is called back to his country from a promising career in Aristotle's school in order to succeed his dying father on the throne. The prince is unlikely to have been a successful student had he not received valuable moral and intellectual training from his parents and compatriots. But such training creates loyalties and dispositions toward public service that the prince cannot ignore without considerable unhappiness. At the same time, abandoning his philosophic career will deny him the opportunities for the more intrinsically desirable activities Aristotle associates with contemplation. Deciding either way will give the prince occasion for regret and unhappiness, for two sources of happiness, practical and contemplative activity, come into conflict here.[19]

Conflicts between contemplative and practical lives are no more resolvable for Aristotle than are the cases of moral conflict considered in the preceding chapter. Each case is unique. It can be decided only with reference to the particular circumstances surrounding it. And each decision will give us some cause for regret, no matter how prudently we weigh competing factors. In each case we will have to give up, to some extent, a component of our happiness.

Moreover, like the moral conflicts considered earlier, these conflicts are an everyday experience rather than an extraordinary, tragic exception. Substitute for our philosophic prince a promising graduate student who is asked by her ailing parents to move back home—thereby giving up a lucrative fellowship at Harvard and transferring to an inferior local university—in order to help out with the family business. The conflict between contemplative and practical activities is no less real in this case, even if it lacks the political consequences and either-or decision associated with the philosophic prince's dilemma.

These examples show that the way in which we deal with conflicts between contemplative and practical activities will often depend on circumstances that we neither control nor choose for ourselves. We often have little control, for example, over the circumstances that determine how badly we are needed to perform duties such as inheriting busi-

18. This example is suggested by R. Kraut, *Aristotle on the Human Good*, 10.
19. Kraut (ibid.), in contrast, treats the example as a case in which duty and personal happiness come into conflict. He uses the example to demonstrate that Aristotle's defense of the contemplative life does not commit him to egoistic disregard for the happiness of others.

nesses or thrones. If our prince has a worthy and publicly acceptable sibling ready to take his place on the throne, then he will have less reason to give up his philosophic studies. If our graduate student were lucky enough to have grown up in the vicinity of a highly ranked research university rather than a second-rate institution, she would have far less reason to resist her parents' request to return home and help run their business.

Most commentary on Aristotle's account of the contemplative and practical lives proceeds as if we were disconnected individuals faced with fitting a choice between two activities into the rational "life plan" that will guide our existence. This procedure is highly misleading and inappropriate, since Aristotle would deny that we are ever in a position to plan our lives in this way. By the time we reach the point in our lives at which it would make any sense to talk about rational "life plans," we have already developed connections and commitments that impinge deeply on our freedom to choose and maintain a form of life for ourselves. Moreover, changing circumstances, such as we are bound to meet, continually interfere with attempts to live our lives according to a rational plan. Aristotle's discussion of the relative merits of the contemplative and practical lives is offered, I suggest, as an aid in dealing with the unavoidable tensions between them that we shall face, rather than as a guide to the best "life plan."

Individuals who are disposed to feel some regret in choosing to sacrifice some element of one of these activities for the other will also probably pursue each of them in a more satisfactory way. Those who recognize some of the limitations of the ethical life will pursue it with greater moderation and modesty than those who do not. If we believe that "man is not the best thing in the world," we are unlikely to pursue the ethical virtues as fiercely and single-mindedly as those, like Kant, whose minds are filled "with ever renewed and growing admiration and awe" at "the moral law" within us.[20] For Aristotle, as for the tragedians of Athens, Kantian awe at human freedom and dignity manifests an

20. "Two things fill the mind with ever renewed and growing admiration and awe: the starry heavens above me and the moral law within me"; I. Kant, *Critique of Practical Reason*, 166. Moreover, for Kant the sublimity that we discover in our experience of immense natural objects such as the night sky and the oceans merely reflects the way in which such objects challenge our moral capacities. "Nature is . . . called sublime merely because it raises the imagination to a presentation of those cases in which the mind can make itself sensible of the appropriate sublimity of the sphere of its own being, even above nature"; *Critique of Judgment*, 150–51. In the end, our capacity for moral freedom is the only thing in this world that fills Kant with awe.

unreasonable and dangerous hubris. Someone who persists in it is likely to pursue the human good without noticing either its fragility or its limitations. Conversely, philosophers who know themselves to be political animals, dependent on others and good fortune for their abilities and happiness, will contemplate better, since they are far less likely to delude themselves about either their own capacities or the relative place of human beings in the natural order of things.

# Conclusion

"Living together and sharing any human concern is always difficult" (*Pol.* 1263a15). Living together and sharing political concerns, I have tried to show, is especially difficult.

Two major goals guide my efforts throughout *The Problems of a Political Animal:* the recovery of some fascinating but neglected insights into the problems of everyday social and political life; and the promotion of a more realistic understanding of the ways in which human sociality constrains the possibilities of moral and political choice. I pursue the first goal by exploring Aristotelian ideas about cooperation and conflict, ideas that have been obscured by overly romantic and moralistic interpretations of his political thought. I pursue the second goal by trying to persuade readers that these ideas have significant advantages over more familiar and popular approaches to a wide variety of social and political phenomena.

In pursuing these goals, I place much greater emphasis on Aristotle's analyses of everyday social and political life than is customary in most contemporary studies of his moral and political philosophy. I emphasize this aspect of Aristotelian social and political thought not only to correct widespread misimpressions about its basic character but also to improve the way in which contemporary moral and political philosophers approach the basic issues of political life. Aristotle is almost unique among the major moral and political philosophers in the way in which he draws political recommendations from a detailed analysis of the structure of ordinary social and political realities. Contemporary moral and political philosophers, in contrast, focus their attention almost exclusively on questions of evaluation and justification, turning to everyday political life only in their discussions of how to apply their ideas to the world. As illustrated throughout this study, their failure to link evaluation and explanatory analysis often leads them to offer implausible descriptions and justifications of the moral and political choices that we need in our lives.

No issue better illustrates the problems created by this failure, as well as the advantages of a more Aristotelian approach to political analysis and evaluation, than recent debates about community and its place in modern political life. Contemporary communitarians rightly point out the implausibility of liberal moral and political theories that abstract from the ways in which our shared practices and institutions shape our moral character and choices. But very few communitarians then turn to the difficult task of identifying and exploring the shared social and political practices that shape modern individuals, as their critique of liberal theories suggests that they should. Instead, the great majority of them jump to an evaluative conclusion: modern liberal societies, like modern liberal theories, eliminate human community itself and must therefore be replaced with more communal social practices. As a result, their critiques of modern liberalism usually succeed only in replacing abstract and implausible accounts of individual choice and character with equally abstract and implausible accounts of community. Unlike these contemporary communitarians, Aristotle clearly recognizes that if we are by nature communal and political animals, we should expect our shared ends and practices to influence our entire social life, not just those exceptional moments when harmony reigns. He thus avoids liberal fantasies about self-constituting individuals without entertaining unrealistic expectations of communal harmony and integration.

Aristotle tries to identify the ways in which community shapes even those social relations in which we pursue self-interest or engage in conflict. In this way he provides us with the basis for a communitarian account of the conflict and competition that are ordinarily experienced by those who participate in political forms of cooperation. He shows us, for example, how even instrumental associations, such as businesses and political communities, promote a limited sense of mutual concern among their members; how the shared practices of mutual accountability associated with political justice shape our character and choice even when we engage in political conflict and competition; how class conflict grows out of the expectations of mutual concern characteristic of political friends; how our reliance on others for our moral character makes moral conflict inevitable and renders absurd contemporary philosophers' talk about a "rational life plan." I have suggested in this study that we need to take heed of insights like these in order both to avoid self-defeating struggles against immovable constraints and to gain a clearer view of real possibilities for social and political improvement in our world.

I have not suggested, however, that an adequate moral and political theory must be fully Aristotelian in character. Shortcomings in the Aristotelian insights explored in this book will undoubtedly emerge as theorists reflect further on the value of these insights and on the ways in which our communal nature shapes the constraints and possibilities of political life. My aim has been to encourage such reflection rather than to present a brief for Aristotelian political philosophy.

Moreover, even if we were persuaded by an Aristotelian understanding of the structural constraints of moral and political life, that understanding provides us with only a framework within which to reason about morality and politics; it does not give us a foundation from which we can deduce our moral and political commitments. Unlike most of Aristotle's contemporary admirers, I do not turn to his works in the hope of finding the objective foundation for our moral and political commitments that is missing from the most influential modern moral and political theories. I fully accept that most of us will continue to seek beyond Aristotelian ideas in order to identify and justify our moral and political commitments. Nevertheless, I remain convinced that further consideration of the Aristotelian insights explored in this book will greatly improve our understanding of the basic problems of moral and political life.

# Bibliography

ARISTOTLE: EDITIONS AND TRANSLATIONS CITED

Translations from Aristotle's texts are my own, although they rely heavily on Carnes Lord's translation of the *Politics,* Martin Ostwald's translation of the *Nicomachean Ethics,* and the translations of Aristotle's other works collected in Jonathan Barnes's edition of *The Complete Works of Aristotle.*

Barker, Ernest, trans. *The Politics of Aristotle.* With an introduction, notes, and appendices. Oxford: Oxford University Press, 1946.
Barnes, Jonathan, ed. *The Complete Works of Aristotle.* Numerous translators. Princeton: Princeton University Press, 1984.
Burnet, John, ed. *The Ethics of Aristotle.* London: Methuen, 1900.
Fritz, Kurt von, and Ernest Kapp, eds. *Aristotle's Constitution of Athens and Related Texts.* With an introduction and notes. New York: Hafner, 1950.
Gauthier, René, and Jean Jolif, eds. *L'Éthique à Nicomaque.* 2 vols. Introduction, traduction et commentaire. Louvain: Publications Universitaires, 1970.
Joachim, Hans, ed. *The Nicomachean Ethics.* Oxford: Oxford University Press, 1951.
Lord, Carnes, trans. *Politics.* With an introduction, notes, and glossary. Chicago: University of Chicago Press, 1984.
Newman, W. L., ed. *The Politics of Aristotle.* 4 vols. Oxford: Clarendon, 1887.
Ostwald, Martin, trans. *Nicomachean Ethics.* With an introduction and notes. Indianapolis: Bobbs-Merrill, 1962.
Rackham, Horace, trans. *Nicomachean Ethics.* Cambridge, Mass.: Loeb Classical Library, 1956.
———. *Politics.* Cambridge, Mass.: Loeb Classical Library, 1956.

Robinson, R., ed. *Aristotle's Politics, Books III and IV*. Translation and commentary. Oxford: Oxford University Press, 1964.
Sinclair, R. K., and Trevor Saunders, trans. *Politics*. London: Penguin, 1989.

OTHER WORKS CITED

Aalders, Georg. *Die Theorie der Gemischten Verfassung im Altertum*. Amsterdam: Hakkert, 1968.
Abramson, Jeffrey. *Liberation and Its Limits: The Moral and Political Thought of Freud*. New York: Free Press, 1984.
Adkins, A. W. H. *From the Many to the One*. Ithaca: Cornell University Press, 1970.
———. *Merit and Responsibility: A Study in Greek Values*. Chicago: University of Chicago Press, 1960.
Allan, D. J. "Individual and State in Aristotle's Ethics and Politics." In *La Politique d'Aristote, Entretiens sur l'antiquité classique* 11:53–96. Geneva: 1965.
Allen, Graham. *Friendship: Developing a Sociological Perspective*. London: Harvester, 1989.
———. *A Sociology of Friendship and Kinship*. London: Allen and Unwin, 1979.
Alpern, K. D. "Aristotle on the Friendships of Utility and Pleasure." *Journal of the History of Philosophy* 21 (1983): 303–15.
Ambler, Wayne. "Aristotle on Nature and Politics: The Case of Slavery." *Political Theory* 15 (1987): 390–410.
Anderson, Benedict. *Imagined Communities: Reflections on the Origins and Spread of Nationalism*. London: Verso, 1983.
Anderson, Perry. *Passages from Antiquity to Feudalism*. London: Verso, 1978.
Andre, Judith. "Nagel, Williams, and Moral Luck." *Analysis* 43 (1983): 202–27.
Aquinas, Thomas. *Commentary on the Nicomachean Ethics*. Chicago: Regnery.
———. *Selected Political Writings*. Edited by P. d'Entrèves. Oxford: Blackwell, 1959.
Arendt, Hannah. *The Human Condition*. Garden City, N.Y.: Doubleday, 1958.
———. *The Origins of Totalitarianism*. New York: Harcourt Brace Jovanovich, 1973.
Arnhart, Larry. "Aristotle, Chimpanzees, and Other Political Animals." *Social Science Information* 29 (1990): 477–551.
———. *Aristotle on Political Reasoning*. De Kalb: University of Northern Illinois Press, 1981.
Ashton, T., and C. Philpin, eds. *The Brenner Debate: Agrarian Class Structure and Economic Development in Pre-Industrial Europe*. Cambridge: Cambridge University Press, 1985.
Austin, M. M., and Pierre Vidal-Naquet. *Economic and Social History of Ancient Greece: An Introduction*. Berkeley and Los Angeles: University of California Press, 1980.
Badian, Ernest. *Publicans and Sinners*. Ithaca: Cornell University Press, 1983.

Baker, Keith. *Inventing the French Revolution*. Cambridge: Cambridge University Press, 1990.
Baker, Keith, François Furet, et al., eds. *The French Revolution and the Birth of Modern Political Culture*. 3 vols. New York: Pergamon, 1987–89.
Barber, Benjamin. *Strong Democracy*. Berkeley and Los Angeles: University of California Press, 1984.
Barker, Ernest. *The Political Thought of Plato and Aristotle*. New York: Dover, 1959.
Barnes, J., M. Schofield, and R. Sorabji, eds. *Articles on Aristotle*. 4 vols. London: Duckworth, 1977.
Bauman, Richard. *Political Trials in Ancient Greece*. London: Routledge and Kegan Paul, 1990.
Bedau, Hugo. "Social Justice and Social Institutions." *Midwest Studies in Philosophy* 3 (1980): 151–76.
Beiner, Ronald. *Political Judgment*. Chicago: University of Chicago Press, 1983.
Bellah, Robert, et al. *Habits of the Heart*. Berkeley and Los Angeles: University of California Press, 1985.
Berti, Enrico. "La notion de société politique chez Aristote." In M. Fischer and O. Gigon, eds., *Antike Rechts- und Sozialphilosophie*. Frankfurt: Peter Lange, 1988.
Bickel, Alexander. *The Least Dangerous Branch*. Indianapolis: Bobbs-Merrill, 1962.
Bien, Gunther. *Die Grundlagen der Politische Philosophie bei Aristoteles*. Munich: Alber, 1973.
Black, Anthony. *State, Community, and Human Desires*. New York: St. Martin's, 1988.
Bluhm, Lawrence. *Friendship, Altruism, and Morality*. London: Routledge and Kegan Paul, 1980.
Blumenberg, Hans. *The Legitimacy of the Modern Age*. Cambridge: MIT Press, 1983.
Bodéüs, Richard. "Deux notions aristotéliciennes sur le droit naturel chez les continentaux d'Amérique." *Revue de metaphysique et morale* 1989:369–89.
———. "Law and the Regime in Aristotle." In Lord and O'Connor, *Essays on the Foundations of Aristotelian Political Science*, 234–48.
———. *Le philosophe et la cité*. Paris: Les Belles Lettres, 1982.
Bradfield, Richard. *The Natural History of Associations: A Study in the Meaning of Community*. 2 vols. London: Duckworth, 1973.
Brown, Wendy. *Manhood and Politics*. New York: Rowman and Allenheld, 1988.
Burnyeat, Miles. "Aristotle on Learning to Be Good." In Rorty, *Essays on Aristotle's Ethics*, 69–92.
Cairns, Huntington. *Legal Philosophy from Plato to Hegel*. Baltimore: Johns Hopkins University Press, 1948.
Calhoun, George. *Athenian Clubs in Politics and Litigation*. New York: Bert Franklin, 1970.
Calvert, Peter. *The Concept of Class*. New York: St. Martin's, 1982.

Canfora, Luciano. *The Vanished Library*. Berkeley and Los Angeles: University of California Press, 1990.
Carter, L. B. *The Quiet Athenian*. Oxford: Clarendon, 1986.
Casey, John. *Pagan Virtue*. Oxford: Clarendon, 1990.
Cashdollar, Sanford. "Aristotle's Politics of Morals." *Journal of the History of Philosophy* 11 (1973): 145–61.
Censer, Jack. "The Coming of a New Interpretation of the French Revolution." *Journal of Social History* 20 (1987): 296–309.
Chambers, John W. *To Raise an Army*. New York: Free Press, 1987.
Charles, David. "Perfectionism in Aristotle's Political Theory: Reply to Martha Nussbaum." In *Oxford Studies in Ancient Philosophy,* supplementary vol., 184–206. Oxford: Clarendon, 1988.
Chroust, Anton-Hermann. *Aristotle: New Light on His Life and on His Lost Works*. 2 vols. Notre Dame: Notre Dame University Press, 1973.
Cicero. *De Officiis*. Cambridge, Mass.: Loeb Classical Library, 1968.
Clapham, Christopher, ed. *Private Patronage and Public Power*. New York: St. Martin's, 1982.
Clark, Stephen. *Aristotle's Man*. Oxford: Oxford University Press, 1975.
Cohen, Eliot A. *Citizens and Soldiers: Dilemmas of Military Service*. Ithaca: Cornell University Press, 1985.
Connor, W. R. *The New Politicians of Fifth Century Athens*. Princeton: Princeton University Press, 1971.
Constant, Benjamin. "The Liberty of the Ancients Compared with that of the Moderns." In his *Political Writings*, edited by B. Fontana, 308–28. Cambridge: Cambridge University Press, 1988.
———. *Les "Principes de Politique" de Benjamin Constant*. 2 vols. Edited by E. Hoffman. Geneva: 1980.
Contiourgos, Georges. *La théorie des révolutions chez Aristote*. Paris: LGDJ, 1978.
Cooley, Charles. *Human Nature and the Social Order*. New York: Macmillan, 1922.
———. *Social Organization*. New York: Macmillan, 1929.
Cooper, John. "Aristotle on Friendship." In Rorty, *Essays on Aristotle's Ethics,* 301–40.
———. "Aristotle on Natural Teleology." In M. Nussbaum and M. Schofield, eds., *Language and Logos,* 197–222. Cambridge: Cambridge University Press, 1982.
———. "Aristotle on the Forms of Friendship." *Review of Metaphysics* 30 (1976–77): 619–48.
———. "Aristotle on the Goods of Fortune." *Philosophic Review* 94 (1985): 173–96.
———. *Reason and the Human Good in Aristotle*. Cambridge: Harvard University Press, 1975.
Dahl, Robert. *Modern Political Analysis*. Englewood Cliffs, N.J.: Prentice Hall, 1963.
Davis, Michael. "Aristotle's Reflections on Revolution." *Graduate Faculty Philosophy Journal* 11 (1986): 49–63.

Day, J. H., and M. Chambers. *Aristotle's History of Athenian Democracy*. Amsterdam: Hakkert, 1965.
Defourny, Maurice. *Études sur la Politique d'Aristote*. Paris: Gabriel Buschesne, 1932.
De Grazia, Sebastian. *The Political Community*. Chicago: University of Chicago Press, 1945.
Dossa, Shiraz. *The Public Realm and the Public Self: The Political Theory of Hannah Arendt*. Waterloo, Ontario: Wilfred Laurier University Press, 1989.
Durkheim, Emile. *The Division of Labor in Modern Society*. New York: Free Press, 1964.
Dworkin, Ronald. *Law's Empire*. Cambridge: Harvard University Press, 1986.
———. *Taking Rights Seriously*. Cambridge: Harvard University Press, 1977.
Eisenstadt, S., and L. Roniger. *Patrons, Clients, and Friends*. Cambridge: Cambridge University Press, 1984.
Elster, Jon. *The Cement of Society*. Cambridge: Cambridge University Press, 1989.
———. "Three Challenges to Class." In J. Roemer, ed., *Analytic Marxism*, 141–61. Cambridge: Cambridge University Press, 1986.
Erikson, Trond Berg. *Bios Theoretikos: Ethica Nicomachea X, 6–8*. Oslo: Universitetsforlaget, 1976.
Everson, Stephen. "Aristotle on the Foundations of the State." *Political Studies* 36 (1988): 89–101.
Farrand, Max, ed. *The Records of the Federal Convention of 1787*. 4 vols. New Haven: Yale University Press, 1954.
Farrar, Cynthia. *The Origins of Democratic Thinking: The Invention of Politics in Classical Athens*. Cambridge: Cambridge University Press, 1988.
Fay, Brian. *Social Theory and Political Practice*. London: George Allen and Unwin, 1975.
Finley, Moses. *The Ancestral Constitution*. Inaugural Lecture. Cambridge: Cambridge University Press, 1971.
———. *The Ancient Economy*. Berkeley and Los Angeles: University of California Press, 1973.
———. *Ancient Slavery and Modern Ideology*. Harmondsworth: Penguin, 1983.
———. "Aristotle and Economic Analysis." In Barnes et al., *Articles on Aristotle 2: Ethics and Politics*, 140–58.
———. *Democracy, Ancient and Modern*. London: Penguin, 1973.
———. "Introduction." In M. Finley, ed., *The Legacy of Greece: A Reappraisal*, 1–21. Oxford: Clarendon, 1981.
———. *Politics in the Ancient World*. Cambridge: Cambridge University Press, 1983.
———. "Was Greek Civilization Based on Slave Labour?" In his *Economy and Society in Ancient Greece*, 97–115. Harmondsworth: Penguin, 1983.
Finnis, John. *Natural Law and Natural Rights*. Oxford: Clarendon, 1980.
Fraisse, J. C. *Philia: La notion de l'amitié dans la philosophie de l'antique*. Paris: PUF, 1974.
Frank, Robert. *Passions Within Reason: The Strategic Role of the Emotions*. New York: Norton, 1988.

Friedrich, Carl J. *The Philosophy of Law in Historical Perspective.* Chicago: University of Chicago Press, 1963.
Frier, Bruce. *The Rise of the Roman Jurists.* Princeton: Princeton University Press, 1985.
Fritz, Kurt von. *The Theory of the Mixed Constitution in Antiquity.* New York: Arno, 1975.
Fuks, Alexander. *The Ancestral Constitution.* Westport, Conn.: Greenview, 1971.
――――. *Social Conflict in Ancient Greece.* Jerusalem: Magnes Press, 1984.
Fuller, Lon. *The Inner Morality of Law.* New Haven: Yale University Press, 1964.
――――. *The Principles of Social Order.* Durham: Duke University Press, 1981.
Furet, François. *Interpreting the Revolution.* Cambridge: Cambridge University Press, 1981.
Fustel de Coulanges, N. D. *The Ancient City.* Garden City, N.Y.: Doubleday, Anchor, 1958.
Gadamer, Hans-Georg. *Truth and Method.* New York: Seabury, 1975.
Gagarin, Michael. *Early Greek Law.* Berkeley and Los Angeles: University of California Press, 1986.
Galston, William. *Justice and the Human Good.* Chicago: University of Chicago Press, 1980.
Garlan, Yvon. *Slavery in Ancient Greece.* Ithaca: Cornell University Press, 1988.
Gehrke, H. J. *Stasis: Untersuchungen zu den inneren Kriegen in den griechischen Staaten.* Munich: C. H. Beck, 1985.
Gould, Stephen Jay. "Human Equality Is a Contingent Fact of History." In his *The Flamingo's Smile,* 185–98. New York: Norton, 1985.
――――. *The Mismeasure of Man.* New York: Norton, 1981.
Hamburger, M. *Morals and Law: The Growth of Aristotle's Legal Theory.* New Haven: Yale University Press, 1951.
Hamilton, Alexander, John Jay, and James Madison. *The Federalist Papers.* New York: Mentor, 1981.
Hampshire, Stuart. *Morality and Conflict.* Cambridge: Harvard University Press, 1983.
Hansen, Mogens. *The Athenian Assembly.* Oxford: Blackwell, 1987.
――――. "The Political Powers of the People's Court in Fourth Century Athens." In Murray and Price, *The Greek City,* 215–43.
Hantz, Harold. "Justice and Equality in Aristotle's *Nicomachean Ethics* and *Politics.*" *Diotima* 3 (1975): 83–92.
Hardie, W. F. *Aristotle's Ethical Theory.* Oxford: Clarendon, 1968.
Hart, H. L. A. *The Concept of Law.* Oxford: Clarendon, 1962.
Havelock, Eric. *The Liberal Temper in Greek Politics.* New Haven: Yale University Press, 1957.
Hayek, Friedrich. *The Constitution of Liberty.* Chicago: University of Chicago Press, 1960.
――――. *Law, Legislation, and Liberty.* 3 vols. Chicago: University of Chicago Press, 1982.

Hegel, G. W. F. *Natural Law*. Philadelphia: University of Pennsylvania Press, 1975.
———. *The Philosophy of Right*. Oxford: Oxford University Press, 1952.
Heidegger, Martin. *Being and Time*. New York: Harper, 1962.
Heinimann, Friedrich. *Nomos und Phusis*. Basel: Friedrich Reinhardt, 1965.
Herman, Gabriel. *Ritualised Friendship and the Greek City*. Cambridge: Cambridge University Press, 1987.
Herodotus. *History*. Chicago: University of Chicago Press, 1987.
Heuss, Alfred. "Das Revolutionsproblem im Spiegel der Antike Geschichte.' *Historische Zeitschrift* 216 (1973): 1–72.
Hobbes, Thomas. *Leviathan*. Edited by C. B. Macpherson. London: Pelican, 1968.
———. *Of the Citizen*. In his *Of Man and Citizen*. Garden City, N.Y.: Doubleday, Anchor, 1972.
Höffe, Ottfried. *Politische Gerechtigkeit*. Suhrkamp: Frankfurt, 1987.
Holmes, Stephen. "Aristippus in and out of Athens." *American Political Science Review* 73 (1979): 112–28.
———. *Benjamin Constant and the Making of Modern Liberalism*. New Haven: Yale University Press, 1984.
———. "Precommitment and the Paradox of Democracy." In J. Elster and R. Slagstad, eds., *Constitutionalism and Democracy*, 195–240. Cambridge: Cambridge University Press, 1988.
Homer. *Iliad*. Translated by Richard Lattimore. Chicago: University of Chicago Press, 1976.
Humphreys, S. C. *Anthropology and the Greeks*. London: Routledge and Kegan Paul, 1978.
———. "The Discourse of Law in Archaic and Classical Greece." *History and Law Review* 6 (1988): 465–93.
———. *The Family, Women, and Death: Comparative Studies*. London: Routledge and Kegan Paul, 1983.
———. "Public and Private Interests in Classical Athens." In her *The Family, Women, and Death*, 22–32.
Hunt, Lynn. *Politics, Culture, and Class in the French Revolution*. Berkeley and Los Angeles: University of California Press, 1984.
Hutchinson, Allan C., and P. Monahan, eds. *Critical Legal Studies*. Totowa, N.J.: Rowman and Littlefield, 1989.
Hutter, Horst. *Politics as Friendship*. Waterloo, Ontario: Waterloo University Press, 1971.
Huxley, George. *On Aristotle and Greek Society*. Belfast, Ireland: Maine, Boyd and Son, 1979.
———. "On Aristotle's Best State." *History of Political Thought* 6 (1985): 139–49.
Irwin, Terence. *Aristotle's First Principles*. Oxford: Clarendon, 1988.
———. "Permanent Happiness: Aristotle and Solon." *Oxford Studies in Ancient Philosophy* 3:89–124. Oxford: Clarendon, 1985.
———. "Reason and Responsibility in Aristotle." In Rorty, *Essays on Aristotle's Ethics*, 117–46.

Jackson, Michael W. *Matters of Justice*. London: Croom Helm, 1986.
Jaeger, Werner. *Aristotle: Fundamentals of the History of His Development*. Oxford: Oxford University Press, 1934.
Jaffa, Harry. "Aristotle." In L. Strauss and J. Cropsey, eds., *History of Political Philosophy*, 2d ed., 64–129. Chicago: Rand McNally, 1972.
———. *Thomism and Aristotelianism*. Chicago: University of Chicago Press, 1952.
Johnson, Curtis. *Aristotle's Theory of the State*. New York: St. Martin's, 1991.
———. "The Hobbesian Conception of Sovereignty and Aristotle's *Politics*." *Journal of the History of Ideas* 46 (1985): 327–47.
Johnson, T., and C. Daneker. "Patronage: Relation and System." In Wallace-Hadrill, *Patronage in Ancient Society*, 219–42.
Jonas, F. *Die Institutionenlehre Arnold Gehlens*. Tübingen, 1966.
Jones, J. W. *The Law and Legal Theory of the Greeks*. Oxford: Clarendon, 1956.
Kairys, David, ed. *The Politics of Law*. New York: Pantheon, 1982.
Kamp, Andreas. *Die Politische Philosophie des Aristoteles und ihre Metaphysischen Grundlagen*. Freiburg and Munich: Alber, 1985.
Kant, Immanuel. *Critique of Judgment*. London: Hafner, 1951.
———. *Critique of Practical Reason*. Indianapolis: Bobbs-Merrill, 1956.
———. *Fundamental Principles of the Metaphysics of Morals*. Indianapolis: Bobbs-Merrill, 1949.
Kekes, John. "Civility and Society." *History of Philosophy Quarterly* 1 (1984): 429–43.
Kelly, Donald. *The Human Measure*. Cambridge: Harvard University Press, 1990.
Keyt, David. "Distributive Justice in Aristotle's *Ethics* and *Politics*." *Topoi* 4 (1985): 23–45.
Keyt, David, and Fred Miller, Jr., eds. *A Companion to Aristotle's Politics*. Oxford: Blackwell, 1991.
Kraut, Richard. *Aristotle on the Human Good*. Princeton: Princeton University Press, 1989.
Kronman, Anthony. "Aristotle's Idea of Political Fraternity." *American Journal of Jurisprudence* 24 (1979): 114–38.
Kullmann, Wolfgang. "Der Mensch als Politische Lebeswesen bei Aristoteles." *Hermes* 108 (1982): 414–43.
———. "Die Politische Philosophie des Aristoteles." In M. Fischer and O. Gigon, eds., *Antike Rechts- und Sozialphilosophie*.
Kurth, Suzanne. "Friendships and Friendly Relations." In G. McCall, ed., *Social Relationships*, 136–70. Chicago: Aldine, 1970.
Labarrière, Jean-Louis. "The Political Animal's Knowledge According to Aristotle." In M. Dascaly, ed., *Knowledge and Politics*, 33–47. Boulder: Westview, 1988.
Larmore, Charles. *Patterns of Moral Complexity*. Cambridge: Cambridge University Press, 1987.
Lear, Jonathan. *Aristotle: The Desire to Understand*. Cambridge: Cambridge University Press, 1988.

Leftwich, Adrian, ed. *What Is Politics?* Oxford: Blackwell, 1984.
Letwin, Shirley. "Justice, Law, and Liberty." In G. Feuer, ed., *Lives, Liberty, and the Public Good*, 225–36. London Macmillan, 1987.
Lewis, Oscar. "The Folk-Urban Ideal Types." In P. Hauser and L. Schnore, eds., *The Study of Urbanization*, 491–517. New York: Wiley, 1965.
Leyden, Walter von. *Aristotle on Equality and Justice*. London: Macmillan, 1985.
Lintott, Andrew. *Violence, Civil Strife, and Revolution in the Classical City*. Baltimore: Johns Hopkins University Press, 1982.
Lloyd-Jones, Hugh. *The Justice of Zeus*. Berkeley and Los Angeles: University of California Press, 1971.
Loenen, Dirk. *Stasis*. Amsterdam, 1953.
Lord, Carnes. *Education and Culture in the Political Thought of Aristotle*. Ithaca: Cornell University Press, 1982.
Lord, Carnes, and David O'Connor, eds. *Essays on the Foundations of Aristotelian Political Science*. Berkeley and Los Angeles: University of California Press, 1991.
Lucas, J. R. *On Justice*. Oxford: Clarendon, 1980.
Lucash, F., ed. *Justice and Equality, Here and Now*. Ithaca: Cornell University Press, 1986.
Luhmann, Niklas. *The Differentiation of Society*. Edited and translated by S. Holmes and C. Larmore. New York: Columbia University Press, 1982.
———. "Moderne Systemtheorien als Form gesamtgesellschaftlicher Analyse." In J. Habermas and N. Luhmann, *Theorie der Gesellschaft oder Sozialtechnologie*, 7–24. Frankfurt: Suhrkamp, 1971.
———. *Soziologische Aufklärung*. Opladen: Westdeutsche Verlag, 1970.
Lukács, Georg. *History and Class Consciousness*. Cambridge: MIT Press, 1971.
Macdowell, D. M. *The Law in Classical Athens*. Ithaca: Cornell University Press, 1978.
Macdowell, John. "The Role of Eudaimonia in Aristotle's Ethics." In Rorty, *Essays on Aristotle's Ethics*, 359–76.
MacIntyre, Alisdair. *After Virtue*. 2d ed. Notre Dame: University of Notre Dame Press, 1984.
———. *Whose Justice? Which Rationality?* Notre Dame: University of Notre Dame Press, 1988.
Maio, Peter. "*Politeia* and Adjudication in Fourth Century Athens." *American Journal of Jurisprudence* 28 (1983): 16–45.
Mansbridge, J. *Beyond Self-Interest*. Chicago: University of Chicago Press, 1990.
Marsilius of Padua. *Defender of the Peace*. Translated by A. Gewirth. New York: Columbia University Press, 1956.
Marx, Karl. *Capital*. Vol. 1. New York: Modern Library, n.d.
———. *The German Ideology*. Vol. 5 of K. Marx and F. Engels, *Collected Works*. New York: International Publishers, 1975.
———. *The Marx-Engels Reader*. Edited by R. Tucker. New York: Norton, 1975.
Masters, Roger. *The Nature of Politics*. New Haven: Yale University Press, 1989.

Mathie, William. "Political and Distributive Justice in the Political Science of Aristotle." *Review of Politics* 49 (1987): 59–84.
Meier, Christian. *The Greek Discovery of the Political*. Harvard: Harvard University Press, 1990. (Partial translation of C. Meier. *Die Entstehung der Politischen bei den Griechen*. Frankfurt: Suhrkamp, 1980.)
Michelkakis, Emmanuel. "Das Naturrecht bei Aristoteles." In E. Berneker, ed., *Zur Griechische Rechtsgeschichte*, 146–71. Darmstadt: Wissenschaftliche Buchgesellschaft, 1968.
Miller, David. *Social Justice*. Oxford: Clarendon, 1976.
Miller, E. F. "Prudence and the Rule of Law." *American Journal of Jurisprudence* 24 (1979): 181–206.
Miller, Fred, Jr. "Aristotle on Natural Law and Justice." In Keyt and Miller, *A Companion to Aristotle's Politics*, 280–304.
Millett, Paul. "Patronage and Its Avoidance in Classical Athens." In Wallace-Hadrill, *Patronage in Ancient Society*, 15–47.
Monan, J. D. *Moral Knowledge and Its Method in Aristotle*. Oxford: Oxford University Press, 1968.
Montesquieu, C. S. de. *Considerations on the Grandeur and Decline of the Romans*. In *Oeuvres complètes* 1:69–209.
———. *Oeuvres complètes*. 2 vols. Dijon: Gallimard, 1951.
Mulgan, Richard. *Aristotle's Political Theory*. Oxford: Oxford University Press, 1977.
Murray, Oswyn. "Life and Society in Classical Greece." In J. Boardman, J. Griffin, and O. Murray, eds., *Oxford History of the Classical World*. Oxford: Oxford University Press, 1987.
Murray, Oswyn, and Simon Price, eds. *The Greek City: Homer to Alexander*. Oxford: Clarendon, 1990.
Nagel, Thomas. "Aristotle on Eudaimonia." In Rorty, *Essays on Aristotle's Ethics*, 7–14.
———. "Moral Luck." In his *Mortal Questions*, 24–38. Cambridge: Cambridge University Press, 1979.
Newell, W. R. "Superlative Virtue: The Problem of Monarchy in Aristotle's Politics." In Lord and O'Connor, *Essays on the Foundations of Aristotelian Political Science*, 191–211.
Nichols, Mary. *Socrates and the Political Community*. Albany: SUNY Press, 1987.
Nietzsche, Friedrich. *Beyond Good and Evil*. Translated by W. Kaufmann. New York: Random House, Vintage, 1972.
Nippel, Wilfried. *Mischverfassungstheorie und Verfassungsrealität in Antike und früher Neuzeit*. Stuttgart: Klett-Cotta, 1980.
Nisbet, Robert. *The Quest for Community*. Oxford: Oxford University Press, 1953.
Nussbaum, Martha. "Aristotelian Social Democracy." In R. Douglass, G. Mara, and H. Richardson, eds., *Liberalism and the Good*, 203–52. London: Routledge and Kegan Paul, 1990.
———. *Aristotle's "De Motu Animalium."* Princeton: Princeton University Press, 1978.

———. *The Fragility of Goodness.* Cambridge: Cambridge University Press.
———. "Human Functioning and Social Justice: In Defence of Aristotelian Essentialism." *Political Theory* 20 (1992): 202–46.
———. "Nature, Function, and Capability: Aristotle on Political Distribution." In *Oxford Studies in Ancient Philosophy*, supplementary vol., 144–84. Oxford: Clarendon, 1988.
———. "A Reply." *Soundings* 72 (1989): 725–81.
———. "Shame, Separateness, and Political Unity: Aristotle's Criticism of Plato." In Rorty, *Essays on Aristotle's Ethics*, 395–435.
Oakeshott, Michael. *On Human Conduct.* Oxford: Clarendon, 1975.
Ober, Josiah. "Aristotle's Political Sociology: Class, Status, and Order in Aristotle's *Politics*." In Lord and O'Connor, *Essays on the Foundations of Aristotelian Political Science*, 112–35.
———. *Mass and Elite in Democratic Athens.* Princeton: Princeton University Press, 1989.
O'Connor, David. "Aristotelian Justice as a Personal Virtue." *Midwest Studies in Philosophy* 13 (1988): 417–27.
Okin, Susan. *Justice, Gender, and the Family.* New York: Basic Books, 1989.
Oldfield, Adrian. *Citizenship and Community: Civic Republicanism and the Modern World.* London: Routledge and Kegan Paul, 1990.
Osborne, Robin. *Demos: The Discovery of Classical Attica.* Cambridge: Cambridge University Press, 1985.
———. "The Demos and Its Divisions in Classical Athens." In Murray and Price, *The Greek City*, 265–93.
Ostwald, Martin. *From Popular Sovereignty to the Sovereignty of Law.* Berkeley and Los Angeles: University of California Press, 1986.
———. "Was There a Concept of *Agraphos Nomos* in Classical Greece?" *Phronesis*, supplement 1 (1973): 70–104.
Owen, G. E. L. "Tithēnai ta phenomena." In his *Logic, Science, and Dialectic: Collected Papers in Greek Philosophy*, 239–51. Ithaca: Cornell University Press, 1986.
Paine, Robert. "Anthropological Approaches to Friendship." *Humanitas* 6 (1970): 139–59.
Parain, Charles. "Les caractères spécifiques de la lutte des classes dans l'Antiquité." *La penseé* 108 (1963): 3–25.
Philips, D. L. *Equality, Justice, and Rectification.* London: Academic Press, 1979.
Pitkin, Hannah. "Justice: On Relating Private and Public." *Political Theory* 9 (1981): 327–52.
———. *Wittgenstein and Justice.* Berkeley and Los Angeles: University of California Press, 1972.
Plato. *Apology of Socrates.*
———. *Republic.* Translated by A. Bloom. New York: Basic Books, 1969.
———. *Statesman.*
Pocock, J. G. A. *The Machiavellian Moment.* Princeton: Princeton University Press, 1975.
Polansky, Ronald. "Aristotle on Political Change." In Keyt and Miller, *A Companion to Aristotle's Politics*, 323–45.

———. "The Dominance of 'Polis' for Aristotle." *Dialogos* 14 (1979): 43–56.
Polybius. *Histories*. 6 vols. Cambridge, Mass.: Loeb Classical Library, 1922.
Price, A. W. *Love and Friendship in Plato and Aristotle*. Oxford: Clarendon, 1989.
Quass, F. *Nomos und Psephisma: Untersuchung zum griechischen Staatsrecht*. Munich: Oscar Beck, 1971.
Rawls, John. "Justice as Fairness: Political, not Metaphysical." *Philosophy and Public Affairs* 15 (1985): 223–51.
———. *A Theory of Justice*. Cambridge: Harvard University Press, 1971.
Raz, Joseph. *The Concept of a Legal System*. Oxford: Oxford University Press, 1970.
———. "The Rule of Law and Its Virtue." In his *The Authority of Law*, 210–29. Oxford: Clarendon, 1979.
Redfield, Robert. *The Little Community: Viewpoints for the Study of a Human Whole*. Chicago: University of Chicago Press, 1955.
Resnick, David. "Justice, Compromise, and Constitutional Rules in Aristotle's *Politics*." In R. Pennock and J. Chapman, eds., *Compromise in Ethics, Law, and Politics, Nomos* 21 (1978): 69–85.
Riedel, Manfred. "Gesellschaft, Gemeinschaft." In R. Koselleck et al., eds., *Geschichtliche Grundbegriffe* 2:801–62. 5 vols. Stuttgart: Klett-Cotta, 1972–84.
———. *Metaphysik und Metapolitik, Studien zu Aristoteles und zur politischen Sprache der neuzeitlichen Philosophie*. Frankfurt: Surhkamp, 1975.
Ritchie, D. G. "Aristotle's Subdivisions of 'Particular Justice.'" *Classical Review* 8 (1894): 185–92.
Ritter, Joachim. *Metaphysik und Politik*. Frankfurt: Suhrkamp, 1969.
Roberts, Jean. "Aristotle on Responsibility for Action and Character." *Ancient Philosophy* 9 (1989): 23–36.
Roemer, John. *A General Theory of Exploitation and Class*. Cambridge: Cambridge University Press, 1982.
Rorty, Amelie O. "The Place of Contemplation in Aristotle's *Nicomachean Ethics*." In Rorty, *Essays on Aristotle's Ethics*, 377–94.
———. "Virtues and Their Vicissitudes." *Midwest Studies in Philosophy* 13 (1988): 136–48.
———, ed. *Essays on Aristotle's Ethics*. Berkeley and Los Angeles: University of California Press, 1980.
Rosen, Frederick. "The Political Context of Aristotle's Categories of Justice." *Phronesis* 20 (1975): 228–40.
Ross, W. D. *Aristotle*. London: Methuen, 1923.
Rousseau, Jean-Jacques. "Discourse on the Arts and Sciences." In his *The First and Second Discourses*, 30–74. Translated by R. and J. Masters. New York: St. Martin's, 1964.
———. *Emile*. Translated by A. Bloom. New York: Basic Books, 1979.
———. *On the Social Contract: With the Geneva Manuscript and Discourse on Political Economy*. Edited by R. Masters. New York: St. Martin's, 1978.
Rowe, Christopher J. "Aims and Methods in Aristotle's Politics." In Keyt and Miller, *A Companion to Aristotle's Politics*, 57–74.

Rybicki, Pawel. *Aristote et la pensée sociale moderne.* Wroclaw, Poland: Ossolineum, 1984.
Ste. Croix, G. E. M. de. *The Class Struggle in the Ancient Greek World.* Ithaca: Cornell University Press, 1981.
Salkever, Stephen. *Finding the Mean: Theory and Practice in Aristotelian Political Philosophy.* Princeton: Princeton University Press, 1990.
Salomon, Max. *Der Begriff der Gerechtigkeit bei Aristoteles.* New York: Arno, 1957.
Sandel, Michael. *Liberalism and the Limits of Justice.* Cambridge: Cambridge University Press, 1982.
———. "The Procedural Republic and the Unencumbered Self." *Political Theory* 12 (1984): 81–96.
Sartre, Jean-Paul. *Existentialism and Humanism.* London: Methuen, 1966.
Saxonhouse, Arlene. "Family, Polity, and Unity." *Polity* 15 (1982): 202–19.
———. *Women in the History of Political Thought: Ancient Greece to Machiavelli.* New York: Praeger, 1985.
Schmalenbach, Herman. "Communion—A Social Category." In his *On Society and Experience,* 64–125. Chicago: University of Chicago Press, 1977.
Schmidt, Steffen W., James Scott, et al., eds. *Friends, Followers, and Factions. A Reader in Political Clientelism.* Berkeley and Los Angeles: University of California Press, 1977.
Schmitt-Pantel, Pauline. "Collective Activity and the Political in the Greek City." In Murray and Price, *The Greek City,* 199–213.
Schroeder, Donald. "Aristotle on Law." *Polis* 4 (1981): 17–31.
Schütrumpf, Edgar. *Die Analyse der Polis durch Aristoteles.* Amsterdam Grüner, 1980.
Sealey, Ralph. *The Athenian Republic: Democracy or the Rule of Law?* University Park: Pennsylvania State University Press, 1987.
Sen, Amartya. "Rational Fools: A Critique of the Behavioral Foundations of Economic Theory." In J. Mansbridge, *Beyond Self-Interest,* 25–43.
Shapiro, Ian. *Political Criticism.* Berkeley and Los Angeles: University of California Press, 1990.
Shapiro, Martin. *Courts.* Chicago: University of Chicago Press, 1981.
Sherman, Nancy. *The Fabric of Character: Aristotle's Theory of Virtue.* Oxford: Clarendon, 1989.
Shklar, Judith. *The Faces of Injustice.* New Haven: Yale University Press, 1990.
———. "Injustice, Injury, and Inequality." In Lucash, *Justice and Equality,* 13–33.
———. *Legalism.* Cambridge: Harvard University Press, 1986.
Shorey, Paul. "Universal Justice in Aristotle's Ethics." *Classical Philology* 19 (1924): 279–80.
Siegfried, Walter. *Der Rechtsgedanke bei Aristoteles.* Zurich: Schultess, 1942.
Silver, Allan. "Friendship and Trust as Moral Ideals: A Historical Approach." *Archives européenes de sociologie* 30 (1989): 274–97.
Simmel, Georg. *Conflict and the Web of Group-Affiliations.* New York: Free Press, 1955.

———. *The Sociology of Georg Simmel*. Edited by K. Wolff. New York: Free Press, 1950.

Simpson, George. *Conflict and Community*. New York: T. S. Simpson, 1937.

Simpson, Peter. "Making the Citizens Good: Aristotle's City and Its Contemporary Relevance." *Philosophical Forum* 22 (1990): 149–66.

Sinclair, R. K. *Democracy and Participation in Democratic Athens*. Cambridge: Cambridge University Press, 1988.

Smiley, Marion. *Moral Responsibility and the Boundaries of Community*. Chicago: University of Chicago Press, 1992.

Smith, Adam. *An Inquiry into the Nature and Causes of the Wealth of Nations*. New York: Modern Library, 1937.

———. *The Theory of Moral Sentiments*. Indianapolis: Liberty Classics, 1976.

Sophocles. *Ajax*.

———. *Oedipus at Colonnus*.

Sorabji, Richard. *Necessity, Cause, and Blame: Perspectives on Aristotle's Theory*. Ithaca: Cornell University Press, 1980.

Springborg, Patricia. "Aristotle and the Problem of Needs." *History of Political Thought* 5 (1984): 409–10.

Stalley, R. F. "Aristotle's Critique of Plato's *Republic*." In Keyt and Miller, *A Companion to Aristotle's Politics*, 182–99.

Steinmetz, Peter, ed. *Schriften zu den Politika des Aristoteles*. Olms Studien 6. Hildesheim and New York: 1973.

Stocker, Michael. *Plural and Conflicting Values*. Oxford: Clarendon, 1990.

Strauss, Barry. *Athens after the Peloponnesian War: Class, Faction, and Policy 403–386*. Ithaca: Cornell University Press, 1986.

———. "On Aristotle's Critique of Democracy." In Lord and O'Connor, *Essays on the Foundations of Aristotelian Political Science*, 212–33.

Strauss, Leo. *The City and Man*. Chicago: University of Chicago Press, 1983.

———. "The Liberalism of Classical Political Philosophy." In his *Liberalism: Ancient and Modern*, 29–64. New York: Basic, 1968.

———. *Natural Right and History*. Chicago: University of Chicago Press, 1953.

Sullivan, William. *Reconstructing Public Philosophy*. Berkeley and Los Angeles: University of California Press, 1986.

Suttles, Gerald. "Friendship as a Social Institution." In G. McCall, ed., *Social Relationships*, 95–135. Chicago: Aldine, 1970.

Taylor, Charles. "The Nature and Scope of Distributive Justice." In Lucash, *Justice and Equality*, 34–67.

Tessitore, Aristide. "Making the City Safe for Philosophy: *Nicomachean Ethics*, Book X." *American Political Science Review* 84 (1990): 1252–62.

Thomas, Laurence. *Living Morally*. Philadelphia: Temple University Press, 1989.

Thucydides. *History of the Peloponnesian War*. Translated by B. Crawley. New York: Modern Library, 1960.

Tocqueville, Alexis de. *Democracy in America*. Garden City, N.Y.: Doubleday, Anchor, 1969.

Tönnies, Ferdinand. *Community and Society*. New York: Harper, 1963.

Trude, Peter. *Der Begriff der Gerechtigkeit in der Aristotelischen Staatsphilosophie*. Berlin: de Gruyter, 1955.

Unger, Roberto. *Law in Modern Society.* New York: Free Press, 1976.
Vernant, Jean-Pierre. "City-State Warfare." In his *Myth and Society in Ancient Greece,* 19–44.
———. "Class Struggle." In his *Myth and Society in Ancient Greece,* 1–18.
———. *Myth and Society in Ancient Greece.* Atlantic Highlands, N.J.: Humanities Press, 1981.
Veyne, Paul. *Bread and Circuses.* London: Penguin, 1990. (Partial translation of P. Veyne. *Le pain et le cirque.* Paris: Editions du Seuil, 1976.)
Voegelin, Eric. *Anamnesis.* Notre Dame: Notre Dame University Press, 1978.
Wallace-Hadrill, A., ed. *Patronage in Ancient Society.* London: Routledge and Kegan Paul, 1989.
Walzer, Michael. *Obligations.* Cambridge: Harvard University Press, 1970.
———. "Philosophy and Democracy." *Political Theory* 9 (1981): 379–99.
———. *Spheres of Justice.* New York: Basic Books, 1983.
Waterlow, Sarah. *Nature, Change, and Agency in Aristotle's Physics,* Oxford: Clarendon, 1982.
Weber, Max. *Economy and Society.* Berkeley and Los Angeles: University of California Press, 1978.
Weil, Raymond. *Aristote et l'histoire.* Paris: Klincksieck, 1960.
Weinrib, Ernest. "The Intelligibility of the Rule of Law." In Allan C. Hutchinson and P. Monahan, eds., *The Rule of Law: Ideal or Ideology,* 59–84. Toronto: Carswell, 1989.
———. "Legal Formalism: On the Immanent Rationality of Law." *Yale Law Journal* 97 (1988): 949–1016.
Wheeler, Marcus. "Aristotle's Analysis of Political Struggle." In Barnes et al., *Articles on Aristotle 2: Ethics and Politics,* 159–69.
Whitehead, David. *The Demes of Attica.* Princeton: Princeton University Press, 1986.
———. *The Ideology of the Athenian Metic. Proceedings of the Cambridge Philological Society,* supplement 4, 1977.
Wieland, Wolfgang. "The Problem of Teleology." In Barnes et al., *Articles on Aristotle 1: Science,* 141–60. London: Duckworth, 1975.
Wilkes, Kathleen. "The Good Man and the Good for Man in Aristotle's Ethics." In Rorty, *Essays on Aristotle's Ethics,* 341–58.
Williams, Bernard. "Conflicts of Values." In his *Moral Luck,* 71–82.
———. *Ethics and the Limits of Philosophy.* Cambridge: Harvard University Press, 1985.
———. "Justice as a Virtue." In Rorty, *Essays on Aristotle's Ethics,* 189–99.
———. "Moral Luck." In his *Moral Luck,* 20–39.
———. *Moral Luck.* Cambridge: Cambridge University Press, 1981.
Winthrop, Delba. "Aristotle and Theories of Justice." *American Political Science Review* 72 (1978): 1201–17.
Wolf, Eric. "Kinship, Friendship, and Patron-Client Relations in Complex Societies." In M. Banton, ed., *The Social Anthropology of Complex Societies,* 1–22. New York: Praeger, 1966.
Wolf, Susan. "Asymmetrical Freedom." *Journal of Philosophy* 77 (1980): 151–66.

Wolff, Francis. "Justice et Politique." *Phronesis* 33 (1988): 273–96.
Wood, Ellen Meiksins. *Mind and Politics*. Berkeley and Los Angeles: University of California Press, 1972.
———. *Peasant-Citizen and Slave: Foundations of Athenian Democracy*. London: Verso, 1988.
Wood, Ellen Meiksins, and Neal Wood. *Class Ideology and Ancient Political Theory*. New York: Oxford, 1978.
Wood, Gordon. *The Creation of the American Republic*. Chapel Hill: University of North Carolina Press, 1969.
Wormuth, Francis. "Aristotle on Law." In his *Essays in Law and Politics*. Port Washington, N.Y.: Kennikat, 1978.
Wright, Erik Olin. *Classes*. London: Verso, 1985.
Wright, George. "Stoic Midwives at the Birth of Jurisprudence." *American Journal of Jurisprudence* 28 (1983): 169–88.
Xenophon. *Memorabilia*.
Yack, Bernard. "Community and Conflict in Aristotle's Political Philosophy." *Review of Politics* 47 (1985): 92–112.
———. "How Good Is the Aristotelian Good Life?" *Soundings* 72 (1989): 607–29.
———. "Injustice and the Victim's Voice." *Michigan Law Review* 89 (1991): 1334–49.
———. "Liberalism and Its Communitarian Critics: Does Liberal Practice 'Live Down' to Liberal Theory?" In C. Reynolds, ed., *Community in America: The Challenges of "Habits of the Heart,"* 149–67. Berkeley and Los Angeles: University of California Press, 1988.
———. *The Longing for Total Revolution: Philosophic Sources of Social Discontent from Rousseau to Marx and Nietzsche*. Berkeley and Los Angeles: University of California Press, 1992.
———. "Natural Right and Aristotle's Understanding of Justice." *Political Theory* 18 (1990): 216–37.
———. "A Reinterpretation of Aristotle's Political Teleology." *History of Political Thought* 12 (1991): 1–19.
———. "Towards a Free Marketplace of Social Institutions: Roberto Unger's 'Super-Liberal' Theory of Emancipation." *Harvard Law Review* 101 (1988): 1961–77.
Yunis, Harvey. "Law, Politics, and the *Graphē Paranomon* in Fourth Century Athens." *Greek, Roman, and Byzantine Studies* 29 (1988): 361–82.

# Index of Citations from Aristotle's Works

*Categories*
14a26 .................. 97n16
*Eudemian Ethics*
1242a6 .... 44, 55, 103, 110–11
1242a15 ................ 63n23
1242a25 .................... 28
1242b .................... 123
1242b23 .................. 112
1242b35 .................. 114
1242b37 ..... 112, 115, 121, 123
1243a42 .................. 115
1244a21 ............... 34, 111
1248b37 .................. 103
*Generation of Animals*
770b ...................... 90
770b9 ..................... 88
*History of Animals*
488a ................... 51–52
*Magna Moralia*
1183b20 ............... 254n33
1211a11 .......... 112, 264n50
*Metaphysics*
993b1 .................... 146
1016b15 ................... 92
1021b10 ................... 98
1041b13 ................... 92
1050a22 .................. 273
*Motion of Animals*
703a28 .................... 94

*Nicomachean Ethics*
1094a27 ................... 18
1094b14 .............. 147, 157
1095a15 .................. 102
1095b4 ................ 3n5, 107
1099a13 .................. 155
1099b2 ................... 253
1099b29 .................. 102
1100a5 ................... 251
1101a .................... 253
1101b2 ................... 253
1101b6 ................... 255
1101b25 .................. 252
1102a5 ................. 96–97
1103a–b ................ 15, 39
1103a15 ................... 97
1103a21 ................... 98
1103a26 ............... 94, 98
1103a30 ................... 98
1103b3 .................... 99
1103b24 ............... 89, 99
1104b8 ................... 155
1105a29 .................. 155
1108a27 .................. 110
1109a28 .................. 145
1109b30 .................. 251
1110a ................ 260–61
1114b22 .................. 247
1125b25 .................. 111

301

*Nicomachean Ethics* (continued)
 1126b15 .................. 110
 1129a32 .................. 159
 1129b ..................... 158
 1129b12 .................. 106
 1129b26 .................. 159
 1129b27 .................. 162
 1130 ...................... 132
 1130a1 ................... 163
 1130a17 .................. 160
 1130b12 ............... 158–59
 1131a25 .............. 165, 221
 1132b ..................... 206
 1132b11 .................. 206
 1132b21 .............. 136, 148
 1132b31 ....... 27, 30, 116, 136
 1132b40 .................. 138
 1134a ...................... 41
 1134a14 ................... 60
 1134a24 .......... 56, 66, 133
 1134a29 ................... 99
 1134b ................. 39, 132
 1134b9 ................... 134
 1134b13 .................. 205
 1134b15 ................... 85
 1134b18 ............... 59, 134
 1134b21 .................. 144
 1134b24 ................ 141–42
 1134b32 .............. 145, 206
 1134b33 ................ 141–42
 1135a5 ........... 142n18, 169
 1135a20 .................. 155
 1136b32 .................. 145
 1137a10 .............. 145, 155
 1137b ..................... 132
 1137b11–24 .......... 180, 193
 1137b22 .................. 194
 1138a2 ................... 194
 1141a21 .................. 269
 1141a25 .................. 182
 1141b24 .................. 198
 1141b28 .................. 180
 1153b19 .............. 251, 276
 1155a19 ................ 180n17
 1155a22 .............. 109, 114
 1155b–57a .............. 103
 1156–57 ................ 29, 36
 1157b28 ................... 36
 1158a11 .............. 103, 113
 1159a29 ................... 30
 1159b25 ................ 27, 30
 1159b27 ................ 29, 34
 1159b30 ............... 36, 103
 1160a3 ............... 1n1, 120
 1160a11 ... 44, 55, 103, 110–12
 1161a24 .................. 113
 1161a25 .................. 122
 1161b5 .................... 106
 1161b11 .................. 103
 1161b18 ................... 64
 1162a16 .................. 119
 1162a31 .................. 123
 1162b7 .................... 112
 1162b16 .................. 112
 1162b18 ................... 64
 1162b21–35 .............. 114
 1162b28 ................ 114–15
 1162b31–37 .............. 116
 1162b35 .................. 117
 1163a28 .................. 226
 1163b1 .................... 227
 1163b12–19 .............. 226
 1163b15 ............... 34, 225
 1164a1 ................... 27n7
 1167b2–5 ................ 114
 1171a16 .................. 111
 1171a18 .................. 113
 1177a–79b .............. 269
 1177b1 .................... 275
 1177b9 ........... 7, 273, 274
 1177b13 .............. 103, 273
 1177b17 .................. 271
 1177b27 .................. 275
 1177b31 ................... 12
 1178a25 .................. 276
 1178b5 .................... 275
 1179b11 ................ 42n42
 1179b24 .................. 107
 1179b31 ......... 204, 242, 248
 1179b–80a ............... 12
 1180a ..................... 180
 1180a14–24 .......... 99, 248
 1180a21 .............. 182, 202
 1180a25 .................. 187
 1180b1 .......... 179, 249n21
 1189a31 .................. 106
*On the Soul*
 433b6 ................. 65n25
*Parts of Animals*
 640b35 .................... 92
 645a15 ................... 108
*Physics*
 192b30 .................... 91
 197a32 .................... 89

198b35 .............. 89, 147
*Politics*
1251b .................... 197
1252a1 ........ 25, 29, 51, 102
1252a17 ................... 92
1252a29 ................... 64
1252b28 ................... 54
1252b29 ........... 54, 64, 96
1253a .......... 40, 51–53, 64
1253a8 ................... 105
1253a15 ................... 66
1253a19 ........... 30, 56, 92
1253a30 ... 62, 94, 98, 184, 188
1253a32 .............. 205, 242
1253a38 .................. 188
1254b16 ............... 68, 139
1254b17 ................... 76
1256b16 .................. 101
1259b1 ............. 66, 138–39
1259b–60a ............ 53, 139
1260a .................... 232
1260a12 ................ 67–68
1260a24 ................... 54
1260b35 ................. 7, 88
1261 .................... 29, 69
1261a .................... 220
1261a30 .................. 136
1261a32 .................. 116
1261b5 .................... 30
1261–62 ................... 15
1262a13 .................. 120
1262b8 ................... 118
1262b14 .............. 119, 122
1262b21 .................. 119
1262b23 ................... 31
1263 ..................... 171
1263a15 .......... 7, 120, 281
1263a30 .................. 119
1263b15 .................. 119
1263b22 .................. 120
1265a14 ................... 72
1267a39 .................. 189
1268b–69a ........... 183, 261
1269a10 .................. 187
1269a20 .................. 184
1271b1 ..................... 7
1272b5 ................... 196
1272b24 ................... 68
1275a23 .................. 189
1276b–78b ................ 262
1278b11 .................. 235
1278b19 ................... 28

1278b21 ................... 54
1279 ..................... 159
1279a10 ....... 66, 100, 138–39
1279b .................... 215
1280a15 .................. 220
1280b10 ................... 97
1281a2 ................ 54, 96
1281a11 .................. 222
1281a15 .............. 156, 159
1281a34 .................. 176
1282 ..................... 238
1282a20 ................... 60
1282b .................... 221
1282b16 .................. 102
1282b20 .................. 223
1282b23 .................. 165
1283a .................... 165
1283a38 .................. 159
1283b ..................... 77
1283b1 ................... 165
1283b27 .................. 165
1283b41 .................. 170
1284a10 .................. 183
1286b ................. 66, 69
1286b32 .................. 180
1287a .................... 203
1287a17 .............. 197, 205
1287a18 .................. 100
1287a30 .................. 183
1287a33 .................. 182
1287b5 ................... 181
1288a .................... 203
1289a3 ................ 232n49
1289b4 ................... 237
1290a .................... 216
1290b1 ................... 215
1290b5 ................... 216
1292a ..................... 75
1292a1 ................... 196
1292a5 ................... 198
1292a15 .................. 222
1292a18 .............. 197, 199
1292a32 .............. 199, 205
1292b1 ................... 196
1292b6 ........... 106n29, 199
1292b8 ................... 222
1292b25 ................... 75
1293a ..................... 75
1293b ................. 74, 235
1294 ..................... 236
1295b5 ................... 238
1295b30 .................. 238

*Politics* (continued)
  1296a9 .................... 74
  1296a12 ................... 237
  1297a35 ................... 236
  1297b4 .................... 237
  1299b15 ................... 235
  1301a25 ................... 220
  1301a28 ................... 221
  1301a38 ................... 224
  1302a1 .................... 223
  1302a9 .................... 237
  1302a23–33 ............... 220
  1303b15 ................... 224
  1304b1 .................... 224
  1310a3 .................... 217
  1310a11 ................... 187
  1315b ..................... 241
  1316a ................233, 239
  1317a35 ................... 235
  1318b ..................... 75
  1320a30 ................... 227
  1323a ..................... 169
  1323a29 ................... 276
  1324b35 ................... 263
  1325b15 ................... 263
  1325b35 ........... 72, 74, 242
  1326a25 ................... 73
  1326b5 .................... 73
  1326b15 ................... 73
  1327b24 ................... 68
  1328a1–15 ................ 120
  1328a10 ............ 1, 38, 224
  1328b35 ................... 168
  1329a31 ................... 83
  1329b32 ................. 68, 74
  1330a25 ............... 168, 242
  1330a32 ................... 168
  1332b ..................... 53
  1333b ..................... 263
  1333b–34b ................ 7
  1336b1 .................... 249
*Refutations of the Sophists*
  167a ................. 134–35
  173a6 ..................... 144
  180b34 ............... 145n26
*Rhetoric*
  1354b .... 144n22, 180, 190–91
  1354b35 .......... 117n14, 192
  1355a27 ................... 146
  1355b26 ................... 146
  1358b ..................... 174
  1365b29 ................... 86
  1367a31 ................... 228
  1367b34 ................... 252
  1368b ................. 188n37
  1368b7 .......... 146n26, 180
  1370a5–12 ................ 99
  1373b ................181, 186
  1373b6 ................145–46
  1374b10 ................... 194
  1374b30 ................... 193
  1375a26 ................... 144
  1375b31 ................... 145
  1378b31 ................40n38
  1379b2 .......... 1n1, 120, 224
  1380b36 ................... 34
  1382–83 ................42n42
  1389 ...................... 117
  1389b16 ................... 7
*Topics*
  100b20 .................... 146
  101b8 ..................... 146
  140a7 ..................... 148

# General Index

Aalders, Georg, 235n57
Adjudication, 184–94
Adkins, A. W. H., 245–46, 251–52
Aquinas, Thomas, 141, 195n46
Arendt, Hannah: definition of politics, 9–10; influence of, 11–13; misinterpretation of Aristotle, 11–13, 62, 67; on political friendship, 113
Aristophanes, 81
Arnhart, Larry, 53n2
Aspasia, 80–81
Athens: its form of democracy, 75, 237; law in, 186–87, 207–8; not a face-to-face society, 55

Badian, Ernest, 80n68
Barber, Benjamin, 2n2, 109n1
Barker, Ernest, 91, 96n15, 141n16, 182–83
Bauman, Richard, 185n26
Bedau, Hugo, 151
Beiner, Ronald, 113n9
Bellah, Robert, 49n55
Best (or ideal) regime: aims at happiness, not justice, 76, 169–70; improbability of, 3, 242–43, 263–64; size of, 72, 74. *See also* Good life
Black, Anthony, 62n20

Blumenberg, Hans, 19n43
Bodéüs, Richard, 205n70, 237n60
Bonald, Louis de, 44
Brown, Wendy, 67
Burke, Edmund, 44
Burnyeat, Miles, 107n31

Cairns, Huntington, 179n12, 183–84
Calvert, Peter, 216n24
Class conflict: in ancient Greece, 210–15; Marx's theory of, 209–14; Marx's theory criticized, 214–18; and perceived injustice 218–22; among political friends, 210, 224–31; political understanding of, 210, 215–18
Collective identity: contrasted with shared identity, 30–31; in Plato's *Republic*, 29–30. *See also* Communion
Communion: contrasted with community, 31–33, 49; and romanticization of community, 32–33
Community (*koinōnia*): distinguished from political community, 26–27; as generic category, 26–29, 43–50; naturalness of, 28–29; as source of conflict, 1–5; translation from Greek, 27.

305

Community (*continued*)
See also Political community
Comradeship: as false ideal of political friendship, 118–21; and fears of betrayal, 121, 124–25; in the French Revolution, 122–24; as symbol of equality, 122
Connor, W. R., 225n39
Constant, Benjamin: as critic of ancient politics, 74, 77–78, 82, 84; as critic of revolutionary comradeship, 122–23
Contemplative life: dependence on moral training, 276; interpretations of, 269–71; superiority of, 269–70, 275. See also Good life
Conventional right: definition of, 142–43. See also Natural right
Cooper, John, 38n34, 101, 252
Crete, 263

Day, J. H., and M. Chambers, 91
Defourny, Maurice, 28n10
Durkheim, Emile, 43, 45
Dworkin, Ronald, 129, 131, 157

Elster, Jon, 34–35
Empedocles, 146
Equity, 193–94
Erikson, Trond, 277n16
Ethics: modern separation from politics, 4, 17–18

Fairness: competing standards of, 164–66; as fidelity or passive justice, 162–66, 171–72; as part of justice, 158–61; seen as whole of justice, 153–54
Farrar, Cynthia, 84
Finley, Moses: on class conflict, 209, 217, 221n34; on Greek invention of politics, 7–8, 57
Finnis, John, 178n11
Forster, E. M., 264
Fraternity. See Comradeship
French Revolution (1789), 48, 78, 239–40
Friedrich, C. J., 185n26
Friendship (*philia*): definition of, 34; in exchange relations, 37–39, 124–25; among family members, 119–20; as feature of community, 33–35; social forms of, 33–39; translation from Greek, 335–36; unequal forms of, 224–31. See also Comradeship; Political friendship
Fustel de Coulanges, N. D., 79, 83–85

Gadamer, Hans-Georg, 19n42, 20
Galston, William, 151, 167–68
Gauthier, R., and J. Jolif, 113, 193
General justice: as active justice, 163–64; as complete virtue, 159, 161–64; contrasted with fairness, 159–64, 171–72; and lawfulness, 159, 262–63
Good life: beauty of, 268–69, 274; dependence on good fortune, 3, 244–45, 251–59; in imperfect political conditions, 242; political contributions to, 96–97; praiseworthiness of, 244–45, 253–54; tensions within, 277–80
Good man vs. good citizen, 262–63
Gould, Stephen Jay, 140n15

Hampshire, Stuart, 260
Hansen, Mogens, 207n73
Happiness (*eudaimonia*). See Good life
Hart, H. L. A., 58
Havelock, Eric, 14
Hayek, Friedrich, 151–52, 176n4
Heidegger, Martin, 13n29
Heraclitus, 108
Herman, Gabriel, 112n5
Herodotus, 225n39
Hobbes, Thomas: on justice, 59, 129, 152; on political friendship, 110, 122, 124–26; on the rule of law, 176; on security, 263; on social conflict, 6, 69–71
Holmes, Stephen, 72n40, 84, 207n72
Homer, 40n38
Household: inequalities within, 53, 66–68, 139–40
Humphreys, S. C., 78–80
Hutter, Horst, 113
Huxley, George, 109n2

General Index

Interpretation: approaches to, 18–24; dialogic approach to, 20–21; as means of self-criticism, 18–20
Irwin, Terence, 3n4, 4n8, 113, 245–46
Isocrates, 228

Jaeger, Werner, 17, 89n4
Jaffa, Harry, 142n18
Joachim, Hans, 254
Johnson, Curtis, 25
Justice: as aspect of community, 33–35, 40; contrasted with friendship, 34–35, 39, 42–43; definition of, 34; extralegal standards of, 129–33, 166–74; forms of, 33–35, 39–43, 57–62; legalist understanding of, 130–31, 172–74; as moral virtue, 39, 150–57; naturalness of, 40; normal model of, 128–33, 150, 162–64; as social practice, 41–43; subject of, 149–57; unqualified (*haplōs*) forms of, 56–67, 133–35. *See also* Fairness; General justice; Natural right; Political justice; Reciprocity

Kamp, Andreas, 92n9
Kant, Immanuel, 12, 256–59, 279
Kekes, John, 115n10
Keyt, David, 90, 91n5
Kraut, Richard, 278n19

Labarrière, J. L., 111n4
Laws: contrasted with decrees, 182, 198–99; defining features of, 180–84; generality of, 99, 180, 193; limited rationality of, 182–84, 205; as means of moral education, 98–100, 107–8, 179–81, 204–5, 250; no systematization of, 184–87; power of compulsion, 99; written and unwritten, 179–81
Lear, Jonathan, 88n1
Letwin, Shirley, 179n14
Lewis, Oscar, 33
Leyden, Walter von, 141n16
Liberal democracy: modern critics of, 1–2, 9–10

Liberal individualism: communitarian critique of, 13–15, 46–50, 282; theoretical weakness of, 47–48, 282
Liturgies, 80, 226–27
Lloyd-Jones, Hugh, 268
Locke, John, 175n1
Lord, Carnes, 28n8
Lucas, J. R., 151, 162n55
Luhmann, Niklas, 27n6, 84

Machiavelli, Niccolò, 232
MacIntyre, Alisdair, 2n2, 6, 10–11, 62, 109n2
Madison, James, 74n46, 217
Maistre, Joseph de, 44
Mann, Thomas, 32
Marx, Karl: on class conflict, 209–18, 221
Masters, Roger, 105n28
Mathie, William, 164n56
Meier, Christian, 75n48
Michelkakis, Emmanuel, 146n7
Miller, David, 151, 158
Mixed regime, 231–39
Monarchy, 85–87
Montesquieu, C. S. de, 14, 127, 273
Moral conflict: between friends and country, 264; as everyday occurrence, 260–61, 265–67, 278; tragic forms of, 265–67
Moral education: in imperfect regimes, 104–8, 243; and moral character, 247–48; political character of, 248–51; role of compulsion in, 248–49
Moral luck, 244–45, 251
Moral responsibility, 245–47
Morris, Gouverneur, 234
Mulgan, Richard, 93n11, 96n15
Murray, Oswyn, 78–79

Natural right: contrasted with natural law, 141–42, 145–57; defining features of, 59, 141–47; naturalness of, 147–49; not a higher standard, 59, 143–45, 156–57
Newell, W. R. 86n81
Newman, W. L., 89n3, 231
Nietzsche, Friedrich, 274–75

Nussbaum, Martha, 3n7, 101, 153, 167–69, 243, 246n13, 266n5, 275n15

Oakeshott, Michael, 49
Ober, Josiah, 207n73, 215n23, 237n62
Osborne, Robin, 55, 75, 81n71

Parain, Charles, 212n10
Patron-client relations, 277–79
Pericles, 80–81, 175n1
Pitkin, Hanna, 9–10, 13
Plato: communitarianism of, 15, 29–30, 83; critique of democracy, 75; interpretations of, 22–23; on political friendship, 118–22; on revolution, 239; on the rule of law, 178, 196–98; understanding of utopia, 76, 169
Polansky, Ronald, 262n48
Polis: as form of political community, 8, 53–55; function of, 89–96, 108; and modern political communities, 71–85; not a face-to-face society, 45, 73; not a natural substance, 89–90
Political animal: meaning of, 6–7, 51–53; non-human species of, 51–53
Political community: as conflict-ridden, 2–3, 71, 222–23, 231–32; defining features of, 7–9, 53–62; dependence on the rule of law, 205; in modern states, 8, 61–62, 71–85; naturalness of, 6–7, 62–71; and the polis, 53–55; and political participation, 74–76; private life within, 77–85; and reasoned speech, 52, 64–66; as shared advantage community, 102–4. *See also* Community; Polis; Political animal
Political friendship: within best regime, 103–4, 117–18; contrasted with virtue friendship, 112–15; defining features of, 54–56, 111–12; relation to justice, 109, 112, 117; and self-sacrifice, 125–27; as shared advantage friendship, 55–56, 103–4, 110–17; as source of conflict, 118–21, 224–31. *See also* Comradeship; Friendship
Political justice: and class conflict, 220; contrasted with domestic justice, 41, 57, 133–35; defining features of, 56–62, 135–36; divided into natural and conventional right, 59, 141–43; indeterminate standards of, 128–31, 154–57, 165–66, 170–74
Political teleology: anthropocentrism of, 100–102; misunderstandings of, 16–17; problems with, 62–63; reinterpretation of, 88–108. *See also* Polis; Political community
Polybius, 233–34
Praise: asymmetries with blame, 254–59
Priam, 251–54

Rawls, John: on extralegal standards of justice, 128–29, 131, 164, 173; on praise and blame, 256–68; on the subject of justice, 150–54, 159
Raz, Joseph, 195n46
Reciprocity: contrasted with natural right, 148–49; distinguished from fairness, 138; as ground of political justice, 136–40, 206; natural standards of, 139–40; and political friendship, 116
Revolution, 239–41
Riedel, Manfred, 29n12
Roberts, Jean, 247n15
Rorty, Amelie, 250–51
Rousseau, Jean-Jacques: as critic of liberal individualism, 14, 44, 52, 82; on fraternity, 110, 122, 125; on socialization, 250
Rule of law: conservative features of, 203; contributions to moral education, 204–5; as enabling constraint, 206–8; as foundation of political rule, 177, 197, 205–8; as moral disposition, 201–3; and popular sovereignty, 175–76, 207–8; as rectitude or regularity, 194–96, 201
Rybicki, Pawel, 27n5, 44n46

Ste. Croix, G. E. M. de, 209, 212–16
Salkever, Stephen, 264n49
Salomon, Max, 144n21
Sartre, Jean-Paul, 265–66
Schmalenbach, Herman, 31–33
Sen, Amartya, 35n28
Shapiro, Martin, 190n39
Sherman, Nancy, 248n19
Shklar, Judith, 128–30, 130n7, 161–62, 180n16
Siegfried, Walter, 141n16
Silver, Allan, 35n29
Simmel, Georg, 1n1, 50n57, 202
Simpson, Peter, 91n5
Smiley, Marion, 219n30, 246n14
Smith, Adam, 35n28, 42n42, 127
Social conflict: communitarian account of, 1–5, 282; in small communities, 33. *See also* Class conflict; Moral conflict
Social heterogeneity: contribution to political conflict, 220; as element of community, 15, 29–30, 53–54
Social theory: Aristotelian approach to, 27, 36, 43–50
Socrates, 81, 118, 176, 276
Sophocles, 144, 146, 258–59, 268
Sparta: limitations of, 7, 82–83, 263

Stocker, Michael, 266n54, 267
Strauss, Barry, 207n73
Strauss, Leo, 145, 177–78
Sullivan, William, 14n33

Taylor, Charles, 164n57, 166n59
Theophrastus, 185n26
Theramenes, 200
Thomas, Laurence, 248n19
Thucydides, 174n70, 175n1, 225n29
Tocqueville, Alexis de, 233–36
Tönnies, Ferdinand, 43–45, 49
Trude, Peter, 141n16

Veyne, Paul, 67–68, 80n65

Walzer, Michael, 126, 129, 131, 173
Weber, Max, 7–8, 43, 45–46
Weinrib, Ernest, 178n11
Wheeler, Marcus, 209n3
Wieland, Wolfgang, 101
Wolf, E. F., 227n43
Wolf, Susan, 256n39
Wood, Ellen M., 77n52
Wood, Ellen M., and Neal Wood, 237
Wormuth, Francis, 143n20, 186, 195n49

www.ingramcontent.com/pod-product-compliance
Ingram Content Group UK Ltd.
Pitfield, Milton Keynes, MK11 3LW, UK
UKHW041655310326
469532UK00002B/33